The Devil's Race-Track:

MARK TWAIN'S
GREAT DARK
WRITINGS

The Devil's Race-Track:

MARK TWAIN'S
GREAT DARK
WRITINGS

The Best from *Which Was the Dream?*
and *Fables of Man*

EDITED BY JOHN S. TUCKEY

University of California Press

BERKELEY · LOS ANGELES · LONDON

University of California Press
Berkeley and Los Angeles, California
University of California Press, Ltd.
London, England
© 1966, 1972, 1980 The Mark Twain Company
ISBN 0-520-03780-4 (cloth)
ISBN 0-520-03893-2 (paper)
Library of Congress Catalog Card Number: 78-62865
Printed in the United States of America

5 6 7 8 9

The paper used in this publication meets the minimum
requirements of American National Standard for Information Sciences—Permanence of Paper for Printed
Library Materials, ANSI Z39.48-1984. ∞

Contents

Contents

A Note on the Texts

For each of the selections included herein, I have used the texts which, as prepared in accordance with the principles of the Center for Editions of American Authors of the Modern Language Association of America, were published by the University of California Press in the Mark Twain Papers Series volumes *Which Was the Dream?* and *Fables of Man*. The appendices of those volumes, as well as most of the editorial notes, have been omitted from this book to provide a clear reading text. I have chosen the following writings of Samuel L. Clemens—Mark Twain:

From *Which Was the Dream?*

"The Passenger's Story"
"The Enchanted Sea-Wilderness"
"Which Was the Dream?"
"The Great Dark"
"The Mad Passenger"
"Which Was It" (excerpt)
"Three Thousand Years Among the Microbes"

From *Fables of Man*

"Little Bessie"
"Little Nelly Tells a Story Out of Her Own Head"
"The Ten Commandments"
"Thoughts of God"
"The Synod of Praise"
"The Refuge of the Derelicts"
"The Fable of the Yellow Terror"
"Passage from 'Glances at History' (suppressed.) Date, 9th century"
"Passage from 'Outlines of History' (suppressed.) Date, 9th century"

"Passage from a Lecture"
"History 1,000 Years from Now"
"Old Age"

Dates of Mark Twain's composition are given in parentheses at the end of each selection.

J. S. T.

Introduction

There is no such figure for the storm-beaten human drift as the derelict," Mark Twain once told his friend and biographer Albert Bigelow Paine. The seas in which he voyaged, in his life and in his writings, were not only the earthly ones with their alluring and forbidding vastnesses and remotenesses. His imagination reached out to the uncharted deeps of the universe in which the globe was but a drifting particle, and also inward to the equally unfathomable inner space of the human psyche immersed in the ocean of the unconscious.

It was after he had passed the age of sixty that Mark Twain wrote all of the pieces that appear in this book. In their focus they range from intensely personal matters to the cosmic situation as he envisioned it. Some deal with the disasters of the mid-1890s that had included financial failure and bankruptcy and the death of his daughter Susy, and these writings are much concerned with sudden turns of fate by which an individual may find himself in calamitous circumstances. Others view the human situation more generally, and sometimes from perspectives remote in time or scale. In "Three Thousand Years Among the Microbes," events are perceived from a micro–macrocosmic viewpoint: the leading character is a germ who inhabits the river-like veins of a living human being that is his "planet" and also his deity.

A number of the writings dealing with personal and family misfortunes represent successive stages of work upon a story of a disastrous sea voyage that he felt compelled to produce, but which gave him trouble in finding the right approach. These various drafts are interesting both in themselves and for what they reveal of the direction and tendency of his thought and work. There are recurring themes. A man long favored by good luck has been pursuing a dream of high success that seems

ix

about to become a reality. Suddenly he experiences a nightmarish time of failure. As his thoughts race around the vicious circle track of his predicament (which Mark Twain was to call the Devil's Race-Track), he becomes confused and disoriented, both as to the passage of time and as to what is dream and what is reality. In several of the drafts, the fallen hero was to have a long dream of a tragedy-laden voyage and then awaken to find that what had seemed the events of terrible years had been the dream of a moment.

The voyage motif partly reflects Mark Twain's extensive sea travels during the globe-circling lecture tour of 1895–96 that he made in order to pay his debts, and from which he returned only to face the loss of Susy. But he had already, when financial ruin had only been impending, used the ship as a symbol of fortune. At a time in 1894 when he believed that the impracticable typesetter in which he had over-invested was finally to succeed, he cabled to his wife Olivia, "A ship visible on the horizon coming down under a cloud of canvas." A few days later, thinking that success had in fact come, he cabled again, *"Our ship is safe in port."* But within another ten days he had to send the woeful message, "Ships that pass in the night." Later in the same year his business advisor Henry H. Rogers had forced him to recognize that the typesetter had almost no commercial value. He wrote to Rogers, "It hit me like a thunder-clap. . . . I went flying here and there . . . , only one clearly defined thought standing up visible and substantial out of the crazy storm-drift—that my dream of ten years was in desperate peril." At this time he also penned some verses that were represented to be the mutterings of a crazed almshouse inmate who considered himself a storm-beaten derelict vessel, "Friendless, forlorn, and forgotten."

Another intertwining theme is that of the loss of the family home, usually by fire, and of the goal of a subsequent return to the once happy home situation that must somehow be achieved, whether in reality or in dream. In 1895, forced to look toward taking the round-the-world tour, he had visited the great house that had been the family center during seventeen more prosperous years but had become too expensive to live in. In a letter headed "At Home, Hartford," he wrote to Olivia, who was then in Paris, of his impressions upon entering the place: "[I]t seemed as if I had burst awake out of a hellish dream, and had never been away, and that you would come drifting down out of those dainty upper regions with the little children tagging after you." He added, "I was seized with a furious desire to have us all in this house again and right away, and never go outside the grounds any more forever—certainly never again to Europe." The desire quickly became a resolve: "I have made up my mind to one thing: if we go around the world we will move into our house when we get back." "At Home" was, thereafter, the title he used for the platform address that he was soon delivering repeatedly; he carried the dream of homecoming around the world with him. But close to the end of the long trip he received word of the death of Susy, of meningitis, on August 18, 1896. She had died in the Hartford house. Susy and he had been especially close, and the loss was for him the worst possible catastrophe. Moreover, her death had blasted the homecoming dream, for now the grieving family could not bear to live in the place at Hartford, and it seemed that there was no longer any goal or purpose to give meaning to their lives. "We are restless and unsettled," Mark Twain wrote early in the following year. "We had a charted course; we have none now. We are derelicts—and derelicts are indifferent to what may happen." It was at about this time that he wrote two story fragments in which a burning ship is made to symbolize a loss of fortune and of family.

In "The Passenger's Story" a sailing vessel is becalmed in the Indian Ocean. At night a fire breaks out, and the sailors are aroused just in time by a splendid and almost humanly intelligent St. Bernard dog, "the pet of the whole crew." All hands quickly take to the lifeboat and are saved—but the dog is left to burn. The captain has tied him to the mast, saying, "He'd be more in the way than a family of *children*—and he can *eat* as much as a family of children, *too*." In the other fragment, "The Enchanted Sea-Wilderness," the incident is developed more fully. Again the wonderful dog rescues the ship's company but is left to burn; again, copied word for word from the earlier draft, there is the captain's observation that the dog would have been as much in the way and would have eaten as much as a family of children. Susy, who had died of a brain–fever during an August heatwave, had almost literally burned up in the Hartford house; it is evident that Mark Twain was blaming himself for having left her behind during his travels.

The action of "The Enchanted Sea-Wilderness" begins with the ship becalmed as "a judgment on the captain" for letting the dog perish. The captain has always considered himself born lucky and for a while he cannot believe that his luck has been reversed. But storm follows calm as his ship is drawn southward into "the whirl and suck of the Devil's Race-Track," an immense circular region "in the midst of the vast ocean solitudes" that is "lashed and tossed and torn by eternal storms, is smothered in clouds and fog, and swept by fierce concentric currents." The Devil's Race-Track involves its victims in endlessly driven motion that goes around and around, arrives nowhere, and achieves nothing— or nothing but destruction. Once caught in its maelstrom forces there is no escape, only the possibility of further and final entrapment into the "Everlasting Sunday," an area of eternal and deathly stillness that lies at the center of the region, inside the storm belt. It is a Sargasso of the Antarctic, a graveyard for derelicts. The relevance of events of Mark Twain's life to the forbidding situation of the Devil's Race-Track and the Everlasting Sunday can easily be seen.

"Which Was the Dream?" was, as he planned it in the spring of 1897, to be a story that would begin with the burning of the family home and continue through a seventeen-year sequence of disasters, including again the voyage of a ship that would get into the Devil's Race-Track and then into the Everlasting Sunday. The narrator was at the end to find that it had all been a fifteen-second dream; yet the dream was to have been so terribly real to him that he would actually have aged by seventeen years and would upon awakening be unable to recognize his own children. Mark Twain did not write the story as planned. After dealing at some length with the business failure and subsequent disgrace of a great public figure and with the impact of these misfortunes upon his family, he left the manuscript incomplete. But in the following year he found a more promising approach. He wrote to William Dean Howells, "I feel sure that all of the first half of the story— and I hope three-fourths—will be comedy; but by the former plan the whole of it (except the first 3 chapters) would have been tragedy and unendurable, almost. I think I can carry the reader a long way before he suspects that I am laying a tragedy-trap." What he was then envisioning became "The Great Dark."

Following his new plan, he did postpone the tragic aspects of his tale
and play for humorous effects. There is, for example, much comic sea
language: his narrator refers to the "mizzen foretop halyards" (much
like referring to a basement penthouse), describes one sailor as "asleep
on the binnacle" and another as "bending on a scuttle-butt," confuses
"Top-sail haul" with "Topsails all," and makes other ludicrous mistakes.
There is also the scene in which the mate Turner is a butt for practical
jokes of the spectral Superintendent of Dreams, who, while remaining
invisible, keeps drinking Turner's coffee. After he had written these
and other comic episodes, Mark Twain next gave further attention to
the dream aspects of his story. It may be seen that he was particularly
interested in the relationship of the waking self and dream self, or conscious and unconscious levels of mind, and the possibility of confusing
dream and reality. Finally, in Book II he began to move toward his
planned ending. But although he had a giant squid, a terrible kraken-
like monster, attack the ship and so alarm the crew that they became
ready to mutiny, he never completed the writing of a tragic outcome. At
the time that the mutineers try to take over the ship, the captain, who
has so far played no prominent part in the story, suddenly discloses himself to be a forceful leader. After calming the rebellious sailors, he
makes a moving speech that ends on a note of high courage:

Are we rational men, manly men, men who can stand up and face hard luck
and a big difficulty that has been brought about by nobody's fault, and say
live or die, survive or perish, we are in for it, for good or bad, and we'll
stand by the ship if she goes to hell! . . . If it is God's will that we pull
through, we pull through—otherwise not. We haven't had an observation
for four months, but we are going ahead, and do our best to fetch up somewhere.

With this strong speech (which may remind one of Huckleberry Finn's
"All right, then, I'll *go* to hell!"), the manuscript stops. Thus, the very
last part of "The Great Dark," as written, expresses strength and reso-
luteness rather than futility and despair. The courageous words of the
captain must have been, for an author supposedly bent upon showing
the hopelessness of life, a difficult act to follow. In projecting a tragedy-
trap Mark Twain had perhaps failed to reckon with his own capacity

for rebound and affirmation. His inability to finish the story as planned was less a failure than a success: one senses the resurgence of latent strengths, just when these had seemed about to capitulate to despair. Having intended to lead his readers on and spring a tragic ending upon them, Mark Twain had himself been trapped by his own returning courage.

In the long story "Which Was It?," only the last part of which has been included here, there is a somewhat different but basically similar trapping of weakness by strength. The cowardly George Harrison, who has committed murder while attempting to rob his way out of financial ruin, finds himself overmastered and "taken over" by the suddenly powerful ex-slave Jasper, who has found proof of Harrison's guilt. Jasper and Harrison can perhaps be viewed as alter egos representing respectively the stronger and the weaker aspects of Mark Twain's own nature (though on the primary level of meaning Jasper is first of all to be taken as a wronged black who is a truly impressive figure and who bears himself with dignity and pride and a good deal of forbearance when the tables are turned on the arrogant white man). In any case, it is evident that strength has asserted itself again in a story intended to show the frailty of human character and the general hopelessness of the situation. And once again it is just at this point of the emergence of a strong character in the story that the manuscript breaks off.

Mark Twain seems in effect to have engaged in a continuing dialogue between his own affirming and negating viewpoints. He had much difficulty in reconciling these, and a sudden reversal would occur when the side that was at a particular time being opposed or suppressed reasserted itself. These alternations must have been most disconcerting, and it is understandable that when they occurred he would be likely to abandon his manuscript and go to work upon a new one—until much the same thing happened again. Such reversals and abandonments can also be disturbing to readers. But a more positive way of looking at it is that Mark Twain was unable to stay for very long in the company of one-sided views and half-truths, especially when they were his own. It is his insistent seeking for the genuinely twofold, the duplicitous view that keeps him so interesting.

The story "Three Thousand Years Among the Microbes" is indeed interesting. In taking up the writing of it in 1905, Mark Twain was returning to a view of the human situation that had been in his thoughts since the time of his work on *Huckleberry Finn*. In August 1884, when he was reading proof for that book, he had noted, "I think we are only the microscopic trichina concealed in the blood of some vast creature's veins, and it is that vast creature whom God concerns Himself about and not us." "Three Thousand Years Among the Microbes" is, as Paine described it, a "fantastic tale . . . , the autobiography of a microbe that had been once a man, and through a failure in a biological experiment transformed into a cholera germ when the experimenter was trying to turn him into a bird. His habitat was the person of a disreputable tramp named Blitzowski, a human continent of vast areas, with seething microbic nations." Curiously, this story appears to have been closely associated in Mark Twain's thought with his voyage-of-disaster writings. It relates especially to "The Great Dark," in which the voyage is taken in a seemingly vast ocean that is actually a drop of water which is under the lens of a microscope. Isabel V. Lyon, his literary secretary, kept a personal diary in which she wrote:

I asked Mr. Clemens how long he'd been turning those marvellous imaginings over in his mind, and he said that the idea had been there for many years—he tried to work it up from a drop of water and a scientist with a powerful microscope; but it wasn't right. He had to become the microbe.

This was to be another story of great personal significance to Mark Twain. It is most interesting to find that in this bizarre narrative he was still attempting to use his early recollections of Hannibal and the Mississippi that had served as the matrix of his best creative work. These Hannibalesque aspects are, however, curiously disguised or transformed. For instance, the narrator, whose microbic name is "Bkshp," eventually becomes known by the nickname "Huck." This "buried" identification is made only after the tale is well in progress, as may be seen by the reproduced page 110 of the manuscript.

There is a further, hidden tie between the names "Huck" and "Bkshp." The latter is represented as the narrator's former earthly name rendered into "microbic orthography." In the microbe nation, the commoners, of

to swear with. They asked me to give them one
one, + I gave them "Huck," an abbreviation of my
American nickname, Huxley. On their side, + to
show their thankfulness, they allowed me change their
names too. I invoiced 45 dictionary ones, + often
borrowed of mine,
considerable drill we selected the ones which they
could pull off with least danger to their jaws. I had
jest
approved therein, + with such names, the stones
or words of it —
(idea) That 8 slaves in the service of the owner; the 6 princes;
*Crest
Simple 20*
Samuel Gulliver, Dot. Pygmies + Head of the Pres.- Grandma Crest,~
Constantlynund. Poin - Dot. Diplocerens, Grammy of Supp--
ration family; Crest, the princes colors.

which Bkshp is one, are not allowed to include vowels in their names. Actually, Bkshp appears to be a coding of "Blankenship," the name of the Hannibal boy who was a childhood acquaintance of Samuel Clemens and who later served as the real-life model for Huckleberry Finn: "In *Huckleberry Finn* I have drawn Tom Blankenship exactly as he was," Mark Twain says in his *Autobiography*. Moreover, the drunken tramp who is the planet of the microbes contains "rivers (veins and arteries)" that "make the Mississippi . . . trifling . . . by comparison." Huck Bkshp, who exists within Blitzowski, is thus in circumstances like those described in the note of August 1884. He is a germ "concealed in the blood of some vast creature's veins." He is a Huckian germ adrift in the Mississippi-like veins of a cosmic Pap Finn!

Mark Twain, writing with great creative exuberance in producing this story, was identifying himself closely with his narrator Huck. On one page of his manuscript, here reproduced, it may be seen that he at first wrote, in a revealing slip of the pen, his own name in place of the appropriate one in a fantastic listing of heraldic crests for an aristocracy of germs. He wrote "Mark Twain" and then substituted "Huck" (next to last line of his page 111).

It is hardly surprising that he should have become so deeply immersed in his story. At last he had found the narrative perspective for the micro-macrocosmic analogy that had for many years been in his thoughts. He was able to express and explore the most comprehensive, even if not the most reassuring, view of the human situation that he had entertained. The tramp-planet-deity of the microbes is infested by the germs that are decaying and devouring him; but he in turn is also the infester and parasite of the greater cosmos, the "vast creature" in whom he moves and has his being. Huck, whose remembered former human life gives him an awareness that his fellow microbes do not share, observes of one of them:

He did not suspect that he, also, was engaged in gnawing, torturing, defiling, rotting and murdering a fellow-creature—he and all the swarming billions of his race. None of them suspects it. That is significant. It is suggestive. It hints at the possibility that the procession of known and listed devourers and persecutors is not complete. It suggests . . . that man is himself a microbe, and his globe a blood-corpuscle drifting with its shining

Rip Van Winkle. Saw ... Brewer: ...

Creat, a window sash.

Guy Manning. Skeptomania. Erysipelas. Creat, a ...

chain.

Dogberry. Acute pneumonia ... Creat, a ...

... Paige. Typhoid. Creat, ...

David Copperfield.

B ... Creat, a ...

Coloned Sellers. Branck — with 3 pomes. Lockjaw. Creat,

a broken needle.

Louis XIV. Consumption. Creat, a ...

King Herod. Diphtheria. Creat, more alphabet ...

... Asiatic Cholera. Creat, group of ... woman.

Don Quixote. Sacrament River. Creat, mass of rain-water 3...

brethren of the Milky Way down a vein of the Master and Maker of all things.

In another story of the same period (written in 1905 and 1906) that he called "The Refuge of the Derelicts," Mark Twain was again concerned with those conditions of life which impose upon everyone the roles of the devoured and the devourers. Old Admiral Stormfield is, like the captain in "The Great Dark" and the better known one in "Captain Stormfield's Visit to Heaven," profane, courageous, opinionated, and generous. Maintaining a home that is fitted out like a ship and run like one, he lets his place serve as a haven for human derelicts. These are persons who are no longer chasing after power and success and are not trying to exploit and victimize their fellow beings. They have refused the role of predator, or at least have tried to do so. But it is shown that even the derelicts, resigned and harmless as they seem to be, are ironically still among the predators. They are feeding upon the bounty of Admiral Stormfield. Fittingly enough, on the occasion of their Plum Duff, an entertainment night with "intellectual raisins in it," they are shown by an illustrated lecture how parasites must treat their host. A sequence of horrific motion-picture close-ups is projected for the derelicts while a sanctimonious lecturer enlarges upon the bounty and goodness of Nature. The pictures, which have been hastily provided, prove to be terribly at variance with the reassuring text of the speaker. A mother spider is shown trusting happily that food will be provided for her little spiderlings; she then learns that *she* is their food: they suddenly begin to devour her. The mother spider is then seized by a mother wasp to provide food for *her* young—and so on. The incident conveys the idea that any creature that survives does so by preying upon another; that no one can decline the grisly banquet—and live.

The same idea that life is so ordered that all must be victimizers and victims appears again in the latest-written selection, "Little Bessie," which was composed in 1908 when Mark Twain was in his seventy-third year. The question that naturally arises when one dwells upon the more grim aspects of life is the old one, older no doubt than the Book of Job, that is ever renewed in the thoughts of living mortals afflicted with pain and sorrow: "What is it all for?" Mark Twain phrased it thus as the query of a precocious little girl, not yet three years old.

The question may be naïve, but behind it there is the vision of the boldly speculative Mr. Hollister whose discussions with Bessie have so disturbed her convention-bound mother. The Hollister viewpoint is a more whole-seeing, or _holistic,_ one that does not blink at disquieting aspects of the human situation. Behind that viewpoint, moreover, there lies the multifaceted and comprehensive awareness, the sagely ironic awareness, of Mark Twain.

There is no need to pretend that everyone has by now become so sophisticated or enlightened that considerations of the darker aspects of life as explored by Mark Twain no longer can shock or distress any readers; even the more venturesomely philosophical reader could well find a few unsettling notions. Yet it would likewise be a mistake to take these later writings always seriously, or to think that Mark Twain was always taking them so. One notices that the tone of the "Little Bessie" dialogues is a felicitously bantering one, and that there are indications that he must have had an enjoyable time with the writing, in which he shows himself to be still a humorist as well as a satirist. Brief as the "Little Bessie" dialogues are, they include much that he dealt with at greater length in other late writings, and they are presented first as a ready entry into these materials and their duplicitous artistry. A few other quite brief pieces have been included for lunch-hour reading.

J. S. T.

The Devil's Race-Track:

MARK TWAIN'S
GREAT DARK
WRITINGS

Little Bessie

Chapter 1

Little Bessie Would Assist Providence

LITTLE BESSIE was nearly three years old. She was a good child, and not shallow, not frivolous, but meditative and thoughtful, and much given to thinking out the reasons of things and trying to make them harmonise with results. One day she said—

"Mamma, why is there so much pain and sorrow and suffering? What is it all for?"

It was an easy question, and mamma had no difficulty in answering it:

"It is for our good, my child. In His wisdom and mercy the Lord sends us these afflictions to discipline us and make us better."

"Is it *He* that sends them?"

"Yes."

"Does He send *all* of them, mamma?"

"Yes, dear, all of them. None of them comes by accident; He alone sends them, and always out of love for us, and to make us better."

"Isn't it strange!"

"Strange? Why, no, I have never thought of it in that way. I have not heard any one call it strange before. It has always seemed natural and right to me, and wise and most kindly and merciful."

"Who first thought of it like that, mamma? Was it you?"

"Oh, no, child, I was taught it."

3

"Who taught you so, mamma?"

"Why, really, I don't know—I can't remember. My mother, I suppose; or the preacher. But it's a thing that everybody knows."

"Well, anyway, it does seem strange. Did He give Billy Norris the typhus?"

"Yes."

"What for?"

"Why, to discipline him and make him good."

"But he died, mamma, and so it *couldn't* make him good."

"Well, then, I suppose it was for some other reason. We know it was a *good* reason, whatever it was."

"What do you think it was, mamma?"

"Oh, you ask so many questions! I think it was to discipline his parents."

"Well, then, it wasn't fair, mamma. Why should *his* life be taken away for their sake, when he wasn't doing anything?"

"Oh, *I* don't know! I only know it was for a good and wise and merciful reason."

"What reason, mamma?"

"I think—I think—well, it was a judgment; it was to punish them for some sin they had committed."

"But *he* was the one that was punished, mamma. Was that right?"

"Certainly, certainly. He does nothing that isn't right and wise and merciful. You can't understand these things now, dear, but when you are grown up you will understand them, and then you will see that they are just and wise."

After a pause:

"Did He make the roof fall in on the stranger that was trying to save the crippled old woman from the fire, mamma?"

"Yes, my child. W*ait!* Don't ask me why, because I don't know. I only know it was to discipline some one, or be a judgment upon somebody, or to show His power."

"That drunken man that stuck a pitchfork into Mrs. Welch's baby when—"

"Never mind about it, you needn't go into particulars; it was to discipline the child—*that* much is certain, anyway."

"Mamma, Mr. Burgess said in his sermon that billions of little creatures are sent into us to give us cholera, and typhoid, and lockjaw, and more than a thousand other sicknesses and—mamma, does He send them?"

"Oh, certainly, child, certainly. Of course."

"What for?"

"Oh, to *dis*cipline us! haven't I told you so, over and over again?"

"It's awful cruel, mamma! And silly! and if I—"

"Hush, oh *hush!* do you want to bring the lightning?"

"You know the lightning *did* come last week, mamma, and struck the new church, and burnt it down. Was it to discipline the church?"

(Wearily). "Oh, I suppose so."

"But it killed a hog that wasn't doing anything. Was it to discipline the hog, mamma?"

"Dear child, don't you want to run out and play a while? If you would like to—"

"Mamma, only think! Mr. Hollister says there isn't a bird or fish or reptile or any other animal that hasn't got an enemy that Providence has sent to bite it and chase it and pester it, and kill it, and suck its blood and discipline it and make it good and religious. Is that true, mother—because if it is true, why did Mr. Hollister laugh at it?"

"That Hollister is a scandalous person, and I don't want you to listen to anything he says."

"Why, mamma, he is very interesting, and *I* think he tries to be good. He says the wasps catch spiders and cram them down into their nests in the ground—*alive*, mamma!—and there they live and suffer days and days and days, and the hungry little wasps chewing their legs and gnawing into their bellies all the time, to make them good and religious and praise God for His infinite mercies. *I* think Mr. Hollister is just lovely, and ever so kind; for when I asked him if *he* would treat a spider like that, he said he hoped to be damned if he would; and then he—"

"My child! oh, do for goodness' sake—"

"And mamma, he says the spider is appointed to catch the fly, and drive her fangs into his bowels, and suck and suck and suck his blood, to discipline him and make him a Christian; and whenever the fly buzzes his wings with the pain and misery of it, you can see by the spider's grateful eye that she is thanking the Giver of All Good for— well, she's saying grace, as *he* says; and also, he—"

"Oh, aren't you *ever* going to get tired chattering! If you want to go out and play—"

"Mamma, he says himself that all troubles and pains and miseries and rotten diseases and horrors and villainies are sent to us in mercy and kindness to discipline us; and he says it is the duty of every father and mother to *help* Providence, every way they can; and says they can't do it by just scolding and whipping, for that won't answer, it is weak and no good—Providence's way is best, and it is every parent's duty and every *person's* duty to help discipline everybody, and cripple them and kill them, and starve them, and freeze them, and rot them with diseases, and lead them into murder and theft and dishonor and disgrace; and he says Providence's invention for disciplining us and the animals is the very brightest idea that ever was, and not even an idiot could get up anything shinier. Mamma, brother Eddie needs disciplining, right away; and I know where you can get the smallpox for him, and the itch, and the diphtheria, and bone-rot, and heart disease, and consumption, and—*Dear* mamma, have you fainted! I will run and bring help! Now *this* comes of staying in town this hot weather."

Chapter 2

Creation of Man

Mᴀᴍᴍᴀ. You disobedient child, have you been associating with that irreligious Hollister again?

Bessie. Well, mamma, he is interesting, anyway, although wicked, and I can't help loving interesting people. Here is the conversation we had:

Hollister. Bessie, suppose you should take some meat and bones and fur, and make a cat out of it, and should tell the cat, Now you are not to be unkind to any creature, on pain of punishment and death. And suppose the cat should disobey, and catch a mouse and torture it and kill it. What would you do to the cat?

Bessie. Nothing.

H. Why?

B. Because I know what the cat would say. She would say, It's my nature, I couldn't help it; I didn't make my nature, *you* made it. And so you are responsible for what I've done—I'm not. I couldn't answer that, Mr. Hollister.

H. It's just the case of Frankenstein and his Monster over again.

B. What is that?

H. Frankenstein took some flesh and bones and blood and made a man out of them; the man ran away and fell to raping and robbing and murdering everywhere, and Frankenstein was horrified and in despair, and said, *I* made him, without asking his consent, and it makes me responsible for every crime he commits. *I* am the criminal, he is innocent.

B. Of course he was right.

H. I judge so. It's just the case of God and man and you and the cat over again.

B. How is that?

H. God made man, without man's consent, and made his nature, too; made it vicious instead of angelic, and then said, Be angelic, or I will punish you and destroy you. But no matter, God is responsible for everything man does, all the same; He can't get around that fact. There is only one Criminal, and it is not man.

Mamma. This is atrocious! it is wicked, blasphemous, irreverent, horrible!

Bessie. Yes'm, but it's true. And I'm not going to make a cat. I would be above making a cat if I couldn't make a good one.

Chapter 3

MAMMA, if a person by the name of Jones kills a person by the name of Smith just for amusement, it's murder, isn't it, and Jones is a murderer?

Yes, my child.

And Jones is punishable for it?

Yes, my child.

Why, mamma?

Why? Because God has forbidden homicide in the Ten Commandments, and therefore whoever kills a person commits a crime and must
suffer for it.

But mamma, suppose Jones has by birth such a violent temper that
he can't control himself?

He *must* control himself. God requires it.

But he doesn't make his own temper, mamma, he is born with it, like
the rabbit and the tiger; and so, why should he be held responsible?

Because God *says* he is responsible and *must* control his temper.

But he *can't*, mamma; and so, don't you think it is God that does the
killing and is responsible, because it was *He* that gave him the temper
which he couldn't control?

Peace, my child! He *must* control it, for God requires it, and that
ends the matter. It settles it, and there is no room for argument.

(*After a thoughtful pause.*) It doesn't seem to me to settle it. Mamma, murder is murder, isn't it? and whoever commits it is a murderer?
That is the plain simple fact, isn't it?

(*Suspiciously.*) What are you arriving at now, my child?

Mamma, when God designed Jones He could have given him a rabbit's temper if He had wanted to, couldn't He?

Yes.

Then Jones would not kill anybody and have to be hanged?

True.

But He chose to give Jones a temper that would *make* him kill
Smith. Why, then, isn't *He* responsible?

Because He also gave Jones a Bible. The Bible gives Jones ample
warning not to commit murder; and so if Jones commits it he alone is
responsible.

(*Another pause.*) Mamma, did God make the house-fly?

Certainly, my darling.

What for?

For some great and good purpose, and to display His power.

What is the great and good purpose, mamma?

We do not know, my child. We only know that He makes *all* things for a great and good purpose. But this is too large a subject for a dear little Bessie like you, only a trifle over three years old.

Possibly, mamma, yet it profoundly interests me. I have been reading about the fly, in the newest science-book. In that book he is called "the most dangerous animal and the most murderous that exists upon the earth, killing hundreds of thousands of men, women and children every year, by distributing deadly diseases among them." Think of it, mamma, the *most* fatal of all the animals! by all odds the most murderous of all the living things created by God. Listen to this, from the book:

> Now, the house fly has a very keen scent for filth of any kind. Whenever there is any within a hundred yards or so, the fly goes for it to smear its mouth and all the sticky hairs of its six legs with dirt and disease germs. A second or two suffices to gather up many thousands of these disease germs, and then off goes the fly to the nearest kitchen or dining room. There the fly crawls over the meat, butter, bread, cake, anything it can find in fact, and often gets into the milk pitcher, depositing large numbers of disease germs at every step. The house fly is as disgusting as it is dangerous.

Isn't it horrible, mamma! One fly produces fifty-two billions of descendants in 60 days in June and July, and they go and crawl over sick people and wade through pus, and sputa, and foul matter exuding from sores, and gaum themselves with every kind of disease-germ, then they go to everybody's dinner-table and wipe themselves off on the butter and the other food, and many and many a painful illness and ultimate death results from this loathsome industry. Mamma, they murder seven thousand persons in New York City alone, every year—people against whom they have no quarrel. To kill without cause is murder—nobody denies that. Mamma?

Well?

Have the flies a Bible?

Of course not.

You have said it is the Bible that makes man responsible. If God didn't give him a Bible to circumvent the nature that He deliberately gave him, God would be responsible. He gave the fly his murderous nature, and sent him forth unobstructed by a Bible or any other restraint to commit murder by wholesale. And so, therefore, God is Himself responsible. God is a murderer. Mr. Hollister says so. Mr. Hollister says God can't make one moral law for man and another for Himself. He says it would be laughable.

Do shut up! I wish that that tiresome Hollister was in H—amburg! He is an ignorant, unreasoning, illogical ass, and I have told you over and over again to keep out of his poisonous company.

Chapter 4

"MAMMA, what is a virgin?"

"A maid."

"Well, what is a maid?"

"A girl or woman that isn't married."

"Uncle Jonas says that sometimes a virgin that has been having a child—"

"Nonsense! A virgin can't have a child."

"Why can't she, mamma?"

"Well, there are reasons why she can't."

"What reasons, mamma?"

"Physiological. She would have to cease to be a virgin before she could have the child."

"How do you mean, mamma?"

"Well, let me see. It's something like this: a Jew couldn't be a Jew after he had become a Christian; he couldn't be Christian and Jew at the same time. Very well, a person couldn't be mother and virgin at the same time."

"Why, mamma, Sally Brooks has had a child, and *she's* a virgin."

"Indeed? Who says so?"

"She says so herself."

"Oh, no doubt! Are there any other witnesses?"

"Yes—there's a dream. She says the governor's private secretary appeared to her in a dream and told her she was going to have a child, and it came out just so."

"I shouldn't wonder! Did he say the governor was the corespondent?"

Chapter 5

B. Mama, didn't you tell me an ex-governor, like Mr. Burlap, is a person that's been governor but isn't a governor any more?

M. Yes, dear.

B. And Mr. Williams said "ex" always stands for a Has Been, didn't he?

M. Yes, child. It is a vulgar way of putting it, but it expresses the fact.

B, (eagerly). So then Mr. Hollister was right, after all. He says the Virgin Mary isn't a virgin any more, she's a Has Been. He says—

M. It is false! Oh, it was just like that godless miscreant to try to undermine an innocent child's holy belief with his foolish lies; and if I could have my way, I—

B. But mama,—honest and true—*is* she still a virgin—a *real* virgin, you know?

M. Certainly she is; and has never been anything *but* a virgin—oh, the adorable One, the pure, the spotless, the undefiled!

B. Why, mama, Mr. Hollister says she *can't* be. That's what *he* says. He says she had five children *after* she had the One that was begotten by absent treatment and didn't break anything and he thinks such a lot of child-bearing, spread over years and years and years, would ultimately wear a virgin's virginity so thin that even Wall street would consider the stock too lavishly watered and you couldn't place it there at any discount you could name, because the Board would say it was wildcat, and wouldn't list it. That's what *he* says. And besides—

M. Go to the nursery, instantly! Go!

Chapter 6

MAMMA, is Christ God?

Yes, my child.

Mamma, how can He be Himself and Somebody Else at the same time?

He isn't, my darling. It is like the Siamese twins—two persons, one born ahead of the other, but equal in authority, equal in power.

I understand it, now, mamma, and it is quite simple. One twin has sexual intercourse with his mother, and begets himself and his brother; and next he has sexual intercourse with his grandmother and begets his mother. I should think it would be difficult, mamma, though interesting. Oh, ever so difficult. I should think that the Corespondent—

All things are possible with God, my child.

Yes, I suppose so. But not with any other Siamese twin, I suppose. *You* don't think any ordinary Siamese twin could beget himself and his brother on his mother, do you, mamma, and then go on back while his hand is in and beget *her*, too, on his grandmother?

Certainly not, my child. None but God can do these wonderful and holy miracles.

And enjoy them. For of course He enjoys them, or He wouldn't go foraging around among the family like that, *would* He, mamma?—injuring their reputations in the village and causing talk. Mr. Hollister says it was wonderful and awe-inspiring in those days, but wouldn't work now. He says that if the Virgin lived in Chicago now, and got in the family way and explained to the newspaper fellows that God was the Corespondent, she couldn't get two in ten of them to believe it. He says they are a hell of a lot!

My child!

Well, that is what he says, anyway.

Oh, I do *wish* you would keep away from that wicked, wicked man!

He doesn't *mean* to be wicked, mamma, and he doesn't blame God. No, he doesn't blame Him; he says they all do it—gods do. It's their habit, they've always been that way.

What way, dear?

Going around unvirgining the virgins. He says our God did not invent the idea—it was old and mouldy before He happened on it. Says He hasn't invented anything, but got His Bible and His Flood and His morals and all His ideas from earlier gods, and they got them from still earlier gods. He says there never was a god yet that wasn't born of a Virgin. Mr. Hollister says no virgin is safe where a god is. He says he wishes he was a god; he says he would make virgins so scarce that—

Peace, peace! *Don't* run on so, my child. If you—

—and he advised me to lock my door nights, because—

Hush, *hush*, will you!

—because although I am only three and a half years old and quite safe from *men*—

Mary Ann, come and get this child! There, now, go along with you, and don't come near me again until you can interest yourself in some subject of a lower grade and less awful than theology.

Bessie, (disappearing.) Mr. Hollister says there *ain't* any.

(1908)

Little Nelly Tells a Story
Out of Her Own Head

Twenty-two-or-three years ago, in Cleveland, a thing happened which I still remember pretty well. Out in the suburbs, it was—on the lake; the Fairbankses had bought a large house and a great place there, and were living sumptuously, after Mr. Fairbanks's long life of struggle and privation in building up the Cleveland Herald to high place and prosperity. I was there a week, and the Severances came out to dinner twice, and they and "Mother Fairbanks" and I talked over the old times we had enjoyed together in the "Quaker City," when we were "Innocents Abroad." Meantime, every day Mother Fairbanks was busy staging a brief little drama of "The Prince and Pauper" and drilling the children from town who were to play it.

One of these children was Nelly (nevermindtherestofthename) and she was a prodigy—a bright and serious and pretty little creature of nine, who was to play Lady Jane Grey. She had a large reputation as a reciter of poetry and little speeches before company in her mother's drawing-room at home; she did her work charmingly, and the sweetest charm about it was the aged gravity and sincerity and earnestness which she put into it. Latterly she had added a new laurel: she had composed a quaint little story, "out of her own head," and had de-

14

lighted a parlor-audience with it and made herself the envy of all the children around.

The Prince and Pauper play was to be given in my honor, and I had a seat in the centre of the front row; a hundred and fifty friends of the house were present in evening costume, old and young and both sexes, the great room was brilliantly lighted, the fine clothes made the aspect gay, everybody was laughing and chatting and having a good time, the curtain was about ready to rise.

A hitch occurred. Edward VI, (to be played by a girl,) had been belated, it would take a quarter of an hour to dress her for her part. This announcement was made, and Mother Fairbanks retired to attend to this function, and took Nelly's mother with her to help. Presently the audience began to call for little Nelly to come on the stage and do her little story. Nelly's twin sister brought her on, and sat down in a chair beside her and folded her pudgy hands in her lap, and beamed upon the house her joy in the ovation which Lady Jane received. Lady Jane got another round when she said she had made a new story out of her own head and would recite it—which she proceeded to do, with none of her sweet solemnities lacking. To-wit:

Once there were two ladies, and were twins, and lived together, Mary and Olivia Scott, in the house they were born in, and all alone, for Mr. and Mrs. Scott were dead, now. After a while they got lonesome and wished they could have a baby, and said God will provide.

(You could feel the walls give, the strain upon suppressed emotion was so great.)

So when the baby came they were very glad, and the neighbors surprised.

(The walls spread again, but held.)

And asked where they got it and they said by prayer, which is the only way.

(There was not a sound in the audience except the muffled volleying of bursting buttons and the drip of unrestrainable tears. With a gravity not of this world, the inspired child went on:)

But there was no way to feed it at first, because it had only gums and could not bite, then they prayed and God sent a lady which had several and showed them how, then it got fat and they were so happy you cannot think; and thought oh, if they could have some more—and prayed again and got them, because whatever you pray for in the right spirit you get it a thousand fold.

(I could feel the throes and quivers coursing up and down the body of the ripe maiden lady at my left, and she buried her face in her hand-kerchief and seemed to sob, but it was not sobbing. The walls were sucking in and bellying out, but they held. The two children on the stage were a dear and lovely picture to see, the face of the one so sweetly earnest, the other's face so speakingly lit up with pride in her gifted sister and with worshipping admiration.)

And God was pleased the way they were so thankful to have that child, and every prayer they made they got another one, and by the time fall came they had thirteen, and whoever will do the right way can have as many, perhaps more, for nothing is impossible with God, and whoever puts their trust in Him they will have their reward, heaped up and running over. When we think of Mary and Olivia Scott it should learn us to have confidence. End of the tale—good bye.

The dear little thing! She made her innocent bow, and retired with-out a suspicion that she had been an embarrassment. Nothing would have happened, now, perhaps, if quiet could have been maintained for a few minutes, so that the people could get a grip upon themselves, but the strain overpowered my old maid partner and she exploded like a bomb; a general and unrestrained crash of laughter followed, of course, the happy tears flowed like brooks, and no one was sorry of the oppor-tunity to laugh himself out and get the blessed relief that comes of that privilege in such circumstances.

I think the Prince and Pauper went very well—I do not remember; but the other incident stays by me with great and contenting vividness —the picture and everything.

(1907)

The Ten Commandments

THE TEN Commandments were made for man alone. We should think it strange if they had been made for *all* the animals.

We should say "Thou shalt not kill" is too general, too sweeping. It includes the field mouse and the butterfly. They *can't* kill. And it includes the tiger, which can't *help* it.

It is a case of Temperament and Circumstance again. You can arrange no circumstances that can move the field mouse and the butterfly to kill; their temperaments will keep them unaffected by temptations to kill, they can avoid that crime without an effort. But it isn't so with the tiger. Throw a lamb in his way when he is hungry, and his temperament will compel him to kill it.

Butterflies and field mice are common among men; they can't kill, their temperaments make it impossible. There are tigers among men, also. Their temperaments move them to violence, and when Circumstance furnishes the opportunity and the powerful motive, they kill. They can't help it.

No penal law can deal out *justice*; it must deal out injustice in every instance. Penal laws have a high value, in that they protect—in a considerable measure—the multitude of the gentle-natured from the violent minority.

For a penal law is a Circumstance. It is a warning which intrudes and stays a would-be murderer's hand—sometimes. Not always, but in many and many a case. It can't stop the *real* man-tiger; nothing can do that. Slade had 26 deliberate murders on his soul when he finally went to his death on the scaffold. He would kill a man for a trifle; or for nothing. He loved to kill. It was his temperament. He did not make his temperament, God gave it him at his birth. Gave it him and said Thou shalt not kill. It was like saying Thou shalt not eat. Both appetites were given him at birth. He could be obedient and starve both up to a certain point, but that was as far as he could go. Another man could go further; but not Slade.

Holmes, the Chicago monster, inveigled some dozens of men and women into his obscure quarters and privately butchered them. Holmes's inborn nature was such that whenever he had what seemed a reasonably safe opportunity to kill a stranger he couldn't successfully resist the temptation to do it.

Justice was finally meted out to Slade and to Holmes. That is what the newspapers said. It is a common phrase, and a very old one. But it probably isn't true. When a man is hanged for slaying *one* man that phrase comes into service and we learn that justice was meted out to the slayer. But Holmes slew sixty. There seems to be a discrepancy in this distribution of justice. If Holmes got justice, the other man got 59 times more than justice.

But the phrase is wrong, anyway. The *word* is the wrong word. Criminal courts do not dispense "justice"—they *can't*; they only dispense protections to the community. It is all they can do.

(1905 or 1906)

Thoughts of God

How OFTEN we are moved to admit the intelligence exhibited in both the designing and the execution of some of His works. Take the fly, for instance. The planning of the fly was an application of pure intelligence, morals not being concerned. Not one of us could have planned the fly, not one of us could have constructed him; and no one would have considered it wise to try, except under an assumed name. It is believed by some that the fly was introduced to meet a long-felt want. In the course of ages, for some reason or other, there have been millions of these persons, but out of this vast multitude there has not been one who has been willing to explain what the want was. At least satisfactorily. A few have explained that there was need of a creature to remove disease-breeding garbage; but these being then asked to explain what long-felt want the disease-breeding garbage was introduced to supply, they have not been willing to undertake the contract.

There is much inconsistency concerning the fly. In all the ages he has not had a friend, there has never been a person in the earth who could have been persuaded to intervene between him and extermination; yet billions of persons have excused the Hand that made him— and this without a blush. Would they have excused a Man in the same circumstances, a man positively known to have invented the fly? On the contrary. For the credit of the race let us believe it would have

19

been all day with that man. Would these persons consider it just to reprobate in a child, with its undeveloped morals, a scandal which they would overlook in the Pope?

When we reflect that the fly was not invented for pastime, but in the way of business; that he was not flung off in a heedless moment and with no object in view but to pass the time, but was the fruit of long and pains-taking labor and calculation, and with a definite and far-reaching purpose in view; that his character and conduct were planned out with cold deliberation; that his career was foreseen and fore-ordered, and that there was no want which he could supply, we are hopelessly puzzled, we cannot understand the moral lapse that was able to render possible the conceiving and the consummation of this squalid and malevolent creature.

Let us try to think the unthinkable; let us try to imagine a Man of a sort willing to invent the fly; that is to say, a man destitute of feeling; a man willing to wantonly torture and harass and persecute myriads of creatures who had never done him any harm and could not if they wanted to, and—the majority of them—poor dumb things not even aware of his existence. In a word, let us try to imagine a man with so singular and so lumbering a code of morals as this: that it is fair and right to send afflictions upon the *just*—upon the unoffending as well as upon the offending, without discrimination.

If we can imagine such a man, that is the man that could invent the fly, and send him out on his mission and furnish him his orders: "Depart into the uttermost corners of the earth, and diligently do your appointed work. Persecute the sick child; settle upon its eyes, its face, its hands, and gnaw and pester and sting; worry and fret and madden the worn and tired mother who watches by the child, and who humbly prays for mercy and relief with the pathetic faith of the deceived and the unteachable. Settle upon the soldier's festering wounds in field and hospital and drive him frantic while he also prays, and betweentimes curses, with none to listen but you, Fly, who get all the petting and all the protection, without even praying for it. Harry and persecute the forlorn and forsaken wretch who is perishing of the plague, and in his terror and despair praying; bite, sting, feed upon his ulcers, dabble your feet in his rotten blood, gum them thick with plague-germs—

feet cunningly designed and perfected for this function ages ago in the beginning—carry this freight to a hundred tables, among the just and the unjust, the high and the low, and walk over the food and gaum it with filth and death. Visit all; allow no man peace till he get it in the grave; visit and afflict the hard-worked and unoffending horse, mule, ox, ass, pester the patient cow, and all the kindly animals that labor without fair reward here and perish without hope of it hereafter; spare no creature, wild or tame; but wheresoever you find one, make his life a misery, treat him as the innocent deserve; and so please Me and increase My glory Who made the fly."

We hear much about His patience and forbearance and long-suffering; we hear nothing about our own, which much exceeds it. We hear much about His mercy and kindness and goodness—in words—the words of His Book and of His pulpit—and the meek multitude is content with this evidence, such as it is, seeking no further; but whoso searcheth after a concreted sample of it will in time acquire fatigue. There being no instances of it. For what are gilded as mercies are not in any recorded case more than mere common justices, and *due*—due without thanks or compliment. To rescue without personal risk a cripple from a burning house is not a mercy, it is a mere commonplace duty; anybody would do it that could. And not by proxy, either—delegating the work but confiscating the credit for it. If men neglected "God's poor" and "God's stricken and helpless ones" as He does, what would become of them? The answer is to be found in those dark lands where man follows His example and turns his indifferent back upon them: they get no help at all; they cry, and plead and pray in vain, they linger and suffer, and miserably die. If you will look at the matter rationally and without prejudice, the proper place to hunt for the *facts* of His mercy, is not where man does the mercies and He collects the praise, but in those regions where He has the field to Himself.

It is plain that there is one moral law for heaven and another for the earth. The pulpit assures us that wherever we see suffering and sorrow which we can relieve and do not do it, we sin, heavily. *There was never yet a case of suffering or sorrow which God could not relieve.* Does He sin, then? If He is the Source of Morals He does—certainly nothing can be plainer than that, you will admit. Surely the Source of law cannot violate law and stand unsmirched; surely the judge upon the bench cannot forbid crime and then revel in it himself unreproached. Nevertheless we have this curious spectacle: daily the trained parrot in the pulpit gravely delivers himself of these ironies, which he has acquired at second-hand and adopted without examination, to a trained congregation which accepts them without examination, and neither the speaker nor the hearer laughs at himself. It does seem as if we ought to be humble when we are at a bench-show, and not put on airs of intellectual superiority there.

(early 1900s)

The Synod of Praise

Animals and Insects

Moderator, the Cow,

        1st Vice—the Giraffe (spectacles)
        2d   ″ —the Rabbit (″   )
        3d   ″ —the Goat   (″   )

Gᴏᴅ—*the Elephant.* Knocks an innocent over now and then or steps on him—this comes out in the speeches—it is always either for His "glory" or to teach some kind of saving lesson, or to over-adequately punish an unknown offence.

Monkey has a disease inherited from his grandfather—is *this* a punishment? Then for what? For a lesson? then how? Evidently God is not moral (sensation). Dull—no perception of justice. No generosity, courtesy, magnanimity.

Invites me to his house, I am his guest. He insults me, maltreats me, cripples me, diseases me, kicks me out when he is tired of me. No gentleman.

Expects me to worship him. A guest worship his host? A guest owes no worship to his host. When hospitably treated he owes acknowledgments, worded in dignified and self-respecting phrase, but no servility, no bending of the knee.

But he has a right to require worship?

Then I his guest am also his slave.

23

The slave says "I belong to my master, he has a right to do what he pleases with me." Which is a lie. The master has no rights at all over his slave. Unless force creates rights. If compulsion over the helpless creates rights, God has rights—he has no other. If the exercise of lawless force is moral, God is moral.

Blame. It is word applicable to God only. Unrequested, he made man, and is responsible for all man's words and deeds. The vote of a continent of Gods could not absolve him from his responsibility nor wash him clean of the stain of any harm that may befal his creature.

Brutes. They cannot enter heaven. Their sufferings are merely to punish their present sins and discipline them.

Grasshopper. Spider fast to his body and sucking its juices.

Caterpillar the same.

Fish with parasites on eye. Etc.

All humbly praise God for these deserved afflictions.

The parasites have parasites and these have others. They all praise.

Cow: He is our loving father.

Monkey. My praise is that we have not two of him.

(early 1900s)

The Passenger's Story.

I T WAS on an American liner—couple of years ago. I was a second cabin passenger. It was after midnight, and very dark—and misty and damp. There was some sea on. I was on the upper deck, away aft, snuggled under the lee of the canvassed rail on the starboard side, doing nothing. That is, *thinking*. Nobody stirring; the whole deck was a solitude. By and by two dim figures came down the port side talking and they stopped and stood there, about opposite me and went on with their talk. One had a heavy voice, the other one had an ordinary voice and a little hacking cough. I couldn't tell what the men were like—except that both were large —they were just shapeless blots in the gloom. The bass voice said—

"But I've always had a good word for *dogs* ever *since*, when I hear people talking against them; because *that dog* saved my life."

(*Hack-hack.*) Is *that so?*

Yes, he *did*. And my whole *crew*, too—14 *men*. Do *you* like *dogs?*

(*H-h*). *Like* them? Well I should *think* so.

All *right*, then. Where *was* I?

(*H-h*) Becalmed in the Indian ocean.

I *know*. But where had I got to about the *dog?*

H. Why, you *started* to tell how you *got* him; but you switched off onto—

O, yes, I remember, now. He came aboard at the dock, racing

25

around with his nose down, hunting for somebody that had been there—his master, I reckon—and the crew captured him and shut him below, and we sailed in a hour. Well, sir, he was just a darling, that dog. Inside of a week he was the pet of the whole crew. He was brim full of play, and fun and affection and good nature. They bedded him like the *aristocracy,* and there warn't a *man* but would divide his dinner with him; and he *was* the lovingest creature and the *gratefulest* you ever *saw.*

Well, that night that I was telling you about, it was *warm,* and *still* and *drowsy* and *lazy;* and the sails hung *idle,* and the deck-watch and the lookout and everybody *else* was sound *asleep.* Well along about an hour after midnight there was a *tremendous* scratching and barking at my door, and *I* jumped *out* and that dog was just *wild* with excitement, and rushed off and just as good as *told* me to come *along,* and come *quick.* Well, sir, she was a*fire* down in the *hold,* and he had *discovered* it. Down I plunged, and *he* went raging off and waking up the *others.*

That *was* the closest fit! Remember the *powder*-kegs I told you about? Why in another two *minutes* the fire would a *had* 'em and we'd a been blown into the *sky.*

H. Good *dog—splen*-did dog!

I had the powder out of danger in half a *second,* and *here* came the men *tearing—*and *white?* Why

[A page of the manuscript is missing.]

was in the boat but *me,* and the flames were soaring up and lighting the whole *ocean,* I tied the dog to the foot of the *main*mast and then got in my*self* and took the *tiller* and said "All *ready—* give *way."*

Why, they all shouted at once—"*What?*—going to leave the *dog?"*

I said, Did you hear the *order?* Give *way.*

Well the *tears* begun to run down their *faces.* And they said, Why he saved our *lives—*we *can't* leave him. I said—

You don't know what you're *talking* about. He'd be more in the way than a family of *children*—and he can *eat* as much as a family

of children, *too*. Now men, *you know me*—and I pulled a
revolver

[A page of the manuscript is missing.]

tugged at his *rope*, and begged and moaned and yelped—why it
was as plain as if he was *saying*, Oh, *don't* leave me, *please* don't
leave me, *I* haven't done any harm. And then presently the fire
swept down on him and he sent up two or three *awful* shrieks and
it was all *over*. And the men sat there sobbing and crying like
children.

H. Is that *true?*

"True as *gospel.*"

H. It was the vilest murder that ever was *done*—and I hope you
will land in hell before you are an hour *older*.

I heard a blow struck, then another and *another;* the ship gave a
heavy *lurch* and the two vague forms came †

(1896)

_____

† Mark Twain here left his sketch incomplete.

The Enchanted Sea-Wilderness

SCATTERED about the world's oceans at enormous distances apart are spots and patches where no compass has any value. When the compass enters one of these bewitched domains it goes insane and whirls this way and that and settles nowhere, and is scared and distressed, and cannot be comforted. The sailor must steer by sun, moon and stars when they show, and by guess when they don't, till he gets past that enchanted region. The worst of these spots and the largest one is in the midst of the vast ocean solitudes that lie between the Cape of Good Hope and the south pole. It is five hundred miles in diameter, and is circular in shape; four-fifths of this diameter is lashed and tossed and torn by eternal storms, is smothered in clouds and fog, and swept by fierce concentric currents; but in the centre there is a circular area a hundred miles across, in whose outer part the storms and the currents die down; and in the centre of this centre there is still a final circular area about fifty miles across where there are but the faintest suggestions of currents, no winds, no whisper of wandering zephyr, even, but everywhere the silence and peace and solemnity of a calm which is eternal.

There is a bronzed and gray sailor on board this ship who has had experience of that strange place, and the other night after midnight I went forward to the forecastle and got him to tell me about it. The hint came from the purser, who said it was a curious and interesting story. I kept it in my memory as well as I could, and wrote it down next day—in my own language, for I could not remember his, of course. He said that the outer great circle where the currents are—as already described by me—is known among sailors as the Devil's Race-Track, and that they call the central calm Everlasting Sunday. Here is his account.

The Enchanted Sea-Wilderness.

We got into that place by a judgment—judgment on the captain of the ship. It was this way. We were becalmed, away down south, dead summer time, middle of December, 1853. The vessel was a brig, and a fairly good sailor; name, *Mabel Thorpe*; loaded with provisions and blasting powder for the new gold mines in Australia; Elliot Cable master, a rough man and hard-hearted, but he *was* master, and that is the truth. When he laid down the law there wasn't pluck enough in the whole ship to take objections to it.

Now to go back a little. About two months before, when we were lying at the dock the day we sailed, a lovely big beautiful dog came aboard and went racing around with his nose down hunting for somebody that had been there—his owner, I reckon—and the crew caught him and shut him up below, and we sailed in an hour. He was a darling, that dog. He was full of play, and fun, and affection and good nature, the dearest and sweetest disposition that ever was. Inside of two days he was the pet of the whole crew. We bedded him like the aristocracy, and there wasn't a man but would divide his dinner with him, and he was ever so loving and grateful. And smart, too; smart and willing. He elected of his own notion to stand watch and watch with us. He was in the larboard watch, and he would turn out at eight bells without anybody having to tell him it was "Yo-ho, the larboard watch!" And he would tug at the ropes and help make sail or take it in, and seemed to know all about it, just like any old veteran. The crew were proud of him—well, of course they would be.

And so, as I was saying, we got becalmed when we were out about two months. It was warm that night, and still and drowsy and lazy; and the sails hung idle, and the deck-watch and the lookout and everybody else was sound asleep, including the dog, for it was his trick below and he had turned in at midnight. Well,

along about an hour after midnight there was a tremendous
scratching and barking at the captain's door, and he jumped out of
his bunk, and that dog was just wild with excitement, and rushed
off, and just as good as *told* the captain to come along and come
quick. You see, the ship was afire down in the hold, and he had
discovered it. Down the captain plunged, and the dog rushed off
waking up the others.

Dear, dear, it was the closest fit! The fire was crowding a pile of
the powder-kegs close, and in another minute or two it would have
had them and we should have been blown into the sky. The
captain snatched the pile of kegs out of reach in half a second, and
we were safe; because the bulk of the powder was away up
forward. And by this time we all came tearing down—white?—oh,
white as ghosts when we saw what a close shave we had had. Well,
then we started in and began to hug the dog. And wasn't he a
proud dog?—and happy?—why, if he had had speech he couldn't
have expressed it any better. The captain snarled at us and said:

"You may well hug him, you worthless hounds! he saved my life,
not you, you lazy rips. I've never cared for dogs before, but next time
I hear people talking against them I'll put in a word for this one,
anyway."

Overboard went that little batch of powder kegs, and then we
flew around getting food and water and compass and sextant and
chart and things for the boat; and the dog helped, just like anybody
else. He did a grown man's work carrying things to the boat, and
then went dancing around *superintending* whilst we launched her.
Bright?—oh, you can't think how bright he was, and intelligent.

When everybody was in the boat but the captain, and the flames
were soaring up and lighting the whole ocean, he tied the dog to
the foot of the mainmast and then got in himself and took the tiller
and said—

"All ready. Give way!"

We were all struck dumb, for a second, then all shouted at
once—

"Oh, *captain!*—going to leave the dog?"

He roared out in a fury—

"Didn't you hear the order? Give way!"

Well, the tears began to run down our faces; and we said, Why, he saved our *lives*—we *can't* leave him. Please, captain! please let him come.

"What, in this little tub of a boat? You don't know what you are talking about. He'd be more in the way than a family of children; and he can eat as much as a family of children, too. Now, men, you know *me*"—and he pulled an old pepper-box revolver and pointed it—"give *way!*"

Well, it was pitiful, the way that poor dog acted. At first he was dancing and capering and barking, happy and proud and gay; but when he saw us going away he stopped and stood still, gazing; it seemed as if he was trying to believe it, and couldn't. And dear, dear, how noble and handsome he was, in that red glare. He was a huge big St. Bernard, with that gentle good face and that soft loving eye that they've got.

Well, pretty soon when he saw that he *was* left, he seemed to go kind of crazy; and he rose on his hind legs in the strong light, and strained and lunged and tugged at his rope, and begged and moaned and yelped—why it was as plain as if he was *saying* Oh, *don't* leave me, *please* don't leave me, I haven't done any harm. And then presently the fire swept down on him and swallowed him up, and he sent up two or three awful shrieks, and it was all over. And the men sat there crying like children.

And deep down in our hearts we believed a judgment would come on the captain for this. And it did; as you will see.

WE WERE in the Indian ocean when we lost the ship—about five hundred miles south of Port Natal, and about the same distance east by south from Cape Town, South Africa. The captain set his course by the stars and struck north, because he believed we were a little south of the track of ships bound for either Natal or

Australia. A smart breeze sprung up and we went along at a good rate. In about four hours day broke, and the first thing that showed up on the westward sea-line was the hazy top-hamper of a ship! She was eastward-bound, and making straight across our course. We raised a cheer, and altered our course to go and meet her. And there wasn't as much heart in the cheer as you might expect, for the thing we were thinking about was, that our poor dog had been done to death for no use; if he had been allowed to come with us he wouldn't have cost us any inconvenience, and no food that we couldn't spare.

The captain had an idea that he was born lucky, and he said something to the mate about it now; he said running across this ship here was pure luck—nobody else could have had such luck. Well, it certainly did look so; but at the same time we said to ourselves, how about this ship's luck that's coming? Our idea was that our captain would bring bad luck to her, and trouble to himself and us, too, on account of the way he treated the dog that saved our lives. And that is what happened, as I have said before.

In about an hour we were aboard that ship; and it happened that we knew her, and knew her crew, too; for she was sister to our ship and belonged to the same house, and was loaded at the same dock with us, and with the same kind of cargo—provisions for the new mines almost altogether, and a few other odds and ends of mining supplies, like candles and powder and fuse, and such things. By name she was the *Adelaide*. She had left port a week or ten days ahead of us, but we could outsail her on a wind. Her captain had been dead about a month, now—died of a sickness of some kind— and Mrs. Moseley, his young widow, was broken-hearted, and cried pretty much all the time, and was in terror lest something should happen to her little girl, and then she would be desolate indeed. Two of the *Adelaide's* crew had died of the sickness, also; so that left mate, second mate and five men aboard. When we joined, that made it seventeen men, one woman and a child.

Our captain took command straight away, and began to give orders, without a by-your-leave to anybody—for that was his style. It wasn't the right way to go about it, and it made bad blood.

The captain allotted the watches and the ship continued on her course for Australia. The wind freshened, the sky grew dark, and inside of an hour there was a terrific gale blowing. We stripped the ship and she drove helpless before it, straight south-east. And so, night and day and day and night for eighteen days we drove, and never got a sight of the sun or the moon or the stars in all that time —hundreds and hundreds and hundreds of miles we wallowed through the wild seas, with never a notion of where we were but what we got from the dead reckoning.

For the last two or three days the captain had got to looking pretty white; and by this time he was just ghastly. Then we found out the reason, from the mates: the captain judged that we must be south of Kerguelan's Land, and maybe nearly half way between that and the Antarctic Circle. Well, that news turned the rest of us white; for if it was true, we were getting into the neighborhood of the Devil's Race-Track!

As that cold dark eighteenth day shut down, everybody was on deck, off-watch and all; and everybody silent; as a rule, nobody saying anything to his neighbor; nobody interested in any but the one thing—the compass. The captain stood over the forward one, watching it and never saying anything; the officers and crew crowded around the after one, watching it and never saying anything. The night shut down black as ink; the wind screamed through the naked rigging; gusts of hail, snow, sleet followed each other right along—a wild night, and bitter cold, and the ship reeling and pitching and tumbling in a most awful way.

You couldn't see a thing; you couldn't see your hand before your face—everything was blotted out; everything except three or four faces bending over the compass-light, and showing in the blackness like ghost-faces that hadn't any bodies.

Then all of a sudden there was a burst of groans and curses, and the faces disappeared and others took their places. You see, the thing everybody was expecting, had happened—the compass was gone crazy, and we were in the whirl and suck of the Devil's Race-Track. Most of us kept the deck all night. Some slept, but it was not much good—just naps and nightmares, and wakings-up with a jerk, in a cold sweat.

When the day came you could hardly tell it, it so little differed from the night. All the day long it was the same; you could hear the sea-birds piping but you couldn't see them, except now and then you would get a dim glimpse of a great white albatross sailing by like a ghost.

We had nine days and nights like this—always the roaring gale and the wild sea and blustering squalls of snow and hail and sleet and the piping of the gulls and the flitting of the dim albatross; and then on the tenth morning the gale began to slacken and the seas to go down and the squalls to get wider apart and less furious, and the blackness to soften up and shred away, and the sea-birds to thin out; and about noon we drifted out of the lofty wall of gloom and clouds into a calm sea and the open day and deep, deep stillness. The sweep of that black wall described an enormous circle; and it was so high that the furthest side of it still stood boldly up above the sea, though it was fifty miles away. We were in a trap; and that trap was the Everlasting Sunday.

There was no need to say it; everybody knew it. And everybody shuddered, too, and was in a cold despair. For a week we drifted little by little around the cloud-wall, and further and further away from it; and when we seemed to have gotten ten or fifteen miles from it we appeared to have stopped dead still. We threw empty bottles overboard and watched them. There was really no motion— at any rate in any one direction. Sometimes a bottle would stay where we threw it; sometimes after the end of an hour we could see that it had moved five or six yards ahead or as many aft.

The stillness was horrible; and the absence of life. There was not a bird or a creature of any kind in sight, the slick surface of the water was never broken by a fin, never a breath of wind fanned the dead air, and there was not a sound of any kind, even the faintest— the silence of death was everywhere. We showed no life ourselves, but sat apart, each by himself, and brooded and brooded, and scarcely ever moved. In that profound inertness, that universal paralysis of life and energy, as far as sentient beings went, there was one thing that was brimming with it, booming with it, crazy with it; and that was the compass. It whirled and whizzed this way and that, and never rested—never for a moment. It acted like a frightened thing, a thing in frantic fear for its life. And so we got afraid of it, and could not bear to look at its distress and its helpless struggles; for we came to believe that it had a soul and that it was in hell.

We never had any more weather—forever that bright sky overhead, with never a shred of cloud in it; not a flake of snow, nor drop of sleet or anything; just a dead still frosty cold, with a glistening white rime coating the decks and spars and rigging—a ship made of sparkling frostwork, she seemed. And as the days dragged on and on and on we grew weary as death of this changeless sky, and watched the vague lightnings playing in the distant cloud-wall with a sort of envy and longing.

Try to escape? Why, none of us wanted to try. What could be the use? Of course the captain tried; it would be just like him. He manned one of the boats and started. He disappeared in the cloud-wall for a while; got lost in it, of course—compass no use—and came near getting swamped by the heavy seas. He was not in there long; the currents soon swept him back into the Everlasting Sunday. Our ship was pretty far away, but still in sight; so he came aboard, and never said a word. *His* spirit was broken, too, you see, like ours; so after that he moped around again, like the rest—and prayed for death, I reckon. We all did.

One morning when we had been in there seven months and gradually getting further and further toward the middle, an inch at a time, there was a sudden stir and excitement—the first we had known for so long that it seemed strange and new and unnatural—like something we hadn't ever experienced before; it was like corpses getting excited—corpses that had been dead many years and had forgotten the feel of it and didn't understand it. A sailor came flying along the deck blubbering and shouting, "A ship! a ship!"

The dull people sitting moping and dreaming here and there and yonder looked up at him in a kind of a drowse, and not pleasantly; for his racket and activity pained their heads and distressed them; and their brains were so blunted and sodden that at first his words couldn't find their way into their understandings, all practice in talk having ceased so long ago. But of course we did understand, presently, and then we woke up and got wildly excited, as I was telling you.

Away off yonder we made out a ship, sure enough; and as the

daylight brightened we made out another; and then another, and
still another and another and another—a whole fleet, scattered
around, a mile or so apart. We were full of amazement. When did
they come, and how did they get there in that sudden way, and so
many of them? We were full of joy; for maybe here was rescue for
us. If they came in there on purpose, they must know the trick of
how to get out again.

Well, everything was bustle and hurry, now. We got out our
boats, and I pulled stroke in the chief mate's. I was twenty-three
and a half years old, and big and strong and an experienced sailor.
We hoisted a flag, first, in the mizzen halliards—union down, of
course—and left the young widow and the little girl standing
under it crying for happiness when we pulled away in the frosty
bright morning.

It was as much as twelve miles to the nearest ship, but we made
it in three hours—without a sail, of course, there being no wind.
When half of the ship's hull showed above the water we began to
wave signals, but didn't get any answer; and about this time we
began to make out that she looked pretty old and crazy. The nearer
we got, the crazier she looked, and there was no sign of life or
movement about her. We began to suspect the truth—and pretty
soon we knew it, and our spirits fell. Why, she was just a naked old
wreck, as you may say, a mouldy old skeleton, with her yards
hanging every-whichway, and here and there a rotten rag of
sailcloth drooping from the clews. As we passed under her stern,
there was her name, in letters so dulled you could hardly spell them
out. The *Horatio Nelson!* I gasped for breath. I knew the ship.
When I was a boy of ten my uncle Robert sailed in her as chief
mate; and from that day to this she had never more been heard of
—thirteen years.

You will know beforehand what we found: barring the frosty litter
of decaying wreckage that strewed the deck, just the counterpart of
our own ship, as you might say—men lying here and there and
yonder, and two or three sitting, with elbow on knee and hand
under chin—just as natural! No, not men—leathery shriveled-up
effigies of them. Dead these dozen years. It was what we had been
seeing for seven months; we would come to be like these, by and

by. It was our fate foreshadowed; that is what we thought. I found my uncle; I knew him by his watch chain. I was young, he had always been kind to me, and it made me cry a little to see him looking like that. That, and that I might be like him soon. I have the watch and chain yet, if you care to look at them. The watch had stopped at twelve minutes to four—whether in the day or in the night I don't know; but he was dead when it ran down—that was all it could tell.

The ship's log left off where we had stopped ours—three days after the entry into the Everlasting Sunday. It told the same monotonous things that ours did, and in nearly the same words; and the blank that followed was more eloquent than the words that went before, in this case as in our own, for it meant despair. By the log, the *Horatio Nelson* had entered the Everlasting Sunday on the 2ᵈ of June, 1840.

We visited ship after ship, and found these dreary scenes always repeated. And always the logs ceased the third or fourth day after the ship got into this death-trap except in a single case. Where one day is exactly like another, why record them? What is there to record? The world continues to exist, but History has come to an end. The *Horatio Nelson* was the latest ship there but one—a whaler from New England. She had been there six years. One English ship which had been there thirty-three years—the *Eurydice*—was overcrowded with men and women. She had 260 of these leathery corpses on board—convicts for Australia and their guards, no doubt, for down below were more than two hundred sets of chains. A Spanish ship had been there sixty years; but the oldest one of all, and in almost the best repair, was a British man-of-war, the *Royal Brunswick*. She perished with all on board the first voyage she ever made, the old histories say—and the old ballads, too—but here she was; and here she had been, since November 10th, 1740—a hundred and thirteen years, you see.

Clean, dry, frosty weather seems to be a good preserver of some things—clothes, for instance. At a little distance you might have thought some of the men in this ship were still alive, they looked so natural in their funny old uniforms. And the Admiral was one—old Admiral Sir John Thurlow; he was a middy in the time of

Marlborough's wars, as I have read in the histories. He had his big
cocked hat on, and his big epaulettes, like as if he was gotten up for
Madam Tussaud's; and his coat was all over gold lace; and it was
real gold, too, for it was not tarnished. He was sitting on a gun
carriage, with his head leant back against the gun in a sick and
weary way; and there was a rusty old leather portfolio in his lap and
a pen and an empty inkstand handy. He looked fine and noble—
the very type of the old fighting British Admiral, the men that
made England the monarch of the seas. By a common impulse, and
without orders, we formed up in front of him and uncovered in
salute. Then Captain Cable stepped up to take the portfolio, but in
his awkwardness he gave a little touch to the Admiral's elbow and
he fell over on the deck. Dear me, he struck as lightly and as
noiseless as if he had been only a suit of clothes stuffed with wool;
and a faint little cloud of leathery dust rose up from him, and we
judged he had gone to pieces inside. We uncovered again and
carried him very reverently to his own cabin and laid him to rest.

And here we had an instance of the difference between navy
discipline and merchant marine. In this ship the log was kept up as
long as an officer was left alive—and that was two months and
sixteen days. That is the grip that authority and duty get upon a
trained man, you see. When the men began to starve and die they
were †

(1896)

_____

† Mark Twain here left his sentence and his story incomplete.

Which Was the Dream?

FROM MRS. ALISON X.'S DIARY.

Mᴀʀᴄʜ *1, 1854, morning.*—It will be a busy day. Tom and the servants and a carpenter or two have already begun to set up the stage and scenery in the north end of the picture gallery *

* We call it the picture gallery because it isn't. It is the ball room.

for Bessie's play—first dress rehearsal to-night. There will be two more before the great occasion—Bessie's eighth birthday—the 19th. The scenery and costumes have cost a great sum, and are very beautiful. It will be a fine show to see that company of pretty children clothed in those rich habits. Tom tried to design Bessie's costume himself; dear man, he is daft about the child; about both of them, indeed. He is vain of the play, and says it is wonderful; and it is, perhaps, for a child of eight to have conjured out of her small head. It lacks coherence, of course, and it has some rather startling feats in it, even for magicians and fairies to do; still it is a remarkable little play, all things considered, and is adorably naïve and quaint.

Tom has often promised me to write a little sketch of his life for the children to have when we are gone, but has always put it off and put it off; but as soon as I suggested that he write it in honor of Bessie's birth-day, that was quite another matter and he was full of it at once. I think I ought to be jealous; anything that Bessie wants, Bessie can have, but poor mamma has to put up with a kiss and a postponement. Of course Tom would find some opportunity in the matter to show Bessie off. He will write the sketch in shorthand tonight, and between this and the birthday Bessie will turn it into long hand, with a little of my help, and then, on the birthnight, after the ball and the play, she—

Mid-afternoon. Dear me, these interruptions! It is a busy day, sure enough. I don't get time to turn around or get a moment's rest, they keep after me so with their How shall we do this? and how shall we do that? and so on. Tom is going to be tired out before night, the way he is working. But he says he won't. And he has devised a surprise of some kind or other for the end of the evening. As soon as the night's rehearsals of the fancy dances and the play are over I am to bring Bessie and Jessie to his study, and then he—

8 p.m. What a darling flock it is! They have all arrived at last, with their troop of mothers. It is going to be a beautiful sight. The gallery never looked so brilliant before, nor so grand and spacious; and it will look finer than ever on the birth-night, with five hundred handsome people in it and all the military and naval uniforms, and the Diplomatic Body in their showy clothes. Washington is a good place for clothes. . . .

I went to the study, and looked in through the glass door. Tom was at his task—since how long, I don't know. He was drowsy, I could see that; I knew he would be tired. But his pen was going. His cigar was lying on the table, and while I looked he fell asleep for a second and his nodding head drooped gradually down till his nose was right over the ascending film of cigar smoke. It woke him with a violent start and a sneeze, and he went straight on with his work again, and I hurried away, amused, to my room, to get a moment's rest before beginning my long task of superintending the costuming of the little people and directing the series of rehearsals. . . . A note—from the White House. The President invites himself for this evening! This *is* an honor. And it is all for Bessie, none of it for Tom. This it is, to be a Chief Magistrate's small sweetheart. Someday it will make the child proud to be able to say that once a President of the United States broke the laws of etiquette that hedge his station for love of her. If he—"Coming!" I am getting tired of that word.

MAJOR GENERAL X.'S STORY.

ALICE (short for Alison) Sedgewick and I (Thomas X.,) were born in the little town of Pawpaw Corners, in the State of Kentucky, I in 1820, she in 1826. When she was five and I eleven, we became engaged. I remember it very well, and so does she. It was the first time we had ever met; for it was only just then that her family had moved into our neighborhood from the other side of the town. We met on the way to school, on a pleasant morning in the early summer time—April, I should say; perhaps toward the end of it. It would be about that time I think, for it was warm enough for even boys connected with "quality" families to begin to hope for leave to go barefoot. The damp was stewing out of the ground, the grass was springing briskly, the wild flowers were thick, and in the woods on Murray Hill early in the mornings there was a musical riot of bird-song in place of the stillness that had reigned there so long. All the common boys had been barefoot for as much as a week already, and were beginning to mock at us for "Miss Nancys," and make fun of us for being under our mother's thumbs and obliged to be unmanly and take care of our health like girls. I had been begging my mother for leave, but she would not give it. She said we were as good blood as the best in the town—good old Virginian stock, like the Sedgewicks and the Dents—and she would not allow her boy to take second place to any offshoot of theirs. She said that I could come out barefoot when Billy Dent and Jeff Sedgewick did, and not a day before. Billy Dent was the county Judge's son, and Mr. Sedgewick was the principal lawyer and had run for Congress once. Mr. Sedgewick was Alice's father and Jeff's uncle, and had a large farm in the country, and owned more negroes than any other man in the town; and Jeff was a playmate of mine, although I had never seen his cousin until now.

I had my new summer suit on, that morning—yellow nankeens —and was proud; proud of the clothes, but prouder still because I was barefoot; the first "quality" boy in the town to be "out." I had been showing off before Jeff and Billy, and making them green with envy: for they had supposed it was by my mother's permission that I was barefoot—supposed it from something I had said, I think. But I knew where my shoes were, and could find them when I wanted to go home.

The schoolhouse stood on a small bare hill, and at that time there was a thicket at the bottom of it, with a clear stream rippling through it; and it was just there that I came upon Alison. She was the dearest and prettiest little thing I had ever seen, and I loved her from that very moment. She had a broad leghorn hat on, with a wide red satin ribbon around it, the long ends dangling down behind; and her little short frock was of thin white summer stuff, and a piece of that same ribbon was tied around her waist for a belt. In one hand she had a Webster spelling-book and first reader, and in the other she had the last winter-apple that was left over.

I wanted to speak to her, but I was all in a quiver and did not know how to begin. She looked timidly up at me out of her brown eyes, then dropped them, and stood there before me silent. I had a marble in my hand—it was a white alley that I had just got in a trade for a China that was so worn that you could hardly see the stripes on it—and my excitement made my hand tremble, and it fell on the ground near by. It was precious property, but I would not take my eyes off that pretty little creature long enough to pick it up; but worked my right foot toward it and closed my toes over it and took it in their grip. That interested her, and broke the ice. She said—

"I didn't know anybody could do that but my cousin Jeff and our Jake. Can you walk with it so? They can."

"Oh, yes—it's easy; anybody can do it."

I made a step or two. Then with my foot I threw up the marble and caught it in my hand.

She was bursting with admiration, and tried to clap her hands, but they were too full of things. She cried out—

"Oh, do it again—do it again!"

I said—

"Shucks, that's nothing—look at this."

I gripped the marble in the toes of my right foot, balanced myself on my left, swung my right forward once or twice, to get impulse, then violently upward and backward, and sent the marble well up into the air above our heads, then made a spring and caught it as it came down.

She was mine! I saw it in her eyes. Her look was the concentrated look which Europe cast upon Napoleon after Austerlitz. She impulsively reached out the apple to me and said—

"There. You may have it all for your own."

I said—

"No, not all of it—we'll have it together. First, you'll take a bite, and then I'll take a bite, and then you'll take a bite, and then—"

I held it to her mouth, she took her bite, then I took mine, and munching we sauntered into the thicket, along the worn path, I holding her by her left hand. And by the stream we sat down together, and took bites turn about, and contentedly munched and talked. I told her my name, she told me hers, and the name of her kitten and its mother's, and some of their habits and preferences and qualities, and I told her how to dig fishing-worms, and how to make a pin-hook, and what to do to keep awake in church, and the best way to catch flies; and at last I asked her if she was engaged, and explained it to her; and when she said she was not, I said I was glad, and said I was not; and she said she was glad; and by this time we had munched down to the core, and I said now we could find out if everything was going to come out right and we get married. So then I took out the apple-seeds one by one and laid them in her small palm, and she listened with deep interest and grave earnestness while I delivered the fateful word that belonged with each:

"One I love, two I love, three I love I say;

Four I love with all my heart, and five I cast away;

Six *he* loves—"

"And *do* you, Tom?"

"Yes. Are you glad?"

"Yes, Tom. Go on."

"Seven *she* loves—*do* you, Alice?"

"Yes, Tom. Go on."

"Eight they *both* love—and they do, *don't* we, Alice?"

"Yes, Tom. Keep on."

"Nine he comes, ten he tarries—"

"What is tarries, Tom?"

"Oh, never mind—t'isn't so, anyway—eleven he courts, and twelve he marries! There, that settles it! It's the very last seed, Alice, dear, and we are going to get married, sure; nothing can ever prevent it."

"I'm *so* glad, Tom. *Now* what do we have to do?"

"Nothing but just kiss. There—another—and one more. Now it's fixed. And it'll stay forever. You'll see, dearie."

And it did stay forever. At least it has stayed until this day and date, March 1, 1854; and that is twenty-three years.†

I will skip a good many years, now. They were filled to the brim with the care-free joys of boyhood, and were followed by four happy years of young manhood, spent at the Military Academy of West Point, whence I was graduated in the summer of 1841, aged 21 years. All those years were a part of my life, it is true, yet I do not count them so. By my count they were merely a preparation for my life—which began in 1845 with my marriage. That was my supreme event; that was happiness which made all previous happinesses of little moment; it was so deep and real that it made those others seem shallow and artificial; so gracious and so divine that it exposed them as being earthy and poor and common. We two were one. For all functions but the physical, one heart would have answered for us both. Our days were a dream, we lived in a world of enchantment. We were obscure, we were but indifferently well off, as to money, but if these were lacks we did not know it, at least did not feel it.

---

† At this point ends the part of the narrative of "X" that was written in May 1897. The rest of it was written about three months later.

In 1846 our little Bessie was born—the second great event in my life. A month later, my wife's father died; within the week afterward coal was discovered on his land and our poverty—to exaggerate the term a little—disappeared in a night. Presently came the war, and through a film of proud tears my Alison, holding our little Bessie up to look, saw her late unnoted 2ᵈ lieutenant, U.S.A., march for Mexico, colonel of a regiment of volunteers. In a little while she began to see his name in the war news, among the crowd of other names; then she saw it gradually and steadily separate itself from the crowd and grow more and more isolated, conspicuous, distinguished; and finally saw it hoisted aloft among the great head-lines, with Scott's and Taylor's for sole company; and in these days it was become as common as theirs upon the world's tongue, and it could be uttered in any assemblage in the land and be depended upon to explode a mine of enthusiasm. She was a proud woman, and glad; and learned to practice deceit, to protect her modesty and save the exultation in her heart from showing in her face—pretending not to hear, when she passed along, and there was a sudden stir upon the pavement, and whispers of, "There—look—the wife of the boy General!" For I was by many years the youngest of that rank in our armies.

And more was to come; the favors of fortune were not exhausted yet. There came a stately addition to that remark—"wife of the boy General—United States Senator—the youngest that was ever elected." It was true. The brief war over, I learned the news from the papers while I was on my way home.

And Alice was a proud woman again when her late obscure 2ᵈ lieutenant entered our village and drove, at the Governor's side, through the massed country multitudes, under triumphal arches, in a rain of rockets, and glare of Greek fire, and storm of cannon-blasts, and crash of bands and huzzahs, to the banquet prepared in his honor; and proud once more when he rose at her side, there, and she saw the house rise at him and fill the air with a snow-tempest of waving napkins and a roar of welcoming voices long continued; and proud yet once more when he made his speech, and carried the house with him, sentence by sentence to the stirring close, and sat down with a dazzling new reputation made. (Her own dear words, and a pardonable over-statement of the facts.)

Those were memorable days, marvelous days for us. More than ever we seemed to be living in a world of enchantment. It all seemed so strange, indeed so splendidly impossible, that these bounties, usually reserved for age, should be actually ours, and we so young; for she was but 22 and I but 28. Every morning one or the other of us laughed and said, "Another day gone, and it isn't a dream *yet!*" For we had the same thought, and it was a natural one: that the night might rob us, some time or other, and we should wake bereaved.

We built a costly and beautiful house in Washington, and furnished it luxuriously. Then began a life which was full of charm for both of us. We did not have to labor our way into society with arts and diplomacies, our position was already established and our place ready for us when we came. We did not need to court, we were courted. We entertained freely, and our house was the meeting ground for all who had done anything, for all who were distinguished in letters, the arts, in politics and fashion, and it was almost the common home of Clay, Webster, Benton, Scott, and some of the other men of conspicuous fame. Alison's beauty and youth attracted all comers to her, and her sterling character and fine mind made them her friends.

And she was the gratefulest creature that ever was. Often she would take my face between her hands, and look into my eyes, and say—

"How dear you are! and it is you that have given me all this wonderful life. But for you I should be nothing—nothing at all. I am so proud of you; so proud, and so glad that you are mine, all mine."

It was her wealth that made this choice life possible; but she always put her hand on my lips when I said that, and would not listen; and said my fame and deeds would have been sufficient.

We are happy, we are satisfied. Fortune has done all for me that was in her power. She would have added the last possible distinction, but was defeated by the Constitution. I should be President and First Citizen of the United States now, if I were of lawful age. It is not I that say this immodest thing—ask your mother. It seems decreed, past all doubt, that I shall ascend to that high post three years hence, but we will not talk of that now, dear; there is no hurry.

POSTSCRIPT.

T HERE—my sketch is done, I have made my promise good. There is enough of it for the purpose. For further particulars, Bessie dear, see the four Biographies. Your mamma is going to give them to you on your birthday morning. And let me whisper to you, Craig's is the best, because it flatters me.

Now I will go on and write something for the mamma. That will be easier work than that which I have just finished—so easy that it will write itself if I merely hold the pen and leave it free, for the text is so inspiring—The Children.

Our Jessie was born in the year of the Californian gold-rush, a cunning black-headed mite that weighed just four pounds, and was as welcome as if she had weighed a hundred. She is above five years old, now, a practical, decisive, courageous, adventurous little soldier, charged to the chin with tireless activities, and never still except when asleep. She is the embodied spirit of cheerfulness; everything that happens to her is somehow convertible into entertainment; and that is what results, no matter what the hap is. This has made it difficult to punish her. Even the dark closet was a failure. It missed her, and merely punished her mother, who kept her shut up a quarter of an hour and then could endure the thought of the little prisoner's sufferings no longer, and so went there to give her the boon of the blessed light again; but found her charmed with the novelty of the darkness and the mystery of the place and anxious to stay and experiment further.

She bears pain with a rare fortitude, for a child—or for an adult. Last summer her forefinger got a pinch which burst the fat front of the main joint, but she cried only a moment, then sat in her mother's lap and uttered no sound while the doctor sewed the ragged edges together—sat, and winced at the proper times, and watched the operation through with a charmed and eager interest, then ran off to her play again, quite ready for any more novelties that might come her way. Tobogganing, last winter in the north, the toboggan ran into a tree, and her ancle was sprained and some of the small bones of her foot broken; but she did not cry—she only whimpered a moment, that was all; and then had as good a time in bed for a week or two as she could have had anywhere.

The other day she was taken to the dentist to have a tooth drawn. Seeing how little she was, the dentist proposed to give her an anaesthetic and make the operation painless, but her mother said it would not be necessary. Alison stepped into the next room, not wishing to see. Presently she heard the dentist say, "There, that one is out, but here is another one that ought to come;" so she stepped in and said, "Here is another handkerchief for you, dear," but [J]essie said, "Never mind, I brought two, mamma, I thought there might be two teeth." She always had a thoughtful business head from the beginning. And she is an orderly little scrap, too. Her end of the nursery is always ship-shape; but poor Bessie's end of it is an exaggeration of chaos.

For Bessie is a thinker—a poet—a dreamer; a creature made up of intellect, imagination, feeling. She is an exquisite little sensitive plant, shrinking and timorous in the matter of pain, and is full of worshiping admiration of Jessie's adventurous ways and manly audacities. Privately we call Bessie "Poetry," and Jessie "Romance" —because in the one case the name fits, and in the other it doesn't. The children could not pronounce these large names in the beginning, therefore they shortened them to Potie and Romie, and so they remain.

Bessie is a sort of little woman, now; and being a thinker, she is learning to put a few modifying restraints upon herself here and there in spots—and they were needed. To start with, she was a dear little baby, with a temper made all of alternating bursts of storm and sunshine, without any detectable intervals between these changes of weather. She was a most sudden creature; always brimming with life, always boiling with enthusiasm, always ready to fly off on the opposite tack without any notice. Her approval was passionate, her disapproval the same, and the delivery of her verdict was prompt in both cases. Her volcano was seldom quiet. When it was, it was only getting ready for an irruption; and no one could tell beforehand whether it was going to illuminate a landscape or bury a city. Fortunately for herself and for us, her exaltations of joy were much more common than her ecstasies of anger. It took both to make her thoroughly interesting; and she was that. And keep us busy; and she did that.

The foundation of her nature is *intensity*. This characteristic is prominently present in her affections. From her babyhood she has made an idol of her mother. She and her mother are sweethearts, lovers, intimate comrades and confidants, and prodigal of endearments and caresses for each other. Nobody but the mother can govern her. She does it by love, by inalterable firmness, by perfect fairness, by perfect justice. While she was still in the cradle Bessie learned that her mother's word could always be depended upon; and that whatever promise her mother made her—whether of punishment, or a holiday, or a gratification, or a benevolence— would be kept, to the letter. She also learned that she must always obey her mother's commands; and not reluctantly and half-heartedly, but promptly, and without complaint. She knew the formula, "Do this, Bessie; do that, Bessie;" but she never had experience of the addition, "If you will, I will give you something nice." She was never hired to obey, in any instance. She early learned that her mother's commands would always be delivered gently and respectfully, never rudely or with show of temper, and that they must be obeyed straightway, and willingly. The child soon learned that her mother was not a tyrant, but her thoughtful and considerate friend —her loving friend, her best friend, her always courteous friend, who had no disposition in her heart or tongue to wound her childish self-respect. And so, this little whirlwind was brought under government; brought under obedience; thorough obedience, instant obedience, willing obedience. Did that save the child something? I think so. If a child—or a soldier—learns to obey promptly and willingly, there is no sting in it, no hardship, no unhappiness. The mother who coaxes or hires her child to obey, is providing unhappiness for it; and for herself as well. And particularly because the mother who coaxes and hires does not always coax and hire, but is in all cases a weak creature, an ill-balanced creature, who now and then delivers herself up to autocratic exhibitions of authority, wherein she uses compulsion—usually in a hot and insulting temper—and so the child never knows just how to take her.

It is a shameful thing to insult a little child. It has its feelings, it has its small dignity; and since it cannot defend them, it is surely an ignoble act to injure them. Bessie was accustomed to polite treatment from her mother; but once when she was still a very little creature she suffered a discourtesy at her hands. Alison and Senator Walker's wife were talking earnestly in the library; and Bessie, who was playing about the floor, interrupted them several times; finally Alice said pretty sharply, "Bessie, if you interrupt again, I will send you at once to the nursery." Five minutes later, Alice saw Mrs. W. to the door. On her way back through the main hall she saw Bessie on the stairs—halfway up, pawing her course laboriously, a step at a time. Alice said—

"Where are you going, Potie?"

"To the nursery, mamma."

"What are you going up there for, dear—don't you want to stay with me in the library?"

Bessie was tempted—but only for a moment. Then she said, with a gentle dignity which carried its own reproach—

"You didn't speak to me right, mamma."

She had been humiliated in the presence of an outsider. Alice felt condemned. She carried Bessie to the library and took her on her lap and argued the matter with her. Bessie hadn't a fault to find with the justice of the rebuke, but she held out steadily against the *manner* of it, saying gently, once or twice, "but you didn't speak to me *right*, mamma." She won her cause. Her mother had to confess that she *hadn't* spoken to her "right."

We require courteous speech from the children at all times and in all circumstances; we owe them the same courtesy in return; and when we fail of it we deserve correction.

These are lovely days that we are living in this pleasant home of ours in Washington, with these busy little tykes for comrades. I have my share of the fun with them. We are great hunters, we. The library is our jungle, and there we hunt the tiger and the lion. I am the elephant, and go on all fours, and the children ride on my back, astride. We hunt Jake. Jake is the colored butler. He belonged to Alison's estate, and is the same Jake whom she mentioned in our engagement-conversation when she was five years old. We brought him and his sister Maria from Kentucky when we first came to Washington. Both are free, by grace of Alice. Jake is thirty-two years old, now; a fine, large, nobly-proportioned man, very black, and as handsome as any man in the city, white or black, I think, and fully twice as good as he is handsome, notwithstanding he is a bigoted Methodist, a deacon in his church, and an incurable gambler on horse-races and prize fights. He is our prey, and we hunt him all over the library and the drawing rooms. He is lion; also tiger; preferably tiger, because as lion his roaring is too competent for Bessie's nerves. Bessie has a passion for hunting the tiger, but as soon as he gives notice that he is going to turn himself into a lion she climbs down and gets behind a chair and Jessie hunts him to his lair alone.

Bessie's mind is my pride, and I am building high hopes upon it. I have said that she is a thinker, and she is; and deep and capable. She has the penetrating mind, the analytical mind—and with it, naturally, precision of speech, intuitive aptitude in seizing upon the right word. Even when she was littler than she is now she often surprised me by the happy ingenuity she showed in choosing the word which would make her meaning clear. For instance. All of us who have labored at a foreign language by *book,* know how hard it is to get rid of the disposition to separate the words and deliver them with over-exactness of enunciation, instead of running them together and making them flow liquidly along, as a person does who has acquired the language by ear in strenuous fun and frolic and quarrel—in the nursery, for example. One day a couple of years ago I was playing with the children, and Bessie glibly—and as I thought, loosely—fluttered off a little German stanza about the

"Vöglein." Then I read it from the *book,* with care and emphasis, to correct her pronunciation, whereupon Jessie corrected *me.* I said I had read it correctly, and asked Bessie if I hadn't. She said—

"Yes, papa, you did—but you read it so *'stinctly* that it 'fused Romie."

It would be difficult to better that, for precision in the choice of the right word for the occasion. At five Bessie was busy enlarging her vocabulary. Some pretty large words got into it, and once she adopted one which presently met with an accident. She told a visitor she was never at church but once—"the time Romie was crucified." Meaning christened.

Bessie has always been dropping her plummet into the deeps of thought, always trying to reason out the problems of life, always searching for light. One day Alison said to her, "There, there, child, you must not cry for little things." A couple of days later Bessie came up out of a deep reverie with the formidable question—

"Mamma, what *is* LITTLE things?"

No one can answer that, for nothing that grieves us can be called little: by the eternal laws of proportion a child's loss of a doll and a king's loss of a crown are events of the same size. Alice was not able to furnish a sufficient answer. But Bessie did not give the matter up. She worked at the problem several days. Then, when Alice was about to drive down town—one of her errands being the purchase of a promised toy watch for Bessie—the child said, "If you should forget the watch, mamma, would that be a little thing?"

Yet she was not concerned about the watch, for she knew it would not be forgotten; what the struggling mind was after was the getting a satisfactory grip upon that elusive and indefinite question.

Like most people, Bessie is pestered with recurrent dreams. Her stock dream is that she is being eaten up by bears. It is the main horror of her life. Last night she had that dream again. This morning, after telling it, she stood apart some time looking vacantly at the floor, absorbed in meditation. At last she looked up, and with the pathos of one who feels that he has not been dealt by with even-handed fairness, said—

"But mamma, the trouble is, that I am never the *bear* but always the *person eaten.*"

It would not occur to everybody that there might be an advantage in being the eater, now and then, seeing that it was nothing but a dream, after all, but there *is* an advantage, for while you are *in* a dream it *isn't* a dream—it is reality, and the bear-bite hurts; hurts in a perfectly real way. In the surprise which I am providing for the children to-night, Bessie will see that her persecuting dream can be turned into something quite romantically and picturesquely delightful when a person of her papa's high capacities in the way of invention puts his mind to work upon it.

Bessie has the gift of concentration. This makes her a good listener, a good audience, for she keeps close track of what is said. And remembers the details, too,—which sometimes makes trouble for me; for I forget my details, and then am brought to book. Every evening I have to tell the children a story after they are in their cribs and their prayers accomplished—and the story has to be invented on the spot; neither of them will put up with any second-hand contributions. Now in all these inventions of mine, from away back, I have had one serious difficulty to contend with, owing to Alison's influence—*nobody in my tale must lie,* not even the villain of the piece. This hampers me a good deal. The blacker and bloodier I paint the villain the more the children delight in him, until he makes the mistake of telling a lie—then down he goes, in their estimation. Nothing can resurrect him again; he has to pack up and go; his character is damaged beyond help, they won't have him around any longer.

Sometimes I try to cover up, or slide over, or explain away, one of these lies which I have blundered into, but it is lost time. One evening during one of our European vacations I was in the middle of the fifth night of a continued story which I intended should last a year and make things easy for my invention-mill; and was gliding along like this—

"But the moment the giant invited him, the grasshopper whispered in Johnny's ear that the food was poisoned; so, Johnny said very politely, 'I am very much obliged to you indeed, sir, but I am not hungry, and—' "

"Why, *papa!* he told a lie!"

(I said to myself, I have made a blunder; Johnny is compromised; I must try to get him out of this scrape.) "Well, you see, Bessie, I reckon he didn't think what he was saying, and—"

"But papa, it couldn't *be;* because he had just said, that very minute, that he was *so* hungry."

"Ye-s, I believe that is true. Yes, that *is* true. Well, I think perhaps he was heedless, and just came out with the first thing that happened in his mind, and—"

"Oh, no, papa, he wasn't ever a heedless boy; it wasn't like him to be heedless; you know how wise and thoughtful he always was. Why, night before last, when all those fairies and enchanted creatures tried their very best, a whole day, to catch him in some little carelessness so they could get power over him, they never *could*. No, papa, all through this story, there never was such a wise boy—he *couldn't* be heedless, papa."

"Well, Potie, I reckon he was so weary, so kind of tired out—"

"Why, papa, he *rode* all the way, on the eagle, and he had been sound asleep all the whole day in the gold-and-ivory bed, with his two lions watching him and taking care of him—why how *could* he be tired, papa, and he so strong? You know the other night when his whale took him to Africa he went ashore and walked all day and all night and wasn't a bit tired; and you know that other time when—"

"Yes, yes, you are right, Bessie, and I was wrong; he couldn't have been tired—but he never intended any wrong; I'm sure he didn't mean what he said; for—"

"Then it *was* a lie, papa, if he didn't mean what he said."

Johnny's days of usefulness were over. He was hard aground, and I had to leave him there. He was a most unprincipled and bloody rascal, and if he could have avoided his one vice he might still be with us, nights, to this day, and as limitlessly happy as we are, ourselves. Romie once said this handsome thing about him—however, I will put that in further along, when I sketch out Romie's little history. I have a little more to say about her sister, yet.

Of instances of Bessie's delicate intuitions there are many in my mind. Here is one which is pleasant to me, and its original sweetness is in no way impaired by my often thinking of it. Last Christmas Eve Alice brought home a variety of presents, and allowed Bessie to see those which were to be sent to the coachman's family. Among these was an unusually handsome and valuable sled for Jimmy. On it a stag was painted, and also the sled's name in showy gilt capitals, "DEER." Bessie was joyously enthusiastic over everything until she came to this sled; then she became sober and silent. Yet this sled was the very thing she was expected to be most eloquent over, for it was the jewel of the lot. Alice was surprised; also disappointed; and said—

"Why Potie, doesn't it please you? Isn't it fine?"

Bessie hesitated; plainly she did not like to have to say the thing that was in her mind; but being pressed, she got it out—haltingly:

"Well, mamma, it *is* fine, and of course it *did* cost a good deal—but—why should that be mentioned?"

Seeing she was not understood, she pointed to that word "deer!" Poor chap, her heart was in the right place, but her orthography wasn't. There is not a coarse fibre in Bessie; she is as fine as gossamer.

From her earliest babyhood her religious training has gone on steadily at her mother's knee, and she has been a willing and interested pupil. But not a slavish one. She has always been searching on her own account, always thinking. There have been abundant evidences of that. I will set down one instance.

For some months, now, the governess has been instructing her about the American Indians. One day, a few weeks ago, Alice, with a smitten conscience, said—

"Potie, I have been so busy that I haven't been in at night, lately, to hear you say your prayers. Maybe I can come in tonight. Shall I?"

Bessie hesitated, waited for her thought to formulate itself, then brought it out—

"Mamma, I don't pray as much as I used to—and I don't pray in the same way. Maybe you would not be pleased with the way I pray now."

"Tell me about it, Potie."

"Well, mamma, I don't know that I can make you understand. But you know, the Indians thought they knew—and they had a great many gods. We know, now, that they were wrong. By and by maybe it will be found out that *we* are wrong, too. So now I only pray *that there may be a God*—and a heaven—OR SOMETHING BETTER."

It is the garnered doubt—and hope—of all the centuries, compacted into a sentence. And by a child.

She is a great treasure to us. Indeed we couldn't do without Bessie. Life would be flat, without her stimulating presence. She is not clay. She is a spirit. Generally in motion, seldom still—a sort of glimpse of frolicking sea-waves flashing in the sun; seldom a cloud-shadow drifting over them in these later times. She is all life, and soap-bubbles, and rainbows, and fireworks—and anything else that has spring and sparkle and energy and intensity for its make-up. She never talks much. I mean, in her sleep.

Now for Jessie—now for the busy brunette. The first day that ever Jessie—

I DID NOT get a chance to finish the sentence. A shriek rang through the house, followed by a confusion of excited cries, and I ran to see what the matter was. The house was on fire. All the upper part of it was burning briskly before the calamity was discovered, for everybody was below, absorbed in the rehearsals.

For a moment the crowd of fifty children and thirty mothers had been in great danger—not from the fire, but from the perils inseparable from panic. There would have been manglings and crushings, if no man had been present. But fortunately, and by a mere chance, there was a man there; and by a still happier chance he was a soldier; a soldier of the best sort, the sort that is coolest in circumstances which make other people lose their heads. This was a young man named Grant, who was a third class man at West Point when I was a first. He had come to see me about something, and entered the ball room only a moment before the alarm was given. He was by the door, and took his place in front of it at once. The mob of women and children were paralyzed with fright for a moment; the next moment they would have made their fatal rush; but Grant did not wait for that. He spoke up in the calm and confident voice which stills troubled human waters by some subtle magic not explicable by the hearer but which compels his obedience, and said—

"Stand as you are! Do not move till I speak. There is no hurry, and there is no danger. Now then, you, madam, take two children by the hands, and move forward; you next, madam—do the same. Next—next—next."

And so on. In orderly procession the column fell in and filed out like a battalion leaving the field on dress parade.

But for West Point's presence there, I should be setting down a pathetic tragedy now. Lieutenant Grant had served under me for a while in the beginning of the Mexican war, and lately he had come to Washington on a business visit from his home in the West, and we had renewed our acquaintanceship. I think he had in him the stuff for a General, or certainly a Colonel; I do not know why he achieved no distinction in the war—but then, such things go a good deal by luck and opportunity. From what he had been telling me about his later fortunes, I judged that he was not born to luck. He remarked upon his Mexican nickname, "Useless," and said the old saying was true, in his case, that fun-nicknames are unwitting disguises of grave fact; for that if ever there was a useless man in the world, and one for whom there was plainly no place and no necessity, he was the one. Before the month was out I had sorrowful occasion to recal this talk of ours. With the Mexican war, his only chance for success in this world passed away; he recognized that, and I recognized it also, and was sorry for him. He was a good fellow, a sterling fellow, and should not have been wasted at West Point in the acquiring of a useless trade. But unfortunately none of us can see far ahead; prophecy is not for us. Hence the paucity of suicides.

We were overwhelmed with kindnesses by our friends; shelter in their houses was freely offered, but it seemed best, on the whole, to take quarters in the hotel, and this we did. The firemen saved the main part of the contents of the ground floor of our house, but nothing from the upper floors—the floors where we had lived, and where every detail was a treasure and precious, because hallowed by association with our intimate and private home life. This was a bitter hardship for us. A battered toy from the nursery would have been worth more to us than all the costly rubbish that was saved from the drawing rooms. Those dumb artificialities could be replaced, but not the historic toys.

The last of our hospitable friends left us at about two in the morning, and then we went to bed, tired out with the labors of the day and the excitements of the night. Alice said—

"I suppose you will rebuild the house just as it was before, Tom?"

"Yes. Jeff can begin tomorrow." That name reminded me of something, and I said, "Why, Alice, I did not see Jeff at the fire—did you?"

"No. And he has not been here in the hotel since we arrived, so far as I know."

"That is very strange. When did you see him last?"

"He left the house about five minutes before the fire alarm, and said he should be back within a quarter of an hour. He must have come back, of course; still, I did not see him."

"Alice! Could he have gone up to his room to save valuables, and got cut off and burned up?"

"He had no valuables in his room."

"No, not of his own, I know, but ours."

"Give yourself no trouble. Jeff Sedgewick has not risked his skin to save valuables of ours. He is not that sort of a man."

"Alice, you do not like your cousin."

"Tom, I have never accused myself of it."

Then we went to sleep. In the morning, still no Jeff Sedgewick. The forenoon wore away, and still he did not come. Everything was at a standstill. There was nobody to make contracts for the rebuilding of the house. Jeff was my business man and confidential secretary. He had begun as my secretary merely, when we first came east; but I knew nothing of business and had an aversion for it, and so, all my matters of that sort gradually drifted into his hands; for he was fond of business, and seemed made for it. In the beginning I franked my public documents myself—a wearisome job; one night I left half the documents unfranked; in the morning they lay in a confused pile, *all* franked. Jeff said—

"I finished the franking myself. Examine the pile, and see if you can tell the genuine signature from the imitation."

I couldn't. I was glad to let him do all the franking after that. In the beginning he wrote my letters from dictation, and I signed them. Later he wrote and signed a letter himself, without dictation, and I saw that he had caught my style exactly, and my hand. After that I was glad to let him do all my letters for me—in "autograph," and out of his own head. Soon he was signing and endorsing checks in "autograph." By and by all of my business was in his hands, every detail of it, and I was a free man and happy. Then came the full power of attorney, quite naturally, and thenceforth I was saved from even the bother of consulting and confirming.

In the very beginning Alice had begged me not to take Jeff to Washington.

"But Alice, he is an old friend, a schoolmate, he is poor and needs help, we are prosperous, we are fortunate, he is smart and capable, I am not, and I need such a person badly."

"But Tom, he is bad; bad to the marrow, and will do you an ill turn some day—the worst turn he can invent. He is envious, malicious, deceitful. He envies you your fame and prosperity, and hates you for it, privately. Every kindness you do him, every step you advance him, he will make record of and charge up against you, and when his opportunity comes he will take his revenge."

I laughed, at the time, at these unreasoning prejudices, and never thought for a moment that a young and inexperienced country girl like Alice could have an opinion that was valuable upon matters like these. I know, now, that her judgment of character was fatally and unfailingly accurate, but I did not find it out as early as I ought to have done.

She did not persecute me with her warnings; it was not her way;

but now and then at intervals she used to drop them when there
seemed opportunity to accomplish something by them. Once in the
early Washington days Jeff came in arrayed in what he thought
was the finest and latest thing in New York fashion. And perhaps it
was the finest and latest thing in the Bowery. He was as pleased as
a child, with his vulgar outfit. I have never had any tact; and that is
why I said—

"I thought the Independent Order of the Fantastics had been
disbanded years ago. When are they going to parade?"

He looked ignorantly embarrassed—like one who suspects that
an offence has been intended him, but is not certain. He said—

"I believe I don't quite get your meaning."

"Isn't that a uniform?"

He went out without saying anything, and did not appear any
more in those clothes. I spoke to Alice of the incident in the
evening. It troubled her, and she said—

"I wish you hadn't done it, Tom. You laugh at it, but it is not
matter for laughing. He is a vulgar, vain fool, and you have hurt
him in a tender place. He will not forget it, nor forgive it. Do get
rid of him, Tom."

Although Jeff had held the power of attorney for years, Alice
never found it out till a month before the fire—for I was too often
unfaithful to her in my business affairs. I hid things from her that I
was ashamed of. Secrecy is the natural refuge of people who are
doubtful about their conduct. She was appalled when I told her the
matter of the power of attorney. She said—

"Oh, Tom, what have you done!" and begged me to abrogate it,
and said Jeff would make beggars of us.

I was able to triumph, this time, and said—

"On the contrary, dear, he has doubled our fortune. Come, now,
you must be just to him at last, and take back some of the hard
judgments you have passed upon him in the bygone times."

She was doubtful still, that was plain; and she asked for
particulars. But I said—

"Wait one month, then you will see."

She sighed and said—

"I will wait, Tom, since you ask it, but even if he should

quadruple the fortune, I should still never be easy until we were rid of him."

I had no fears. I was preparing a pleasant surprise for Alice, and was sure I could spring it upon her in a few weeks. Jeff had made some brilliant speculations for me, of late years, and my confidence in his wisdom and shrewdness had grown in consequence until now they were boundless. He had sold out Alice's estate and invested her fortune in a Californian gold mine; for many months the mine had been swallowing money wholesale, but recent reports from its chief engineer showed that it was now on the point of paying back the fortune, with a hundred per cent interest. I had never liked the name of it—the "Golden Fleece"—but that was Jeff's taste; he named it.

Next morning we created a parlor and an office by having the beds cleared out of a couple of large chambers, and furniture proper to their new functions put in. In our house, Sedgewick's office had been on the ground floor, consequently all my business books and papers were saved. Alice soon arranged these in our new quarters. It was common for people whose houses had been burned down to send the firemen a donation and a word or two of compliment and gratitude, therefore in deference to this custom Alice asked me to draw a check for her to forward to the fire marshal. It was customary to disproportion the donation to the service rendered; therefore at Alice's request I made the check large. At least I considered it large; it was for $3,000. But then it was to help the company buy a new engine and build a new engine house.

Before Alice could finish writing her note of compliment and gratitude—she did not expect me to do any clerical work that could be shifted to somebody else—company began to pour in again. The stream continued until mid-day; then dinner interrupted it for an hour and a half; then the flow was resumed. About mid-afternoon or a little later Alice stole a moment and wrote the note, and sent it to the marshal by Jake. Still no Jeff appeared. Alice knew I was uneasy, for she knew the signs of all my moods, and with her native generous forbearance she left Jeff unmentioned. She never made a sore place of mine worse by meddling with it at the inopportune time. This is a beautiful trait; indeed it may be called a noble trait; and we all know it to be a rare one. I was never able to learn it, never able to make it a possession of mine. By taking thought I could *practice* it, momentarily, at wide intervals, but that was all. It was a *part of* Alice, and she did not have to think about it; but it refused to become a part of me. I was born small and selfish; Alice and the children were not. In nine cases in ten, when Alice had a sore place, I hastened with an insane eagerness to bruise it, and grieve her heart—and yet I loved her so, and had such a deep reverence for her beautiful character. I hurried to bruise it, knowing, when I did it, that when I saw the wounded look in her eyes I should be blistered with remorse and shame, and would give anything if I had not done it. But I could not help it, for deep down in the very web and woof of my nature I was ignoble and ungenerous.

How little the world knows us; indeed how little any except our nearest friends know us. You who are reading these lines—your world loves you and honors you. But suppose it knew you as you know yourself? Be humbly thankful that it does not.

Supper. Still no Jeff. My uneasiness was steadily growing.

I had not been out, all day. In fact, I had even kept away from the windows, I did not know why. I knew I should see a crowd of waiting strangers from different regions of the Union on the opposite sidewalk. I was used to it, had been used to it ever since I came back from Mexico with my military glories upon me; and had always been pleased with it, happy in it. But the thought of it troubled me, now. I was accustomed to driving or walking, every day, and accustomed to be flocked after and cheered, as I went along, and no more minded it than did the stately General Scott; in fact dearly liked it and enjoyed it, as he did. But to-day, for some reason, I shrank from the thought of it. There was a vague, indefinable, oppressive sense of impending trouble in the air.

After supper came the marine band—a serenade. The idea of it, to take friendly notice of our little mishap. I was in the room which had been set apart as a nursery, and was employed as usual at that hour of the evening—inventing a blood-curdling story for the children; a child seated on each arm of my chair, their feet in my lap, their elbows on their knees, their chins crutched in their plump hands, their eyes burning duskily through their falling cataracts of yellow hair and black. For ten minutes I had been wandering with these two in a land far from this world; in the golden land of Romance, where all things are beautiful, and existence is a splendid dream, and care cannot come. Then came that bray of the brazen horns, and the vision vanished away; we were prisoners in this dull planet again. I was for ignoring the serenade, and getting back to that shining land with my story, and Jessie was for supporting me in that impropriety; but Bessie had inherited higher instincts than we, and larger principles; and she said—

"No, no, papa, mamma would not approve. You must go, papa."

"And make a speech? Somehow it seems impossible to-night."

"Oh, no it isn't, papa. It is nothing. Don't be afraid. Make the same speech you always make. Everybody says it is a good one. Mr. Pierce likes it better every time; he says so his own self."

Out of the unconscious lips of babes and sucklings are we satirized. I walked slowly away into my banishment, leaving happiness behind me. For I left a dispute behind me; and where no care is, that is joy. I heard Bessie say—

"Papa didn't say that. He *couldn't* say it, because there's no sense in it. You've got two things mixed up, Romie."

"I haven't. He did say it. I heard him; I heard the very words. He said it is foolish to kill the goose that lays the golden calf."

It would have been a joy to me—an old and familiar and beloved joy—to go back and take a solemn hand in the discussion and mix it all up till the puzzled little rascals could make neither head nor tail of it, but this boon was not for me. From outside went up a crashing cheer which lifted my spirits away up into the sunshine, and set my pulses to leaping, and for a moment I was myself again. But for a moment only. Then at the door a bank president touched me on the shoulder and whispered—

"Senator, can I have a word with you presently?"

"Yes," and I passed on. But there was something in his manner which blotted out my sunshine and made my heart cold. I stepped out on the balcony, and gazed out, dazed and hardly conscious, over the wide sea of flaring torches and uplifted faces; and the explosions of welcome which went up sounded muffled and far away in my dulled ears. I made my speech—no, it made itself, automatically; and it was as if it was some one else talking, and I scarce noting what was said. Then the cheers burst out again, as in a dream, and I—as in a dream—bowed, and went my way.

I took the bank president into my office, closed the door, and said—

"What is it?"

He answered, apologetically—

"I am sorry to disturb you with such a matter, Senator, but the fire marshal handed in a check just as we were closing the bank, and—and—"

"Very well. Go on."

"And—and—well, the fact is, Senator, your account is over-drawn."

What a load it lifted off my breast. And what a relief it was, to hear myself laugh once more; it had seemed to me that I had forgotten how.

"Oh, dear me," I said, "is that all? What of it? It isn't uncommon."

But he did not laugh. He remained ominously grave. He was silent a moment, gathering courage for a disagreeable duty, then he spoke out and named the amount of the overdraft.

I staggered as I have seen a soldier do when hit in the breast with a spent ball. After a little I rallied, and said, "I am amazed. I never could have imagined this. I don't know what Sedgewick can have been thinking of. Let us square up at once; and pray don't ever let this happen again—by his authority or any one else's." I sat down at the desk and said, "I will give you a check on Riggs's."

Nothing but a deadly silence followed this remark. I turned in my chair. My guest said, reluctantly—

"I am sorry, but it would do no good."

"Oh, what *do* you mean?"

"We bankers have been together this evening to look over the situation, and unfortunately we find—we find—"

"Well, well, you find—what do you find?"

"That you are heavily overdrawn all around."

He told me the several amounts. It made my head swim, for a moment. Then I pulled myself together, and said—

"After all, Simmons, it is merely embarrassing, not serious; and in no sense alarming. By good luck our house has burned down; the insurance-money will far more than pay you gentlemen, and henceforth I shall keep clear of this kind of thing. Even if I owed a million or two I should still be solvent, by grace of my Californian mining venture."

The banker asked me if I would mind telling him, in confidence, something about the Golden Fleece. I said I should be very glad to tell him *all* about it; that there was no occasion for concealment. So I got out the mining manager's long series of carefully detailed reports, and we examined them patiently from the first one to the last. Mr. Simmons was very much pleased, indeed. He said the reports were remarkably clear, orderly and candid, and that I was fortunate in having a manager who was courageous enough to put in the bad news as well as the good. He conceded that I was demonstrably worth above a million and a half, and prospectively worth indefinitely more. Then he confessed that when Sedgewick began to overdraw rather heavily, sometime back, and had spoken mysteriously of the wonders of the Golden Fleece, he had felt a little uneasy and had written his brother, a banker in Grass Valley for particulars concerning the mine. He had had no answer as yet, but he could forsee, now, that it would be a satisfactory one when it came.

Then a letter was brought up which completed my comfort. It was from the lost Sedgewick. I read it aloud. It said—

"No doubt you have wondered what was become of me. When I returned and found that the house was doomed, I hurried to the station and caught the midnight train for New York; for there was an informality in one of the insurance policies which—however I will explain how it happened when I get back. As to $102,000 of the insurance, there will be no trouble. I think there will be none

about the rest—$38,000—but I shall stay here two or three days
and see. Meantime, through the luck of coming here just a[t] this
time I am likely to bring back, from another source, $80,000 which
I had long ago given up as an irremediable loss. Indeed it is not
merely likely, I feel that I may regard it as sure."

Mr. Simmons and I parted on very pleasant terms, and I went to
bed a serene and contented man.

Nᴇxᴛ ᴅᴀʏ I presided, for half an hour, at a session of the
Committee on Military Affairs, then went back to Willard's, and
Alice and I excused ourselves to callers and spent the whole happy
day planning little improvements in the proposed new house, the
architect helping and suggesting. Alice, who was conservative,
wanted the cost kept within the former house's figure, but I said we
could afford a more expensive one; and I talked her out of her
reluctances and gained my point. She had been used to money all
her life, therefore the possession of it did not turn her head or
incline her to vain shows and display; but I was a kind of beggar on
horseback, and had no sense of financial proportion, no just notion
of values, and—but you know the kind of man I was. We did not
get through until midnight; then the architect went away with a
house in his pocket which charmed him and me, and made Alice
shudder.

Two or three more days went pleasantly by, then came Mr.
Simmons, Mr. Riggs, and Mr. Fulton, bankers, and with them a
Mr. Collins from New York. Their manner was a warning; it
spread a frost over the summer that was teeming in my heart, and
the chill of it invaded my spirits. Trouble was coming; I felt it.
They wished to see me in my private office. Arrived there, they sat
down, and there was a moment or two of silence; then one said to
another, with solemnity—

"Will you begin?"

"No, you, if you prefer."

"Perhaps it will be best that Mr. Simmons open the matter."

It was so agreed. Every face there was hard and set, every eye frankly unfriendly. Mr. Simmons cleared his throat and said—

"General X., you will pardon me if I ask you one or two blunt questions."

"Go on, sir."

"What property do you own, aside from the Golden Fleece?"

"None."

The men glanced at each other; Riggs and Fulton twisted nervously in their chairs.

"Has your wife any property other than the Golden Fleece?"

"None."

The color left the faces of Riggs and Fulton at that, then came back in a purple flush, and Fulton put up his hand and loosened his collar.

"One more question, Senator X." This in a slightly rising voice. "When you showed me the reports of your mining manager, was it your purpose to deceive me?"

I flushed, but said, with as much calmness as I could command—

"Mr. Simmons, have a care. I must remind you that you are going too far."

"I am, am I?" said he, excitedly. "My brother's letter has arrived from Grass Valley. Read it!"

I read it. Read it again; and still again, not able to believe my eyes. There was one italicized line in it which seemed written in fire, it glared so, and burnt me so: *"There is no such mine as the Golden Fleece."* The life was all gone out of me, and I said—

"I am a ruined man, gentlemen. I realize it—absolutely ruined. But my destruction does not injure you. The insurance-money will more than pay everything I owe."

"That is your whole resource, then?"

"Yes."

"Are you certain that your house was insured?"

"Certain of it? Of course. It has always been insured, from the first; and in the same companies. Here is the record. The last entry, as you see, is of date a year ago, and insures the house for three years."

"Mr. Collins is the agent through whom your policies were always taken out. Mr. Collins, will you speak?"

Collins addressed himself to me, and said—

"You may remember, sir, that something more than a year ago, I wrote you two personal letters. In the first one I reminded you; in the second I urged you, to renew your insurance, for that I was not able to get Mr. Sedgewick's attention. My letters were confidential, as I did not wish to get your representative's ill will. You remember my letters?"

"Quite well. In the case of the first one I asked Sedgewick to answer you and re-insure; in the second I gave him a peremptory order to do it."

"Have you your policies there?"

"Yes."

"Last year's, too?"

"I suppose so. I will see. N-no. Not last year's."

"It is because that last-year entry is fraudulent. Your house was not insured. The loss is total."

My God, the words went through me like a bullet. If they were true, they meant that I was not merely and only a pauper, but a hundred times worse than that—*in debt.* For a time, no one spoke. The stillness was oppressive, smothering. All were waiting for me; but I was dumb, I could not find my voice. When it came back to me at last, I said—

"I am to blame. I am to blame, I confess it freely. I trusted Sedgewick as no human being ought to be trusted, and I have my reward. He has destroyed me."

There was no word of response. I was ashamed. I had expected at least a recognition of my remark, the mere courtesy of a comment of some kind or other; I was used to this much deference—and entitled to it. My dignity was wounded. I glanced up at the faces about me, and was cut to the heart; for if I could read what was written there, it was contempt! It seemed unbelievable, it had been so many years since any face had delivered me a message like that. I gathered my pride together, and said—

"Do not mistranslate me, gentlemen; I was not begging for sympathy."

Simmons made a gesture of impatience, and said—

"This is not a time for womanish sentimentalities, General X., with these strange facts—shall I say, these suspicious facts?— before us. You must see it yourself."

"What do you mean, sir?" I said with some little heat—I could not keep it all down. "Please explain yourself."

He amended his manner, then, leaving nothing of discourtesy in it or in his tones. But his words were knives.

"I ought not to forget, and I do not, that of the three or four men of towering eminence in the Union, you are one; that your great services deserve the country's gratitude and have it; and that until now your public and private conduct has been above the reach of suspicion; but—but—" He stopped for a moment, troubled as to how to go on; then added reluctantly, and with the manner of one who is saying a thing which he does not want to say, but which he does not know how to get around, "but these insurance-entries, which are—I hate to use the word—fraudulent—why did you make them?"

"*I* make them! *I* didn't make them."

The kindness faded out of the banker's face, and stupefaction took its place—stupefaction, mixed with surprise and unbelief; and he said with offended severity—

"I beg your pardon. I know your hand well."

For the first time, I saw my whole peril. The earth seemed to be opening under me, and said in a voice which made my words sound like a lie even to me, so sapped of force were they by my despairing conviction that I was not going to be believed—

"I give you my word of honor—oh, more, I give you my oath— that I never wrote—"

"*Don't!* Stop where you are, for God's sake!"

"I implore you to believe me! Gentlemen, I call God to wit—"

"Stop where you are! Do not make it worse than it already is. Remember what you are. Go on, and say what you can in palliation of this unfortunate act—even in plausible explanation of it, if such a thing may be possible—but for your own pride's sake leave out denials backed by oaths."

I went back to the beginning of my connection with Sedgewick, and told the tale all down to date; told them the simple truth, the plain, straightfor[war]d, humiliating facts—burning up with self-contempt while I did it, and watching those marveling and incredulous faces for any relenting sign, as wistfully as ever a prisoner on trial for his life watched the faces of the jury.

The sign never came. When I finished, the group looked at each other and said, plainly, though without words, "It is pitiable to see an illustrious man degrade himself to the manufacture of such trash as this." I read the words in their faces, and knew that my good name was gone, now, as well as my bread. After a considerable silence, Mr. Fulton said, with chill deliberation—

"As I understand it, sir, you ask credit for these several most extraordinary asseverations, to-wit, that you, an educated man, a man of the world, a general of the army, a statesman, a grown person, put yourself, body and soul, together with your wife's whole property and your own, unreservedly into the hands of a man—*any* man—empowering him to originate and write letters for you in your own handwriting, sign and endorse your name upon checks, notes, contracts, in your own hand, and speculate in anything he pleased, with the family's money—and all without even your casual supervision of what he was doing, or inquiry into it? Am I right?"

Detailed, item by item, in that cold direct fashion, it seemed incredible, impossible, even to me. And yet it was true, every shameful detail of it; and I said so. Mr. Fuller spoke out with what sounded like an almost generous enthusiasm—

"For the honor I bear your great name I will do you the reverence to believe not one damned word of it!"

I fought, and fought long, and the best I could, to save some shred of that name, but it was a lost battle. These men *could* not believe me. To them, it was impossible that a full grown man could be the fool I had professed myself to be. Their minds were soon made up that Sedgewick and I were partnership swindlers—pals.

They almost used that word; I was sure of it. From that conviction no arguments of mine were able to move them. They summed our affairs concisely up in this way: we had speculated in New York stocks and lost money and been obliged to sell Alice's estate; we had speculated further, and gotten deeper in; we had invented the Golden Fleece to postpone the crash and gain time to recoup; we continued to go from bad to worse; when the house burned, I had seen that the game was up, and had hurried Sedgewick off to scrape up what money he might for our joint benefit before the exposure should fall, and take it to some far country, leaving me to put all the irregularities upon him—he not minding that, since it could not hurt his pocket.

I said that my own statement of my conduct—if true—proved me a fool; but that this new solution of it—if true—proved me insane. I urged that a General of the Army, Senator, and prospective President of the United States could not by any possibility commit the crimes imputed to me unless he were insane, and that the gentlemen here present must know this themselves. I felt a hopeful glow at the heart for a moment, for I said to myself, *that* is an argument which will spike their guns; it is unanswerable.

But how little I knew the religion of commerce and its god. The argument fell flat; more—it was received with disdain—disdain of the sort evoked when a person intrudes a triviality into a serious discussion. Mr. Simmons brushed it aside as indifferently as if he were squelching the ignorant prattle of a schoolboy—

"Men will do anything for money."

From the moment that those men arrived at the conviction that I was a swindler and Sedgewick my tool and partner, my reasonings went for nothing. It untangled every tangle, it laid bare the core of every mystery, it explained and accounted for every move in the odious game that had been played.

If I said that I couldn't know that the mining reports exhibited to me as coming from Grass Valley were manufactured in Washington,—why, true,—yes, quite so—etc., etc.; which being translated, meant that my word, as to that, was not valuable, in the circumstances.

If I referred to Sedgewick's letter from New York (about the insurance) as having been received by me in perfect and unsuspecting good faith, the comment I got was merely noddings of the head which meant "Oh, certainly, certainly, quite so—pray do not think we doubt it."

I started, once, to inquire how *I* was to be benefited by making false entries in my insurance-list, and—

But they interrupted me impatiently, with a "There, it isn't worth while to go into *that* again," meaning, "Oh, it is quite simple —part of the game, dear sir, part of the game—any one can understand it."

I had tried all things, said all things, that might help me; there was nothing more that I could do, nothing more that I could say. I was lost. There was no help for me. The consciousness of this settled down upon me and wrapped me as in a darkness. There was a long silence. Then I broke it.

"Gentlemen, I comprehend that I am a ruined man—bankrupt in purse, and, in your belief, in character also. It may be that I shall never be able to retrieve myself financially, though I shall try my best while I live to do that and clear away the debts put upon me by a trusted subordinate; but I am *not* a dishonest man, whatever you may think, and I will bring that man before the courts and fasten all these swindles upon him, where they belong."

"When?" asked Mr. Collins.

"When? Why, at once."

"He sailed for the other side of the world the day he wrote you the letter; a friend of mine saw him go." Then he could not deny himself the pleasure of adding—as if to himself, and not intended for me to hear, "But it may be that this is not news."

Anybody could insult me now, with impunity—even that poor thing. Being pleased with himself for his boldness in kicking the dead lion, and detecting condescending approval in the faces of the bankers, he thought he saw his opportunity to ingratiate himself further with these high deities of his heaven; so he jauntily covered himself. But Mr. Riggs said, angrily—

"Uncover! Have you no shame? Respect what he *was*."

What he *was!* It lit up my whole vast ruin, from horizon to horizon; it compacted my colossal disaster into a single phrase. I knew that those words were burnt in; that no lapse of time, no mental decay, would ever rid my memory of them.

But why were these men still waiting? Was there more? More! The idea was almost able to make *me* smile. More? Was not Pelion piled upon my Ossa? More, indeed! The possibilities had been exhausted. I stirred in my chair, to indicate that I was ready for the interview to terminate if they were. Nobody moved. Then I said—

"I suppose we have finished, gentlemen." Still, nobody moved. The situation was embarrassing; and so, with a groping idea of relieving it, I added in a wan and sickly attempt at playfulness, "I seem to have committed about all the crimes there are; still, if by chance one has been overlooked, let us complete the tale. Pray bring it out."

Mr. Riggs began to wash his hands nervously; Simmons glanced at me, and dropped his eyes; Fulton, without passion or even emphasis, spat out the word—

"Forgery!"

I sprang at him—and remembered no more.

W HEN I CAME to myself I had the feeling of one who has slept heavily, is lazily comfortable, but not greatly refreshed, and is still drowsy. My mind was empty of thought, and indifferent. My eyelids began to droop slumbrously, and I was drifting pleasantly toward unconsciousness, when I heard Jake's voice cry out—apparently in the next room—

"No indeed it ain't, honey—it's a jay-bird. Wait till I come. Don't make a noise; you'll scare him."

My eyes came open, and then there was a surprise. I was stretched upon a bed, in a log cabin. The sharp March weather was gone, summer was in the air. The floor was of earth, packed hard and clean swept; at one end was a vast fire-place, built of undressed stones; in it a couple of great smouldering logs six or seven feet long; swinging above them, from an iron chimney-hook, a large iron pot; on rude unpainted shelves, on one side, some old but brightly polished tin pans, plates, pint cups, candle-sticks and a coffee pot, some bone-handled knives and forks, some tin cans, some wooden and pasteboard boxes such as candles and groceries come in, and some brown paper parcels; against the logs on that side, under a small square window, a coverless deal table that had paper and pens on it and half a dozen old books; for sole ornament, a crippled tumbler containing a bouquet of fresh wild flowers; against the logs, beside the window, was fastened a diamond-shaped piece of looking-glass, and under it was a shelf with cheap combs and brushes on it. On the other side of the fireplace, by the door, was a small wooden bench, with a piece of bar soap on it in a common white saucer, a tin wash-basin inverted, and a wooden pail of water with a tin dipper in it; under the ceiling, above the bench, hung half of a side of bacon; on the floor on that side was an open sack of flour, and another of navy beans. Nailed to the wall opposite the bed was a deep long stretch of curtain calico which bulged, and I knew by that sign that it was the wardrobe. Along the wall, above the bed, four cheap lithographs were tacked to the logs—the Battle of Buena Vista, the storming of San Juan d'Ulloa, (I took part in both), and portraits of Scott and Taylor in uniform. Overhead was a ceiling made of flour-sacks sewed together; it was a frescoed ceiling, so to speak, for the sacks bore the names and addresses of the mills, loudly stenciled in blue capitals. Across the room, past the head of the bed, ran a flour-sack partition, also frescoed. It was the picture gallery; against it was pinned a number of steel engravings from Godey's Lady's Book.

Everything about the place was beautifully neat and clean and trim—and unimaginably inexpensive. I examined the bedstead. It was made of small poles—only tolerably straight, and the bark still on—laid close together along a frame supported by posts—the bark still on—driven into the ground. There was but one mattrass; it was filled with straw; there were pillows, filled with something or other; their cases and the sheets were of coarse white cotton; a cheap white blanket completed the bed.

I had on an old pair of blue jeans breeches and a private soldier's blue army shirt.

Where was I? I had no idea.

A glory of sunny hair appeared in the open door, now, and with it a bright young face—Bessie's.

"Come here, dear," I said, "and read me this riddle."

"Why, *papa!*"

She came cautiously in, and slowly approached, her eyes big with glad wonder—and doubt. She hesitated, then stopped, in the middle of the little room, four feet from me, and said wistfully—

"Papa—do you know me?"

"Do I *know* you? Why, Bessie, what—"

With a spring she was in my arms and covering my face with frantic kisses. Presently she had flashed away again, with the suddenness of a ray of light, and I heard her calling—outside—excitedly:

"Run here—run—run!"

Then she came flying back and stood, expectant, in the middle of the room, her eyes and cheeks glowing; and in a moment or two more Jessie was at her side, a speaking picture of childish interest and curiosity. Bessie put her mouth close to Jessie's ear, whispered a word, then stepped back to observe the effect. Jessie looked startled, but said promptly—

"I don't believe it."

The effect seemed to be all that could have been desired, for Bessie clapped her hands like a gratified showman and said—

"I knew you wouldn't. Now you'll see. Papa, who is this?"

"Come, what kind of game are you little rascals playing? Do you suppose I don't know Romie?"

And now they were both in my arms, and for some reason or other seemed to be mad with delight. Presently I said—

"It's a charming piece, and I am playing my part of it as well as I can, but I am in the dark, you know. Why am I in jeans and army shirt? And why are you two in these little linsey-woolsey frocks, and why are you barefooted? And why are we in this log cabin? Is it all in the piece? And how much do we get for it? But first of all, where *are* we?"

The children looked troubled and disappointed, and a little apprehensive, and Bessie said—

"But papa, I thought you would know *everything*, now. Don't you?"

"Dear me, no, apparently I don't. I am reveling in mysteries. Really, I don't seem to know much of anything."

Jessie said, as one who is trying to offer encouragement—

"Oh, no, papa, you mustn't say that. You know *us*—you know you do."

"Oh indeed, yes, if that is large learning, I am not at the foot of the class yet. I can say my lesson. You are Bessie and Jessie, and I am Thomas X."

Their soft hands covered my mouth at once, and they said in a frightened way—

" 'sh! papa! You mustn't say that!"

"Mustn't say it? Why?"

"Because it isn't your name. You've got another name, now. Don't you know your other name?"

"Oh, you mean my stage name. No, I don't know what it is. What is it?"

"Jacobs—Edward Jacobs; and you mustn't forget it, papa; you mustn't *ever* forget it. Promise."

"All right, I promise. Jacob Edwards—it's a very pretty name, too."

"No, no—Edward *Jacobs*. Say it again, papa; and keep saying it till you learn it good."

"All right, I'll begin now. Are you ready?"

"Yes, papa—and do be careful; and don't hurry."

And they fixed their grave eyes upon me; eyes charged with hope, hope just touched with a pathetic shade of doubt. I couldn't help toying with it.

"Yes, I will be very careful, because always it is best to get a thing right in the first place, then after that it comes easier. And in the case of a difficult name like Jacob Edwards—"

"Oh, papa!"—this with a sort of anguish; and the tears sprang into their eyes.

I gathered the abused pair to my breast and cried out—

"Bless your hearts I was only fooling. I didn't know it was any matter to you. I won't do it any more. I wasn't in earnest, upon my word I wasn't. I can say it without any trouble; listen: Edward Jacobs, Edward Jacobs, Edward Jacobs—"

The sunshine was come again, and I thought I would not play any more treacheries like that for the present. I said—

"But come. You know you haven't told me where we are."

"Why, we are in a town, papa."

"No we are not, Potie, we are only in the edge of it."

"Well, in the edge of it, then—it's all the same. And its name— don't you know its name, papa?"

"I think I can tell better when I hear it. What is it, Bessie?"

She hesitated, and said—

"Mamma only just calls it *the town*; and so that is what we call it, too; but the people—they—well, the people call it—"

"Hell's Delight," said Jessie, gravely.

It nearly startled me out of my army shirt, for it suggested some tremendous possibilities. My breath came short and quick, now, and in insufficient quantity for a person who was full of questions and in a hurry to ask them; but I got them out, and as fast as I could:

"Are we in California?"

"Yes, papa."

"What time of the year is it?"

"The middle of August."

"How old are you, Bessie?"

"Nearly nine and a half, papa."

"This is amazing. I have been asleep eighteen months! Amazing —incredible—impossible. And how you children have grown—I was supposing it was your mean disguises that were deceiving my eyes. What—"

"Mamma's come, mamma's come! Oh, mamma, he's in his right mind!"

We two had been separated just an hour—by the clock—but in the *true* sense a whole year and a half. What the meeting was like, there is no art to tell. The ignorant cannot imagine it, but only such as have lived it.

W HEN A PERSON has been absent from the planet a year and
a half, there is much news to hear when he gets back. It took
Alison many hours to tell me her story. She had had a hard life of
it, and heavy work and sharp privations, and this had aged her body
a little, but not her spirit. Her spirit was [as] it had always been; its
courage, its hopefulness, its generosities, its magnanimities had
suffered no impairment, her troubles had not soured its native
sweetness nor embittered its judgments of men and the world. She
had no complaints to make about her poverty; and as for upbraid-
ing me for causing it, she never thought of such a thing. It shamed
me to see this, knowing how quick I should be to upbraid her if our
places had been changed, and how meanly prone to keep her
reminded of it—and sincerely repent, in sackcloth and ashes for it
—and then do it again the next day, and the next, and the next,
and all the days.

She told me her tale. When she found that we were ruined and
in debt she left the hotel at once and got three cheap rooms and a
kitchen on the fourth floor of a tenement house, and discharged
Jake and Maria. They declined the discharge. Maria remained and
did the housework, and Jake went out to service and made her take
and use almost all the money he earned. It helped to save us alive,
in those first days before Alice had found work for herself. She
presently got copying to do; and so great was the sympathy which
her calamities excited that she was soon overrun with this kind of
work, and was able to employ several assistants. All our friends
stood by her, none of them discarded her; new ones came; and new
and old together would have helped her out of their pockets if she
would have consented. She said it was worth while to know
poverty, because it so enlarged and ennobled one's estimates of the
world in general as well as of one's friends. Almost every paper in
the land used me generously. There was but one man who was

bitter against me; even the injured bankers made no trouble, and ceased from saying harsh things about me. The officers of the army believed my story, and believed it entirely. They said that a man trained at West Point might be a fool in business matters, but never a rascal and never a liar; that he was a gentleman, and would remain one. General Scott said I was a good soldier, none better; and that even the best soldier could botch a trade which he was not fitted for.

(1897)

The Great Dark

BEFORE IT HAPPENED.

STATEMENT BY MRS. EDWARDS.

WE WERE in no way prepared for this dreadful thing. We were a happy family, we had been happy from the beginning; we did not know what trouble was, we were not thinking of it nor expecting it.

My husband was thirty-five years old, and seemed ten years younger, for he was one of those fortunate people who by nature are overcharged with breezy spirits and vigorous health, and from whom cares and troubles slide off without making any impression. He was my ideal, and indeed my idol. In my eyes he was everything that a man ought to be, and in spirit and body beautiful. We were married when I was a girl of 16, and we now had two children, comely and dear little creatures: Jessie, 8 years old, and Bessie, 6.

The house had been in a pleasant turmoil all day, this 19th of March, for it was Jessie's birthday.† Henry (my husband) had romped with the children till I was afraid he would tire them out and unfit them for their party in the evening, which was to be a children's fancy dress dance; and so I was glad when at last in the edge of the evening he took them to our bedroom to show them the grandest of all the presents, the microscope. I allowed them fifteen minutes for this show. I would put the children into their costumes, then, and have them ready to receive their great flock of

---

† Olivia Susan Clemens—Mark Twain's Susy—was born on 19 March 1872.

80

little friends and the accompanying parents. Henry would then be free to jot down in short-hand (he was a past-master in that art) an essay which he was to read at the social club the next night. I would show the children to him in their smart costumes when the party should be over and the good-night kisses due.

I left the three in a state of great excitement over the microscope, and at the end of the fifteen minutes I returned for the children. They and their papa were examining the wonders of a drop of water through a powerful lens. I delivered the children to a maid and they went away. Henry said—

"I will take forty winks and then go to work. But I will make a new experiment with the drop of water first. Won't you please strengthen the drop with the merest touch of Scotch whisky and stir up the animals?"

Then he threw himself on the sofa and before I could speak he uttered a snore. That came of romping the whole day. In reaching for the whisky decanter I knocked off the one that contained brandy and it broke. The noise stopped the snore. I stooped and gathered up the broken glass hurriedly in a towel, and when I rose to put it out of the way he was gone. I dipped a broomstraw in the Scotch whisky and let a wee drop fall upon the glass slide where the water-drop was, then I crossed to the glass door to tell him it was ready. But he had lit the gas and was at his table writing. It was the rule of the house not to disturb him when he was at work; so I went about my affairs in the picture gallery, which was our house's ballroom.

STATEMENT BY MR. EDWARDS

W‍E WERE experimenting with the microscope. And pretty ignorantly. Among the little glass slides in the box we found one labeled "section of a fly's eye." In its centre was faintly visible a dot.

We put it under a low-power lens and it showed up like a fragment of honey-comb. We put it under a stronger lens and it became a window-sash. We put it under the most powerful lens of all, then there was room in the field for only one pane of the several hundred. We were childishly delighted and astonished at the magnifying capacities of that lens, and said, "Now we can find out if there really are living animals in a drop of water, as the books say."

We brought some stale water from a puddle in the carriage-house where some rotten hay lay soaking, sucked up a dropperful and allowed a tear of it to fall on a glass slide. Then we worked the screws and brought the lens down until it almost touched the water; then shut an eye and peered eagerly down through the barrel. A disappointment—nothing showed. Then we worked the screws again and made the lens *touch* the water. Another disappointment—nothing visible. Once more we worked the screws and projected the lens hard *against* the glass slide itself. *Then* we saw the animals! Not frequently, but now and then. For a time there would be a great empty blank; then a monster would enter one horizon of this great white sea made so splendidly luminous by the reflector and go plowing across and disappear beyond the opposite horizon. Others would come and go at intervals and disappear. The lens was pressing *against* the glass slide; therefore how could those bulky creatures crowd through between and not get stuck? Yet they swam with perfect freedom; it was plain that they had all the room and all the water that they needed. Then how unimaginably little they must be! Moreover, that wide circular sea which they were traversing was only a small part of our drop of stale water; it was not as big as the head of a pin; whereas the entire drop, flattened out on the glass, was as big around as a child's finger-ring. If we could have gotten the whole drop under the lens we could have seen those gruesome fishes swim leagues and leagues before they dwindled out of sight at the further shore!

I threw myself on the sofa profoundly impressed by what I had seen, and oppressed with thinkings. An ocean in a drop of water—

and unknown, uncharted, unexplored by man! By man, who gives all his time to the Africas and the poles, with this unsearched marvelous world right at his elbow. Then the Superintendent of Dreams appeared at my side, and we talked it over. He was willing to provide a ship and crew, but said—

"It will be like any other voyage of the sort—not altogether a holiday excursion."

"That is all right; it is not an objection."

"You and your crew will be much diminished, as to size, but you need not trouble about that, as you will not be aware of it. Your ship itself, stuck upon the point of a needle, would not be discoverable except through a microscope of very high power."

"I do not mind these things. Get a crew of whalers. It will be well to have men who will know what to do in case we have trouble with those creatures."

"Better still if you avoid them."

"I shall avoid them if I can, for they have done me no harm, and I would not wantonly hurt any creature, but I shan't run from them. They have an ugly look, but I thank God I am not afraid of the ugliest that ever plowed a drop of water."

"You think so *now*, with your five feet eight, but it will be a different matter when the mote that floats in a sunbeam is Mont Blanc compared to you."

"It is no matter; you have seen me face dangers before—"

"Finish with your orders—the night is slipping away."

"Very well, then. Provide me a naturalist to tell me the names of the creatures we see; and let the ship be a comfortable one and perfectly appointed and provisioned, for I take my family with me."

Half a minute later (as it seemed to me), a hoarse voice broke on my ear—

"Topsails all—let go the lee brace—sheet home the stuns'l boom —hearty, now, and all together!"

I turned out, washed the sleep out of my eyes with a dash of cold water, and stepped out of my cabin, leaving Alice quietly sleeping

in her berth. It was a blustering night and dark, and the air was
thick with a driving mist out of which the tall masts and bellying
clouds of sail towered spectrally, faintly flecked here and there aloft
by the smothered signal lanterns. The ship was heaving and
wallowing in the heavy seas, and it was hard to keep one's footing
on the moist deck. Everything was dimmed to obliteration, almost;
the only thing sharply defined was the foamy mane of white water,
sprinkled with phosphorescent sparks, which broke away from the
lee bow. Men were within twenty steps of me, but I could not
make out their figures; I only knew they were there by their voices.
I heard the quartermaster report to the second mate—

"Eight bells, sir."

"Very well—make it so."

Then I heard the muffled sound of the distant bell, followed by a
far-off cry—

"Eight bells and a cloudy morning—anchor watch turn out!"

I saw the glow of a match photograph a pipe and part of a face
against a solid bank of darkness, and groped my way thither and
found the second mate.

"What of the weather, mate?"

"I don't see that it's any better, sir, than it was the first day out,
ten days ago; if anything it's worse—thicker and blacker, I mean.
You remember the spitting snow-flurries we had that night?"

"Yes."

"Well, we've had them again to-night. And hail and sleet
besides, b'George! And here it comes again."

We stepped into the sheltering lee of the galley, and stood there
listening to the lashing of the hail along the deck and the singing of
the wind in the cordage. The mate said—

"I've been at sea thirty years, man and boy, but for a level ten-
day stretch of unholy weather this bangs anything I ever struck,
north of the Horn—if we *are* north of it. For I'm blest if I know
where we are—do you?"

It was an embarrassing question. I had been asked it very
confidentially by my captain, long ago, and had been able to state

that I didn't know; and had been discreet enough not to go into any particulars; but this was the first time that any officer of the ship had approached me with the matter. I said—

"Well, no, I'm not a sailor, but I am surprised to hear *you* say you don't know where we are."

He was caught. It was his turn to be embarrassed. First he began to hedge, and vaguely let on that perhaps he did know, after all; but he made a lame fist of it, and presently gave it up and concluded to be frank and take me into his confidence.

"I'm going to be honest with you, sir—and don't give me away." He put his mouth close to my ear and sheltered it against the howling wind with his hand to keep from having to shout, and said impressively, "Not only I don't know where we are, sir, but by God the captain himself don't know!"

I had met the captain's confession by pretending to be frightened and distressed at having engaged a man who was ignorant of his business; and then he had changed his note and told me he had only meant that he had lost his bearings in the thick weather—a thing which would rectify itself as soon as he could get a glimpse of the sun. But I was willing to let the mate tell me all he would, so long as I was not to "give it away."

"No, sir, he don't know where he is; lets on to, but he don't. I mean, he lets on to the crew, and his daughters, and young Phillips the purser, and of course to you and your family, but here lately he don't let on any more to the chief mate and me. And worried? I tell you he's worried plumb to his vitals."

"I must say I don't much like the look of this, Mr. Turner."

"Well, don't let on, sir; keep it to yourself—maybe it'll come out all right; hope it will. But you look at the facts—just look at the facts. We sail north—see? North-and-by-east-half-east, to be exact. Noon the fourth day out, heading for Sable island—ought to see it, weather rather thin for *this* voyage. *Don't* see it. Think the dead reckoning ain't right, maybe. We bang straight along, all the afternoon. No Sable island. *Damned if we didn't run straight over it!* It warn't there. What do you think of that?"

"Dear me, it is awful—awful—if true."

"*If* true. Well, it *is* true. True as anything that ever was, I take my oath on it. And then Greenland. We three banked our hopes on Greenland. Night before last we couldn't sleep for uneasiness; just anxiety, you know, to see if Greenland was going to be there. By the dead reckoning she was due to be in sight along anywhere from five to seven in the morning, if clear enough. But we staid on deck all night. Of course two of us had no business there, and had to scuttle out of the way whenever a man came along, or they would have been suspicious. But five o'clock came, seven o'clock, eight o'clock, ten o'clock, and at last twelve—and then the captain groaned and gave in! He knew well enough that if there had been any Greenland left we'd have knocked a corner off of it long before that."

"This is appalling!"

"You may hunt out a bigger word than that and it won't cover it, sir. And Lord, to see the captain, gray as ashes, sweating and worrying over his chart all day yesterday and all day to-day, and spreading his compasses here and spreading them there, and getting suspicious of his chronometer, and damning the dead-reckoning—just suffering death and taxes, you know, and me and the chief mate helping and suffering, and that purser and the captain's oldest girl spooning and cackling around, just in heaven! I'm a poor man, sir, but if I could buy out half of each of 'em's ignorance and put it together and make it a whole, blamed if I wouldn't put up my last nickel to do it, you hear *me*. Now—"

A wild gust of wind drowned the rest of his remark and smothered us in a fierce flurry of snow and sleet. He darted away and disappeared in the gloom, but first I heard his voice hoarsely shouting—

"Turn out, all hands, shorten sail!"

There was a rush of feet along the deck, and then the gale brought the dimmed sound of far-off commands—

"Mizzen foretop halyards there—all clue-garnets heave and away—now then, with a will—sheet home!"

And then the plaintive notes that told that the men were handling the kites—

"If you get there, before I do—
Hi-ho-o-o, roll a man down;
If you get there before I do,
O, give a man time to roll a man down!"

By and by all was still again. Meantime I had shifted to the other side of the galley to get out of the storm, and there Mr. Turner presently found me.

"That's a specimen," said he. "I've never struck any such weather anywheres. You are bowling along on a wind that's as steady as a sermon, and just as likely to last, and before you can say Jack Robinson the wind whips around from weather to lee, and if you don't jump for it you'll have your canvas blown out of the cat-heads and sailing for heaven in rags and tatters. I've never seen anything to begin with it. But then I've never been in the middle of Greenland before—in a *ship*—middle of where it *used* to be, I mean. Would it worry you if I was to tell you something, sir?"

"Why, no, I think not. What is it?"

"Let me take a turn up and down, first, to see if anybody's in earshot." When he came back he said, "What should you think if you was to see a whale with hairy spider-legs to it as long as the foretogallant backstay and as big around as the mainmast?"

I recognized the creature; I had seen it in the microscope. But I didn't say so. I said—

"I should think I had a little touch of the jimjams."

"The very thing *I* thought, so help me! It was the third day out, at a quarter to five in the morning. I was out astraddle of the bowsprit in the drizzle, bending on a scuttle-butt, for I don't trust that kind of a job to a common sailor, when all of a sudden that creature plunged up out of the sea the way a porpoise does, not a hundred yards away—I saw two hundred and fifty feet of him and his fringes—and then he turned in the air like a triumphal arch, shedding Niagaras of water, and plunged head first under the sea with an awful swash of sound, and by that time we were close aboard him and in another ten yards we'd have hit him. It was my belief that he tried to hit *us*, but by the mercy of God he was out of practice. The lookout on the foc'sle was the only man around, and thankful I was, or there could have been a mutiny. He was asleep on the binnacle—they always sleep on the binnacle, it's the best place to see from—and it woke him up and he said, "Good land, what's that, sir?" and I said, "It's nothing, but it *might* have been, for any good a stump like you is for a lookout." I was pretty far gone, and said I was sick, and made him help me onto the foc'sle; and then I went straight off and took the pledge; for I had been going it pretty high for a week before we sailed, and I made up my mind that I'd rather go dry the rest of my life than see the like of that thing again."

"Well, I'm glad it was only the jimjams."

"Wait a minute, I ain't done. Of course I didn't enter it on the log—"

"Of course not—"

"For a man in his right mind don't put nightmares in the log. He only puts the word 'pledge' in, and takes credit for it if anybody inquires; and knows it will please the captain, and hopes it'll get to the owners. Well, two days later the chief mate took the pledge!"

"You don't mean it!"

"Sure as I'm standing here. I saw the word on the book. I didn't say anything, but I felt encouraged. Now then, listen to this: day before yesterday I'm dumm'd if the *captain* didn't take the pledge!"

"Oh, come!"

"It's a true bill—I take my oath. There was the word. Then we begun to put this and that together, and next we began to look at each other kind of significant and willing, you know; and of course giving the captain the pre* cee*dence, for it wouldn't become *us* to begin, and we nothing but mates. And so yesterday, sure enough, out comes the captain—and we called his hand. Said he was out astern in a snow-flurry about dawn, and saw a creature shaped like a wood-louse and as big as a turreted monitor, go racing by and tearing up the foam, in chase of a fat animal the size of an elephant and creased like a caterpillar—and saw it dive after it and disappear; and so he begun to prepare *his* soul for the pledge and break it to his entrails."

"It's terrible!"

"The pledge?—you bet your bottom dollar. If I—"

"No, I don't mean the pledge; I mean it is terrible to be lost at sea among such strange, uncanny brutes."

"Yes, there's something in that, too, I don't deny it. Well, the thing that the mate saw was like one of these big long lubberly canal boats, and it was ripping along like the Empire Express; and the look of it gave him the cold shivers, and so he begun to arrange *his* earthly affairs and go for the pledge."

"Turner, it is dreadful—dreadful. Still, good has been done; for these pledges—"

"Oh, they're off!"

"Off?"

"Cert'nly. Can't be jimjams; couldn't all three of us have them at once, it ain't likely. What do you want with a pledge when there ain't any occasion for it? *There* he goes!"

He was gone like a shot, and the night swallowed him up. Now all of a sudden, with the wind still blowing hard, the seas went down and the deck became as level as a billiard table! Were *all* the laws of Nature suspended? It made my flesh creep; it was like being in a haunted ship. Pretty soon the mate came back panting, and sank down on a cable-tier, and said—

"Oh, this is an awful life; I don't think we can stand it long. There's too many horribles in it. Let me pant a little, I'm in a kind of a collapse."

"What's the trouble?"

"Drop down by me, sir—I mustn't shout. There—now you're all right." Then he said sorrowfully, "I reckon we've got to take it again."

"Take what?"

"The pledge."

"Why?"

"Did you see that thing go by?"

"What thing?"

"A *man*."

"No. What of it?"

"This is four times that *I've* seen it; and the mate has seen it, and so has the captain. Haven't you ever seen it?"

"I suppose not. Is there anything extraordinary about it?"

"Extra-ordinary? Well, I should *say!*"

"How is it extraordinary?"

He said in an awed voice that was almost like a groan—

"Like this, for instance: you put your hand on him and *he ain't there.*"

"What do you mean, Turner?"

"It's as true as I'm sitting here, I wish I may never stir. The captain's getting morbid and religious over it, and says he wouldn't give a damn for ship and crew if that thing stays aboard."

"You curdle my blood. What is the man like? Isn't it just one of the crew, that you glimpse and lose in the dark?"

"You take note of *this:* it wears a broad slouch hat and a long cloak. Is that a whaler outfit, I'll ask you? A minute ago I was as close to him as I am to you; and I made a grab for him, and what did I get? A handful of air, that's all. There warn't a sign of him left."

"I do hope the pledge will dispose of it. It must be a work of the imagination, or the crew would have seen it."

"We're afraid they have. There was a deal of whispering going on last night in the middle watch. The captain dealt out grog, and got their minds on something else; but he is mighty uneasy, because of course he don't want you or your family to hear about that man, and would take my scalp if he knew what I'm doing now; and besides, if such a thing got a start with the crew, there'd be a mutiny, sure."

"I'll keep quiet, of course; still, I think it must be an output of imaginations overstrung by the strange fishes you think you saw; and I am hoping that the pledge—"

"I want to take it now. And I will."

"I'm witness to it. Now come to my parlor and I'll give you a cup of hot coffee and—"

"Oh, my goodness, there it is again! . . . It's gone. . . . Lord, it takes a body's breath . . . It's the jimjams I've got—I know it for sure. I want the coffee; it'll do me good. If you could help me a little, sir—I feel as weak as Sabbath grog."

We groped along the sleety deck to my door and entered, and

there in the bright glare of the lamps sat (as I was half expecting)
the man of the long cloak and the slouch hat, on the sofa,—my
friend the Superintendent of Dreams. I was annoyed, for a
moment, for of course I expected Turner to make a jump at him,
get nothing, and be at once in a more miserable state than he
already was. I reached for my cabin door and closed it, so that Alice
might not hear the scuffle and get a fright. But there wasn't any.
Turner went on talking, and took no notice of the Superintendent.
I gave the Superintendent a grateful look; and it was an honest
one, for this thing of making himself visible and scaring people
could do harm.

"Lord, it's good to be in the light, sir," said Turner, rustling
comfortably in his yellow oilskins, "it lifts a person's spirits right
up. I've noticed that these cussed jimjam blatherskites ain't as apt
to show up in the light as they are in the dark, except when you've
got the trouble in your attic pretty bad." Meantime we were
dusting the snow off each other with towels. "You're mighty well
fixed here, sir—chairs and carpets and rugs and tables and lamps
and books and everything lovely, and so warm and comfortable and
homy; and the roomiest parlor I ever struck in a ship, too. Land,
hear the wind, don't she sing! And not a sign of motion!—rip goes
the sleet again!—ugly, you bet!—and here? why here it's only just
the more cosier on account of it. Dern that jimjam, if I had him in
here once I bet you I'd sweat him. Because I don't mind saying that
I don't grab at him as earnest as I want to, outside there, and ain't
as disappointed as I ought to be when I don't get him; but here in
the light I ain't afraid of *no* jimjam."

It made the Superintendent of Dreams smile a smile that was
full of pious satisfaction to hear him. I poured a steaming cup of
coffee and handed it to Turner and told him to sit where he pleased
and make himself comfortable and at home; and before I could
interfere he had sat down in the Superintendent of Dreams' lap!—
no, sat down *through* him. It cost me a gasp, but only that, nothing
more. [The] Superintendent of Dreams' head was larger than
Turner's, and *surrounded* it, and was a transparent spirit-head

fronted with a transparent spirit-face; and this latter smiled at me as much as to say give myself no uneasiness, it is all right. Turner was smiling comfort and contentment at me at the same time, and the double result was very curious, but I could tell the smiles apart without trouble. The Superintendent of Dreams' body enclosed Turner's, but I could see Turner through it, just as one sees objects through thin smoke. It was interesting and pretty. Turner tasted his coffee and set the cup down in front of him with a hearty—

"Now I call that prime! 'George, it makes me feel the way old Cap'n Jimmy Starkweather did, I reckon, the first time he tasted grog after he'd been off his allowance three years. The way of it was this. It was there in Fairhaven by New Bedford, away back in the old early whaling days before I was born; but I heard about it the first day I *was* born, and it was a ripe old tale then, because they keep only the one fleet of yarns in commission down New Bedford-way, and don't ever re-stock and don't ever repair. And I came near hearing it in old Cap'n Jimmy's own presence once, when I was ten years old and he was ninety-two; but I didn't, because the man that asked Cap'n Jimmy to tell about it got crippled and the thing didn't materialize. It was Cap'n Jimmy that crippled him. Land, I thought I sh'd die! The very recollection of it—"

The very recollection of it so powerfully affected him that it shut off his speech and he put his head back and spread his jaws and laughed himself purple in the face. And while he was doing it the Superintendent of Dreams emptied the coffee into the slop bowl and set the cup back where it was before. When the explosion had spent itself Turner swabbed his face with his handkerchief and said—

"There—that laugh has scoured me out and done me good; I hain't had such another one—well, not since I struck *this* ship, now that's sure. I'll whet up and start over."

He took up his cup, glanced into it, and it was curious to observe the two faces that were framed in the front of his head. Turner's was long and distressed; the Superintendent of Dreams' was wide, and broken out of all shape with a convulsion of silent laughter. After a little, Turner said in a troubled way—

"I'm dumm'd if *I* recollect drinking that."

I didn't say anything, though I knew he must be expecting me to say something. He continued to gaze into the cup a while, then looked up wistfully and said—

"Of course I must have drunk it, but I'm blest if I can recollect whether I did or not. Lemme see. First you poured it out, then I set down and put it before me here; next I took a sup and said it was good, and set it down and begun about old Cap'n Jimmy—and then—and then—" He was silent a moment, then said, "It's as far as I can get. It beats me. I reckon that after that I was so kind of full of my story that I didn't notice whether I—." He stopped again, and there was something almost pathetic about the appealing way in which he added, "But I *did* drink it, *didn't* I? You *see* me do it—*didn't* you?"

I hadn't the heart to say no.

"Why, yes, I think I did. I wasn't noticing particularly, but it seems to me that I saw you drink it—in fact, I am about certain of it."

I was glad I told the lie, it did him so much good, and so lightened his spirits, poor old fellow.

"Of course I done it! I'm such a fool. As a general thing I wouldn't care, and I wouldn't bother anything about it; but when there's jimjams around the least little thing makes a person suspicious, you know. If you don't mind, sir—thanks, ever so much." He took a large sup of the new supply, praised it, set the cup down—leaning forward and fencing it around with his arms, with a labored pretense of not noticing that he was doing that—then said—

"Lemme see—where was I? Yes. Well, it happened like this. The Washingtonian Movement started up in those old times, you know, and it was Father Matthew here and Father Matthew there and Father Matthew yonder—nothing but Father Matthew and temperance all over everywheres. And temperance societies? There was millions of them, and everybody joined and took the pledge. We had one in New Bedford. Every last whaler joined—captain, crew and all. All, down to old Cap'n Jimmy. He was an old bach, his grog was his darling, he owned his ship and sailed her himself, he was independent, and he wouldn't give in. So at last they gave it up and quit pestering him. Time rolled along, and he got awful lonesome. There wasn't anybody to drink with, you see, and it got unbearable. So finally the day he sailed for Bering Strait he caved, and sent in his name to the society. Just as he was starting, his mate broke his leg and stopped ashore and he shipped a stranger in his place from down New York way. This fellow didn't belong to any society, and he went aboard fixed for the voyage. Cap'n Jimmy was out three solid years; and all the whole time he had the spectacle of that mate whetting up every day and leading a life that was worth the trouble; and it nearly killed him for envy to see it. Made his mouth water, you know, in a way that was pitiful. Well, he used to get out on the peak of the bowsprit where it was private, and set there and cuss. It was his only relief from his sufferings. Mainly he cussed himself; but when he had used up all his words and couldn't think of any new rotten things to call himself, he would turn his vocabulary over and start fresh and lay into Father Matthew and give *him* down the banks; and then the society; and so put in his watch as satisfactory as he could. Then he would count the days he was out, and try to reckon up about when he could hope to get home and resign from the society and start in on an all-compensating drunk that would make up for lost time. Well, when he was out three thousand years—which was *his* estimate, you know, though really it was only three years—he came rolling down the home-stretch with every rag stretched on his poles. Middle of winter, it was, and terrible cold and stormy. He made the landfall just at sundown and had to stand watch on deck all night of course, and the rigging was caked with ice three inches thick, and the yards was bearded with icicles five foot long, and the snow laid nine inches deep on the deck and hurricanes more of it being shoveled down onto him out of the skies. And so he plowed up and down all night, cussing himself and Father Matthew and the society, and doing it better than he ever done before; and his mouth was watering so, on account of the mate whetting up right in his sight all the time, that every cuss-word come out damp, and froze solid as it fell, and in his insufferable indignation he would hit it a whack with his cane and knock it a hundred yards, and one of them took

the mate in the mouth and fetched away a rank of teeth and lowered
his spirits considerable. He made the dock just at early breakfast
time and never waited to tie up, but jumped ashore with his jug in
his hand and rushed for the society's quarters like a deer. He met
the seckatary coming out and yelled at him—

" 'I've resigned my membership!—I give you just two minutes to
scrape my name off your log, d'ye hear?'

"And then the seckatary told him he'd been black-balled three
years before—*hadn't ever been a member!* Land, I can't hold in, it's
coming again!"

He flung up his arms, threw his head back, spread his jaws, and
made the ship quake with the thunder of his laughter, while the
Superintendent of Dreams emptied the cup again and set it back in
its place. When Turner came out of his fit at last he was limp and
exhausted, and sat mopping his tears away and breaking at times
into little feebler and feebler barks and catches of expiring
laughter. Finally he fetched a deep sigh of comfort and satisfaction,
and said—

"Well, it *does* do a person good, no mistake—on a voyage like
this. I reckon—"

His eye fell on the cup. His face turned a ghastly white—

"By God she's empty again!"

He jumped up and made a sprawling break for the door. I was
frightened; I didn't know what he might do—jump overboard,
maybe. I sprang in front of him and barred the way, saying,
"Come, Turner, be a man, be a man! don't let your imagination
run away with you like this"; and over his shoulder I threw a
pleading look at the Superintendent of Dreams, who answered my
prayer and refilled the cup from the coffee urn.

"Imagination you call it, sir! Can't I *see?*—with my own eyes?
Let me go—don't stop me—I can't stand it, I can't stand it!"

"Turner, be reasonable—you know perfectly well your cup isn't
empty, and *hasn't* been."

That hit him. A dim light of hope and gratitude shone in his eye,
and he said in a quivery voice—

"Say it again—and say it's true. *Is* it true? Honor bright—you
wouldn't deceive a poor devil that's—"

"Honor bright, man, I'm not deceiving you—look for your-self."

Gradually he turned a timid and wary glance toward the table; then the terror went out of his face, and he said humbly—

"Well, you see I reckon I hadn't quite got over thinking it happened the first time, and so maybe without me knowing it, that made me kind of suspicious that it would happen again, because the jimjams make you untrustful that way; and so, sure enough, I didn't half look at the cup, and just jumped to the conclusion it *had* happened." And talking so, he moved toward the sofa, hesi-tated a moment, and then sat down in that figure's body again. "But I'm all right, now, and I'll just shake these feelings off and be a man, as you say."

The Superintendent of Dreams separated himself and moved along the sofa a foot or two away from Turner. I was glad of that; it looked like a truce. Turner swallowed his cup of coffee; I poured another; he began to sip it, the pleasant influence worked a change, and soon he was a rational man again, and comfortable. Now a sea came aboard, hit our deck-house a stunning thump, and went hissing and seething aft.

"Oh, that's the ticket," said Turner, "the dummdest weather that ever I went pleasure-excursioning in. And how did it get aboard?—You answer me that: there ain't any motion to the ship. These mysteriousnesses—well, they just give me the cold shudders. And that reminds me. Do you mind my calling your attention to another peculiar thing or two?—on conditions as before—solid secrecy, you know."

"I'll keep it to myself. Go on."

"The Gulf Stream's gone to the devil!"

"What do you mean?"

"It's the fact, I wish I may never die. From the day we sailed till now, the water's been the same temperature right along, I'll take my oath. The Gulf Stream don't exist any more; she's gone to the devil."

"It's incredible, Turner! You make me gasp."

"Gasp away, if you want to; if things go on so, you ain't going to forget how for want of practice. It's the wooliest voyage, take it by and large—why, look here! You are a landsman, and there's no telling what a landsman can't overlook if he tries. For instance, have you noticed that the nights and days are exactly alike, and you can't tell one from tother except by keeping tally?"

"Why, yes, I have noticed it in a sort of indifferent general way, but—"

"Have you kept a tally, sir?"

"No, it didn't occur to me to do it."

"I thought so. Now you know, you couldn't keep it in your head, because you and your family are free to sleep as much as you like, and as it's always dark, you sleep a good deal, and you are pretty irregular, naturally. You've all been a little seasick from the start— tea and toast in your own parlor here—no regular time—order it as each of you pleases. You see? You don't go down to meals—*they* would keep tally for you. So you've lost your reckoning. I noticed it an hour ago."

"How?"

"Well, you spoke of *to-night*. It ain't to-night at all; it's just noon, now."

"The fact is, I don't believe I have often thought of its being day, since we left. I've got into the habit of considering it night all the time; it's the same with my wife and the children."

"There it is, you see. Mr. Edwards, it's perfectly awful; now ain't it, when you come to look at it? Always night—and such dismal nights, too. It's like being up at the pole in the winter time. And I'll ask you to notice another thing: this sky is as empty as my sou-wester there."

"Empty?"

"Yes, sir. I know it. You can't get up a day, in a Christian country, that's so solid black the sun can't make a blurry glow of *some* kind in the sky at high noon—now can you?"

"No, you can't."

"Have you ever seen a suspicion of any such a glow in this sky?"

"Now that you mention it, I haven't."

He dropped his voice and said impressively—

"Because there ain't any *sun*. She's gone where the Gulf Stream twineth."

"Turner! Don't talk like that."

"It's confidential, or I wouldn't. And the moon. She's at the full —by the almanac she is. Why don't *she* make a blur? Because there *ain't* any moon. And moreover—you might rake this on-completed sky a hundred year with a drag-net and you'd never scoop a star! Why? Because there *ain't* any. Now then, what is your opinion about all this?"

"Turner, it's so gruesome and creepy that I don't like to think about it—and I haven't any. What is yours?"

He said, dismally—

"That the world has come to an end. Look at it yourself. Just look at the facts. Put them together and add them up, and what have you got? No Sable island; no Greenland; no Gulf Stream; no day, no proper night; weather that don't jibe with any sample known to the Bureau; animals that would start a panic in any menagerie, chart no more use than a horse-blanket, and the heavenly bodies gone to hell! And on top of it all, that jimjam that I've put my hand on more than once and he warn't there—I'll swear it. The ship's bewitched. You don't believe in the jim, and I've sort of lost faith myself, here in the bright light; but if this cup of coffee was to—"

The cup began to glide slowly away, along the table. The hand that moved it was not visible to him. He rose slowly to his feet and stood trembling as if with an ague, his teeth knocking together and his glassy eyes staring at the cup. It slid on and on, noiseless; then it rose in the air, gradually reversed itself, poured its contents down the Superintendent's throat—I saw the dark stream trickling its way down through his hazy breast—then it returned to the table, and without sound of contact, rested there. The mate continued to stare at it for as much as a minute; then he drew a deep breath, took up his sou-wester, and without looking to the right or the left, walked slowly out of the room like one in a trance, muttering—

"I've *got* them—I've had the proof."

I said, reproachfully—

"Superintendent, why do you do that?"

"Do what?"

"Play these tricks."

"What harm is it?"

"Harm? It could make that poor devil jump overboard."

"No, he's not as far gone as that."

"For a while he was. He is a good fellow, and it was a pity to scare him so. However there are other matters that I am more concerned about just now."

"Can I help?"

"Why yes, you can; and I don't know any one else that can."

"Very well, go on."

"By the dead-reckoning we have come twenty-three hundred miles."

"The actual distance is twenty-three-fifty."

"Straight as a dart in the one direction—mainly."

"Apparently."

"Why do you say apparently? Haven't we come straight?"

"Go on with the rest. What were you going to say?"

"This. Doesn't it strike you that this is a pretty large drop of water?"

"No. It is about the usual size—six thousand miles across."

"Six thousand miles!"

"Yes."

"Twice as far as from New York to Liverpool?"

"Yes."

"I must say it is more of a voyage than I counted on. And we are not a great deal more than halfway across, yet. When shall we get in?"

"It will be some time yet."

"That is not very definite. Two weeks?"

"More than that."

I was getting a little uneasy.

"But how *much* more? A week?"

"All of that. More, perhaps."

"Why don't you tell me? A month more, do you think?"

"I am afraid so. Possibly two—possibly longer, even."

I was getting seriously disturbed by now.

"Why, we are sure to run out of provisions and water."

"No you'll not. I've looked out for that. It is what you are loaded with."

"Is that so? How does that come?"

"Because the ship is chartered for a voyage of discovery. Ostensibly she goes to England, takes aboard some scientists, then sails for the South pole."

"I see. You are deep."

"I understand my business."

I turned the matter over in my mind a moment, then said—

"It is more of a voyage than I was expecting, but I am not of a worrying disposition, so I do not care, so long as we are not going to suffer hunger and thirst."

"Make yourself easy, as to that. Let the trip last as long as it may, you will not run short of food and water, I go bail for that."

"All right, then. Now explain this riddle to me. Why is it always night?"

"That is easy. All of the drop of water is outside the luminous circle of the microscope except one thin and delicate rim of it. We are in the shadow; consequently in the dark."

"In the shadow of what?"

"Of the brazen end of the lens-holder."

"How can it cover such a spread with its shadow?"

"Because it is several thousand miles in diameter. For dimensions, that is nothing. The glass slide which it is pressing against, and which forms the bottom of the ocean we are sailing upon, is thirty thousand miles long, and the length of the microscope barrel is a hundred and twenty thousand. Now then, if—"

"You make me dizzy. I—"

"If you should thrust that glass slide through what you call the 'great' globe, eleven thousand miles of it would stand out on each side—it would be like impaling an orange on a table-knife. And so—"

"It gives me the head-ache. Are these the fictitious proportions which we and our surroundings and belongings have acquired by being reduced to microscopic objects?"

"They are the proportions, yes—but they are not fictitious. You do not notice that you yourself are in any way diminished in size, do you?"

"No, I am my usual size, so far as I can see."

"The same with the men, the ship and everything?"

"Yes—all natural."

"Very good; nothing but the laws and conditions have undergone a change. You came from a small and very insignificant world. The one you are in now is proportioned according to microscopic standards—that is to say, it is inconceivably stupendous and imposing."

It was food for thought. There was something overpowering in the situation, something sublime. It took me a while to shake off the spell and drag myself back to speech. Presently I said—

"I am content; I do not regret the voyage—far from it. I would not change places with any man in that cramped little world. But tell me—is it always going to be dark?"

"Not if you ever come into the luminous circle under the lens. Indeed you will not find *that* dark!"

"If we ever. What do you mean by that? We are making steady good time; we are cutting across this sea on a straight course."

"Apparently."

"There is no apparently about it."

"You might be going around in a small and not rapidly widening circle."

"Nothing of the kind. Look at the tell-tale compass over your head."

"I see it."

"We changed to this easterly course to satisfy—well, to satisfy everybody but me. It is a pretense of aiming for England—in a drop of water! Have you noticed that needle before?"

"Yes, a number of times."

"To-day, for instance?"

"Yes—often."

"Has it varied a jot?"

"Not a jot."

"Hasn't it always kept the place appointed for it—from the start?"

"Yes, always."

"Very well. First we sailed a northerly course; then tilted easterly; and now it is more so. How is *that* going around in a circle?"

He was silent. I put it at him again. He answered with lazy indifference—

"I merely threw out the suggestion."

"All right, then; cornered; let it stand at that. Whenever you happen to think of an argument in support of it, I shall be glad to hear about it."

He did not like that very well, and muttered something about my being a trifle airy. I retorted a little sharply, and followed it up by finding fault with him again for playing tricks on Turner. He said Turner called him a blatherskite. I said—

"No matter; you let him alone, from this out. And moreover, stop appearing to people—stop it entirely."

His face darkened. He said—

"I would advise you to moderate your manner. I am not used to it, and I am not pleased with it."

The rest of my temper went, then. I said, angrily—

"You may like it or not, just as you choose. And moreover, if my style doesn't suit you, you can end the dream as soon as you please —right now, if you like."

He looked me steadily in the eye for a moment, then said, with deliberation—

"The dream? *Are you quite sure it is a dream?*"

It took my breath away.

"What do you mean? *Isn't* it a dream?"

He looked at me in that same way again; and it made my blood chilly, this time. Then he said—

"You have spent your whole life in this ship. And this is *real* life. Your other life was the dream!" †

---

† This answer of the Superintendent of Dreams represents a substantive departure from the previous transcription by Bernard DeVoto, which here prints

It was as if he had hit me, it stunned me so. Still looking at me, his lip curled itself into a mocking smile, and he wasted away like a mist and disappeared.

I sat a long time thinking uncomfortable thoughts.

We are strangely made. We think we are wonderful creatures. Part of the time we think that, at any rate. And during that interval we consider with pride our mental equipment, with its penetration, its power of analysis, its ability to reason out clear conclusions from confused facts, and all the lordly rest of it; and then comes a rational interval and disenchants us. Disenchants us and lays us bare to ourselves, and we see that intellectually we are really no great things; that we seldom really know the thing we think we know; that our best-built certainties are but sand-houses and subject to damage from any wind of doubt that blows.

So little a time before, I *knew* that this voyage was a dream, and nothing more; a wee little puff or two of doubt had blown against that certainty, unhelped by fact or argument, and already it was dissolving away. It seemed an incredible thing, and it hurt my pride of intellect, but it had to be confessed.

When I came to consider it, these ten days had been such intense realities!—so intense that by comparison the life I had lived before them seemed distant, indistinct, slipping away and fading out in a far perspective—exactly as a dream does when you sit at breakfast trying to call back its details. I grew steadily more and more nervous and uncomfortable—and a little frightened, though I would not quite acknowledge this to myself.†

"I give you ten years to get over that superstition in!" In the holograph, just before this statement, Mark Twain wrote "OVER" and then, on an inserted page 59½, at first wrote the following statements: "You have spent two-thirds of your life in this ship. And this is *real* life. Your other life was the dream!" Thereafter he struck out "two-thirds of" and added "whole" in the first sentence. Following the revised reply, he recopied on page 59½ the rest of what he had already written on page 59 below the direction "OVER." He recopied smoothly, picking up two minor alterations that he had previously made. Although he did not actually strike lines through the superseded passage, there seems to be little reason to doubt that what he rewrote and recopied on the inserted page represents his later intention.

† On the reverse side of page 61 of the holograph (which includes the preceding paragraph), he noted, "And now another past began to rise dim and spiritual before me and stretch down and down and down into dreaming remotenesses of bygone years—a past spent in a ship!"

Then came this disturbing thought: if this transformation goes on, how am I going to conceal it from my wife? Suppose she should say to me, "Henry, there is something the matter with you, you are acting strangely; something is on your mind that you are concealing from me; tell me about it, let me help you"—what answer could I make?

I was *bound* to act strangely if this went on—bound to bury myself in deeps of troubled thought; I should not be able to help it. She had a swift eye to notice, where her heart was concerned, and a sharp intuition, and I was an impotent poor thing in her hands when I had things to hide and she had struck the trail.

I have no large amount of fortitude, staying power. When there is a fate before me I cannot rest easy until I know what it is. I am not able to wait. I want to know, right away. So, I would call Alice, now, and take the consequences. If she drove me into a corner and I found I could not escape, I would act according to my custom—come out and tell her the truth. She had a better head than mine, and a surer instinct in grouping facts and getting their meaning out of them. If I was drifting into dangerous waters, now, she would be sure to detect it and as sure to set me right and save me. I would call her, and keep out of the corner if I could; if I couldn't, why—I couldn't, that is all.

She came, refreshed with sleep, and looking her best self: that is to say, looking like a girl of nineteen, not a matron of twenty-five; she wore a becoming wrapper, or tea gown, or whatever it is called, and it was trimmed with ribbons and limp stuff—lace, I suppose; and she had her hair balled up and nailed to its place with a four-pronged tortoise-shell comb. She brought a basket of pink and gray crewels with her, for she was crocheting a jacket—for the cat, probably, judging by the size of it. She sat down on the sofa and set the basket on the table, expecting to have a chance to get to work by and by; not right away, because a kitten was curled up in it asleep, fitting its circle snugly, and the repose of the children's kittens was a sacred thing and not to be disturbed. She said—

"I noticed that there was no motion—it was what waked me, I think—and I got up to enjoy it, it is such a rare thing."

"Yes, rare enough, dear: we do have the most unaccountably strange weather."

"Do you think so, Henry? Does it seem strange weather to you?"

She looked so earnest and innocent that I was rather startled, and a little in doubt as to what to say. Any sane person could see that it was perfectly devilish weather and crazy beyond imagination, and so how could she feel uncertain about it?

"Well, Alice, I may be putting it too strong, but I don't think so; I think a person may call our weather by any hard name he pleases and be justified."

"Perhaps you are right, Henry. I have heard the sailors talk the same way about it, but I did not think that that meant much, they speak so extravagantly about everything. You are not always extravagant in your speech—often you are, but not always—and so it surprised me a little to hear you." Then she added tranquilly and musingly, "I don't remember any different weather."

It was not quite definite.

"You mean on *this* voyage, Alice."

"Yes, of course. Naturally. I haven't made any other."

She was softly stroking the kitten—and apparently in her right mind. I said cautiously, and with seeming indifference—

"You mean you haven't made any other this year. But the time we went to Europe—well, that was very different weather."

"The time we went to Europe, Henry?"

"Certainly, certainly—when Jessie was a year old."

She stopped stroking the kitty, and looked at me inquiringly.

"I don't understand you, Henry."

She was not a joker, and she was always truthful. Her remark blew another wind of doubt upon my wasting sand-edifice of certainty. Had I only *dreamed* that we went to Europe? It seemed a good idea to put this thought into words.

"Come, Alice, the first thing you know you will be imagining that we went to Europe in a dream."

She smiled, and said—

"Don't let me spoil it, Henry, if it is pleasant to you to think we went. I will consider that we did go, and that I have forgotten it."

"But Alice dear we *did* go!"

"But Henry dear we *didn't* go!"

She had a good head and a good memory, and she was always truthful. My head had been injured by a fall when I was a boy, and the physicians had said at the time that there could be ill effects from it some day. A cold wave struck me, now; perhaps the effects had come. I was losing confidence in the European trip. However, I thought I would make another try.

"Alice, I will give you a detail or two; then maybe you will remember."

"A detail or two from the dream?"

"I am not at all sure that it was a dream; and five minutes ago I was sure that it wasn't. It was seven years ago. We went over in the *Batavia*. Do you remember the *Batavia*?"

"I don't, Henry."

"Captain Moreland. Don't you remember him?"

"To me he is a myth, Henry."

"Well, it beats anything. We lived two or three months in London, then six weeks in a private hotel in George Street, Edinburgh—Veitch's. Come!"

"It sounds pleasant, but I have never heard of these things before, Henry."

"And Doctor John Brown, of *Rab and His Friends*—you were ill, and he came every day; and when you were well again he still came every day and took us all around while he paid his visits, and we waited in his carriage while he prescribed for his patients. And he was so dear and lovely. You *must* remember all that, Alice."

"None of it, dear; it is only a dream."

"Why, Alice, have you ever had a dream that remained as distinct as that, and which you could remember so long?"

"So long? It is more than likely that you dreamed it last night."

"No indeed! It has been in my memory seven years."

"Seven years in a dream, yes—it is the way of dreams. They put seven years into two minutes, without any trouble—isn't it so?"

I had to acknowledge that it was.

"It seems almost as if it couldn't have been a dream, Alice; it seems as if you ought to remember it." †

"Wait! It begins to come back to me." She sat thinking a while, nodding her head with satisfaction from time to time. At last she said, joyfully, "I remember almost the whole of it, now."

"Good!"

"I am glad I got it back. Ordinarily I remember my dreams very well; but for some reason this one—"

"*This* one, Alice? Do you really consider it a dream, yet?"

"I don't consider anything about it, Henry, I know it; I know it positively."

The conviction stole through me that she must be right, since she felt so sure. Indeed I almost knew she was. I was privately becoming ashamed of myself now, for mistaking a clever illusion for a fact. So I gave it up, then, and said I would let it stand as a dream. Then I added—

"It puzzles me; even now it seems almost as distinct as the microscope."

"Which microscope?"

"Well, Alice, there's only the one."

"Very well, which one is *that?*"

"Bother it all, the one we examined this ocean in, the other day."

"Where?"

"Why, at home—of course."

"What home?"

"Alice, it's provoking—why, *our* home. In Springport."

---

† As the manuscript was first written, Alice was not to recall any part of what Henry remembered. After his assertion that she "ought to remember it," her answer was, "Why, Henry, if it had really happened, the nurse and Delia and George would have been with us." Deleting this reply, Mark Twain wrote on an inserted page the passage beginning with "Wait! It begins to come back to me," and continuing through "So I gave it up. . . ." In the latter part of Book I he made other revisions, representing Henry as remembering former events of the voyage and Alice as remembering the events of an earthly existence she had lived in her dreams.

"Dreaming again. I've never heard of it."

That was stupefying. There was no need of further beating about the bush; I threw caution aside, and came out frankly.

"Alice, what do you call the life we are leading in this ship? Isn't it a dream?"

She looked at me in a puzzled way and said—

"A dream, Henry? Why should I think that?"

"Oh, dear me, *I* don't know! I thought I did, but I don't. Alice, haven't we ever had a home? Don't you remember one?"

"Why, yes—three. That is, dream-homes, not real ones. I have never regarded them as realities."

"Describe them."

She did it, and in detail; also our life in them. Pleasant enough homes, and easily recognizable by me. I could also recognize an average of 2 out of 7 of the episodes and incidents which she threw in. Then I described the home and the life which (as it appeared to me) we had so recently left. She recognized it—but only as a dream-home. She remembered nothing about the microscope and the children's party. I was in a corner; but it was not the one which I had arranged for.

"Alice, if those were dream-homes, how long have you been in this ship?—you say this is the only voyage you have ever made."

"I don't know. I don't remember. It *is* the only voyage we have made—unless breaking it to pick up this crew of strangers in place of the friendly dear men and officers we had sailed with so many years makes two voyages of it. How I do miss them—Captain Hall, and Williams the sail-maker, and Storrs the chief mate, and—"

She choked up, and the tears began to trickle down her cheeks. Soon she had her handkerchief out and was sobbing.

I realized that I remembered those people perfectly well. Damnation! I said to myself, are we real creatures in a real world, all of a sudden, and have we been feeding on dreams in an imaginary one since nobody knows when—or how *is* it? My head was swimming.

"Alice! Answer me this. Do you know the Superintendent of Dreams?"

"Certainly."

"Have you seen him often?"

"Not often, but several times."

"When did you see him first?"

"The time that Robert the captain's boy was eaten." †

"*Eaten?*"

"Yes. Surely you haven't forgotten that?"

"But I have, though. I never heard of it before." (I spoke the truth. For the moment I could not recal the incident.)

Her face was full of reproach.

"I am sorry, if that is so. He was always good to you. If you are jesting, I do not think it is in good taste."

"Now don't treat me like that, Alice, I don't deserve it. I am not jesting, I am in earnest. I mean the boy's memory no offence, but although I remember him I do not remember the circumstance—I swear it. Who ate him?"

"Do not be irreverent, Henry, it is out of place. It was not a *who*, at all."

"What then—a *which?*"

"Yes."

"What kind of a which?"

"A spider-squid. *Now* you remember it I hope."

"Indeed and deed and double-deed I don't, Alice, and it is the real truth. Tell me about it, please."

"I suppose you see, now, Henry, what your memory is worth. You can remember dream-trips to Europe well enough, but things in real life—even the most memorable and horrible things—pass out of your memory in twelve years. There is something the matter with your mind."

It was very curious. How *could* I have forgotten that tragedy? It must have happened; she was never mistaken in her facts, and she

---

† This statement is at the bottom of page 74 of the holograph, which has *verso* some notes by which Mark Twain worked out the inversion of dream and reality that was to occur in the story. The Superintendent of Dreams "says his proper title is S[uperintendent] of R[ealities], and he is so-called in the other planets, but here we reverse the meanings of many words, and we wouldn't understand him." He noted, regarding Alice, "Where does she get her notions of mountain, valley, etc. if she has never been ashore? The S. of D. has taken her many a time —in dreams. But none of those things—permanent as they are—are substantial; they and the people are made of dream stuff. . . ."

never spoke with positiveness of a thing which she was in any degree uncertain about. And this tragedy—*twelve years* ago—

"Alice, how long *have* we been in this ship?"

"Now how can I know, Henry? It goes too far back. Always, for all I know. The earliest thing I can call to mind was papa's death by the sun-heat and mamma's suicide the same day. I was four years old, then. Surely you must remember that, Henry."

"Yes. . . . Yes. But it is so dim. Tell me about it—refresh my memory."

"Why, you must remember that we were in the edge of a great white glare once for a little while—a day, or maybe two days,—only a little while, I think, but I remember it, because it was the only time I was ever out of the dark, and there was a great deal of talk of it for long afterwards—why, Henry, you *must* remember a wonderful thing like that."

"Wait. Let me think." Gradually, detail by detail the whole thing came back to me; and with it the boy's adventure with the spider-squid; and then I recalled a dozen other incidents, which Alice verified as incidents of our ship-life, and said I had set them forth correctly.

It was a puzzling thing—my freaks of memory; Alice's, too. By testing, it was presently manifest that the vacancies in my ship-life memories were only apparent, not real; a few words by way of reminder enabled me to fill them up, in almost all cases, and give them clarity and vividness. What had caused these temporary lapses? Didn't these very lapses indicate that the ship-life was a dream, and not real?

It made Alice laugh.

I did not see anything foolish in it, or anything to laugh at, and I told her so. And I reminded her that her own memory was as bad as mine, since many and many a conspicuous episode of our land-life was gone from her, even so striking an incident as the water-drop exploration with the microscope—

It made her shout.

I was wounded; and said that if I could not be treated with respect I would spare her the burden of my presence and conversation. She stopped laughing, at once, and threw her arms about my neck. She said she would not have hurt me for the world, but she supposed I was joking; it was quite natural to think I was not in earnest in talking gravely about this and that and the other dream-phantom as if it were a reality.

"But Alice I *was* in earnest, and I *am* in earnest. Look at it—examine it. If the land-life was a dream-life, how is it that you remember so much of it exactly as *I* remember it?"

She was amused again, inside—I could feel the quiver; but there was no exterior expression of it, for she did not want to hurt me again.

"Dear heart, throw the whole matter aside! Stop puzzling over it; it isn't worth it. It is perfectly simple. It is true that I remember a little of that dream-life just as you remember it—but that is an accident; the rest of it—and by far the largest part—does not correspond with your recollections. And how *could* it? People can't be expected to remember each other's dreams, but only their own. You have put me into your land-dreams a thousand times, but I didn't always know I was there; so how could I remember it? Also I have put you into my land-dreams a thousand times when you didn't know it—and the natural result is that when I name the circumstances you don't always recal them. But how different it is with this real life, this genuine life in the ship! Our recollections of it are just alike. You have been forgetting episodes of it to-day—I don't know why; it has surprised me and puzzled me—but the lapse was only temporary; your memory soon rallied again. Now it hasn't rallied in the case of land-dreams of mine—in most cases it hasn't. And it's not going to, Henry. You can be sure of that."

She stopped, and tilted her head up in a thinking attitude and began to unconsciously tap her teeth with the ivory knob of a crochet needle. Presently she said, "I think I know what is the matter. I have been neglecting you for ten days while I have been grieving for our old shipmates and pretending to be seasick so that I might indulge myself with solitude; and here is the result—you haven't been taking exercise enough."

I was glad to have a reason—any reason that would excuse my memory—and I accepted this one, and made confession. There was no truth in the confession, but I was already getting handy with these evasions. I was a little sorry for this, for she had always trusted my word, and I had honored this trust by telling her the truth many a time when it was a sharp sacrifice to me to do it. She looked me over with gentle reproach in her eye, and said—

"Henry, how can you. be so naughty? I watch you so faithfully and make you take such good care of your health that you owe me the grace to do my office for me when for any fair reason I am for a while not on guard. When have you boxed with George last?"

What an idea it was! It was a good place to make a mistake, and I came near to doing it. It was on my tongue's end to say that I had never boxed with anyone; and as for boxing with a colored man-servant—and so on; but I kept back my remark, and in place of it tried to look like a person who didn't know what to say. It was easy to do, and I probably did it very well.

"You do not say anything, Henry. I think it is because you have a good reason. When have you fenced with him? Henry, you are avoiding my eye. Look up. Tell me the truth: have you fenced with him a single time in the last ten days?"

So far as I was aware I knew nothing about foils, and had never handled them; so I was able to answer—

"I will be frank with you, Alice—I haven't."

"I suspected it. Now, Henry, what can you say?"

I was getting some of my wits back, now, and was not altogether unprepared, this time.

"Well, Alice, there hasn't been much fencing weather, and when there was any, I—well, I was lazy, and that is the shameful truth."

"There's a chance now, anyway, and you mustn't waste it. Take off your coat and things."

She rang for George, then she got up and raised the sofa-seat and began to fish out boxing-gloves, and foils and masks from the locker under it, softly scolding me all the while. George put his head in, noted the preparations, then entered and put himself in boxing trim. It was his turn to take the witness stand, now.

"George, didn't I tell you to keep up Mr. Henry's exercises just the same as if I were about?"

"Yes, madam, you did."

"Why haven't you done it?"

George chuckled, and showed his white teeth and said—

"Bless yo' soul, honey, I dasn't."

"Why?"

"Because the first time I went to him—it was that Tuesday, you know, when it was ca'm—he wouldn't hear to it, and said he didn't want no exercise and warn't going to take any, and tole me to go 'long. Well, I didn't stop there, of course, but went to him agin, every now and then, trying to persuade him, tell at last he let into me" (he stopped and comforted himself with an unhurried laugh over the recollection of it,) "and give me a most solid good cussing, and tole me if I come agin he'd take and thow me overboard—there, ain't that so, Mr. Henry?"

My wife was looking at me pretty severely.

"Henry, what have you to say to that?"

It was my belief that it hadn't happened, but I was steadily losing confidence in my memory; and moreover my new policy of recollecting whatever anybody required me to recollect seemed the safest course to pursue in my strange and trying circumstances; so I said—

"Nothing, Alice—I did refuse."

"Oh, I'm not talking about that; of course you refused—George had already said so."

"Oh, I see."

"Well, why do you stop?"

"Why do I stop?"

"Yes. Why don't you answer my question?"

"Why, Alice, I've answered it. You asked me—you asked me—What *is* it I haven't answered?"

"Henry, you know very well. You broke a promise; and you are trying to talk around it and get me away from it; but I am not going to let you. You know quite well you promised me you wouldn't swear any more in calm weather. And it is such a little thing to do. It is hardly ever calm, and—"

"Alice, dear, I beg ever so many pardons! I had clear forgotten it; but I won't offend again, I give you my word. Be good to me, and forgive."

She was always ready to forgive, and glad to do it, whatever my crime might be; so things were pleasant again, now, and smooth and happy. George was gloved and skipping about in an imaginary fight, by this time, and Alice told me to get to work with him. She took pencil and paper and got ready to keep game. I stepped forward to position—then a curious thing happened: I seemed to remember a thousand boxing-bouts with George, the whole boxing art came flooding in upon me, and I knew just what to do! I was a prey to no indecisions, I had no trouble. We fought six rounds, I held my own all through, and I finally knocked George out. I was not astonished; it seemed a familiar experience. Alice showed no surprise, George showed none; apparently it was an old story to them.

The same thing happened with the fencing. I suddenly knew that I was an experienced old fencer; I expected to get the victory, and when I got it, it seemed but a repetition of something which had happened numberless times before.

We decided to go down to the main saloon and take a regular meal in the regular way—the evening meal. Alice went away to dress. Just as I had finished dressing, the children came romping in, warmly and prettily clad, and nestled up to me, one on each side, on the sofa, and began to chatter. Not about a former home; no, not a word of that, but only about this ship-home and its concerns and its people. After a little I threw out some questions—feelers. They did not understand. Finally I asked them if they had known no home but this one. Jessie said, with some little enthusiasm—

"Oh, yes, dream-homes. They are pretty—some of them." Then, with a shrug of her shoulders, "But they *are* so queer!"

"How, Jessie?"

"Well, you know, they have such curious things in them; and they fade, and don't stay. Bessie doesn't like them at all."

"Why don't you, Bessie?"

"Because they scare me so."

"What is it that scares you?"

"Oh, everything, papa. Sometimes it is so light. That hurts my eyes. And it's too many lamps—little sparkles all over, up high, and large ones that are dreadful. They could fall on me, you know."

"But I am not much afraid," said Jessie, "because mamma says they are not real, and if they did fall they wouldn't hurt."

"What else do you see there besides the lights, Bessie?"

"Ugly things that go on four legs like our cat, but bigger."

"Horses?"

"I forget names."

"Describe them, dear."

"I can't, papa. They are not alike; they are different kinds; and when I wake up I can't just remember the shape of them, they are so dim."

"And I wouldn't wish to remember them," said Jessie, "they make me feel creepy. Don't let's talk about them, papa, let's talk about something else."

"That's what I say, too," said Bessie.

So then we talked about our ship. That interested them. They cared for no other home, real or unreal, and wanted no better one. They were innocent witnesses and free from prejudice.

When we went below we found the roomy saloon well lighted and brightly and prettily furnished, and a very comfortable and inviting place altogether. Everything seemed substantial and genuine, there was nothing to suggest that it might be a work of the imagination.

At table the captain (Davis) sat at the head, my wife at his right with the children, I at his left, a stranger at my left. The rest of the company consisted of Rush Phillips, purser, aged 27; his sweetheart the Captain's daughter Lucy, aged 22; her sister Connie (short for Connecticut), aged 10; Arnold Blake, surgeon, 25; Harvey Pratt, naturalist, 36; at the foot sat Sturgis the chief mate, aged 35, and completed the snug assemblage. Stewards waited upon the general company, and George and our nurse Germania had charge of our family. Germania was not the nurse's name, but that was our name for her because it was shorter than her own. She was 28 years old, and had always been with us; and so had George. George was 30, and had once been a slave, according to my record, but I was losing

my grip upon that, now, and was indeed getting shadowy and
uncertain about all my traditions.

The talk and the feeding went along in a natural way, I could
find nothing unusual about it anywhere. The captain was pale, and
had a jaded and harassed look, and was subject to little fits of
absence of mind; and these things could be said of the mate, also,
but this was all natural enough considering the grisly time they had
been having, and certainly there was nothing about it to suggest
that they were dream-creatures or that their troubles were unreal.

The stranger at my side was about 45 years old, and he had
the half-subdued, half-resigned look of a man who had been under
a burden of trouble a long time. He was tall and thin; he had
a bushy black head, and black eyes which burned when he was
interested, but were dull and expressionless when his thoughts
were far away—and that happened every time he dropped out of
the conversation. He forgot to eat, then, his hands became idle, his
dull eye fixed itself upon his plate or upon vacancy, and now and
then he would draw a heavy sigh out of the depths of his breast.

These three were exceptions; the others were chatty and cheerful, and they were like a pleasant little family party together.
Phillips and Lucy were full of life, and quite happy, as became
engaged people; and their furtive love-passages had everybody's
sympathy and approval. Lucy was a pretty creature, and simple in
her ways and kindly, and Phillips was a blithesome and attractive
young fellow. I seemed to be familiarly acquainted with everybody,
I didn't quite know why. That is, with everybody except the
stranger at my side; and as he seemed to know me well, I had to let
on to know him, lest I cause remark by exposing the fact that I
didn't know him. I was already tired of being caught up for
ignorance at every turn.

The captain and the mate managed to seem comfortable enough
until Phillips raised the subject of the day's run, the position of the
ship, distance out, and so on; then they became irritable, and sharp
of speech, and were unkinder to the young fellow than the case
seemed to call for. His sweetheart was distressed to see him so
treated before all the company, and she spoke up bravely in his
defence and reproached her father for making an offence out of so

harmless a thing. This only brought her into trouble, and procured for her so rude a retort that she was consumed with shame, and left the table crying.

The pleasure was all gone, now; everybody felt personally affronted and wantonly abused. Conversation ceased and an uncomfortable silence fell upon the company; through it one could hear the wailing of the wind and the dull tramp of the sailors and the muffled words of command overhead, and this made the silence all the more dismal. The dinner was a failure. While it was still unfinished the company began to break up and slip out, one after another; and presently none was left but me.†

I sat long, sipping black coffee and smoking. And thinking; groping about in my dimming land-past. An incident of my American life would rise upon me, vague at first, then grow more distinct and articulate, then sharp and clear; then in a moment it was gone, and in its place was a dull and distant image of some long-past episode whose theatre was this ship—and then *it* would develop, and clarify, and become strong and real. It was fascinating, enchanting, this spying among the elusive mysteries of my bewitched memory, and I went up to my parlor and continued it, with the help of punch and pipe, hour after hour, as long as I could keep awake. With this curious result: that the main incidents of both my lives were now recovered, but only those of one of them persistently gathered strength and vividness—our life in the ship! Those of our land-life were good enough, plain enough, but in minuteness of detail they fell perceptibly short of those others; and in matters of feeling—joy, grief, physical pain, physical pleasure— immeasurably short!

Some mellow notes floated to my ear, muffled by the moaning wind—six bells in the morning watch. So late! I went to bed. When I woke in the middle of the so-called day the first thing I thought of was my night's experience. Already my land-life had faded a little—but not the other.

---

† The "Mad Passenger" variant (the following selection) was cut out of the story at this point.

BOOK II

CHAPTER I

I HAVE long ago lost Book I, but it is no matter. It served its purpose—writing it was an entertainment to me. We found out that our little boy set it adrift on the wind, sheet by sheet, to see if it would fly. It did. And so two of us got entertainment out of it. I have often been minded to begin Book II, but natural indolence and the pleasant life of the ship interfered.

There have been little happenings, from time to time. The principal one, for us of the family, was the birth of our Harry, which stands recorded in the log under the date of June 8, and happened about three months after we shipped the present crew, poor devils! They still think we are bound for the South Pole, and that we are a long time on the way. It is pathetic, after a fashion. They regard their former life in the World as their real life and this present one as—well, they hardly know what; but sometimes they get pretty tired of it, even at this late day. We hear of it now and then through the officers—mainly Turner, who is a puzzled man.

During the first four years we had several mutinies, but things have been reasonably quiet during the past two. One of them had really a serious look. It occurred when Harry was a month old, and at an anxious time, for both he and his mother were weak and ill. The master spirit of it was Stephen Bradshaw the carpenter, of course—a hard lot I know, and a born mutineer I think.

In those days I was greatly troubled, for a time, because my wife's memories still refused to correspond with mine. It had been an ideal life, and naturally it was a distress not to be able to live it over again in its entirety with her in our talks. At first she did not feel about it as I did, and said she could not understand my interest in those dreams, but when she found how much I took the matter to heart, and that to me the dreams had come to have a seeming of reality and were freighted with tender and affectionate impressions besides, she began to change her mind and wish she could go back in spirit with me to that mysterious land. And so she tried to get back that forgotten life. By my help, and by patient probing and searching of her memory she succeeded. Gradually it all came back, and her reward was sufficient. We now had the recollections of two lives to draw upon, and the result was a double measure of happiness for us. We even got the children's former lives back for them—with a good deal of difficulty—next the servants'. It made a new world for us all, and an entertaining one to explore. In the beginning George the colored man was an unwilling subject, because by heredity he was superstitious, and believed that no good could come of meddling with dreams; but when he presently found that no harm came of it his disfavor dissolved away.

Talking over our double-past—particularly our dream-past—became our most pleasant and satisfying amusement, and the search for missing details of it our most profitable labor. One day when the baby was about a month old, we were at this pastime in our parlor. Alice was lying on the sofa, propped with pillows—she was by no means well. It was a still and solemn black day, and cold; but the lamps made the place cheerful, and as for comfort, Turner had taken care of that; for he had found a kerosene stove with an ising-glass front among the freight, and had brought it up and lashed it fast and fired it up, and the warmth it gave and the red glow it made took away all chill and cheerlessness from the parlor and made it homelike. The little girls were out somewhere with George and Delia (the maid).

Alice and I were talking about the time, twelve years before, when Captain Hall's boy had his tragic adventure with the spider-squid, and I was reminding her that she had misstated the case when she mentioned it to me, once. She had said the squid *ate* the boy. Out of my memory I could call back all the details, now, and I remembered that the boy was only badly hurt, not eaten.

For a month or two the ship's company had been glimpsing vast animals at intervals of a few days, and at first the general terror was

so great that the men openly threatened, on two occasions, to seize
the ship unless the captain turned back; but by a resolute bearing
he tided over the difficulty; and by pointing out to the men that the
animals had shown no disposition to attack the ship and might
therefore be considered harmless, he quieted them down and
restored order. It was good grit in the captain, for privately he was
very much afraid of the animals himself and had but a shady
opinion of their innocence. He kept his gatlings in order, and had
gun-watches, which he changed with the other watches.

I had just finished correcting Alice's history of the boy's
adventure with the squid when the ship, plowing through a
perfectly smooth sea, went heeling away down to starboard and
stayed there! The floor slanted like a roof, and every loose thing in
the room slid to the floor and glided down against the bulkhead.
We were greatly alarmed, of course. Next we heard a rush of feet
along the deck and an uproar of cries and shoutings, then the rush
of feet coming back, with a wilder riot of cries. Alice exclaimed—

"Go find the children—quick!"

I sprang out and started to run aft through the gloom, and then I
saw the fearful sight which I had seen twelve years before when
that boy had had his shocking misadventure. For the moment I
turned the corner of the deck-house and had an unobstructed view
astern, there it was—apparently two full moons rising close over
the stern of the ship and lighting the decks and rigging with a
sickly yellow glow—the eyes of the colossal squid. His vast beak
and head were plain to be seen, swelling up like a hill above our
stern; he had flung one tentacle forward and gripped it around the
peak of the main-mast and was pulling the ship over; he had
gripped the mizzen-mast with another, and a couple more were
writhing about dimly away above our heads searching for something to take hold of. The stench of his breath was suffocating
everybody.

I was like the most of the crew, helpless with fright; but the
captain and the officers kept their wits and courage. The gatlings
on the starboard side could not be used, but the four on the port
side were brought to bear, and inside of a minute they had poured

more than two thousand bullets into those moons. That blinded the
creature, and he let go; and by squirting a violent Niagara of water
out of his mouth which tore the sea into a tempest of foam he shot
himself backward three hundred yards and the ship forward as far,
drowning the deck with a racing flood which swept many of the
men off their feet and crippled some, and washed all loose deck-
plunder overboard. For five minutes we could hear him thrashing
about, there in the dark, and lashing the sea with his giant tentacles
in his pain; and now and then his moons showed, then vanished
again; and all the while we were rocking and plunging in the
booming seas he made. Then he quieted down. We took a thankful
full breath, believing him dead.

Now I thought of the children, and ran all about inquiring for
them, but no one had seen them. I thought they must have been
washed overboard, and for a moment my heart stopped beating.
Then the hope came that they had taken refuge with their mother;
so I ran there; and almost swooned when I entered the place, for it
was vacant. I ran out shouting the alarm, and after a dozen steps
almost ran over her. She was lying against the bulwarks drenched
and insensible. The surgeon and young Phillips helped me carry
her in; then the surgeon and I began to work over her and Phillips
rushed away to start the hunt for the children. It was all of half an
hour before she showed any sign of life; then her eyes opened with
a dazed and wondering look in them, then they recognized me and
into them shot a ghastly terror.

"The children! the children!" she gasped; and I, with the heart
all gone out of me, answered with such air of truth as I could
assume—

"They are safe."

I could never deceive her. I was transparent to her.

"It is not true! The truth speaks out all over you—they are lost,
oh they are lost, they are lost!"

We were strong, but we could not hold her. She tore loose from
us and was gone in a moment, flying along the dark decks and
shrieking the children's names with a despairing pathos that broke
one's heart to hear it. We fled after her, and urged that the flitting

lanterns meant that all were searching, and begged her for the children's sake and mine if not for her own to go to bed and save her life. But it went for nothing, she would not listen. For she was a mother, and her children were lost. That says it all. She would hunt for them as long as she had strength to move. And that is what she did, hour after hour, wailing and mourning, and touching the hardest hearts with her grief, until she was exhausted and fell in a swoon. Then the stewardess and I put her to bed, and as soon as she came to and was going to creep out of her bed and take up her search again the doctor encouraged her in it and gave her a draught to restore her strength; and it put her into a deep sleep, which was what he expected.

We left the stewardess on watch and went away to join the searchers. Not a lantern was twinkling anywhere, and every figure that emerged from the gloom moved upon tip-toe. I collared one of them and said angrily—

"What does this mean? Is the search stopped?"

Turner's voice answered—very low: "—'sh! Captain's orders. The beast ain't dead—it's hunting for us."

It made me sick with fear.

"Do you mean it, Turner? How do you know?"

"Listen."

There was a muffled swashing sound out there somewhere, and then the two moons appeared for a moment, then turned slowly away and were invisible again.

"He's been within a hundred yards of us, feeling around for us with his arms. He could reach us, but he couldn't locate us because he's blind. Once he mighty near had us; one of his arms that was squirming around up there in the dark just missed the foremast, and he hauled in the slack of it without suspecting anything. It made my lungs come up into my throat. He has edged away, you see, but he ain't done laying for us." Pause. Then in a whisper, "He's wallowing around closer to us again, by gracious. Look—look at that. See it? Away up in the air—writhing around like a crooked mainmast. Dim, but—there, *now* don't you see it?"

We stood dead still, hardly breathing. Here and there at little distances the men were gathering silently together and watching and pointing. The deep hush lay like a weight upon one's spirit. Even the faintest quiver of air that went idling by gave out a ghost of sound. A couple of mellow notes floated lingering and fading down from forward:

Booooom——booooom. (Two bells in the middle watch.)

A hoarse low voice—the captain's:

"Silence that damned bell!"

Instantly there was a thrashing commotion out there, with a thundering rush of discharged water, and the monster came charging for us. I caught my breath, and had to seize Turner or I should have fallen, so suddenly my strength collapsed. Then vaguely we saw the creature, waving its arms aloft, tear past the ship stern first, pushing a vast swell ahead and trailing a tumultuous wake behind, and the next moment it was far away and we were plunging and tossing in the sea it made.

"Thank God, *he's* out of practice!" said Turner, with emotion.

The majestic blind devil stopped out there with its moons toward us, and we were miserable again. We had so hoped it would go home.

I resumed my search. Below I found Phillips and Lucy Davis and a number of others searching, but with no hope. They said they had been everywhere, and were merely going over the ground again and again because they could not bear to have it reported to the mother that the search had ceased. She must be told that they were her friends and that she could depend upon them.

Four hours later I gave it up, wearied to exhaustion, and went and sat down by Alice's bed, to be at hand and support her when she should wake and have to hear my desolate story. After a while she stirred, then opened her eyes and smiled brightly and said—

"Oh, what bliss it is! I dreamed that the children—" She flung her arms about me in a transport of grief. "I remember—oh, my God it is true!"

And so, with sobs and lamentations and frantic self-reproaches she poured out her bitter sorrow, and I clasped her close to me, and could not find one comforting word to say.

"Oh, Henry, Henry, your silence means—oh, we cannot live, we cannot bear it!"

There was a flurry of feet along the deck, the door was burst in, and Turner's voice shouted—

"They're found, by God they're found!"

A joy like that brings the shock of a thunderbolt, and for a little while we thought Alice was gone; but then she rallied, and by that time the children were come, and were clasped to her breast, and she was steeped in a happiness for which there were no words. And she said she never dreamed that profanity could sound so dear and sweet, and she asked the mate to say it again; and he did, but left out the profanity and spoiled it.

The children and George and Delia had seen the squid come and lift its moons above our stern and reach its vast tentacles aloft; and they had not waited, but had fled below, and had not stopped till they were deep down in the hold and hidden in a tunnel among the freight. When found, they had had several hours' sleep and were much refreshed.

Between seeing the squid, and getting washed off her feet, and losing the children, the day was a costly one for Alice. It marks the date of her first gray hairs. They were few, but they were to have company.

We lay in a dead calm, and helpless. We could not get away from the squid's neighborhood. But I was obliged to have some sleep, and I took it. I took all I could get, which was six hours. Then young Phillips came and turned me out and said there were signs that the spirit of mutiny was abroad again and that the captain was going to call the men aft and talk to them. Phillips thought I would not want to miss it.

He was right. We had private theatricals, we had concerts, and the other usual time-passers customary on long voyages; but a speech from the captain was the best entertainment the ship's talent could furnish. There was character back of his oratory. He was all sailor. He was sixty years old, and had known no life but sea life. He had no gray hairs, his beard was full and black and shiny; he wore no mustache, therefore his lips were exposed to view; they fitted together like box and lid, and expressed the pluck and resolution that were in him. He had bright black eyes in his old bronze face and they eloquently interpreted all his moods, and his moods were many: for at times he was the youngest man in the ship, and the most cheerful and vivacious and skittish; at times he was the best-natured man in the ship, and he was always the most lovable; sometimes he was sarcastic, sometimes he was serious even to solemnity, sometimes he was stern, sometimes he was as sentimental as a school-girl; sometimes he was silent, quiet, withdrawn within himself, sometimes he was talkative and argumentative; he was remarkably and sincerely and persistently pious, and marvelously and scientifically profane; he was much the strongest man in the ship, and he was also the largest, excepting that plotting, malicious and fearless devil, Stephen Bradshaw the carpenter; he could smile as sweetly as a girl, and it was a pleasure to see him do it. He was entirely self-educated, and had made a vast and picturesque job of it. He was an affectionate creature, and in his family relations he was beautiful; in the eyes of his daughters he was omniscient, omnipotent, a mixed sun-god and storm-god, and they feared him and adored him accordingly. He was fond of oratory, and thought he had the gift of it; and so he practiced it now and then, upon occasion, and did it with easy confidence. He was a charming man and a manly man, with a right heart and a fine and daring spirit.

Phillips and I slipped out and moved aft. Things had an unusual and startling aspect. There were flushes of light here and there and yonder; the captain stood in one of them, the officers stood a little way back of him.

"How do matters stand, Phillips?"

"You notice that the battle-lanterns are lit, all the way forward?"

"Yes. The gun-watches are at their posts; I see that. The captain means business, I reckon."

"The gun-watches are mutineers!"

I steadied my voice as well as I could, but there was still a quaver in it when I said—

"Then they've sprung a trap on us, and we are at their mercy, of course."

"It has the look of it. They've caught the old man napping, and we are in a close place this time."

We joined the officers, and just then we heard the measured tramp of the men in the distance. They were coming down from forward. Soon they came into view and moved toward us until they were within three or four paces of the captain.

"Halt!"

They had a leader this time, and it was he that gave the command—Stephen Bradshaw, the carpenter. He had a revolver in his hand. There was a pause, then the captain drew himself up, put on his dignity, and prepared to transact business in a properly impressive and theatrical way. He cleared his voice and said, in a fatherly tone—

"Men, this is your spokesman, duly appointed by you?"

Several responded timidly—

"Yes, sir."

"You have a grievance, and you desire to have it redressed?"

"Yes, sir."

"He is not here to represent himself, lads, but only you?"

"Yes, sir."

"Very well. Your complaint shall be heard, and treated with justice." (Murmur of approbation from the men.) Then the captain's soft manner hardened a little, and he said to the carpenter, "Go on."

Bradshaw was eager to begin, and he flung out his words with aggressive confidence—

"Captain Davis, in the first place this crew wants to know where they *are*. Next, they want this ship put about and pointed for home —straight off, and no fooling. They are tired of this blind voyage, and they ain't going to have any more of it—and that's the word with the bark on it." He paused a moment, for his temper was rising and obstructing his breath; then he continued in a raised and insolent voice and with a showy flourish of his revolver. "Before, they've had no leader, and you talked them down and cowed them; but that ain't going to happen this time. And they hadn't any plans, and warn't fixed for business; but it's different, now." He grew exultant. "Do you see this?"—his revolver. "And do you see that?" He pointed to the gatlings. "We've got the guns; we are boss of the ship. Put her about! That's the order, and it's going to be obeyed."

There was an admiring murmur from the men. After a pause the captain said, with dignity—

"Apparently you are through. Stand aside."

"Stand aside, is it? Not till I have heard what answer you—"

The captain's face darkened and an evil light began to flicker in his eyes, and his hands to twitch. The carpenter glanced at him, then stepped a pace aside, shaking his head and grumbling. "Say your say, then, and cut it short, for I've got something more to say when you're done, if it ain't satisfactory."

The captain's manner at once grew sweet, and even tender, and he turned toward the men with his most genial and winning smile on his face, and proceeded to take them into his confidence.

"You want to know where you are, boys. It is reasonable; it is natural. If we don't know where we are—if we are lost—who is worst off, you or me? You have no children in this ship—I have. If we are in danger have I put us there intentionally? Would I have done it purposely—with my children aboard? Come, what do you think?"

There was a stir among the men, and an approving nodding of heads which conceded that the point was well taken.

"Don't I know my trade, or am I only an apprentice to it? Have I sailed the seas for sixty years and commanded ships for thirty to be taught what to do in a difficulty by—by a damned carpenter?"

He was talking in such a pleading way, such an earnest, and moving and appealing way that the men were not prepared for the close of his remark, and it caught them out and made some of them laugh. He had scored one—and he knew it. The carpenter's back was turned—he was playing indifference. He whirled around and covered the captain with his revolver. Everybody shrank together and caught his breath, except the captain, who said gently—

"Don't be afraid—pull the trigger; it isn't loaded."

The carpenter pulled—twice, thrice, and threw the pistol away. Then he shouted—

"Fall back, men—out of the way!" They surged apart, and he fell back himself. The captain and the officers stood alone in the circle of light. "Gun 4, fire!" The officers threw themselves on their faces on the deck, but the captain remained in his place. The gunner spun the windlass around—there was no result. "Gun 3, fire!" The same thing happened again. The captain said—

"Come back to your places, men." They obeyed, looking puzzled, surprised, and a good deal demoralized. The officers got up, looking astonished and rather ashamed. "Carpenter, come back to your place." He did it, but reluctantly, and swearing to himself. It was easy to see that the captain was contented with his dramatic effects. He resumed his speech, in his pleasantest manner—

"You have mutinied two or three times, boys. It is all right—up to now. I would have done it myself in my common-seaman days, I reckon, if my ship was bewitched and I didn't know where I was. Now then, can you be trusted with the facts? Are we rational men, manly men, men who can stand up and face hard luck and a big difficulty that has been brought about by nobody's fault, and say live or die, survive or perish, we are in for it, for good or bad, and we'll stand by the ship if she goes to hell!" (The men let go a tol[erably] hearty cheer.) "Are we men—grown men—salt-sea men —men nursed upon dangers and cradled in storms—men made in the image of God and ready to do when He commands and die when He calls—or are we just sneaks and curs and carpenters!" (This brought both cheers and laughter, and the captain was happy.) "There—that's the kind. And so I'll tell you how the thing stands. *I* don't know where this ship is, but she's in the hands of God, and that's enough for me, it's enough for you, and it's enough for anybody but a carpenter. If it is God's will that we pull through, we pull through—otherwise not. We haven't had an observation for four months, but we are going ahead, and do our best to fetch up somewhere."

                                                            (1898)

The Mad Passenger

THE DINNER was a failure. While it was still unfinished the company began to† break up and slip out, one after another; and presently none was left but the stranger at my side and me. We were sipping black coffee and smoking. The stranger said, with a sigh—

"Ah, well, that is the way with them. They are mad—that captain and that mate."

"Mad?"

"Well, on the way to it. I have noticed it for days."

"I think, myself, that they are disturbed about something, but I don't see any suggestion of madness about it."

"But you haven't been around. You have been shut up a good deal lately and haven't seen what has been going on. Let me tell you a few things." He was speaking in a low voice. A rattling of dishes attracted his attention—a steward was clearing the other end of the table. "Come to my cabin—this place lacks privacy. Bring your coffee."

---

† In writing "The Great Dark" Mark Twain introduced a character called The Mad Passenger a few pages before the end of Book I. To account for his sudden presence he made use of an incident involving a man snatched from the taffrail of his ship by the bowsprit of another vessel, which he had noted during November 1897 as material to be added to "Which Was the Dream?" Its appearance in a variant of "The Great Dark" suggests that he thought of this later narrative as another draft of the earlier one. He wrote twenty-five manuscript pages concerning The Mad Passenger but later cut them out of the story at the point here indicated.

It was a roomy and comfortable cabin, and had a good lamp in it, also a locker and a swinging table. He locked the door and we sat down. He began to speak again—still in a guarded voice, a precaution not needed, now, and so I judged that it was habit or nature that made him do this.

"These new people have got a name for me which you may not have heard; they call me the Mad Passenger. I do not mind this insult, I give you my word. It is a secret bitterness to me, true, but as it hasn't its source in malice, but only in ignorance it is of course not blameworthy. O dear, think of the irony of it—they call me mad—*they!* Do you know what these people are doing? They've got a chart of *Dreamland,* and they are navigating this ship by it!"

I tried to look incredulous. He laid his hand on my arm and said with great earnestness—

"You don't believe me. It was not to be expected that you would. But I have said only the truth. I have seen the chart myself; and I have peeped in through the chart-room window when no one was near, and seen them working over it and trying to compass-out a course over it. It is perfectly true. Along at first, any one could go and look; but not now. They don't allow any but themselves to enter that place; and they've curtained the window. You see now, don't you, why they flew out so at the purser and the girl?"

"Well—er—"

"Dear me, it's an amazing thing, when you come to think of it. It's a chart of one particular part of Dreamland—Jupiter. No, not Jupiter—Saturn. No, I'm wrong again. I can't call the name to mind, now, but I know many of the details, land and sea; in fact am tolerably familar with them, for I have often been there in dreams, with the Superintendent. It may be that you have been there, too, and will remember whether it is a planet or a fixed star, if I mention a detail or two. On the chart are countries called England, America, and so on, and an ocean called Atlantic. Come—does it suggest anything? Can you help?"

It troubled me. It was a confusing situation. I said—

"Yes, I have been there. It is called the World, and—"

"That's it, that's it! It had slipped my memory for the moment—"

"But dear sir, are you *sure* it is a part of Dreamland?"

He looked frightened; and edged away from me a little, and sat apparently dazed and ill at ease. I didn't know anything to say, so there was an uncomfortable silence. Presently he said, haltingly and timidly—

"You—you won't be offended—but—but are you mad, too? They all are."

I said to myself, "It is of no use to struggle. Something has happened to me, I don't know what. It seems manifest, from all sorts of evidences, that I have been under a delusion since I don't know when. Years, no doubt. I think I have lived in dreams so long that now that I have at last got back among realities I have lost the sense of them and *they* seem dreams, too." I wished I knew of some good way to get back this man's confidence; no doubt he could wake up my dead memory for me and bring to life in it things of interest to me and thus save me from surprising Alice with my ignorances at every turn. Presently I ventured this—

"No, I am not mad, but a thing has happened to me which is nearly as serious. I can trust you, I think, and I will. Will you let me tell you something in strict confidence—something which I have confessed to no one, not even my wife?"

It pleased him to the marrow—I could see it.

"It is good of you to show me this distinction; but you have always been good to me, these twenty-two years—I say it gratefully. Whatever the secret is, I promise to keep it faithfully."

"I believe you will. It is this. I have lost my memory."

"Lost—your—memory?"

"Lost it wholly."

"Why—it is terrible. Was it from the fall?"

"Fall? Have I had a fall?"

"Yes. Ten or eleven days ago."

"I remember nothing of it."

"Yes, you slipped and fell on the deck,—there was a heavy sea at the time. I was with you. I helped you up, and you laughed and

said you were not hurt but your clothes were wet and you would go
and change them. I haven't seen you since to speak with you till to-
day; but George always said you were well, when I inquired, but
chose to keep to your quarters most of the time."

"It must have been the fall. I remember everything that has
happened today, but not a single previous experience of my whole
life."

"Dear me, it is a fearful thing, an amazing thing."

"And a misery beyond imagination. My wife knows that something has happened to me, but she does not suspect the serious
extent of it. Of course I wouldn't have her know, for anything.
She terrifies me by reminding me of things which I ought to be
familiar with, then I have to scramble out of the scrape the best I
can; and of course I do it awkwardly. But I am safe now. When I
want to get over one of those obstacles I shall come to you. You will
post me?"

"Gladly. Nothing has happened to you in twenty-two years that
I am not acquainted with. We shall have no trouble."

"This makes me easy. You will tell me my history. It ought to
interest me, for every detail of it will be new. And you must tell me
about yourself, too. She spoke of you to-day, and I supposed I was
hearing of you for the first time."

"*Isn't* it astonishing!"

We had a long talk together and he told me a great deal of my
history, and I found it curious and entertaining; and he told me a
great deal about Alice, whom he had known ever since she was
three years old. He posted me in the details of the devouring of
Captain Hall's boy by the spider-squid, and in other matters which
I needed to know in order not to be embarrassed when trading
reminiscences with my family and the servants.

We became comrades, and I came to like him better and better
every day. I spent an hour or two in his cabin daily, and he an hour
or so in my quarters. Alice had always liked him very well; and now
he was become very near to her, for outside of our family he was
the only relic left of her former life and its lost and lamented
comradeships. He had a name of a jaw-breaking sort, but no one

called him by it in these recent days; even the family and our servants had dropped it for the one used by the rest of the ship. This was "M.P.," (mad passenger.) It was simple and easy. He was sane, I thought, but as long as the ship thought differently, the title was well enough, and did no harm.

After a couple of weeks I noticed that when I wanted him and couldn't find him in his cabin there was no occasion to go groping everywhere—he was pretty sure to be in one certain place. On the forecastle—sitting on the mizzen-hatch. Sitting there and peering wistfully out ahead through the gloom, and looking melancholy. At last, one day in his cabin I asked him why he did that. A pathetic expression came into his face, and he muttered an ejaculation or two in his own strange language, then said in English—

"I am looking for my country."

"Your country?"

"I have done it every day for twenty-two years. It is long to wait, long to wait!"

The poor devil. It was sort of heart-breaking to hear him.

"What country is it? Where is it?"

He told me the tough name of it—it was an Empire of some sort —then added—

"It isn't anywhere in particular—it floats."

"Floats?—isn't fixed, isn't anchored?"

He smiled, and said—

"Why should it be? It isn't Dreamland. Of course it floats."

"Tell me about it. It must be dreadful there. In the eternal night."

"No, it isn't. It is a fair land, and beautiful. And it is not night there, but eternal day—a mellow rich light, and enchanting; for it circles forever and ever around outside the Great White Glare, and just the right distance away from it—like the other wandering Empires. Tradition says one vaguely glimpses one or another of them now and then at intervals of a century or two.

"It is curious. What keeps your Empire just the right distance away?"

"Attraction and repulsion. But for the attraction it would drift into the darkness; but for the repulsion it would drift into the Glare —and then!"

"I wish I could see that country. Do you expect to see it again?"

A passion of longing lighted his face for a moment, then faded out and he said despondently—

"No, it is too good to hope for. At first I hoped—all the first years. But that is all gone by, now—oh, yes, that is all over, years and years ago; I watch for it now from old habit, not from hope." He was silent awhile, then sighed and added, "But it is better so, perhaps. My girl-wife has broken her heart with waiting, no doubt; my little child is a woman, now—she would not remember me. She was half as old as your little Bessie—yes, and like her a little, and had the same cunning ways; and sometimes there flashes into Bessie's face an expression when we are playing together that is exact! When I see that, I have to put the child down and go away; I cannot endure the joy of it—and the pain. But let us talk of other things. Say something—anything! Ask me a question."

"I will. Of course I have forgotten about your coming aboard the ship; how did it happen?"

"Curse that day—forever! I had a great yacht, and I used to take my family and friends with me and make cruises out into the cold weather and the darkness; and once we walked the deck a good while laughing and chatting; then a storm began to brew and the snow to fly, and they all went below to arrange for some games and prepare something hot and wait a quarter of an hour for me. We were shortening sail, and I wanted to superintend a little. I was standing astern, backed up against the taffrail and staring up toward the flapping kites—which I could not see for the gloom— when your ship's invisible bowsprit swept past me, and the dragging bight of the main-brace caught me around the body and carried me off my feet. I seized it and saved myself; the bowsprit dipped me into the sea, but when it rose again I was astride it, and my yacht had vanished in the blackness and the storm."

"You never saw it again?"

"No, never. And now I was among strangers; we did not know each other's language, of course, and I could not explain how I got there; but they were friendly to me and hospitable. They taught me the language; they taught me how to divide time, and measure it off into seconds, minutes, hours, days, weeks, months, years, and a hundred other strange and interesting things; and so, as I was always something of a scholar, these twenty-two years have not been dull and stupid to me. But I would they could have had less of heart-break in them!"

It was a pathetic history, and I was touched by it. I was moved to try to say some hopeful things to the poor exile, but he courteously put all that aside, and said he found it wholesomest to keep the subject out of his mind when he had the opportunity to do it—and that was only when he had a chance to talk. Talk could deal with other matters, and was a good medicine. So then we drifted into a discussion of language, its curiosities and peculiarities, and it presently came out that in his tongue there were no exact equivalents for our words *modesty, immodesty, decency, indecency, right, wrong, sin.* He said that in most details the civilization of his country was the counterpart of that which prevailed among the highest civilizations of dreamlands like the World, and that a citizen of that unreal planet would be quite at home in his Empire, and would find it quite up to date in matters of art, erudition, invention, architecture, etc.

That seemed strange, but he said there was properly nothing strange about it, since dreamlands were nothing but imitations of real countries created out of the dreamer's own imagination and experience, with some help, perhaps, from the Superintendent of Dreams. At least that was his belief, he said, and he thought it reasonable and plausible. He had noticed that in Jupiter, Uranus, and in fact in all other dream-countries he found things about as they were at home, and apparently quite real and natural as long as the dream lasted. In the World, it was true, there were a few details that it had a monopoly of, but they were not important, and not pleasant.

"For instance?"

"Well, for instance they have what they term Religions; also curious systems of government, and an interesting but most odd code of morals. But don't you know about these things? Haven't you been there with the Superintendent? Come in!"

It was the children. They had come with Germania to be entertained.

M. P. was good at that. He told them a quaint and charming tale whose scene was laid in his lost country, then he and I had a game of romps with them. In the course of the romps Bessie hurt herself, and in her anger she tried to break things, and did break a glass. I said—

"Tut-tut, why did you do that, Bessie?—it's wrong."

"No-no, not wrong," said M. P.; "don't call it that."

"What then?"

"Inexpedient."

I remembered. It was the nearest that his native tongue could come to furnishing an equivalent for our word "wrong."

He petted Bessie into a good humor, then set the children to rummaging the drawers of his bureau and the compartments of his locker. In one of these latter they found a microscope. M. P. began to arrange it for an exhibition, and a curious feeling came over me. It seemed to me that I had seen the same thing done before; even that I had done it myself—in a dream. It was a strange sensation, and troubled me. Then M. P. put a drop of water on a glass slide, threw a circle of white light under it from the reflector, screwed the lens down tight against it, and soon the children were exclaiming over the hideous animals they saw darting about and fighting in the bit of moisture.

I dropped into a whirl of thinkings and dim and shadowy half-reminiscences, and wholly lost myself. After a while the children reached up and kissed me good-bye—I was hardly conscious of it—and then they went away with the nurse and with M. P., who said the sea was rising and he would help them home and then come back. I presently got up to stretch my legs, and noticed a portfolio lying in the open locker. Pictures, I judged, for M. P. was a good amateur artist—there were several small portraits and photographs of his wife and children pinned to the wall which were his own work, he had told me. I opened the portfolio and found a number of pictures; pictures of himself, his family, and many lady and gentleman friends: in some cases beautifully clothed, but in most cases naked!

I heard him coming. I put the book away, and prepared myself to look like a person who had not discovered a disgraceful secret and who was not shocked. I arranged a pleasant smile and—

(1898)

Which Was It?

Editor's Note: The last section of Mark Twain's lengthy but unfinished novel *Which Was It?* is here presented. The village aristocrat George Harrison, having robbed and then murdered while attempting to save a dwindling family estate, finds he is too cowardly to confess when his friend and benefactor Squire Fairfax is accused of the crime. Believing his actions have gone undetected, he maintains an anguished silence. Finally, when Harrison seems about to rationalize away his sense of guilt, the ex-slave Jasper comes to confront him and involve him in further degradations.

TROUBLES are only mental; it is the mind that manufactures them, and the mind can forget them, banish them, abolish them. Mine shall do it. Nothing is needed but resolution, firmness, determination. I will exert it. It is the only wisdom. I will put all these goblins, these unrealities behind me, I have been their slave long enough; if I have done wrong I have atoned for it, I have paid the cost and more, I have sweated blood, I have earned my freedom, I have earned peace and a redeemed and contented spirit, and why should I not have them? I will lift up my head, it is my right. I am honored and esteemed by all. Yes, by all. I can say it truly. There is not a person in the community who does not look up to me and—"

There was a knock on the front door. Harrison stepped to it and opened it, and found Jasper standing there in the humble attitude of his caste, with his ancient slouch hat in his hand.

"Kin I see you a minute, seh?" he asked.

Harrison said, with ruffled dignity—

"Where are your manners, you dog? Take yourself to the back door."

138

He closed the front one in Jasper's face and returned to his seat. Presently Jasper entered by the back one, without knocking, came forward, and began:

"I wanted to ast you, seh—"

"Take your hat off!"

"I begs yo' pahdon, seh—I fo'got, deed I did, seh, I's in sich trouble en so worried."

"Now then, go on. And cut it short. What is it you want? Wait —put that stick on the fire."

Jasper dropped his hat on the floor and obeyed. But the stick slipped from his hands, and scattered the coals in every direction. While he brushed them up George scolded his clumsiness and superintended his work, correcting, fussing, finding fault, and giving new orders before the mulatto could finish the old ones. At last there was an end, and George said—

"I think I never saw such an awkward brute."

Jasper explained.

"I ain't allays so, Marse Hahson, but I been laid up in de bed considable many days, en I's stiff en ain't got de full use er myseff."

"What laid you up?"

"De constable, he done it. He gimme thutty-nine."

"You needed it, I reckon. Step out back and fetch in an armful of wood, then tell me what your business is, here—and be quick about it, you hear? it's getting late."

This all seems harsh, coming from so kind-hearted a man as Harrison was, but it was merely custom, the habit of the time, in dealing with the colored man, and had less depth to it and feeling in it than a stranger to the country would have supposed. The whites imagined that the negroes did not mind it. They judged by the negro's outside, and forgot to inquire within. Jasper brought the wood and piled it, and Harrison said—

"You were out without a pass—was that it?"

"Yes, seh."

"How was that?"

"You know, seh, I's de Squiah's g'yardener, en so now dey ain't nobody to gimme a pass."

"Then you're here without one! Speak up—is that so?"

Jasper—humbly:

"Yes, seh. I ain't got no fren's, en—"

"I'll have you jailed to-morrow! Upon my word, the impudence of a free nigger beats anything that ever—look here, my man, what's your business here? Come, speak out—speak out."

Jasper dropped on his knees and put up his hands and began to plead.

"Oh, marse Hahson, if I can't git nobody to he'p me I doan' know what gwyneter become er me. Workin' in de greenhouse ain't gwynter save me if I ain't got no pass. Dey'll drive me outen de State, en if I's to try to stay dey'd take en sell me, en if I resis' dey'll lynch me, caze I ain't got no fren's en nobody to stan' by me. Won't *you*, marse Hahson?—won't you stan' by me?"

"What!"

"You's de mos' pow'ful genlman in de whole deestrick, now; you's de only one dey dasn't stan' out agin, de only one dat kin say 'You keep yo' han's off'n him' and dey dasn't say a word. Don't you reckon, seh—"

"No—I don't. I don't like the law that sells and banishes free niggers, but if the people wish to enforce it it is their right, and as a Christian citizen it is my duty to bow to their will and not obstruct the law in its course."

Jasper rose slowly up, and stood on his feet. Harrison turned his eyes away, and stroked his jaw nervously and uncomfortably with his hand; he was not proud of himself. There was a pause, then the negro said—

"Ain't dey noth'n better'n bein' a Christian, seh?"

"You blasphemous scoundrel! You—"

"I means, *dat* kind of a Christian, seh."

Harrison turned an outraged eye upon him and motioned toward the door with his hand, saying sharply—

"I've had enough of this—quite enough; I don't like your tone; there's the door; move along!"

Jasper picked up his hat and stood fumbling it, with his head bowed, Harrison watching him with rising choler. After a moment or two the drooping head came up—and the hat was on it! Harrison could not speak. He could only stare, and wonder if this miracle of insolence was real, or only a fantastic delusion. Jasper turned slowly away, saying, absently—

"Po' Jake Bleeker. If de law would let a nigger testify in a cote—"

Any reference to the tragedy which had wrecked Harrison's life was enough—it took the man all out of him, it filled his imagination with formless shapes and ghastly terrors. He rose up sick and trembling, steadying himself with his hand on his chair-back, and said, with a weak counterfeit of mere curiosity—

"Wait a moment. What's that?"

Jasper moved a step, saying—

" 'Tain't no matter, seh." Still moving: " 'Course de law—"

"Wait, I tell you," said Harrison. "This is a matter of interest to every public-spirited citizen; nothing concerning it—however seemingly trivial it may seem—is unimportant. What are you hinting at? Suppose niggers could testify—what then?"

Jasper's hat was still on. Harrison ignored it. Jasper turned toward him, and said—

"Marse Hahson, you reckon dey's any doubt dat de Squiah done it?"

Harrison answered with as easy a confidence as he was able to assume—

"Oh, no, there seems to be none. No, none at all, I am afraid."

He wished the mulatto would not keep his eyes bent on him so steadily; the effect was uncomfortable.

"Dey say de Squiah tole Miss Helen he never done it; dey say he tole her dat de man 'at done it was a stranger in de place. Does you reckon dat could happen, seh?"

"Why, yes. Why, certainly, it *could* happen."

Jasper was silent a moment, then he said—

"I hearn a man say he reckon it could a been a stranger, en said he b'lieve it *was*, en said he wisht he could find dat man."

Harrison could not say anything; the remark made him shiver. The silence that followed oppressed him; it seemed to bear down on him like a weight. Presently Jasper said, in an indifferent tone—

"I reckon marse Tom would, too, becaze he's gwyne to marry in de fambly."

Harrison—relieved:

"Ah, yes, yes, indeed he would!"

" 'Course—hit stan' to reason. En you'd like to find de man, too."

"Ye-s."

In an instant Jasper snatched him by the shoulders and whirled him in front of the mirror.

"Dah he is!"

Harrison's terror paralysed his voice for a moment, then it freed itself in a passion of fright and indignation mixed, and he broke away, panting, and stood at bay and began to pour out a torrent of threats and curses and insults upon the mulatto, who listened with the look of one who is hearing pleasant music; listened intently, tranquilly, contentedly: then, in the midst of it all, he fished around in his coat pocket in a leisurely way and got out a white handkerchief with two holes in it and blood stains upon it, and shook it out and held it up by two corners!

The tornado stopped, and Harrison sank into a chair, white and breathless, and dumbly staring. Jasper folded the handkerchief carefully, slowly, elaborately, and returned it to his pocket. Then he nodded toward Harrison and said—

"You is my meat."

Harrison moaned in his misery, but no words came. He realized that a formidable disaster had befallen him. How formidable it might be he could not estimate, it was but matter for guesswork as yet, and his brain was too much stunned to work capably, now, upon the materials at hand. It tried to guess, of course, but its efforts were so dominated by fright that they were the opposite of tranquilizing. Presently these thought-processes suffered an interruption which changed their drift and raised the temperature of Harrison's blood by several degrees: the negro coolly sat down in his presence! This was too much. For a moment Harrison forgot all other things in the indignation bred in him by this monstrous insult, and he straightened up and said—

"How dare you? Get up!"

For all reply the negro got out the red-stained mask again, and spread it upon his knees. In an instant Harrison had snatched it and sprung toward the fire with it; but in the next moment his wrists were prisoners in the vise-like grip of the yellow athlete's brawny hands. He struggled, and raged, and wept—a vain waste of wind and strength, it was but a case of rabbit and wolf; Jasper held him, waited, and said nothing. When he saw that his prey was exhausted, he crushed him into his chair, freed him, and said, picking up the fallen mask and pocketing it—

"Set dah en pant whilst I talks to you, Hahson."

Harrison allowed this fresh affront to pass; there could be no profit in discussing it, in the circumstances.

"Now den, in de fust place, some niggers is fools. De mos' of 'em is. Well, I ain' no fool. You gwyneter fine it out 'fo' I's done wid you. I's gwyneter ast you some questions. Answer 'em right out squah en plain—I ain' gwyneter 'low no foolin'. You knowed de hankcher was missin'?"

"Yes."

"Didn't you reckon it was cur'us it didn't turn up at de inques'?"

"Yes."

" 'Course! What did you reckon was de reason?"

"Thought an enemy had it."

"*White* enemy?"

"Yes."

The negro chuckled.

"You ain' *got* none! Hain't it so?"

"Well—yes. I believe it is."

"Den it was a dam fool reason. He'd a brung it to de inques', so's he kin git revenge. But *I* never brung it to de inques'. Does you know de reason?"

"No."

"Becaze I warn't ready. Does you know why I brung it now?"

"No."

"Becaze I *is* ready."

"I don't know how you are more ready now than you were on the fourth of November. I don't see any reason for it."

"Den I's gwyneter tell you. Nigger evidence ain't no good in cote?"

"N-no." Harrison felt a sinking sensation at the pit of his stomach.

"I had to rummage out de *white* witness, en I done it!"

Harrison sank back with a gasp, and a half-smothered "Ah, my God!" He looked so ghastly that Jasper jumped for water and sprinkled some in his face, thinking he would die if help was not promptly afforded. He watched his patient with absorbing interest and solicitude until he saw him revive, then he resumed his talk and his tortures.

"Does you know, Hahson, if I couldn't *make* dat white man tell what he seen en what he hearn dat night, he wouldn't go a step to de cote? Becaze—well, *I* knows why. You's pow'ful strong en 'spectable en looked up to, Hahson, you's got a mighty good name in dis town."

The persecutor chuckled again.

"But *he* knows I kin fetch de white folks dat'll jail him down dah in de Souf any time I says de word, en so if I tell him to go to de cote en swah agin you, he *got* to."

Harrison was about to pluck up a little imitation spirit and cast contempt upon this possibly imaginary witness, when Jasper added, in an indifferent tone—

"But I ain' gwyneter sen' him to no cote."

Joyful words! So joyful that Harrison was half afraid, for a moment, that he had mis-heard. But before he could reassure himself and utter his gratification, Jasper was speaking again. What he said dismissed the fickle sunshine and brought the clouds once more.

"Dat man ain' gwyne to no cote, Hahson—not if I knows it. You b'longs to me, now. You's my proppity, same as a nigger, en I ain' gwyneter was'e you. By God, I kin hang you any minute I wanter! Git up en fetch yo' marster a dram!"

Through Harrison's half-paralysed brain flitted the shameful reflection, "Slave of an ex-slave! it is the final degradation; there is nothing below this." It is win or lose, now—this moment will never come again; he must act a man's part, now—resist, free himself, risk his life on it, or remain a slave! He said in his heart he *would*, and bravely raised his eyes; they met the stern gaze of the master, wavered there a moment, then fell. He was conquered, and knew it. He rose, and passed unsteadily by his tamer, and at the other end of the room began his menial labors.

"Make it strong—you heah? En put sugar in it."

Harrison's eye fell upon the gun—double-barrelled—loaded for robbers. He glanced cautiously around, hopeful, excited, trembling from his hair to his heels: Jasper's back was to him! stirring the toddy noisily with one hand, he reached for the gun with the other, got it and faced about, cocking it. Jasper heard the clicks, turned, and looked down the barrels. Harrison pulled the triggers. Jasper burst into an unfeeling laugh.

"I never see sich a fool," he said; "didn't you reckon I knowed de gun was dah—right whah anybody kin see it? I done fix' dat gun befo' de constable laid me up. Been yo' ole father, *he'd* a foun' it out, but I could 'pen' 'pon you, *you* doan' take notice er noth'n. I drove pins in de nipples en filed 'em down. Stan' her up in de cornder. When I's done wid you you kin have some mo' guns if you want 'em—dey ain't gwyne to worry *me* none. *You's* gwyne to p'oteck me, yo' own seff—you'll see; yes, en you's gwyneter be mighty k'yerful uv me, too, *dat* you is. Fetch de dram!"

He tasted it. "Put in some mo' sugar." He tasted again. "Put in mo'—dah, dat's enough." He had his feet in Harrison's chair. "Whah is yo' paper en pen? Git 'em. Git a cheer. Now, den, you write what I tells you. En don't you try to come no games, er I'll make you sorry."

George wrote from Jasper's dictation, doctoring the English as he went along:

"This is my body-servant, Jasper. Let him pass at all hours of the day and night. I make myself responsible for his behavior.
George L. P. Harrison."

Jasper folded the pass and put it in his pocket.

"Now den," he said, "write agin." He furnished the words. The pen dropped from Harrison's paralysed fingers.

"Write *that?* Oh, my God," he cried, "I can't—I can't!"

"You can't?" said Jasper, dispassionately.

"How *can* I? Have some mercy! What are you going to do with it?"

"Gwyne to make you *safe*—dat's de idear. Hit'll go to dat witness —alonger dish-yer hankcher dat I's got. If anything happen' to me, *he'll* know what to do wid it. If noth'n don't happen to me, he on'y jist hide it en wait, en keep mum. Well, dey ain't noth'n gwyne to happen to me. You's gwyneter take pow'ful good k'yer o' dat, *I* bet you!"

"Yes, I will, with my hand on my heart I promise I will and—"

"*I* doan' want none o' yo' promises," said Jasper, scornfully, "I wouldn't give a dern for 'em."

"I'll do anything you say—anything, *everything* you tell me to—"

"Mp! Dey ain't no 'casion for you to tell me dat, I 'low to *make* you."

"—but spare me this—I can't, oh, I *can't* write it!"

Jasper got up and moved lazily away, remarking in a careless tone—

"Dat's all right—dat's all right."

"Wait!" cried Harrison in a panic; "oh, don't go! Where are you going?"

"Whah is I gwyne? You knows mighty well whah I's a gwyne, Jawge Hahson."

"Stop, for God's sake, don't go! I'll write it—I will, I will!"

"Well, den, *do* it. En I can tell you dis: if I starts *agin*—"

"There it is! it's written. Now be kind, be merciful; I've signed away my life, my good name, my liberty, all my spiritual riches—"

"En you's a slave!—dat's what you is; en I lay I'll learn you de paces! I been one, en I *know* 'em; slave to de meanest white man dat ever walked—en he 'uz *my father*; en I bought my freedom fum him en paid him for it, en he took 'vantage of me en stole it back; en he sold my mother down de river, po' young thing, en she a cryin' en a beggin' him to let her hug me jist once mo', en he wouldn't; en she say 'cruel, cruel,' en he hit her on de mouf, God damn his soul!—but it's my turn, now; dey's a long bill agin de low-down ornery white race, en you's a-gwyneter *settle* it."

He held up the fateful paper and contemplated it a long minute, his nostrils faintly dilating; and when at last he ceased from this contemplation he was visibly a changed man. The meek slouch of the slave was gone from him, and he stood straight, the exultation of victory burning in his eyes; and not even his rags and tatters could rob his great figure of a certain state and dignity born in this moment to it of the pride of mastership and command that was rising in his heart. He *looked* the master; but that which had gone from him was not lost, for his discarded droop and humble mien had passed to his white serf, and already they seemed not out of place there, but fit, and congruous, and pathetically proper and at home.

He resumed his chair and sat dreaming, musing, and unconsciously fondling and caressing the puissant bit of paper that had lifted him so high and brought that other man so low. Harrison was submerged in thinkings, too. Presently he stirred, and something like a moan escaped him. It roused Jasper, who said—

"Hahson?"

Harrison—wearily, sadly:

"Yes?"

"Yes?" (mimicking him). "Is dat yo' manners?"

Harrison looked up, inquiringly.

"I—I don't understand."

"You don't? Well, den, I'll learn you. Does servants say Yes, to dey marster, and stop dah?"

The word stuck in Harrison's throat; it refused to come.

"Hahson!"

By this help he got it out:

"Yes . . . sir?"

"Now den, don't you fo'git again. I lay if you do I'll make you sorry. You's a servant—you unnerstan'?—en I's gwyneter make you know yo' place en *keep* it. Say it agin!"

"Yes, sir."

"Dat's all right. Practice! You heah?"

"Yes, sir."

The mulatto's eyes spat fire for a while, filling Harrison's soul with nameless fears and discomforts, and he wished he could forecast this exacting master's requirements and save himself sorrow by meeting them before the orders came. He was alert, now, and pitifully anxious to do almost anything that could protect him from the pain and shame of uttered insults.

"Hahson?"

Harrison—with a timorous eagerness:

"Yes, sir?"

"Hain't I a talkin' to you?"

"Yes, sir."

A pause—with a penetrating look of inquiry and disapproval. Then—

"Well den!"

"I—I'm afraid I don't understand, sir. I—"

"Does servants *set down* when dey marsters is talkin' to 'em?"

Harrison rose and stood, with the red sign of humiliation stealing into his gray and tired face. Jasper contemplated his serf's misery with deep and healing satisfaction: studying it, weighing it, measuring it, so to speak, his mind traveling back over bitter years and comparing it with the thousand instances wherein he himself had been the unoffending victim and had looked like that, suffered like that. Then he began to speak.

"Hahson, hit do me good to look at you like dat. My father serve' me so, many's de time, en I not doin' any harm, no mo' dan what you is. En him a white man, en treat my po' little mother so, en rob' me like a thief—I hope he's a-roastin' in hell! Hahson?"

"Yes, sir."

"You's white, en I's gwyneter take it outer *you.* You en de res'. Ev'ry time I gits a chance. Now den, I done made my plans, en I's gwyneter tell you. I been run outer two States, or dey'd a sold me to de nigger-traders or lynch' me. Some folks hint aroun' dey gwyneter drive me outer *dis* one. Lemme see 'em try it!—it'll cost *you* heavy. Dey hints if I don't go, dey gwyneter put me on de block en sell me. Lemme see 'em try it!—it'll cost *you* heavy. Dey hints if I resis' dey gwyneter lynch me. Lemme see 'em try it! Let 'em try jist *one* un um—en straight off dish-yer paper goes to Miss Helen!"

"Oh, for God's sake! Oh—"

"Shet up! Git up off'n de flo'!—a-clawin' en a-wallerin' aroun' like a cat in a fit; you oughter be 'shame' er yoself, en you a grown pusson. Dah, now, set on de flo' if you can't stan' up—dad burn you, you ain' got no mo' grit 'n a rabbit. I reckon you's a right down coward, Hahson. Fac' I knows you is; for *I* knows you—knows you by de back, same as de gamblers knows de k'yards. Stop dat whinin' en blubberin', Hahson; stop it! you *heah* me?"

Jasper sat looking down at him in measureless contempt. Presently he took up his discourse again.

"Hahson, made de way you is, *you* ain't in no danger—not de least."

"Oh, I am so thankful for—"

"Thank yo'seff! Dat's whah it b'longs. *You* ain't gwyneter git yo'seff in no danger—lawd, I knows *you*. Becaze you knows better'n to let anybody do *me* any harm, bless yo' soul you does! Now, den, you listen. Hahson, I can't stay wid you to-night, caze I got to go en give de white witness de hankcher en de paper en 'splain to him what to do case any harm come to me whilst I's in dis deestrick; but I's a-comin' back in de mawnin', en den I's gwyneter stay wid you all yo' life. When dey's anybody aroun', I's yo' servant, en pow'ful polite, en waits on you, en waits on de table, en wah's good clo'es, en runs arrants, en sleeps over yo' stable, en gits ten dollars a week; en when dey ain't nobody aroun' but me en you, you's *my* servant, en if I don't sweat you!—well, nemmine 'bout dat, *I'll* show you! Hahson?"

"Yes, sir."

"You ain' got no manners."

"I know, but I can soon—"

"Learn? You better bet you kin—if you knows what's good for you. Hahson?"

"Yes, sir."

"When I's a waitin' on de quality, you keep yo' eye on me, en notice de way I does, en de way I 'spress myseff, en de way I bows, en all dat; den you study it by yo'seff, en practice. You ain't fitten for shucks de way you is, becase you ain't had no breedin', but I's gwyneter make you wuth two dollars a week befo' I's done wid you. Does you unnerstan' de whole plan, now?"

"Yes, sir."

"Gimme de fust week. Ten dollars. Don't you fo'git 'bout de clo'es, ner 'bout de stable—you heah? Git up en open de do' for me."

When he was gone Harrison put his face in his hands and sobbed, moaning and muttering, and saying, "Oh, my God, I cannot bear it, the burden is too heavy; *why* was I born with a man's form and a rabbit's heart? why haven't I the courage to kill myself? who but I would keep a life that is become an agony?"

AT DAWN in the morning Jasper arrived at Harrison's kitchen with a banjo, a jewsharp, a mouth-harp, and not much other baggage. He uncovered the fire, built it up, brought in a load of wood, fetched a bucket of water from the well, filled the kettle, hung it on the hook, found the breakfast coffee in the mill, and was beginning to grind it when old Martha entered from her room to see who was making the noise. She threw up her hands in astonishment, and said—

"Well, fo' de lan' sake if it ain't you! What brung *you* heah, Jasper?"

"What brung me? Bless yo' soul, honey, I's de new servant."

"No!—you don't say!"

"True for a fac', my darlin'. Marse Hahson done hire me las' night."

"Well—well—well—*is* dat so? Now ain't you in luck, sho' nuff?"

"Deed I is, en so is you. Caze you ain' got no sweetheart, en I's gwyneter cote you—dat I is, honey. You's de gal for me!"

"Shet up yo' impudence, er I'll take en bat you over de head, you long-laigged yaller-jacket! I's ole enough to be yo' mother."

Then they broke out and laughed a rollicking laugh in cordial admiration of their powers of repartee, and Jasper plunged at Martha saying he was just "honing" for a kiss, and a three-minute struggling and scuffling and laughing followed, which ended in Jasper's getting the kiss and a sounding cuff; then Martha wiped her eyes on her apron and said—

"*Allays* a humbuggin' en a carryin' on, I never see sich a nigger; hain't you ever serious *no* time?"

"What I gwyneter be serious 'bout? I ain't only thutty-five; what *I* got to be serious 'bout?"

"Nemmine, nemmine, Jasper, you wait ontel you's fifty, de way I is—"

"Den I'll be serious de way *you* is, you ole cat!"

"Jasper, what you needs is some trouble; I lay dat'll take de friskies outen you when it come—you'll see."

"G'long wid you! Trouble! didn't dat constable take de hide off'n me?"

Martha set her hands on her hips and gave him a look that was full of pity of his ignorance.

"Took de hide off'n you! What's dat! 'Tain't nothin'. Who gwyneter mind a little thing like dat? You doan' know nothin' 'bout real trouble; you wait ontel you has some *real* trouble, den you'll know!"

"Well, den, what you *call* real trouble?"

"A heart dat's broke! dat's what's real trouble. If you'd a had a father to lose, er a mother to lose. . . . Look at marse George. *Dah's* trouble! Jasper, mo'n half de time he jist can't res', on accounts er ole marster a-dyin'."

It seemed to impress Jasper, and he said—

"Well, I reckon it is turrible hard. But Martha, he was sich a ole man. I's pow'ful sorry for marse Hahson, but if he ain't got no troubles but dat—"

"Can't you see, yo'seff, dat it's enough? He couldn't stan' no mo' if he *had* 'em, you yaller fool!"

"Well, *I* ain't sayin' he could, I 'uz on'y jist sayin' he—"

"Shet up, you doan' know nothin' what you talkin' 'bout. You wait tell you's had trouble; up to den you can't talk nothin' 'bout it but foolishness."

"Martha, how kin you say dat? Hain't I *seen* people dat's had it? Look at Bridget; look at de Squiah—my, dat's trouble, sho-nuff trouble. You see, if marse Hahson had troubles like *dem*—"

It went to Martha's compassionate old heart, and she said—

"Oh, yes, Gawd knows he ain't had no troubles like *dem* po'

creturs has. 'Twould kill marse George, he got sich a good heart en
so sof'. Why Jasper, jist *hearin'* 'bout what de Squiah done 'most
killed him. Laws, it make me feel turrible down, talkin' like dis.
Wake up de banjo."

"Camptown Races?"

"Dat's it. Go it!"

Pul-lunky plunk-plunk plunk-plunk. Jasper poured out the gay
song in great style, and when the chorus came round, Martha, all
enthusiasm, added the rich voice that is the birthright of her
race.

> "I's boun' to run all night,
>   I's boun' to run all day,
> I bet my money on de bobtail nag,
>   If somebody bet on de bay."

Other songs followed, and rattling dance-tunes, and light-
hearted laughter; and Harrison recognized the voices, and one of
them carried dread and misery to his heart. An hour passed, and
Martha said she must carry up the shaving-water now, and set the
table; but Jasper said—

"What you talkin' 'bout? What is I for?"

"Why, bless you, Jasper, I clean fo'got you's hired. Ain't dat
good! 'Tain't gwyneter be lonesome en mo'nful in dis kitchen no
mo', now. I's pow'ful glad, Jasper. Heah—take de hot water. You
got a good marster, now—jist as kind. He'll cuff you roun' a little
when he's cross, but don't you mind, 'tain't much, en he don't mean
nothin' by it."

Jasper answered bravely—

"I doan' k'yer noth'n for cuffin', I kin stan' all he'll gimme."

He departed with the water. Martha liked that reply of his; it
showed the right spirit, the spirit of a slave, and made her doubt if
free niggers were quite as black as they had been commonly
painted—for certainly here was one that was rational, and worthily
constructed. She felt sure that Jasper's sunny spirit would have a
good influence upon the master, and that the importing it into the
shadowed homestead would turn out to have been a fortunate idea
on the master's part. She recognized, too, that there was profit for

herself in the arrangement—her labor-burdens eased, and lively company at hand in place of loneliness. Jasper was gone ten minutes.

"What kep' you so long?" she asked, when he returned.

Jasper's white teeth radiated a gleaming smile, and he answered—

"Well, he's feelin' prime, smawnin', en hatter jist let go en talk, he couldn't he'p it, he feelin' so gay."

"Dah, now!" exclaimed Martha, "hit's jist as I's a-sayin' no longer ago 'n dis minute. Las' night he was a feelin' jesso, en I turn' in en cher'd him up good, en I says to myseff, hit ain't takin' all *dis* time to tote up dat shavin' water, I lay Jasper's a cherin' him up some mo'—warn't I right, hey, warn't I?"

"Dat you wuz, sho's you bawn; he's jist gay, now, I tell you!"

This was not true. However, Martha, innocently taking it at par, laughed out her happy thankfulness over it, and said—

"I jist know'd how 'twould be. Jasper, I do b'lieve befo' you's done wid marse George he's gwyneter be a diff'nt man to what he was."

He responded, with modest confidence—

"*I* bet you!"

She rewarded him with a buttered biscuit hot from the reflector. His eye chanced to fall upon the breakfast dishes, and he felt a sense of disappointment. He said—

"Martha, is *dat* all?"

She chuckled, and answered—

"Bless yo' soul, honey, hit shows you doan' know what sorrer is. *He* doan' eat nothin'. My, if a body could *git* him to!"

Jasper—argumentatively, persuasively—and with a watering mouth:

"Martha, hit's diff'nt, smawnin', you know. He's a feelin' like a bird. Hain't dat gwyneter raise his appertite, don't you reckon?"

"Well, well, well, what *is* de matter of me! gracious I never thought. 'Course it will! Jasper, how much you reckon you kin 'suade him to eat?" and she began to load up her pans and ovens again, in great excitement and joy, Jasper helping, without invitation.

"Pile 'em in, pile 'em in," he said, with fervor, "doan' you 'feered, Martha, you ain' gwyneter see 'em no mo'."

"We-ll, if dat ain't de bes' news I ever—Lan', Jasper, why dis is enough for a hoss!"

"His very words! Martha, he *said* he could eat a hoss!"

"Dem's blessed words, Jasper, jist blessed—I doan' wanter heah no mo' blesseder ones. Laws, if he kin on'y git away wid dis stack it'll be de makin' of him."

Jasper—with placid conviction:

"Look yo' las' on it, honey—look yo' las'."

Some little time afterward Jasper was sitting solitary in the dining room—at the head of Harrison's table. The snowy table-cloth was almost hidden under its prodigal freightage of hot and appetising good things; the coffee pot was steaming, and a generous hickory fire was sending a sheet of flame up the chimney. Jasper was listening—listening with evil satisfaction to a descending step on the stair, a slow and lifeless step, a weary and halting step. And now Harrison appeared. Wan, old, gaunt, broken, humble—he seemed rather a spectre than a man. Jasper's mind slipped back over long years, and he saw the duplicate of this apparition: himself. It was when he went to his father to ask for a new bill of sale in place of the one which had burned up with his cabin, and his father mocked him, laughed in his face and said, "Out of my presence, you bastard, and keep mum, or I'll sell you South, as I did your sniveling mother!"

The mulatto sat studying the meek apparition, and musing, with a hardening heart. This was a Harrison, *that* was a Harrison—the hated blood was in his own veins! The thought stung him, galled him. He spoke up sharply—

"Hahson!"

Harrison—timidly:

"Yes, sir."

"You's makin' a po' start. You's kep' me a waitin'. I ain' gwyneter have it!"

"I—"

"Shet up, when I's a talkin'. Got no mo' manners 'n a animal. You wait till somebody asts you to mix in." He paused, to see if

Harrison's judgment would fail him again, but it didn't. "Now den, git to work. En doan' you wait for me to give you de orders; you watch en 'scover what I wants befo' I tells you."

Harrison poured the coffee, then furnished beefsteak, spare-ribs, home-made sausages, corn-pone, biscuits, winter-stored vegetables —one after the other, with encores, and in generous quantity—and kept a sharp lookout, as commanded, saying nothing, and moving constantly and with his best briskness, for this devourer was more than a mere man, he was a mill. When about half of the food had been devoured there was a light knock on the door, and by force of habit Harrison called out before he had had time to think—

"Come in!"

Jasper scowled darkly upon him and said—

"Has anybody ast you to make yo'seff so dam brash?"

"Oh, I beg pardon, sir."

"De do's bolted. I done it." He got up with deliberation and said, "Hit's Martha. She's comin' in wid de batter-cakes." He had risen from his chair. He pointed to it, and added: "Set down here. I's servant, now—you is marster; you *un'stan'?* Doan' you fo'git yo'seff, less'n you wanter be sorry. Look cherful! you heah?"

Harrison took the seat, and Jasper went to the door. Martha, entering, said, reprovingly—

"What you fasten de do' for?"

Jasper chuckled, in what seemed to be a sort of embarrassed but pleasant confusion, and explained.

"Nev' you mine 'bout de do', honey: marse Hahson feelin' prime, smawnin', en tellin' 'bout de times when he's young; en he say shet de do', 'tain't suitable for ladies to heah. Bless you, he's feelin' dat gay—look at him laugh!"

Harrison, obeying a threatening side look, delivered himself of a ghastly travesty of a laugh which sent a shudder through Martha, and would have made her drop her platter of cakes but that it was already reaching the refuge of Jasper's hands. Martha soliloquised audibly, and unconsciously—

"De Lawd God!" and stood staring, rather vacantly yet admiringly, while Jasper, all smiling servility, most politely helped the master to one cake and purposely dropped another in his lap, at the same time whispering, "Raise hell 'bout it! you *heah?*"

"Curse your lumbering awkwardness, *now* look what you've done!" responded the obedient master.

Jasper mimicked the proper consternation while he nervously and clumsily repaired the mishap, meanwhile whispering " 'Buse me, 'buse me, Hahson—keep it up!" and Harrison, obeying, poured out severities the best he could, and trembled to his marrow in apprehension of what he might have to pay for them. Martha chimed in—

"Give it to him good, marse George, hit boun' to do you good, stirrin' yo'seff up like dat; tain't gwyneter do *him* no harm, en he 'zerve it, anyway."

Privately she was puzzled at Harrison's haggard appearance, and could not understand why he should look like that, now when he was so gay—so unnaturally gay that he was even obliged to break out in tales not proper for ladies to hear, to get relief, an extravagance of high spirits which he surely had never risen to before. She was minded to speak of this curious thing, and inquire if the gayety was solid and real; but she glanced at the table and held her peace. She remarked to herself:

"I reckon he's all right. He's et enough to bust a tavern."

She passed out, and master and servant changed places again.

"Pass 'em, pass 'em along!" cried Jasper, indicating the tower of hot batter-cakes, "en de m'lasses; I's pow'ful hongry, yit; I ain't had no sich breakfus' as dis sence de cows come home."

But there was a brisk stamping of feet at the front door, now, and Jasper jumped from his seat and thrust Harrison into it just in time. Dug Hapgood burst in with an eager shout—

"Say, George, there's a stranger at the tavern. Get it? *stranger,* I said. Been there a couple of days. How he managed it without me finding it out, blamed if *I* know." He was busy shedding his wraps, and quite unaware that Jasper was obsequiously receiving them and hanging them up. But he noticed the mulatto now, and shouted in great surprise, "Why, what in the nation are *you* doing here?" Jasper grinned in a flattered and thankful way and answered,

"Marse Hahson done hire me, Misto Dug."

"Well, by gracious if that ain't just like you, George Harrison! There ain't anybody too low down for you to come up to the rack and give him a lift when he's in trouble, even a free nigger! I just honor you, George Harrison, I do, that's the fact." He went forward blinking the sympathetic water out of his eyes, and wrung Harrison's hand cordially. "George derned if I don't think you are just a brevet angel, that's what *I* think—just a noble generous tadpole-angel, as you may say, and likely to sprout legs any time and feather-out and jine the choir. Shake again!" He turned to Jasper: "Looky here, yaller-belly, do you know you've had a mighty close shave? You bet you! Why, George, it was all put up yesterday to run him out of the State to-night—sho! what am I talkin' about; you found it out and that's why he's here. Now how in the nation *did* you, and you shut up in the house all the time?"

Jasper cut in, and saved Harrison the necessity of answering:

"I foun' it out myself, Misto Dug, en come en tole him, en he up 'n say 'You's my nigger, now—jist let 'em tetch you!' he says."

"Well, George, I'll say it again, you're the bravest devil that ever was, when you want to be. You're the only man in the whole deestrict that could a saved this cuss, and the only one that's good-hearted enough. Jasper!"

"Yes, seh."

"Are you grateful?"

" 'Deed I is, Misto Dug."

"All right, then; some niggers ain't." His eye fell on the table, and his mouth watered. "That looks good. Pity to let *that* go to waste. George, I'll see what I can do, if you don't mind," and he sat down and began an assault on the remaining half of the breakfast that meant victory and annihilation, Jasper serving him with zeal and exterior eagerness accompanied by a running fire of curses inside his breast. "Say, George, he's a whole team and a yeller dog under the wagon, when it comes to telling fortunes. Bowles says he lays over Confucius, oh, to hell and gone! Says he told *him* things in his life he hadn't thought of for so long he'd about forgotten them. And he told my fortune, too, and it's plumb wonderful the way he does it. It's a new way: just looks in your hand, and there it's all wrote out and he can read it like print—everything you've

ever done or going to do. Say, George, he told Frances Osgood's
fortune, and in one place he looked awful sorrowful, and says
'You've had a dreadful calamity in your life, poor lady,' and put her
hand away and didn't want to go on; but she made him, and then
he started in and told her all about the fire where she lost her twin
and you lost your house and family, just as straight as if he'd been
there and seen the whole thing himself—ain't it wonderful!" A
potatoe, impaled on a fork, was approaching his mouth, which was
falling open in welcome and anticipation. It stopped where it was,
and the mouth began to close. These were signs that a vast idea had
been born to Dug. He laid the potatoe down and said impressively—

"George!"

"Well?"

"He's the very man!"

"How the very man?" said Harrison, wearily.

"To root out the bottom facts of Jake Bleeker's murder."

It made Harrison gasp, it hit him with such power and
suddenness.

"Bottom facts?" he said, as indifferently as he could, "what
bottom facts?"

"Well, I'll tell you. You see, he could get right down into the
details. There *ain't* any details, up to now. This cuss could lay it all
just as bare as your hand. By gracious, it's a grand idea!" He sprang
from the devastated table and began to throw on his things.
Harrison shouted—

"Stop! what are you going to do?"

"Going to have him come here tomorrow afternoon and—"

"Oh, stop, *stop*, I tell you!"

But Dug was gone. Harrison plunged toward the door, but
Jasper stepped in his way and said—

"Stay whah you is. Hain't you ever gwyneter git any sense?
S'pose you stop dat deef jackass—how you gwyneter 'splain it?
Does you want to raise a lot er s'picions? Let de man come. I's
gwyneter be in dat closet dah, en notice what he say. He ain't
gwyneter jail you en spile yo' good name en yo' power, not if *I*
knows it—I can't 'ford it. If he gits down to de bottom facks, I's

gwyneter buy his mouf shet, en you's gwyneter pay de bill. Cler up de table—hustle! Stack up de dishes; I's gwyneter tote 'em to de kitchen en git some mo' grub, dad burn dat greedy gut!"

Dug spread the news of Jasper's redemption, and it made a sensation in the village, which had had nothing to buzz about and get excited over for some little time. It was diligently discussed. Harrison's judgment was discounted, and his conduct in some degree censured; but his courage was frankly admired and extolled, and there was none but had a fervent word of praise for the nobility of his nature and the never-failing goodness of his heart. His act would have heavily damaged any other citizen, but it raised Harrison a shade in the public reverence and affection, and was recognized as a natural and proper thing for him to do. When some persons did things, the public customarily hunted for a doubtful motive, and generally believed it had found it; in Harrison's case it always premised a good motive, and of course it always found it. What one expects to find and wants to find is easy to find, as a rule. Reputation is a formidable force in this world.

People flocked to Harrison's house all day; partly to recognize his pluck and praise it, and partly out of curiosity to see Jasper, gardener, perform as a house servant. Their praises were vinegar to Harrison's wounds, and the pain was the greater for that Jasper was there to see and enjoy the sufferings the others did not suspect and could not see. Everybody was surprised and a little disappointed to find that Jasper did not seem very much out of place in his new office, and many were candid enough to say so, and fling him a compliment as well. Tom and Helen were of these. Tom said, heartily—

"You are performing really well, Jasper, and I mean what I say. All you've got to do is to behave yourself, and show yourself worthy of what my father has done for you, and you'll have in him a protector that is not afraid to stand by you against the whole town."

Jasper was so moved, and so grateful for these gracious words that Tom was quite touched, and gave him a dime, which he gave to Harrison that night, at the same time mimicking the son's manner and paraphrasing his speech:

"You's p'fawmin' real good, Hahson, en I means what I says. All you got to do is to behave, en show yo'seff wuthy of what I's went en done for you, en I's gwyneter be a p'tector dat'll—yah-yah-yah! I couldn't scasely keep fum laughin' to heah dat goslin' talk 'bout you p'tectin' *me!*"

Frances Osgood was there in the afternoon, and shook George by the hand, and said—

"George, you are so different from other people! Happiness, good fortune and an applauding conscience make some persons hard or indifferent, but they only furnish you new impulses toward—"

"No, Frances, no, you—"

"There, I will spare you, but I had to say it, because I feel it. If Alison and the children could come back now from the grave, how proud they would be of you, and what love and worship they—"

Jasper was hearing all this and storing it up for sarcastic use. He was always hovering in Harrison's neighborhood when it was handy to do it; partly to listen, but mainly because his listening sharpened his slave's miseries.

Ann Bailey cordially endorsed Frances Osgood's remarks, and so did Sol and his brother the minister; the widow Wilkinson and Axtell the consumptive joined the group and added their praises, and General Landry and Asphyxia Perry did likewise while Tom and Helen listened in charmed contentment and pride, all unaware that these compliments which were heaven to them were hell to Harrison; unaware, too, that he would have to hear them again, toward midnight, with Jasper to serve them up, in a new edition revised and improved.

(1902)

3,000 Years Among the Microbes

BY A MICROBE
B. b. Bkshp
With Notes Added by the Same Hand
7,000 Years Later*

Translated from the Original Microbic

By

MARK TWAIN

1905.

PREFACE.

ALTHOUGH THIS WORK is a History, I believe it to be true. There is internal evidence in every page of it that its Author was conscientiously trying to state bare facts, unembellished by fancy. While this insures irksome reading, it also insures useful reading; and I feel satisfied that this will be regarded as full compensation by an intelligent public which has long been suffering from a surfeit of pure History unrefreshed by fact. Among the thousands of statements put forth in this Work there are but two that have a

---

* NOTE, *7,000 years later.* I had been a microbe 3,000 years (microbe-years) when I resolved to do this Narrative. At first I was minded to save time and labor by delivering it into the mechanical thought-recorder, but I gave up that idea because I might want to deal in some privacies—in fact I should *have* to do it—and a body might as well publish a secret and be done with it as put it into a machine which is ready to reveal its privacies to any thief that will turn the crank, let the thief's language and nationality be what they may. So I decided to write my book in my own tongue. Not many sooflaskies would be able to read it if they got hold of it; besides, I was beginning to forget my English, and this labor would presently bring it back to me as good as new, no doubt.   *B.b.B.*

161

doubtful look, and I think these divergences—if they are divergences—are forgivable for the reason that there are indications that the Author made them with regret and was afterward pursued by remorse for having made them at all. But for this pair of slight and indeed inconsequential blemishes, there had been no occasion for apologies from me.

The Translator.

PREFACE.

I HAVE TRANSLATED the author's style and construction, as well as his matter. I began by reforming these, but gave it up. It amounted to putting evening dress on a stevedore and making him stand up in the college and lecture. He was trim, but he was stiff; he delivered strict English, polished English, but it seemed strained and artificial, coming from such a source, and was not pleasant, not satisfactory. Elegant, but cold and unsympathetic. In fact, corpsy. It seemed best to put him back into his shirt-sleeves and overalls, and let him flounder around after the fashion that he was used to.

His style is loose and wandering and garrulous and self-contented beyond anything I have ever encountered before, and his grammar breaks the heart. But there is no remedy: let it go.

The Translator.

His title-page is incorrect.

xxxxx. But really no one was to blame, it was an accident.†

---

† The narration begins thus abruptly, outside of the formal structure of the story, to convey the disorienting effect of the miscarried experiment that is then described in Chapter I. The following notes with asterisks are Mark Twain's own.　Ed.

I.

THE MAGICIAN's experiment miscarried, because of the impossibility of getting pure and honest drugs in those days, and the result was that he transformed me into a cholera-germ when he was trying to turn me into a bird.

At first I was not pleased. But this feeling did not last. I was soon interested in my surroundings, and eager to study them and enjoy them. I was peculiarly well equipped for these pleasures, for certain reasons: to wit, I had become instantly naturalized, instantly endowed with a cholera germ's instincts, perceptions, opinions, ideals, ambitions, vanities, prides, affections and emotions; that is to say, I was become a real cholera germ, not an imitation one; I was become intensely, passionately, cholera-germanic; indeed, I out-natived the natives themselves, and felt and spoke and acted like those girls of ours who marry nobilities and lose their democracy the first week and their American accent the next; I loved all the germ-world—the Bacilli, the Bacteria, the Microbes, etc.,—and took them to my heart with all the zeal they would allow; my patriotism was hotter than their own, more aggressive, more uncompromising; I was the germiest of the germy. It will be perceived, now, that I could observe the germs from their own point of view. At the same time, I was able to observe them from a human being's point of view, and naturally this invested them with an added interest for me. Another thing: my human measurements of time and my human span of life remained to me, right alongside of my full appreciation of the germ-measurements of time and the germ span of life. That is to say, when I was thinking as a human, 10 minutes meant 10 minutes, but when I was thinking as a microbe, it meant a year; when I was thinking as a human, an hour meant an hour, but when I was thinking as a mircrobe it meant 6 years; when I was thinking as a human, a day meant a day, but when I was thinking as a microbe it meant 144 years; when I was thinking as a human, a week meant a week, but when I was thinking as a microbe it meant 1,008 years; when I was thinking as a human, a year meant a year, but when I was thinking as a microbe it meant 52,416 years. When I was using microbe-time, I could start at the cradle with a tender young thing and grow old with her: follow her fortunes second by second, minute by minute, hour after hour; see her bud into sweet maidenhood, see her marry an idolized husband, see her develop into the matron's noble estate, see her lovingly watch over her millions of babes, see her rear them in honesty and honor, see her mourn the loss of millions of them by early death, see her rejoice over the happy nuptials of more fortunate millions of them, see old age and wrinkles and decrepitude descend gradually upon her, and finally see her released from the griefs and the burden of life and laid to rest in the hallowed peace of the grave, with my benediction and my tears for farewell—all this in 150 years by microbe-count, about 24 hours by human time.

II.

THE ERRING magician introduced me into the blood of a hoary and mouldering old bald-headed tramp. His name is Blitzowski—if that isn't an alias—and he was shipped to America by Hungary because Hungary was tired of him. He tramps in the summer and sleeps in the fields; in the winter he passes the hat in cities, and sleeps in the jails when the gutter is too cold; he was sober once, but does not remember when it was; he never shaves, never washes, never combs his tangled fringe of hair; he is wonderfully ragged, incredibly dirty; he is malicious, malignant, vengeful, treacherous, he was born a thief, and will die one; he is unspeakably profane, his body is a sewer, a reek of decay, a charnel house, and contains swarming nations of all the different kinds of germ-vermin that have been invented for the contentment of man. He is their world, their globe, lord of their universe, its jewel, its marvel, its miracle, its masterpiece. They are as proud of their world as is any earthling of his. When the soul of the cholera-germ possesses me I am proud of him: I shout for him, I would die for him; but when the man-nature invades me I hold my nose. At such times it is impossible for me to respect this pulpy old sepulchre.

I have been a microbe about 3 weeks, now. By microbe-time it is 3 thousand years. What ages and ages of joy, prosperity, poverty, hope, despair, triumph, defeat, pain, grief, misery, I have seen, felt, experienced in this lagging and lingering slow drift of centuries! What billions of friends I have made, and loved, and clung to, only to see them pass from this fleeting life to return no more! What black days I have seen—but also what bright ones!

III.

WHEN I BECAME a microbe, the transformation was so complete that I felt at home at once. This is not surprising, for men and germs are not widely different from each other. Of germs there are many nationalities, and there are many languages, just as it is with mankind. The germs think the man they are occupying is the only world there is. To them it is a vast and wonderful world, and they are as proud of it as if they had made it themselves. It seems a pity that this poor forlorn old tramp will never know that, for compliments are scarce with him.

IV.

OUR WORLD (the tramp) is as large and grand and awe-compelling to us microscopic creatures as is man's world to man. Our tramp is mountainous, there are vast oceans in him, and lakes that are sea-like for size, there are many rivers (veins and arteries) which are fifteen miles across, and of a length so stupendous as to make the Mississippi and the Amazon trifling little Rhode Island brooks by comparison. As for our minor rivers, they are multitudinous, and the dutiable commerce of disease which they carry is rich beyond the dreams of the American custom-house.

Well, and why shouldn't our tramp seem imposing and majestic to us little creatures? Think what a wee little speck a man would be if you stood the American Continent up on end in front of him. Standing there with his back to the waves,—standing there on the arching roof of the continent's big toe, (Cape Horn), he would naturally lift his eyes skyward; and how far up that dimming huge frontage would his vision carry? Half way to the knees? No. Not a tenth of the distance! Evanishment would quickly supervene, the colossus would be swallowed up and lost in the sky! If you should stand one of us microscopic specks upon the roof of our tramp's big toe and say "look up"—well, you'd have the same result over again.

There are upwards of a thousand republics in our planet, and as many as thirty thousand monarchies. Several of these monarchies have a venerable history behind them. They do not date back to the actual moment of Blitzowski's birth, for a human child is born pure of disease-germs, and remains pure of them for a matter of three or four hours—say eighteen or twenty years, microbe-time—but they do date back to the earliest invasions, and have sturdily maintained and preserved their regal authority in full force through all vicissitudes from that remote period until now, a stretch approximating four and a half million years. In one case *the same dynasty* holds the throne to-day that established it twenty-five hundred thousand years ago. This is the Pus family,—Pus being the family name, just as Romanoff is the family name of the Czars; the official title is, His August Majesty Henry, D.G. Staphylococcus Pyogenes Aureus * CMX—that is to say, he is the One Hundred and Ten Thousandth monarch of the Pus lineage that has occupied that throne. They have all used the one name, HENRY. In this they

---

* Latin. "D.G.," (Deus gratias,) means *by the grace of God*. The long word means *pus-tank*. The next word—when used in a scientific sense—means *principal;* politically it means *imperial;* in the slang of the common people it means *brick*, and is a term of admiration. Aureus means *gold*. Hence the title, when occurring in a State paper, could be translated *Henry by the grace of God Imperial Pus-Tank*, while in the endearing speech of the common people it would be shortened to *Henry the Gold Brick*.

have been imitated by the Princes of Reuss, of Germany: all Princes of Reuss are named Henry. Reuss is a fine old royal house, and its blood can be traced back, right alongside the Guelf and the Hohenzollern to the dim antiquity of ten centuries ago.

The English monarchy—the *real* English monarchy—has been in existence about 840 years; its 36 reigns have averaged about 23 years each. Pretty nearly the same average obtains here. At least it is so with the great monarchy of which I have been speaking—the greatest, in population, and the most ambitious, in all Blitzowski. In my 3,000 years here I have walked, uncovered and sincerely sorrowing, at the end of the funeral pageants of 121 sovereigns of this venerable line, and have been permitted to assist in the rejoicings which followed the coronations of their successors. It is a stern and noble race, and by diplomacy and arms has pushed its frontiers far. Wherever it has deprived a conquered nation of its liberties and its religion it has replaced these with something better. It is justly claimed for this great House that it has carried the blessings of civilization further than has any other imperial power. In honor of this good work many of our microbe nations have come to speak of pus and civilization as being substantially the same thing.*

---

* NOTE: *5,000 [Years] Later.* The microbe's name for himself is not Microbe, it is *Sooflasky.* It would bankrupt the Unabridged to furnish definitions enough to damage *all* its meanings and make you afraid of the word forever after. Oh, that worthless, worthless book, that timid book, that shifty book, that uncertain book, that time-serving book, that exasperating book, that unspeakable book, the Unlimited Dictionary! that book with but one object in life: to get in more words and shadings of the words than its competitors. With the result that nearly every time it gets done shading a good old useful word it means everything in general and nothing in particular. When, in my human life, we first borrowed the word *unique,* for instance, it was strong and direct, it meant *sole, only,* the *one and only* "joker"—not another one in the pack; the *one and only* existent example of whatever thing the user of the word was referring to: then the Dictionary took hold of it, and hitched to it every careless user's definition of it that it could hunt out—and look at that whilom virgin now! I am not as particular as I might be, perhaps, but I should not like to be caught going around in public with that trollop.

Now as to that word Sooflasky. Straitly translated, it means in Blitzowski what the word Man—as chief creature in the scheme of Creation—means in the human World: that is to say, The Pet, The Chosen One, The Wonderful One, The Grand Razzledazzle, The Whole Thing, The Lord of Creation, The Drum Major, The Head of the Procession. The word Sooflasky means all that, includes all those shades. To construct an English equivalent that would hold them all and not leak was exceedingly difficult, for me, but I believe

Bullyboywithaglasseye came nearest. I often applied it to my fellow-microbes, from the very first, and they liked it. Partly because it was long and fine-sounding and foreign, and partly because of the modified translation I furnished along with it. I told them it was the form employed by our best Major Molar poets, and meant "the Deity's Delight." On these terms I worked it into universal use among the grateful clergy, the poets, the great orators, and the rest of our best people. Quaintly and prettily accented, and delivered lingeringly and lovingly and impressively in a sermon, or with fire and thunder and gush in a great oration, it is certainly one of the nobbiest things I know of. But the first time I heard it wafted from the pulpit it took me unprepared, and it was all I could do to keep from being over-affected by it.

I often used the term Microbe, applying it freely to myself and to the others; and this without offence. If I had explained its real meaning—its mean little patronizing microscopic meaning—there would have been trouble, but I did not do that. I saved myself early. I said it was Major Molar for "the Creature With The Moral Sense," and was the cold scientific term employed to technically describe the Lord Paramount of Animated Nature. There are times when guff is better than fact, and you get more for the price.

"*The* Creature With The Moral Sense." The *the* got them—the *the* captured them—the *the* took them into camp. You know, I thought it would. To be *a* "the" is something, to Man and Microbe; but to be *the* "the"—oh, well, that is a bait which they can't resist at all. I was always a daring person, I never could help it, and I played that 'ansome title on them for a compliment. They did the natural thing, the thing which the honestest of us does when he is on uncertain ground: they looked wise and unsurprised, and let on to know all about it. Without doubt they thought I had brought that jewel from some deep well of erudition in the Major Molar. If they thought that, one thing was sure: they wouldn't expose their ignorance by *asking* me. No, they would keep still; they wouldn't even risk asking if it was a custom there to keep such things in wells.

My instinct was right; that is to say, my knowledge was right—my knowledge of the furtive and cautious ways of Man and Microbe: they didn't ask any questions. Not public ones, at any rate. One inquirer did approach me, but he came privately. He wanted to talk frankly and freely, he said, but hoped I would let the conversation be and remain confidential. He said—

"I will be candid, for I am inviting candor. You supposed, of course, that your '*the* Creature With The Moral Sense' was not new to us, but it was; our calm manner of receiving it was a deception; we had never heard of it before. It has gone into currency; it is accepted, and purred over, and I think it is safe to say that everybody is vain of it, the learned and the ignorant alike. So—"

"Dear sir," I said, with some complacency, interrupting, "I was not altogether deceived—I was doing a little pretending on my own account; I perceived that the restricting of the Moral Sense to the Bullyboywithaglasseye was a new idea to them, and—"

"Oh, bless you, no!" cried he, "not *that*. That was not new."

"Ah-h," said I, a little squelched, "what was it that was new, then?"

"Why, the *the*—used as you used it. You see, that emphasis was the striking thing. I mean, the way you *said* it. It made it sound like a title of honor, a compliment. Making a compliment of it was a new idea, you see. We haven't ever doubted that the Moral Sense is restricted to the Higher Animals, but—look here, give me some help. Our idea of the Moral Sense is, that it teaches us how to distinguish right from wrong; isn't that your idea of it, the Major Molar idea of it?"

"Yes."

"Also, it enables us to find out what is right, and *do* it."

"Correct."

"Also, it enables us to find out what is wrong, and do *that.*"

"Correct."

"Also, without *it* we couldn't find out what was wrong, and therefore couldn't *do* wrong. There wouldn't *be* any wrong; everything we did would be right. Just as it is with the Lower Animals."

"Correct, again."

"Rationally stated, then, the function of the Moral Sense is to *create* WRONG —since without it all conduct would be right."

"Correct."

"It creates wrong, points it out, and so enables us to *do* it."

"Yes."

"Therefore the special and particular office of the Moral Sense is to suggest, instigate and propagate wrong-doing."

"Also, *right*-doing, dear sir—admit it, please."

"Excuse me, we could do that *without* it. But we couldn't do *wrong* without it."

"Very true. But dear sir, to be *able* to do wrong is a high distinction—it lifts us far above the other animals. It is a good deal of a distinction, isn't it?"

"Yes: the distinction between a dial and a tin watch."

x x x He went away pretty sour. All the same, the *the* was planted, and it stayed. Ever since then, these nations look complacently down upon the Lower Animals because they can't do wrong, and complacently up at themselves because they *can*. The Microbes are my own people, and I loyally and patriotically admire them and am proud of them; yet I know in my secret heart that when it comes to reasoning-power they are not really a shade less comical than Man. *B.b.B.*

P.S., *2,000 years still later.* That note was an error. I had not given the matter sufficient thought at that time. I am aware now that the Moral Sense is a valuable possession, indeed inestimably valuable. Without it we could not be what we are. Life would be monotonous, it would consist of sleeping and feeding, only, it would have no lofty ambitions, no noble ideals, there would be no missionaries, no statesmen, no jails, no crime, no soldiers, no thrones, no slaves, no slaughter,—in a word, no Civilization. Without the Moral Sense, Civilization is impossible. *B.b.B.*

I have often been in the actual presence of our Emperors. More, I have been spoken to by them. This great honor has never been vouchsafed to any other foreigner of my degree in all the vast stretch of time during which the present Family has occupied the throne. It was accorded only once before, in all history. That was nearly three million years ago. There is a monument, to preserve the memory of it. It is rebuilt every five hundred years, by voluntary contributions exacted by the State. This is in obedience to an edict promulgated by the emperor of that ancient day and dynasty, who was of a lofty nature and noted for his benevolence. It is a matter of pride to me to know that the subject of that distinction was of my own race—a cholera germ. Beyond this fact nothing is known of him except that he was a foreigner. From what part of Blitzowski he came, history does not say, nor what procured him the memorable honor which the emperor bestowed upon him.

Foreigners are not hated, here; I may say they are not even disliked—they are tolerated. The people treat them courteously, but are indifferent to them. They look down upon them, without being distinctly conscious of it. Foreigners are regarded as inferiors everywhere under the Blitzowski skies. Substantially that, though there are some exceptions. One at least—Getrichquick, the principal republic. There, a third-rate foreign microbic celebrity easily outranks a first-rate native one, and is received with a worshipful enthusiasm which astonishes him away down in his private soul, and he gets more champagne than he gets beer at home. In a Blitzowskan monarchy it is the other way: there, a Getrichquick first-rate ranks as a fifth-rate. But he is solaced: he is a shade prouder of being fifth-rate there than first-rate at home.

Everywhere throughout the planet of Blitzowski the foreigner ranks as an inferior, except—as I have just said—in the mighty Republic of Getrichquick, universally known as the greatest of all the democracies. It occupies a prodigious domain. Under its flag is the whole of Blitzowski's stomach, which is the richest country, the most fertile, the most productive and the most prodigally and variously endowed with material resources in all the microbic world. In that world it is one of the two or three conspicuously great centres of trade. Its commerce, both domestic and foreign, is colossal. Its transportation-facilities are quite extraordinary; these make it a distributing-centre of imposing importance. In manufactures it heads all the countries in Blitzowski. It imports raw materials from the North and ships the manufactured product to all the great nations lying toward the South. For ages it was selfish; it cared for the prosperity and happiness of its own people only, and steadily refused to extend its dominions in the interest of remote and suffering little nations. Many of its best people were ashamed of this. They saw great Heartland sending the refreshing blood of her gracious Civilization to many a dark and neglected nation rotting in debasing indolence and oriental luxury upon the confines of Blitzowski and requiring nothing in return but subjection and revenue; they saw imperial Henryland, far away in the desolate North gradually and surely spreading its dominion down the planet's flat expanse from the Shoulder Range to the lofty land of the Far South—the "Majestic Dome" of the poet and the traveler—distributing happiness and pus all the way, and in return requiring nothing of the benefited peoples except what they had; they saw these things and were ashamed. They were ashamed, and they rose and fought that policy at the polls and replaced it with a higher and holier one, which they baptised with the noble name of Benevolent Assimilation. It was an epoch-making achievement. It lifted Getrichquick out of her obscure and selfish isolation, the moment she was worthy, and throned her in the august company of the Pirate Powers. This was in very recent times—hardly three hundred and fifty thousand years ago, indeed. Far away, in the midst of the shoreless solitudes of the Great Lone Sea† was a collection of mud islets inhabited by those harmless bacilli which are the food of the fierce *hispaniola sataniensis,* whose excretions are the instrument appointed to propagate disease in the human trigonum. This archipelago was benevolently assimilated by the puissant Republic. It was first ingeniously wrested from its owners, by help of the unsuspicious owners themselves, then it was purchased from its routed and dispossessed foreign oppressors at a great price. This made the title perfect, even elegant. Also it added a Great Power to Blitzowski's riches and distinctions of that sort. The new Great Power was really no greater than it was before; the addition of the mud-piles was about the equivalent of adding a prairie-dog village to a mountain range, but the artificial expansion produced by the addition was so vast that it may justly be likened to

---

†The holograph here reads "Great Stale Sea"; however, Mark Twain recorded in his working notes his intention of changing this name, wherever it appears in the story, to "Great Lone Sea." This later intention has been followed.

a case of "before and after": the great Captive Balloon of Paris lying flat and observed of no passer-by, before filling, and the same balloon high in the air, rotund, prodigious, its belly full of gas, the wonder and admiration of a gazing world.

The native bacilli of the islets are of the kind called "benevolent" by the Blitzowski scientist. That is to say, they are not disease-producers. They are unusually little creatures. I have seen several of them. They were hardly more than five feet in diameter. I mean, as seen by my present eye—the eye of a microbe. Ordinary bacilli can be seen by a human being with a microscope magnifying ten or twelve hundred times; but he would not be able to see these little creatures without magnifying them considerably more than that. If you bunch a million ordinary bacilli together on a glass slide they will appear to the naked human eye like a minute stain, but I doubt if a similar crowd of these little Great Lone Sea islanders could be detected at all by the naked human eye. Yes, they are small, like their archipelago, but to hear the Republic talk about the combination, you would think she had been annexing four comets and a constellation.

The first of my imperial masters I was privileged to see was Henry the Great. Not the first one bearing that title—no, I do not mean that; mine was the 861st Henry the Great. By law and usage he was called Seiner Kaiserlichedurchlaustigstehochbegabtergot-tallmächtiger Eight-Sixty-One des Grossen. It sounds like German, but it isn't. Many of the 861 Greats earned the envied title by begetting heirs in a time of scarcity, several earned it by general-ship in war and other forms of massacre, others earned it by illustrious achievements in the line of Benevolent Assimilation, still others by acting as the Church's harlot, others still by enriching the nobility with State lands and with large pensions and gratuities bilked from the public till; the rest earned it by sitting still, looking wise, accepting the credit of the great achievements of their ministers of State—and *not meddling*. These latter are held in imperishable honor by the grateful nation. They have their monuments. Built by the people, by voluntary contributions—real voluntaries. And rebuilt by the people whenever time moulders them to ruin.

As I have already remarked, my own Henry the Great was No. 861. This was about 3,000 years ago—when I first came. That I should have the distinction of appearing before the emperor was a most extraordinary thing. Because I was a foreigner, and (at that time) not noble. My sept—the Cholera Microbes—is one of the Malignant Septs, therefore nobilities may be chosen from it, but I myself was neither noble nor received by persons of noble degree. So it naturally made a great sensation when I was commanded to the presence.

The event came about in this way. By some strange circumstance the egg of an American flea got into Blitzowski's blood and was hatched out and drowned. Then it became fossilized. This was about four million years ago, when the tramp was a boy. On earth I was a scientist by profession, and I remained one after I was transformed into a microbe. Paleontology was a passion with me. I was soon searching for fossils. I found several new ones, and this good fortune gave me the entré into scientific society. Local, I mean. It was humble and obscure, but in its heart burned the same passion for science that was consuming my own.

NOTE. *Seven Thousand Years Later.* Many things have gone from my memory in the 7,000 years that have passed since then, but I still remember little incidents connected with my introduction to that pleasant comradeship. We had a little banquet, a very modest one, of course, for we were all poor and earned our living by hard work in common handicrafts, but it was very good, what there was of it. Exceedingly good, I may say. The word is not too strong, for we were more used to fasting than feasting. We had both kinds of corpuscles, and they were served up in six different ways, from soup and raw down to pie. The red ones were a little high, but Tom Nash made us all laugh by wittily saying it wasn't any matter, because the *bill* was so low that—that— well, it has gone from me, but I still consider it one of the wittiest things I have ever heard in my life. And he said it offhand—he did not have to stop and think, just flirted it out without any study, and perfectly easy and composed, the same as if he might be saying any little thing; and he . . . but *was* it Tom? . . . Ah, well, it could have been Sam Bowen . . . or maybe John Garth or Ed. Stevens. . . . Anyway it was one of them, I remember it perfectly. Yes, it was a quite memorable event, for young fellows like us. Ah, little did we suspect that we were making history! But we were. Little did we foresee that our poor little banquet was going to live forever in song and story, and in text-book and grave chronicle, and that my most careless words were destined to be remembered, and treasured and reverently repeated until the last

I no longer regretted lost America, I was among friends, admirers, helpers, and was happy.

In all ways I was enviably situated in those days. I lived in the country, in a dozing village, an easy distance from the capital, and had for neighbors a kindly and innocent peasantry whose quaint habits and quainter speech I loved to study. There were some billions of them, in the village and around it, yet they seemed few and scattering, for billions count for nothing among germs. The region was healthful and attractive; on every hand a receding and diminishing perspective of fair fields and gardens and parks, threaded with limpid streams and musical with the songs of birds, stretched away to a stately mountain rampart which lifted its rugged and broken sky-line against the western horizon—a prospect ever serene, contenting and beautiful, and never curtained, never blotted out, for in Blitzowski there is no night. What would be the blackest darkness to a human eye is noonday—a noonday as of fairyland, soft and rich and delicate—to the microbe's. The microbe's mission is urgent, exacting, he seldom sleeps, until age tires him.

What would my rugged mountains be, to the human eye? Ah, they would hardly even rank as warts. And my limpid and sparkling streams? Cobweb threads, delicate blood-vessels which it could not detect without the aid of the microscope. And the soaring arch of my dream-haunted sky? For that coarse eye it would have no existence. To my exquisite organ of vision all this spacious landscape is *alive*—alive and in energetic motion—unceasing

---

germ shall fall silent and be gathered to his rest. I think the finest part of my speech was where I said, in concluding a lofty and impassioned tribute to the *real* nobility of Science and her devotees, "Ah, gentlemen," I said, "in the— the . . . in the—." I will look it up, in one of the Universal Histories. Here it is: "Ah, gentlemen, in the laboratory there are no fustian ranks, no brummagem aristocracies; the domain of Science is a republic, and all its citizens are brothers and equals, its princes of Monaco and its stonemasons of Cromarty meeting, barren of man-made gauds and meretricious decorations, upon the one majestic level!"

Of course the boys did not understand the references, and I did not explain at that time, but it was a grand peroration and the eloquence of it carried them clear off their feet. Eloquence is the essential thing in a speech, not information. B.b.B.

motion—every detail of it! It is because I can see the individual molecules that compose it, and even the atoms which compose the molecules; but no microscope is powerful enough to reveal either of these things to the human eye. To the human mind they exist only in *theory*, not in demonstrated fact. The human mind—that wonderful machine—has measured the invisible molecule, and measured it accurately, without seeing it; also it has counted the multitudinous electrons that compose it, and counted them correctly, without having seen one of them; certainly a marvelous achievement.

Take a man like Sir Oliver Lodge, and what secret of Nature can be hidden from him? He says: "A billion, that is a million millions, of atoms is truly an immense number, but the resulting aggregate is still excessively minute. A portion of substance consisting of a billion atoms is only barely visible with the *highest* power of a microscope; and a speck or granule, in order to be visible to the naked eye, like a grain of lycopodium-dust, *must be a million times bigger still.*"

The human eye could see it then—that dainty little speck. But with my microbe-eye I could see *every individual* of the whirling billions of *atoms* that *compose* the speck. *Nothing is ever at rest*— wood, iron, water, everything is alive, everything is raging, whirling, whizzing, day and night and night and day, nothing is dead, *there is no such thing as death*, everything is full of bristling life, tremendous life, even the bones of the crusader that perished before Jerusalem eight centuries ago. There are no vegetables, *all things are* ANIMAL; each electron is an animal, each molecule is a collection of animals, and each has an appointed duty to perform and a soul to be saved. Heaven was not made for man alone, and oblivion and neglect reserved for the rest of His creatures. He gave them life, He gave them humble services to perform, they have performed them, and they will not be forgotten, they will have their reward. Man—always vain, windy, conceited—thinks he will be in the majority there. He will be disappointed. Let him humble himself. But for the despised microbe and the persecuted bacillus, who needed a home and nourishment, he would not have been created. He has a mission, therefore—a reason for existing: let him do the service he was made for, and keep quiet.

Three weeks ago I was a man myself, and thought and felt as men think and feel; but I have lived 3,000 years since then, and I see the foolishness of it now. We live to learn; and fortunate are we when we are wise enough to profit by it.

V.

IN MATTERS pertaining to microscopy we necessarily have an advantage, here, over the scientist of the earth, because, as I have just been indicating, we see with our naked eyes minutenesses which no man-made microscope can detect, and are therefore able to register as facts many things which exist for him as theories only. Indeed, we know as facts several things which he has not yet divined even by theory. For example he does not suspect that there is no life but *animal* life, and that all atoms are *individual animals*, each endowed with a certain degree of consciousness, great or small, each with likes and dislikes, predilections and aversions— that, in a word, each has a *character*, a character of its own. Yet such is the case. Some of the molecules of a stone have an aversion for some of those of a vegetable or any other creature, and will not associate with them—and would not be allowed to, if they tried. Nothing is more particular about society than a molecule. And so there are no end of castes; in this matter India is not a circumstance.

I often think of a talk I once had upon some of these things with a friend of mine, a renowned specialist by the name of Bblbgxw, a name which I have to modify to Benjamin Franklin because it is so difficult for me to pronounce that combination right; but that is near enough anyway, because when a foreigner pronounces it it always sounds a little like Franklin, when it doesn't sound like Smith. As I was saying, I was discussing those things with him, and

I still remember some of the remarks he made; others have faded
out of my memory, but no matter, I wrote down the talk at the
time, and will insert that record here:

THE RECORD.

FRANKLIN is a Yellow-fever germ, but speaks a broken and fiendishly
ungrammatical thyroid-diphthyritic which I am able to follow, and
could follow better if his accent were less homicidal. I wish he knew
Latin—however, he doesn't. It is curious, the way these bacilli stick to
their own tongues and avoid foreign ones. And yet it is not so very
curious, perhaps, seeing there is such a multitude of foreign tongues
in Blitzowski that a learner hardly knows where to begin on them. As
for me, I have a talent for languages, and I like to learn them. The
time-cost is nothing to me. I can learn six in an hour, without
difficulty. (Microbe-time, of course, confound these troublesome
time-tables!)

I may well say that, for they make my head ache. I have no trouble
with *microbe*-time, for I have used no other, nor had occasion to use
any other, for several centuries; and so the familiarity with human
time which I once possessed has ceased to be a familiarity, and I
cannot now handle its forms with easy confidence and a sure touch
when I want to translate them into microbe-equivalents. This is
natural. Since ever so long ago, microbe time has been *real* to me,
and human time a dream—the one present and vivid, the other far
away and dim, very dim, wavering, spectral, the substantiality all
gone out of it. Sometimes I shut my eyes and try to bring back the
faces that were so dear to me in my human days in America. How
immeasurably remote they are, and vague and shadowy, glimpsed
across that gulf of time—mere dream-figures drifting formless through
a haze! Indeed, all things are dim to me, I think, that lie beyond it.
Why, when I first began to write this little statement a half a second
ago, I had to keep stopping to dig down into my memory for old
forgotten human measurements of time that I had not used nor
thought of for lifetimes and lifetimes! My difficulties were so great
and my mistakes so frequent and vexatious that for comfort's sake
and accuracy's sake I stopped writing, and labored out a tabulated

translation of microbe time-divisions into human ones for my guidance and protection. Like this:

TIME—EQUIVALENTS.

Human.		Microbe.
¼ of a second is (roughly)	. 3 hours.
½ " " " " "	. 6 "
1 second " "	. 12 "
2 " " "	. 24 "
15 " " "	. 1 week.
30 " " "	. 1 fortnight.
60 " " "	. 1 month.
10 minutes " "	. 1 year
1 hour " "	. 6 years
1 day " "	. 144 "
1 week " "	. 1,008 "
1 year " "	. 52,416 "

A Pause for Comment.
Record Suspended, Meantime.

As far as the table deals in seconds and minutes it is inexact. The microbe month is *more* than 60 human seconds; it is 1 human minute, and 12 seconds over. But I use the rough measurement because it is handy, and near enough for all ordinary purposes. I wanted to translate a microbe hour into its human equivalent, but it kept shrinking and diminishing and wasting away, and finally disappeared from under my pen, leaving nothing behind that I could find again when I wanted it. As nearly as I could get at it, a microbe hour seemed to be the fiftieth part of human second. We will let it go at that. I used to be the best mathematician in Yale when I was in the class of '53, and to-day I am considered the best one in Blitzowski—that is, in microbe mathematics—but I can do nothing with human mathematics now. I have tried lately to get back the art, but my memory refuses. In the Yale days I was perfect in it; indeed I was called wonderful. Justly, too, perhaps, for people used to come from great distances to see me do eclipses, and occultations of Venus, and such things. I could do twelve simultaneously, blindfold, and keep the run of them all, just in my head. It was in those days that I invented the logarhythyms, but I cannot even spell it without embarrassment now, let alone put up a hand in them that a soph can't beat. Great days—yes, they were great days. They will come no more. In this pathetic life all things pass, nothing abides. Even the human multiplication table has gone from me—almost utterly. It has been more than seven thousand years since I could say it beyond 4 times 9 is 42. But it is no matter, I shall never need it after I get done writing this. And besides, if I should need multiplications in this, it may be that I can use the local multiplication table and then translate it into human. No—that will hardly answer, everything is so small here, as compared with human dimensions. It is not likely that 4 times 9 in microbe would amount to enough in English to be worth while. It would not convey enough of the idea for the reader to get it.

Having clarified the atmosphere on the time-limit and removed the confusions and perplexities that were vexing it, I will now return to the conversation I had with Franklin.

The Record Resumed.

"FRANKLIN," I asked, "is it certain that each and every existing *thing* is an individual and alive—every *plant*, for instance?"

"Yes," he answered.

"And is each molecule that composes it an individual too, and alive?"

"Yes."

"And is each atom that composes the molecule an individual also, and alive?"

"Yes."

"Now then, has the whole plant—a tree, for instance—feelings, sympathies and so on, *as* a tree?"

"Yes."

"Whence do they come?"

"They are imparted by the combined feelings and sympathies that exist separately in the molecules that compose the tree. They are the tree's soul. They make the tree feel like a tree instead of like a rock or a horse."

"Have rocks, trees and horses any feelings that are common to the three?"

"Yes. The feelings which are the product of oxygen are shared in greater or lesser degree by all three. If the chemical compounds of a rock were the same as those of a tree and in the same proportions, it wouldn't look like a rock, nor feel like a rock, and—"

"Well?"

"Well, it wouldn't *be* a rock. It would be a tree."

"I do believe it. Tell me: Inasmuch as oxygen enters into the composition of pretty much everything that exists, it would interest me to know if it imparts a *special and particular feeling*—a feeling not imparted to a creature by any other kind of molecule?"

"Indeed it does. Oxygen is *temper,* and is the sole source of it. Where there is but little of it there is but little passion; where there is more of it, there is more temper; where there is more still, still more temper; add still more oxygen, degree by degree, keep on adding, and you warm that temper up and up, stage by stage, till by and by you reach the ultimate of fury. Some plants are very quiet and peaceable —you have noticed that?"

"I have."

"It is because they contain but little oxygen. Others contain more, others more still. Some are more heavily charged with oxygen than with any other chemical. We know the result: the rose is sweet-tempered, the nettle is hasty, the horse-radish is violent. Observe the bacilli: Some are gentle—it means lack of oxygen. Then look at the tuberculosis-germ, and typhoid: loaded to the mandibles with oxygen! I have some temper myself, but I am thankful to say I do not act like those outlaws. When I am at my angriest, I am still able to remember that I am a gentleman."

Well, we are curious creatures. Sometimes I wonder if there *is* anybody who is not a self-deceiver. He believed what he was saying, he was perfectly sincere about it; yet everybody knows that when a yellow-fever germ's temper is up, there is no real difference between him and an insurrection. He evidently expected me to concede that he was a kind of a saint, and so I had discretion enough to do it, for I take no pleasure in mutilations, and I am going to be unusually anxious for trouble before ever I throw out any remark that is likely to stir up *his* oxygen. Presently, I said—

"Tell me, Franklin, is the ocean an individual, an animal, a creature?"

"Sure."

"Then water—any water—is an individual?"

"Sure."

"Suppose you remove a drop of it? Is what is left an individual?"

"Yes, and so is the drop."

"Suppose you divide the drop?"

"Then you have two individuals."

"Suppose you separate the hydrogen and the oxygen?"

"Again you have two individuals. But you haven't water, any more."

"Of course. Certainly. Well, suppose you combine them again, but in a new way: Make the proportions equal—one part oxygen to one of hydrogen?"

"But you know you can't. They won't combine on equal terms."

I was ashamed to have made that blunder. I was embarrassed; to cover it, I started to say we used to combine them like that where I came from, but thought better of it, and stood pat.

"Now then," I said, "it amounts to this: water is an individual, an animal, and is alive; remove the hydrogen and *it* is an animal and is alive; the remaining oxygen is also an individual, an animal, and is alive. Recapitulation: the two individuals combined, constitute a third individual—and yet each *continues* to be an individual."

I glanced at Franklin, but . . . upon reflection, held my peace. I could have pointed out to him that here was mute Nature explaining the sublime mystery of the Trinity so luminously that even the commonest understanding could comprehend it, whereas many a trained master of words had labored to do it with speech and failed. But he would not have known what I was talking about. After a moment, I resumed—

"Listen—and see if I have understood you rightly. To-wit—All the atoms that constitute each oxygen molecule are separate individuals, and each one is a living animal; all the atoms that constitute each hydrogen molecule are separate individuals, and each one is a living animal; each drop of water consists of millions of living animals, the drop itself is an individual, a living animal, and the wide ocean is another. Is that it?"

"Yes, that is correct."

"By George, it beats the band!"

He liked the expression, and set it down in his tablets.

"Franklin, we've got it down fine. And to think—there are other animals that are still smaller than a hydrogen atom, and yet *it* is so small that it takes five thousand of them to make a molecule—a molecule so minute that it could get into a microbe's eye and he wouldn't know it was there!"

"Yes, the wee creatures that inhabit the bodies of us germs, and feed upon us, and rot us with disease. Ah, what could they have been created for? they give us pain, they make our lives miserable, they murder us—and where is the use of it all, where the wisdom? Ah, friend Bkshp, we live in a strange and unaccountable world; our birth is a mystery, our little life is a mystery and a trouble, we pass and are seen no more; all is mystery, mystery, mystery; we know not whence we came, nor why, we know not whither we go, nor why we go. We only know we were not made in vain, we only know we were made for a wise purpose, and that all is well! We shall not be cast aside in contumely and unblest, after all we have suffered. Let us be patient, let us not repine, let us trust. The humblest of us is cared for —oh, believe it!—and this fleeting stay is not the end!"

You notice that? He did not suspect that he, also, was engaged in gnawing, torturing, defiling, rotting, and murdering a fellow-creature —he and all the swarming billions of his race. None of them suspects it. That is significant. It is suggestive—irresistibly suggestive—insistently suggestive. It hints at the possibility that the procession of known and listed devourers and persecutors is not complete. It suggests the possibility, and substantially the certainty, that man is himself a microbe, and his globe a blood-corpuscle drifting with its shining brethren of the Milky Way down a vein of the Master and Maker of all things, Whose body, mayhap,—glimpsed partwise from the earth by night, and receding and lost to view in the measureless remotenesses of Space—is what men name the Universe.

VI.

"WELL, FRANKLIN," I said, "Carpe diem—quam minimum credula postero." *

He was very much pleased when I translated it for him; and got me to write it down in his tablets, so that he could make an illuminated motto of it and stick it up in his parlor like a God-Bless-Our-Home and have its admonition ever under his eye, for he was profoundly struck by its wisdom. While I was complying, he took *two* drinks. I did not say anything, but it seemed to me that when it came to wisdom he already had enough for the practical purposes of this brief life.

I excused myself from going to the door with him—being shy, for I had long been intolerably renowned and sought after. He understood, for he could see, himself, that the usual multitude had massed itself, black and solid, for hundreds of yards around, hoping to get a glimpse of me. He took a snap with his instantaneous multograph, looked at the record, and called back to me that the number of persons present was 648,342,227,549,113. It interested him, and he put up his hand and flung back, with a flirt or two of his fingers, the sign-language remark, "This is the penalty for being illustrious, magister!"

Oh, dear, how many million times I have heard and seen that shop-worn remark since I became famous. Each person that utters it thinks he's the first that thought of it; thinks it's a cute phrase and felicitous, and is as vain of it as if he had cornered the fourth dimension. Whereas it is the *obvious* remark; any person who was alive and not in the asylum would think of it. It is of the grade of the puns which small wits make upon people's names. Every time they are introduced to a person named Terry they dazzle-up like the sun bursting out of a cloud and say, "I am not going to hurt you, don't look so *terr*ified!" and then they almost perish with cackling over that poor little addled egg that they've laid. Why doesn't it occur to them

* Latin. It means, "Be thou wise: take a drink whilst the chance offers; none but the gods know when the jug will come around again."

that in the very nature of things Terry has seen it laid every day since he was born? Twain . . . Twain . . . what was his other name? Mike? I think it was Mike, but it was long ago, centuries ago, that I used to hear of him in that almost forgotten world that I used to inhabit; and I read his books, too, but I do not remember what they were about, now . . . no, it wasn't books, it was pictures . . . pictures or agriculture . . . agri . . . yes, it *was* agriculture, I remember it perfectly, now. He was a Californian, and his middle name was Burbank; he did miracles in the invention and propagation of new and impossible breeds of flowers and fruits and timber, and became known all over the world, and was finally hanged, many thought unjustly. He was coming out of a saloon sometimes one day, and one of the times that he was coming out of it a stranger was introduced to him, and dazzled-up like the sun bursting out of a cloud, and shouted, "Aha! he-he! he-he! if a man require thee to go with him a mile, go *with* him, Twain!" and Twain shot him in five places and he crumpled up on the sidewalk and died, many people looking on, and some regretting it. The whole State joined in an effort to get the death-sentence commuted to a term in Congress or jail, I do not remember which it was, now, and the governor was quite willing if the agriculturist would say he was sorry, but he said he could not tell a lie, and some believed him, because he had once chopped down a cherry tree because he couldn't; and then it came out that he had already killed dozens of persons of every sex for making that remark and had concealed it for one reason or another, and so it was judged best, on the whole, to let the sentence stand, although everybody, even Grovenor Rossfelt, President of the United States, conceded that such people were not necessary.

Well, certainly memory is a curious machine and strangely capricious. It has no order, it has no system, it has no notion of values, it is always throwing away gold and hoarding rubbish. Out of that dim old time I have recalled that swarm of wholly trifling facts with ease and precision, yet to save my life I can't get back my mathematics. It vexes me, yet I am aware that everybody's memory is like that, and that therefore I have no right to complain. There was an odd instance of it the other day: Wzprgfski * the historian was here, and was telling about ancient times, and all of a sudden the bottom fell out of the back end of his memory and spilt every proper

---

* Pronounced Tolliver.

name he ever knew. During the interval that the infirmity lasted, he was short on generals, poets, patriarchs and all the rest of his venerated celebrities, and long on lies and legends and battles and revolutions and other incorporeate facts only. Presently he got his proper-name memory back, then another piece of bottom fell out and spilt a hatful of verbs. When it happened he was just starting to say, "And so, in the fulness of time Ggggmmmdw.* . . ." But there he went aground; the word he wanted was gone. I had to supply it myself and start him along again. It was *hfcn̈zz*. With that umlaut over the *n* it means "began to disintegrate;" without the umlaut, the word is an active transitive past participle, and means that the disintegration has been completed; thus it means—substantially—that the man is *dead*: but not exactly that, but not *really*, because in Blitzowski, as I have previously remarked, there is no such thing as death. The umlauted word is restricted to poetry; but even in poetry it does not mean that life has *ceased*; it has *departed*—that is all; we do not know its new habitat, but we know it is still with us, still near us. Of the molecules which constituted its late dwelling and gave it motion and feeling— that is to say, *life*—many have wandered away and joined themselves to new plasmic forms, and are continuing their careers in the bodies of plants, birds, fishes, flies, and other creatures; in time the rest will follow, till the last bone has crumbled to dust, in the far future, and dismissed its atoms, each to seek its kind and go on with its functions indefinitely. And so our people here have no word to signify that either a person or his spirit is *dead*, in our sense of that term; no, his oxygen molecules are gradually deserting and wandering away, in groups and companies, to furnish temper to the horse-radish, the tiger and the rabbit, each in the degree required; his hydrogen, (humor, hope, cheer) as fast as it is released, will carry its happy spirit whither it is needed, and will lift up the drooping flower and whatever other thing is despondent; his glucose, his acetic acid, his— well, everything he has got will go out and seek and find a new home, and each will continue its vocation. Nothing will be lost, nothing will perish.

Franklin realizes that no atom is destructible; that it has always existed and will exist forever; but he thinks all atoms will go out of this world some day and continue their life in a happier one. Old Tolliver thinks no atom's life will ever end, but he also thinks

---

* Pronounced nearly like the Welsh name Llthwbgww.

Blitzowski is the only world it will ever see, and that at no time in its eternity will it be either worse off or better off than it is now and always has been. Of course he thinks the planet Blitzowski is itself eternal and indestructible—at any rate he says he thinks that. It could make me sad, only I know better. D. T. will fetch Blitzy yet, one of these days.

But these are alien thoughts, human thoughts, and they falsely indicate that I do not want this tramp to go on living. What would become of me if he should disintegrate? My molecules would scatter all around and take up new quarters in hundreds of plants and animals; each would carry its special feelings along with it, each would be content in its new estate, but where should *I* be? I should not have a rag of a feeling left, after my disintegration—with his—was complete. Nothing to think with, nothing to grieve or rejoice with, nothing to hope or despair with. There would be no more *me*. I should be musing and thinking and dreaming somewhere else—in some distant animal, maybe—perhaps a cat; by proxy of my oxygen I should be raging and fuming in some other creature—a rat, perhaps; I should be smiling and hoping in still another child of Nature—heir to my hydrogen—a weed, or a cabbage, or something; my carbonic acid (ambition) would be dreaming dreams in some lowly wood-violet that was longing for a showy career; thus my details would be doing as much feeling as ever, but I should not be aware of it, it would all be going on for the benefit of those others, and I not in it at all. I should be gradually wasting away, atom by atom, molecule by molecule, as the years went on, and at last I should be all distributed, and nothing left of what had once been Me. It is curious, and not without impressiveness: I should still be alive, intensely alive, but so scattered that I would not know it. I should not be dead,—no, one cannot call it that—but I should be the next thing to it. And to think what centuries and ages and aeons would drift over Me before the disintegration was finished, the last bone turned to gas and blown away! I wish I knew what it is going to feel like, to lie helpless such a weary, weary time, and see my faculties decay and depart, one by one, like lights which burn low, and flicker, and perish, until the ever-deepening gloom and darkness which—oh, away, away with these horrors, and let me think of something wholesomer!

My tramp is only 85; there is good hope that he will live ten years longer—500,000 of my microbe years. So may it be.

The Ancient Record Continued.

VII.

As SOON as I was sure Franklin was out of sight I stepped out on the balcony: looked surprised to find that people were waiting in the hope of getting a glimpse of me—fell into an attitude of embarrassment and consternation which is very effective in Kodak-snaps and illustrations, and which I have perfected by practice before the glass —then I allowed the usual thunder-crash of salutation and welcome to astonish me into another and quite stunning attitude of surprise— surprise mixed with almost childish gratification—really a most fetching thing when it is done well—then I scudded away like a dear little shy maid who has been caught with nothing on but a blush, and vanished into my quarters, thus making the most taking and delightful effect of all, for it always leaves the mighty multitude rent with storms of happy and grateful laughter, and they shout "oh, isn't he *too* sweet for anything!"

Oh shocked and scornful reader, be gentle with me! Can't you see *yourself* in that disgraceful picture? For it *is* you. There has never been anybody who would not like to be in that place; there has never been any one who would throw away the chance to occupy it if he had it. The baby microbe shows off before company; the microbe lad shows off, with silly antics, before the little bacillus girls; also he plays pirate, soldier, clown—anything to be conspicuous. After that— well, after that, his appetite for notice and notoriety remains— remains always—but he lyingly and hypocritically lets on that he has lost it. He hasn't lost it, he has only lost his honesty.

Now then, be gentle with me, for that is all that I have lost; all that you and I have lost. Otherwise we are what we were when we were babies and used to crow and cackle and carry on in mommer's lap and glance at the company to collect the applause. The company were poignantly ashamed of the baby, and you have been as poignantly ashamed of me—that is, you thought you were ashamed of me, but that was not so—you were ashamed of yourself, as exposed in me.

We can't help our nature, we didn't make it, it was made for us; and so we are not to blame for possessing it. Let us be kind and compassionate toward ourselves; let us not allow the fact to distress us and grieve us that from mommer's lap to the grave we are all shams and hypocrites and humbugs without an exception, seeing that we did not make the fact and are in no way responsible for it. If any teacher tries to persuade you that hypocrisy is not a part of your blood and bone and flesh, and can therefore be trained out of you by determined and watchful and ceaseless and diligent application to the job, do not you heed him; ask him to cure himself first, then call again. If he is an honorable person and is meaning well, he will give the medicine you have recommended to him an earnest and honest and sincere trial, but he will not call again.

For centuries I have held unchallenged the reputation of being a celebrity who is so shy and modest by nature that he shrinks from public notice and is pained by it. Very well, I have earned it. By thoughtful and deeply-reasoned arts. I have played my game every day for a lengthy procession of centuries, and played it well; I have my reward. I have copied the way of the kings; they do not make themselves common to the public eye. A king's most valued and valuable asset is public notice. Without it the chief charm of his difficult and burdensome office would be wanting, and he would mourn and sigh, and wish he could trade his post for one with more show to it and less work to do. Tradition puts this frank retort into the mouth of old Henry MMMMMDCXXII, surnamed The Untamed: "Yes, I *am* fond of praises, processions, notice, attentions, reverence, fuss and feathers! *Vanities,* are they? There was never a creature, particularly a god, that did not like them."

I started to tell how I came to be celebrated, but I have wandered far from my course. It is partly because I have long been unused to writing, and thereby have lost the art and habit of concentration. And so I scatter too much. Then there was another difficulty: I wanted to write in English, but could not manage it to my satisfaction, because the words, the grammar, the forms, the spelling and everything else connected with the language had faded and become unfamiliar to me. And the phrasing! Phrasing is everything, almost. Oh, yes, phrasing is a kind of photography: out of focus, a blurred picture; in focus, a sharp one. One must get the focus right—

that is, frame the sentence with exactness and precision, in his mind
—before he pulls the string.*

(*End of Extract from the Ancient Record.*)

VIII.

IT SEEMED best to fall back on the microbe tongue, and so I
did it. I went back to the start and put this History into that
language, then laboriously translated it into English, just as you see
it now. It is very good, not many could do it better, yet in brilliancy
and effectiveness it is but the lightning-bug to the lightning, when
compared with the microbic original. Among microbe authors I
hold the belt for phrasing, and I could hold it in English if I was a
mind to take the trouble.

The way I came to be celebrated was this. When I first arrived in
Blitzowski I was poor and a stranger; and as all could see that I was
a foreigner, my society was not sought after. I took cheap board
with a humble family** and by their kindly help I was enabled to
hire a hand-organ and a monkey. On credit. On a royalty. I was
very industrious, performing all day and studying the family's
language all night, with the children for teachers, for they never
slept, there being no night for them; and indeed none for me
except the conventional one invented by myself.

At first I gained but few pennies, but I soon struck a good idea. I
began to sing. In English. It was not very good singing, and was
avoided; but only for a little while; for when the germs noticed that

---

* Alas, alas! Well, I was certainly pretty young when I wrote that, away
back yonder, ages ago; pretty young and self-satisfied. It makes me ashamed.
Still, I believe I will let it stand. Why should I care? it is not giving *me* away,
it is giving away a silly youth who *was* me, but is no more me now than is the
once-sapling the present oak.   B.b.B.

** Named Taylor, but spelt different.

I was using a strange tongue, and one which they had never heard before, they were interested. I sang "Sally in Our Alley" and "I don't 'low no Coon to Fool roun' Me," and other simple anthems, and then the crowds began to follow me around, and couldn't get enough.

I prospered. By the end of the first year I was past master in the family's language, then I went to work on a new one. I was still so American that that microbe year of ten minutes and twelve seconds seemed astonishingly brief; but after that, each year that went by seemed considerably longer than its immediate predecessor. This constantly lengthening process continued for ten years; after that, the microbe year was become fully as long to me as the half of any American year had ever been. The older crops of Taylor children had grown so, meantime, that several of the girls were 40 and marriageable. A microbe girl at 40 is about where an American girl is at 20 or 25, for the climate is wonderfully healthy and the food nutricious, and many a person lives to be 150, which is a shade more than an entire human day.

Yes, I had prospered. But Sally and the Coon-song were beginning to show wear and invite rocks; so, out of prudence I reorganized my program and pulled off another prosperous ten with "Bonny Doon" and "Buffalo Gals Can't You Come out To-night." Microbes like sentimental music best.

Pretty early I had to explain what *kind* of a foreigner I was. This was a delicate business. I could have told inquirers the truth, of course, for I was in practice, but there would have been no takers. I could market a lie if I built it with judgment, but to say I was an American and came of a race of star-bumping colossi who couldn't even see an average microbe without a microscope, would have landed me in the asylum.

The local name of the cholera microbe is *Bwilk*—a word equivalent to the Latin word *lextalionis*, which means—well, I don't remember, now, what it means, but bwilk is a good name and much respected here. I found that there was no one in our neighborhood that had ever seen a native of the Major Molar, or knew what the language of that region sounded like. The Major

Molar is Blitzowski's furthest-aft tooth on the port side. In the dentine of that tooth there are some exceeding delicate nerve-threads that traverse it horizontally, crossing the cane-brake of perpendicular ones at right angles, and I pretended that I was a native of one of those—the north-west one. After I had said it and it was too late to mend the statement, I remembered that Blitzowski's Major Molar was at the dentist's—awaiting redemption and not likely to get it, for Blitzowski is not given to paying for services or redeeming undesirable securities so long as he can dodge. But no one noticed, and my statement passed. Some good-hearted people thought it a pity that a respectable race should be so straitened as to be obliged to live in such a remote and desolate country. This touched me deeply, and I took up a collection for them.

I was fond of the Taylor children, they had grown up under my eye, many crops of them had been dear little pets and housemates of mine from their cradle-days, and it caused me a pang when they began to leave the safe haven of their home and embark upon the uncertain sea of matrimony. In the case of the boy-microbes, I did not so much mind it, but it was very hard to lose the girls, indeed I could hardly bear to think of it. And to make it the harder, the first to give her heart away was my favorite. This was Maggie (my love-name for her, and used by none but her and me). I gave her that sacred name out of the secretest chamber of my heart, when she was a little thing; and in after-years when she came to have a budding sense of the sweetest and tenderest of all the passions and I told her why that name was the name of names to me, her eyes filled and she expressed with a kiss the pitying words her quivering lips could not frame. The marriage made a great gap in the family, for 981,642 of her sisters were married at the same time, and many brothers—over a million, I do not remember the exact number, but I think I am within 30 or 35 of it. None can know the desolation of a day like that who has not lived it. I had an honored place at the wedding solemnities, and assisted in deepening their impressiveness by singing one of the dear old early songs; but when I tried to sing the other one the strain upon my feelings was too great and I broke down. Neither could Maggie bear it. From that day to this I have never been able to sing "I Don't 'Low No Coon" through to the end without my voice breaking.

That wedding carried my mind back to other scenes and other days, and filled it with images painfully sweet and unforgetable. Turning the pages of my mouldy diaries now, to refresh my memory for these chapters, I find this entry, whose pathos moves me still, after all these centuries:

> May 25, Y. H. 2,501,007. Yesterday, Maggie's wedding. Last night I dreamed of that other Maggie, that human Maggie, whose dear face I shall look upon no more in this life. In that sweet vision I saw her as I had seen her last—oh, dream of loveliness, oh, radiant creature, oh, spirit of fire and dew, oh, fairy form, transfigured by the golden flood of the sinking sun! . . . God forgive me, I hurt her with a cruel speech! How could I commit that crime! And how had I the heart to note unmoved the reproach in those gentle eyes and go from that sweet presence unforgiven?

I wrote that passage 7,000 years ago. There is a very curious thing connected with it: I have had that same dream, its glory unfaded, its pain unsoftened, once in every century since that recorded date—and always on the 24th of May of the hundredth year. When this had recurred two or three times I took courage to hope it was a sign—a sign that it would continue to recur after the lapse of each century; when it had blessed me five times I felt sure it would continue; after that, I never had a doubt. So sure was I, that when the sixth century drew toward its close, I began to tally off the decades, then the years, the months, the days, with ever increasing impatience and longing, until the hallowed day came and again upon my slumbering mind the beautiful vision rose. I have always watched with confidence for the dream since, as each century waned toward the memorable date, and in no instance have I been disappointed. Always in the dream I hear distant music— distant and faint, but always sweet, always moving: "Bonny Doon." It was Margaret's favorite, therefore it was mine too.

There is one very curious effect: in the dream the beautiful human girl is as beautiful to me as she was when I was of her own race. This is quite unaccountable, there is no way to explain it. Do I become human again, in the dream, and re-acquire human notions of what is beautiful and what isn't? Really it has a plausible look, yet it is pretty fanciful, pretty far-fetched, not very persuasive, not very likely, when one examines it soberly. When I am awake, my standards of beauty and and loveliness are microbic, and microbic only, and this is natural. When I am awake and my memory calls up human faces and forms which were once beautiful to me, they are still beautiful, but not with the beauty that exists by grace of *race*-ship—no, it is merely the sort of beauty which I see in a flower, a bird, or other comely thing not of my own kind. To the young gentleman-caterpillar no human being nor any other creature approaches in charm and beauty and winsomeness the lissome and rounded young lady-caterpillar whom he loves. What is Cleopatra to him? Nothing. He would not go out of his way to look at her. To him she would seem fluffy, gross, unshapely, she could not fire his passions. To the vain and happy mother-octopus, the bunch of goggled and squirming fringes which she has given birth to is beautiful beyond imagination, she cannot take her eyes off it, whereas I would not give a damn for a ton of them. Indeed, to me any octopus is insufferable, and I would not live with one for anything a person could give me. This is not unreasoning prejudice, it is merely nature. We do not invent our tastes in this matter, they come to us with our birth, they are of the many mysteries of our being.

I am a microbe. A cholera microbe. For me there is comeliness, there is grace, there is beauty findable, some way or some where, in greater or lesser degree, in every one of the nationalities that make up the prodigious germ-world—but at the head I place the cholera-germ. To me its beauty has no near competitor. I still remember that in the human world each of the nationalities had a beauty of its own: there was the Italian style, the German style, the French, the American, the Spanish, the English, the Egyptian, the Dahomian, the red Indian, the East Indian and a thousand other styles, civilized and savage, and I also remember that each thought its own style the finest and best—a condition which is repeated here in Blitzowski, from one end of him to the other. From the scrapings of his teeth you can gather, oh, such an array of self-complacent tribes! and from the rotting dollar-bill in his pocket you can accumulate another swarm; and I give you my word that every naked savage in the lot would pass indifferently by Maggie Taylor, the germ-belle of Henryland, if she were still existent, and go into ecstasies over the imagined beauty of some frumpy squaw of his own particular breed who could no more stir me than a cow could. I speak from experience. With my own eyes I have seen a he-buccalis maximus lose his mind over a she-one, accidentally encountered, while right in sight were a dozen surpassingly lovely little cholera-germ witches, each and every of them more tantalizingly delicious to look at than her comrades, if possible. Of course, to my mind that spirilla was a fool; and of course, to his mind I was another one.

It is the way we are made, and we can't help it. I have never married, I shall never marry. Is it because I lost my heart irrecoverably when I lost it to Margaret Adams in America three thousand years ago? It must be so. I think it is so. Once in every century she comes to me in my dream, clothed in immortal youth and imperishable beauty; and in the dream she is as erst my idol, and I adore. But when the dream passes, I am myself again and she but a dim and fair unthrilling memory; I am myself again, and my worship of the budding and beautiful of my own loved microbic race comes back to me, and I know that for another century I shall have no homage for any charm but that which looks out from the blue eyes and plays in the winsome smile of the college-maid whose high privilege it is to carry in her veins the blood of the cholera-germ—oldest and noblest and most puissant of all the race of germs, save only the Plague-Bacillus, at sound of whose mighty name the nations uncover!

I cannot be sure of my human dear one's age, for it was long ago, but I think she was eighteen or nineteen. I think I was three or four years older than she was, but I find myself unable to be exact about it, all such things are so dim in my memory now. I have an impression that the first Napoleon was reigning at the time, or that he had lately fallen at Marathon or Philippi, whichever it was, for I am clear that a world-convulsing event was filling all men's mouths then, and I think it must have been that one. I remember that I had just graduated—class of '53 *—a vast event for me, and not lightly to be misplaced in my memory I should think, and *that* was the year that General Washington went North to assume command of the Hessians, the only time I ever saw him, so far as I remember. I depend mainly on historical events to preserve my connection with my human life, because they stay with me better than minor happenings do, on account of their prominence and importance, and because I have a natural fondness for history and an aptness for mastering its details which Professor Tolliver regarded as quite remarkable, a verdict which greatly pleased me, since history was that learned and illustrious germ's specialty.

I must explain that that "Y.H.," in the above diary-date stands for "year of the Henriad." It was like this arrogant House to cancel and wipe out the preceding ages when it captured the throne, and second-stage history with a new Year One. Speaking as a microbe, and with a microbe's ideas of propriety, I think it was not seemly. Indeed I had felt the same way before I was ever a microbe, for I was among the dissenters when the American Revolution ended successfully and Sir John Franklin and his brother Benjamin got the Diet of Worms to establish a new Year One and name the months *Germinal*, and *Fructidor*, and all that nonsense. Such tremendous readjustments of time should be the prerogative of religions only, I think. Religions achieve real and permanent epochs, whereas no political epoch can be of that character, the very law of all political entities being change, change, unceasing change,—sometimes advancement, sometimes retrogression, but never rest, never repose, never fixity. Religions are of God, and they come from His hand perfect, therefore unimprovable, but policies are of men and microbes, and unstable, like their creators. Evolution is the law of policies: Darwin said it, Socrates endorsed it, Cuvier proved it and established it for all time in his paper on "The Survival of the Fittest." These are illustrious names, this is a mighty doctrine:

---

* NOTE. *Seven thousand years later.* This is the second time this statement has crept in, I do not know how. I wrote it, but I think it is untrue. I do not think I was ever at Yale, except to receive honorary degrees. B.b.B.

nothing can ever remove it from its firm base, nothing dissolve it, but evolution.

IX.

THOSE TAYLOR weddings are a land-mark in my career. It was there that I met a teacher of music whom I was permitted to call Thompson, his right name being too difficult for me. He was a cream-ripening bacullus of good character and considerable education, and was attracted by my singing, because it was so different. He came of his own accord and introduced himself. It made me happy beyond words, for I had long been starving for intellectual companionship. We soon became intimates. He was not a person of importance, therefore he could not advance my material interests, but he introduced me to educated friends of his, and that was service enough. Among these were some humble scientists. Was I happy now? Indeed I was, and most grateful. We were young, and full of enthusiasm; we lost no opportunity of being together. We foregathered as often as the bread-and-butter requirements of our several trades permitted, and in happy comradeship we searched after Nature's secrets.

Sometimes we stole a day from shop, counting-room, hand-organ, etc., and made excursions—botanical, insectivorous, mammiferous, piscatorial, paleontological, and the like, and every now and then, as the years danced by on joyous wing, we had the luck to make quite fortunate discoveries. This went on for ten years. Then all of a sudden came the discovery of discoveries—the fossil flea heretofore mentioned.

X.

W<small>E BOYS</small> had good times in those days. I say boys, because we still felt like boys, and because the term had stayed with us, from old habit, after we had crossed the strictly "young-chap" (boy-) frontier; and naturally enough, for we had crossed it without noticing it. We had been training together ten years. I was 78 (microbe-time), but looked just as I had looked 30 years earlier when I first arrived: that is to say I looked my human age of that date—about 26 or 27. Their age was about 50 when we first met, and they had then looked as humans of 25 to 28 look; the 10 years they had since added, showed: one could see that they had grown older. In my case no shade of change was detectible. My sojourn of 30 years had seemed a life-long stretch of time, to me, yet exteriorly it had not aged me by a day. My face, my figure, my strength, my young vivacity and animation—all these had kept their youth. The boys wondered, and so did I. I puzzled over it privately a good deal. Was there something human left in me? I had been a microbe a considerable part of a human day; could it be that my consciousness was keeping microbe time and my body keeping human time? I couldn't tell, I didn't know anything about it; and moreover, being happy,—and just a little frivolous by nature, perhaps—I didn't care. The mystery of my stuck-fast youth was a valued riddle for the boys: whenever they ran out of science-conundrums they could always fall back upon that and subject it to a new discussion.

Naturally they wanted me to help them do the theorizing, and naturally I dearly wanted to, for the echte † scientist would rather theorize than eat; but I was reluctant. To be fair and honest I should have to do as the scientist always does—I should have to honorably contribute to the discussion every fact within my possession which could by any possibility be related to the matter;

---

† Mark Twain here uses this word from the German language in the sense of "genuine." Ed.

and so I should be obliged to reveal the secret of my earlier existence, and frankly furnish all the particulars. It is not easy to exaggerate the embarrassment of the situation. I wanted to keep the respect of my comrades: to tell them a colossal lie would not be a good way to do that, and certainly the chances were a thousand to one, in my opinion, that they would put just that estimate upon my statement.

Well, we are mere creatures of Circumstance. Circumstance is master, we are his slaves. We cannot do as we desire, we have to be humbly obedient and do as Circumstances command. Command—that is the word; Circumstance never requests, he always commands: then we do the thing, and think *we* planned it. When our circumstances change, we have to change with them, we cannot help it. Very well, there came a time when mine changed. The boys began to get suspicious of me. *Why* did I always shirk, and fumble, and change the subject whenever they wanted me to help theorize upon the mystery of my persistent youthfulness? They took that up, and began to whisper apart. When I appeared among them no face lighted with a welcome for me, I got perfunctory greetings in place of the old hearty ones, the group soon broke up and went away and I was left solitary and depressed. I had been happy always, before; I was always miserable, now.

Circumstances had changed. They commanded a change on my part. Being their slave, I had to obey. There was but one course to pursue if I would get back the boys' confidence and affection: I must frankly empty my human history into the debated mystery and take the consequences. Very well, I shut myself to think out the best way to proceed in the matter. Ought I to make my statement to the comradeship assembled in a body, or would it be wisest to try my history on a couple of the boys, make converts of them, if possible, and get their help in converting the rest? After much thought I inclined toward the latter course.

There were twelve of us. I will remark here that we were all of "good stock," to use the common phrase. We were nobodies, we were not noble, but by descent we were of the blood twelve of the great families or classes from which all the monarchies in Blitzowski drew their hereditary aristocracies. Not one of us had a vowel in his name, but our blood entitled us to acquire vowels, whereas this was not the case with persons of meaner extraction. Mainly, vowels went by favor, of course,—among the high-up,— as in all aristocracies, but minor persons of the Blood could acquire them by merit, purchase, the arts of corruption, and so forth. There was a mighty hunger for these gauds and distinctions, but that was natural, and is one of the indications that the difference between microbes and men is more a matter of physical bulk than anything else.

There was hardly a name among us that I could pronounce, on account of the absence of vowels, and the boys had a deal of trouble in managing my microbe-name, for I used an alias, painstakingly invented by myself, to cover accidents; I had said I was a native of the Major Molar, and so, as that was a far-off and quite unknown country it was rather necessary to have a name that would inspire confidence in the hearer—that is to say a name strange enough to properly fit a strange country. I made it out of a Zulu name and a Tierra del Fuegan name combined, and it consisted of three clucks and a belch, and was one of the most trying names I have ever struck. I could not pronounce it twice the same way myself; and as for the boys they presently gave it up, and only used it, after that, to swear with. They asked me to give them an easier one, and I gave them "Huck," an abbreviation of my American middle name, Huxley. On their side, and to show their thankfulness, they allowed me to change their names, too. I invoiced 45 literary ones, favorites of mine, and after considerable drill we selected the eleven which they could pull off with least danger to their jaws. I here append them; and with each name, the strain of great ancestral blood, or branch of it, that flowed in the veins of the owner; also, family crest:

LEMUEL GULLIVER. *Dôt-Pyogenes. Head of the Pus-breeders.* Crest, *Single dot.*

LURBRULGRUD. *Pair-Dot, Diplococcus,* branch of Suppuration family. Crest, the printer's *colon.*

RIP VAN WINKLE. *Sarcina branch: cuboidal masses.* Crest, *a window-sash.*

GUY MANNERING. *Streptococcus. Erysipelas.* Crest, a *looped chain.*

DOGBERRY. *Acute pneumonia* branch. Crest, *a lance.*

SANCHO PANZA. *Typhoid.* Crest, *jackstraws.*

DAVID COPPERFIELD. Branch—with cilia. Crest, *a radish, with roots adhering.*

COLONEL MULBERRY SELLERS. Branch—with spores. *Lockjaw.* Crest, *a broken needle.*

LOUIS XIV. *Consumption.* Crest, *a ruined spider-web.*

KING HEROD. *Diphtheria.* Crest, *Morse alphabet, wrecked.*

HUCK. *Asiatic Cholera.* Crest, *Group of earth-worms.*

DON QUIXOTTE. *Recurrent Fever.* Crest, *maze of hair-snakes.*

Nobody knows the origin of these illustrious crests, there is no record of the great events which they were intended to commemorate and preserve from oblivion; the events occurred such ages and ages ago that history cannot remember them, and even legend itself has forgotten them. Now then, for an odd thing! I distinctly remember that under the microscope, in the earth, each of these families of microbes *looks like its crest,* whereas when you observe them here, with the microbe eye, they are strikingly beautiful in form and feature, and have not even a remote resemblance to their crests. This is certainly very odd, and to my mind it is most interesting. I think that as a coincidence it ranks away up. There was a time, long ago, when I came near to telling the boys about this curious thing, I was so anxious to examine it and discuss it with them, but I restrained myself. It would not have been prudent. They were a sensitive lot, and I doubt if they would have been pleased. Another thing: they—

But never mind that, for the present; I must get back to the real business of this chapter. In the end, I concluded to take a couple of the boys into my confidence, and let the others wait a while. I chose Gulliver and Louis XIV. I would have preferred Guy Mannering and David Copperfield, for certain reasons, but we were not living in a republic, and I had to think a little about etiquette and precedence. In Gulliver's veins was a quarter of a molecule of the blood of the reigning House, the imperial Henries; and although the imperial Henries did not know it and would not have cared for it if they had, Gulliver cared for it and kept himself—and others— reminded of it. So I had to choose Gulliver, and choose him *first*. Louis XIV had to come next. This was imperative, on account of his great blood—what he had of it. Of course if we had had a Plague bacillus—but we hadn't, so there is no occasion to go into that. Gulliver was clerk in a feed-store, Louis XIV was a pill-constructor in the pharmacy.

I invited that pair to my poor quarters, and they came. It was the evening of the day of the splendid discovery of the monster flea— the discovery of the point of his prodigious claw, to be exact. It was a good time, for our enthusiasm over the discovery had drawn us together again, and we had been like our old selves once more. For days I had been on the point of calling Lem and Louis, but had lost courage every time I had tried to do it, but now I knew the conditions were favorable, and I struck while the iron was hot.

The boys came, and they came in good spirits. I gave them an old-time welcome which touched them, and even brought the moisture to their eyes. I chunked up the poor little cheap fire and made it look its cheerfulest, and we bunched ourselves in front of it with lighted pipes, and with hot punches thereto.

"Oh, come, this is great!" said Louis "this is like old times!"

"Here's to their resurrection!" cried Gulliver; and "drink hearty!" cried I, and we did accordingly.

Then we chatted along, and chatted along, stowing the liquor between paragraphs, for punctuation, until we were become properly mellow and receptive, then I broke ground.

"Boys," I said, "I'm going to make a confession." They glanced at me with interest, not to say apprehension. "You have all wanted me to take a hand and help unriddle the mystery of my arrested development in the matter of age-indications, and I have avoided that subject—not out of perversity, I give you my word, but for a better reason, which I mean to lay before you to-night, and try to convince you that my course was fair and justifiable."

Their eyes beamed gratification, and their tongues put it into cordial words:

"Shake!" they said, and we shook.

"Without a doubt you have all suspected that I had invented an elixir of life, and was preserving my youth with it. Isn't it so?"

They hesitated, then said it was so. They said they had been forced to that conclusion because all their other theorizings had come to nothing. Then they quoted a remark of mine which I had long ago forgotten: a hint which I had thrown out to the effect that perhaps an elixir might be distilled from the chyle in the veins of a ram which—

"Well, you know," continued Louis, who had instanced the remark, "you did throw that out. When you wouldn't talk any more, we took hold of that hint and tried to get at your secret for ourselves. We believed, for a time, that we had succeeded. We made the elixir, and tried it on a lot of decrepit and tottering bacilli, and at first the results were splendid. The poor old things brisked up in a surprising way, and began to go to balls, and do the trapeze, and win foot-races, and show off in all sorts of antic improprieties, and it was the most pathetic and ridiculous spectacle of the century. But all of a sudden every lunatic of them collapsed and went to rags and ruin."

"*I* remember it! Was it you boys that got up the famous sheep-elixir that made such an immense noise for a little while?"

"Yes," said Lem Gulliver, "and we believed you could correct it and perfect it for us if you would, and it grieved us to think you were keeping such a sublime secret to yourself, when the honorable traditions of science required you to reveal it and confer it free of reward upon the public."

"Boys," I said, "I am going to ask you, for old friendship's sake, to believe two things, taking them from my lips without other evidence of their truth. First, that I invented no elixir of life; second, that if I had invented one I would have given it freely to the public. Do you believe?" They answered up promptly:

"By the beard and body of Henry the Great, 861, we do, Huck, and are *glad* to! Shake!"

Which we did.

"Now then," I said, "I will ask you to believe one more thing— which is this: *I don't know the secret of my persistent youth myself.*"

I saw the chill descend upon them. They gazed steadily at me, sorrowfully, reproachfully—until my eyes fell. I waited—and waited—hoping that in charity they would break the miserable silence, but they would not. At last I said—

"Friends, old comrades, hear me, and be kind. You do not believe me, yet upon my honor I have spoken the truth. And now I come to my confession—according to the promise which I made. Possibly it may throw light upon this mystery—I hope it may. I believe there is light in it, but I am not certain, and, as a scientist, I am not permitted to accept anything, howsoever plausible, which cannot meet and conquer the final test, the test of tests—*demonstration.* The first article of my confession is this: *I was not always a cholera-germ.*"

The surprise of it made them gasp—I had suspected it would. But it lifted the solemnities a bit, and that was a good thing.

XI.

YES, IT DID THAT. That remark delivered a blast of ozone into the atmosphere. It was a remark that would fresh-up the curiosity of any person that ever lived. Naturally you couldn't throw it at a pair of trained scientists and not get attention. The new, the unheard-of, the uncanny, the mysterious—how the dullest head welcomes them! The old mystery was riches, here was the match of it, piled on top of it. The scientist is not permitted to exhibit surprise, eagerness, emotion, he must be careful of his trade-dignity—it is the law. Therefore the boys pulled themselves together and masked their eagerness the best they could. There was a studied scientific pause, then Louis, in a voice trembling with calm, opened the engagement—

"Huck, have you spoken figuratively, or are we [to] take that statement on a scientific rating?"

"Scientific."

"If you were not always a cholera-germ, what were you before?"

"An American."

"A what?"

"American."

"This seems—well, it seems vague. I do not understand. What is an American?"

"A man."

"Er—that is vague, too. Lem, do you get it?"

"Search me!" He said it despairingly. Louis returned to the inquest:

"What is a man, Huck?"

"A creature you are not acquainted with. He does not inhabit this planet, but another one."

"*Another* one!"

"*Another* one!" echoed Gulliver. "What do you mean by that, Huck?"

"Why, I mean what I said."

He chuckled amusedly, and said—

"The Major Molar a *planet!* Well, that *is* good, upon my word. Here they've been trying for centuries to track-out and locate the original habitat of the modesty-germ, and . . . *say,* Huck, *that's* settled!"

It irritated me, but I kept the most of my temper down, and said:

"Lem, I never called it so. I wasn't referring to the Major Molar, at all."

"Oh, is *that* so! Say, Huck—"

"I don't know anything *about* the Major Molar, and I don't *care* anything about it. I was never there in my life!"

"What! you were nev—"

"No! I never was. I—"

"Sho! where'd you get that heart-breaking name?"

"Invented it. My real name doesn't resemble it."

"What is your real name?"

"B. b. Bkshp."

"Why, Huck," said Louis, "what did you want to tell so many lies for? What was the good of it?"

"I *had* to."

"Why?"

"Because if I had told the truth they would have put me in the asylum, thinking I was out of my head."

"I don't see how that could happen. Why should the truth have such an effect?"

"Because it would not have been understood, and would have been considered a lie. And a crazy one, at that."

"Come, Huck, you are straining your fancy. I guess you wouldn't have been misunderstood. You—"

"Oh, I like that! Only a minute ago I told *you* two or three truths and you didn't understand me. And when I said I came from another planet, Lem thought I was talking about the Major Molar, that humble little backwoods province! whereas I was referring to —to—hang it, I meant what I *said*—another *planet*. Not Blitzowski, but *another* one."

Then Gulliver broke in:

"Why, you muggins, there *isn't* any other. Lots of germs like to play with the *theory* that there's others, but you know quite well it's only theory. Nobody takes it seriously. There's nothing to support it. Come, Huck, your attitude is distinctly unscientific. Be reasonable—throw that dream-stuff out of your system."

"I tell you it *isn't* dream-stuff; there *is* another planet, and I was reared to maturity in it."

"If that is so, you must know a good deal about it. And perhaps you'll enrich us with as much of it as—"

"You needn't mock! I *can* enrich your knowledge-treasury as it was never enriched before, if you will listen and reflect, instead of making fun of everything I say."

Louis said—

"It isn't fair, Lem. Stop chaffing. How would you like to be treated so?"

"All right. Go on, Huck, tell us about the new planet. Is it as big as this one?"

I found I was going to laugh; so I pretended some smoke went down the wrong way, and this enabled me to cough past the danger-point. Then I said—

"It is bigger."

"Bigger, your granny! How much bigger?"

It was delicate ground, but I thought it wisest to go right on.

"It—well, it is so much bigger that if you were to mislay this planet in it and didn't tie a string to it or mark the place, it would take you a good four thousand years to find it again. In my opinion, *more* than that."

They stared at me a while most thankfully, then Louis got down on the floor so that he could laugh with spacious enjoyment, and Gulliver went behind the door and took off his shirt and brought it and folded it up and laid it in my lap without saying anything. It is the microbe way of saying "that takes the chromo." I threw the shirt on the floor, and told both of them they were as mean as they could be.

That sobered them, and Lem said, "Why, Huck, *I* didn't suppose you were in earnest," and Louis sat up on the floor and began to wipe the tears away, and said, "I didn't either, Huck—I *couldn't*, you know—and it came so sudden, you see."

Then they took their seats again, and tried to look repentant, and *did* look sorry, and Lem asked me to bite off another piece. If it had been almost any one else I would have struck him, but a prudent person doesn't hit one of those deadly pus-breeders when arbitration will do. Louis reproved Gulliver, then the pair set themselves to work to smooth my feathers down and get me in a good humor again; and the kind things they said soon had that effect, for one can't pout long when voices beloved for ten years are playing the old tunes on his heart—so to speak, for the metaphor is mixed. Soon the inquest was going along again, all right. I furnished several minor planetary facts, then Louis said—

"Huck, what is the actual size of that planet, in straight figures?"

"Figures! oh, I couldn't ever! There isn't room enough in this one to hold them!"

"Now there you go again, with your extrav—"

"Here! Come to the window—both of you. Look. How far can you see, across that plain?"

"To the mountains. Sixty-five miles."

"Come to this opposite side. Now how far do you see?"

"There being no mountain-barrier, we can't tell. The plain melts into the sky; there's no way to measure."

I said—

"Substantially, it's limitless receding and fading spaciousness, isn't it?"

"Just so."

"Very well. Let *it* represent that other planet; drop a single mustard seed in the middle of it, and—"

"O, fetch him a drink!" shouted Lem Gulliver; "and fetch it quick, his lie-mill's a-failing him!"

There spoke the practical mind, the unsentimental mind—the railroad mind, it may be called, perhaps. It has large abilities, but no imagination. It is always winter there. No, not just that—call it about the first week of November: no snow, only threats; cloudy, occasional drizzles, occasional wandering fogs drifting along; all aspects a little doubtful, suspicious, counseling wariness, watchfulness; temperature not vicious, not frosty, only chilly; average, about 45 F. It is the kind of mind that does not invent things itself, and does not risk money and worry on the development of another man's invention, and will not believe in its value until other people's money and labor have proved it; but it has been watching, all the time, and it steps promptly forward, then, and is the first to get in on the ground floor and help rake in the profits. It takes nothing on trust, you can't get it to invest in a dream at any discount, nor believe in it; but if you notice you will find that it is always present when the dream comes true—and has a mortgage on it, too.

To Lem Gulliver my planet was a dream, and would remain one, for the present. But to Louis, who had sentiment and imagination it was a poem, and I a poet. And he *said* that handsome thing, too. He said it was plain that I was endowed with a noble and beautiful gift, and that my planet was a majestic conception, a grand and impressive foundation, so to speak, lying ready for the architect's hand; and he said he believed that the genius that could imagine such a foundation was competent to build upon it a very palace of enchantment—a tumult of airy domes and towers, without, a golden wilderness of wonders within, where the satisfied soul might wander and worship, unconscious of the flight of time, uncon—

"O, rats!" said Lem Gulliver, breaking in, "that's just your style, Louis XIV—always jumping in to build a cathedral out of a hatful of bricks. Because he has spread out a big foundation, that's enough for you, you can already see the summer-hotel he's going to put up on it. Now I am not made in that way; I'm ready and willing to take stock in that joint *when* it's built, but—finance it at this stage? oh, I think I *see* myself!"

"Oh, yes," retorted Louis, "that *is* your style, Lem Gulliver, we all know it, and we know what comes of it, too. You are always keeping us back, with your doubts; you discourage everything. If Huck can go on as he has begun, it will be the sublimest poem in all the literatures; and anybody but you would believe that the mind that was able to imagine that mighty foundation is able to imagine the palace too, and furnish the rich materials and put them divinely together. Lie-mill, indeed! You may live to see the day when you will wish God had given *you* such a mill, Lem Gulliver!"

"Oh, go it! all down but nine, set 'em up on the other alley! I'm crushed—I'm routed; but all the same, I copper the hotel—at the present date. If you think he's got the materials for it, all right, it's your privilege; but as for me, I reason that when a person has laid down a foundation the size of that one, it isn't argument that it's a sample, it's argument that you've got his pile. He's empty, Louis—you'll see."

"I don't believe it. You're *not* empty, are you, Huck?"

"Empty? No. I haven't begun, yet."

"There, now, Lem Gulliver, what do you say to that?"

"I say his saying it is no proof. Let him start-up his mill again, that's all. Let him venture!"

Louis hesitated. Lem noticed it, and said, mockingly—

"You're right, Louis, I wouldn't over-strain him."

"I wasn't hesitating on account of fear, Lem Gulliver, and you needn't think it. I was recognizing that it wasn't fair. He is entitled to a recess, to recuperate in. Inspirations are not a mechanical affair, they do not come by command. It may well be—"

"Oh, don't apologize. It's all right; he's empty. I'm not wanting to crowd him. Give him a rest; let him recuperate. It's just as you say: inspirations are not mechanical things—no, they are spiritual. Pass him the jug."

"I don't need it," said I, recognizing that I ought to come to Louis' help. "I can get along without it."

Louis brightened up at that, and said—

"*Do* you think you can go ahead, Huck? do you think you can?"

"I don't only think it, I know it!"

Lem chuckled derisively, and told me to fetch on my "empty-ings."

XII.

So the inquest began again. I was asked to describe my planet. I said—

"Well, as to shape, it is round, and—"

"*Round?*" said Gulliver, interrupting. "What a shape for a planet! Everybody would slide off—why, a cat couldn't stay on it! *Round!* Oh, cork the jug—*he* doesn't need any inspiration! Round! Say, Cholera—"

"Let him alone!" cried Louis, sharply. "There's neither right nor dignity in criticizing the fanciful creations of poesy by the standards of cold reason, Lem Gulliver, and you know it."

"Well, that *is* so, Louis, and I take it back. You see, it sounded just as if he were throwing out a straight fact, and so—well, it caught me off my base."

"I *was* throwing out a fact," I said. "If it must pass as poetry I can't help that, but it's fact, just the same, and I stand by it and stick to it. Louis, it *is* fact, I give you my word of honor it is."

It dazed him. He looked a good deal jumbled up, for a while, then he said, resignedly—

"Well, I feel all adrift. I don't quite know what to do with a situation like this, it's clear out of my experience. *I* don't understand how there could be a round planet, but I believe you *think* there is such a thing, and that you honestly believe you have been in it. I can say that much, Huck, and say it sincerely."

I was pleased, and touched, and said—

"Out of my heart I thank you for that, Louis. It cheers me, and I was needing it, for my task is not an easy one."

This was too sentimental to suit the pus-germ, and he said—

"*Dear* girlies! Oh—oh—*oh,* it is *too* touching! Do it some more."

I do not see how a person can act like that. To me it is a mark of coarseness. I coldly ignored it, I would not condescend to notice it. I reckon that that showed him what I thought about it. I now went calmly on with my work, just as if I was not aware that there had been any interruption. I judged it cut him, but I was cold and stern, and did not care. I remarked that my planet was called the World; that there were many countries and oceans spread over its vast surface—"

"O, hold on!" said Gulliver. "Oceans?"

"Yes—oceans."

"And they are facts too, are they?"

"Certainly."

"Well, then, perhaps you will be good enough to tell me how *they* stay on? What keeps them from spilling off?—those that are on the under side, I mean—in case there *are* any on the under side —and certainly there ought to be, to keep up the uniformity of insanity proper to such a crazy invention as that."

"There *isn't* any under side," I said. "The world keeps turning over in the air all the time."

"Turning over—in the air! Come—is that introduced as a fact, too?"

"Yes—and it is a fact."

"Turns over in the air, and doesn't fall! Is that it?"

"Yes."

"Doesn't rest on anything? Is that it?"

"Yes."

"What's it made out of? Is it gas, in a soap bubble?"

"No. Rocks and dirt."

"Turns over in the air, doesn't rest on anything, is made out of rocks and dirt, and doesn't fall! Seems too good to be true! What's the reason it doesn't fall?"

"It is kept in its place by the attraction of other worlds in the sky; and the sun."

"*Other* worlds!"

"Yes."

"Well! So there's more, then?"

"Yes."

"How many?"

"Nobody knows. Millions."

"Millions! Oh, sweet Maria!"

"You can make as much fun as you want to, Lem Gulliver, but all the same it's true. There are millions of them."

"Say—couldn't you knock off a few? just a few, you know, for cash?"

"I've told you—and you can believe it or not, just as you please."

"Oh, *I* believe it—oh, yes indeedy! I could believe a little thing like that with both hands tied behind me. Are they big, Huck, or little?"

"Big. The world is a puny little thing compared to the most of them."

"How handsome of you to allow it! Now *that's* what I call *real* magnanimity. It humbles me. I bow to it."

He was going on with his mean sarcasms, but Louis was so ashamed of him, and so outraged to see me treated so ungenerously when I was evidently speaking the truth, or at least speaking what I believed to be the truth, that he cut in and shut Gulliver off in the midst of his small-arm gun-play.

"Huck," he said, "what are the components of the World, and their proportions?"

"Offer an amendment!"—this from the tiresome pustule—"call it the Bubble. If it flies, that's what it is; if it's solid, it's a lie; either a lie or supernatural. Supernatural lie, *I* think."

I took no notice of his drivel, I would not stoop to it. I addressed my answer to Louis:

"Three-fifths of the World's surface is water. Seas and oceans. That is to say, salt water and undrinkable."

Of course Lem broke in:

"Oh, my land, *that* won't do! it would take ten million mountain ranges of pure salt to keep it up to standard, and *then* it wouldn't. Come—what *makes* it salt? That's it. Out with it—don't stop to invent. What *makes* it salt?"

I simply answered—

"I don't know."

"Don't *know!* The idea! Don't know!"

"No, I don't. *What makes your Great Lone Sea rancid?*"

I scored, that time! He couldn't say a word. It crumpled him up like sitting down on a plug hat. I was tickled to the pericardium; so was Louis, for it was a corker, now I tell you! You see, Science had been fussing for ages over the riddle of what supplies the waters of the Great Lone Sea; the riddle of whence they could come in such miraculous quantity was persistently and exasperatingly insolvable —just as was the case with earthscience in its effort to find the source of the sea's salt-supply.

After a little, Louis said—

"Three-fifths of the surface is a mighty quantity. If it should overflow its banks there would be a catastrophe that would be remembered."

"It did it once," I said. "There was a rain-storm which lasted forty days and forty nights, and buried the whole globe out of sight, mountains and all, for eleven months."

I thought the pathos of the stupendous disaster to life would stir them; but no—with the true scientist, science always comes first, the humanities later. Louis said—

"Why didn't it *stay* buried? What reduced the water?"

"Evaporation."

"How much of it did evaporation carry off?"

"The water covered mountains six miles high, which overlooked ocean-valleys five miles deep. Evaporation carried off the upper six miles."

"Why didn't it get the rest? What stopped it?"

I had not thought of that before, and the question embarrassed me. But I did not show it, beyond a catching of the breath, and maybe an anxious look in the face, and before these had time to rouse suspicion I had scraped up an emergency-answer:

"There,"—with a just-perceptible pressure on the word—*"there* the law of evaporation is restricted to the upper six miles. Below that line it can't work."

The boys looked at me so sadly, and withal so reproachfully, that I was sorry for myself, and dropped my eyes. There was one of those oppressive silences, for a time,—the kind, you know, that start at a weight of 30 pounds to the square inch and add 30 per second—then Lem Gulliver fetched a deep sigh and said—

"Well, it certainly is the insanest country that ever *I've* struck. But I make no moan; I'm getting hardened to its freaks. Hand me another, Huck. Sock it to me! One—two—three—let her go, Gallagher! *Say*—three-fifths is salt water; what's the next detail?"

"Ice and desert. But there's only one-fifth of that."

"Only! Only's good! *Only* one-fifth ice and desert! Oh, *what* a planet! *Only* one-f—"

The scorn of it was unendurable, it scorched me like fire. In a fury I threw up my hand—he stopped—and almost to my tongue's end leaped the words—

"Look at *your* planet! A third of it is—" †

But I caught myself in time. Slowly I closed my mouth, slowly I lowered my threatening hand. I was bred in an atmosphere of refinement, I was refined by nature and instinct, and I could not sully my lips with the word. We are strange beings, we seem to be free, but we go in chains—chains of training, custom, convention, association, disposition, environment—in a word, Circumstance— and against these bonds the strongest of us struggle in vain. The proudest of us and the meanest meet upon a common level, the

---

† Cancelled word was "guts."

rankless level of servitude. King, cobbler, bishop, tramp—all are slaves, and no slave in the lot is freer than another.

I was burning, I was blazing! I had been caring nothing for my lost World; at bottom I was even despising it, so loyal was I in my admiration for the planet which was become so dear to me by reason of my microbe blood; but this scorn of that lost home of mine turned me into its champion, and I jumped to my feet, white to the lips with anger, and burst out with—

"Silence, and listen! I have spoken the truth—and only the truth, so help me God! That World *is,* as compared with your planet, as is that horizonless plain yonder to a grain of sand! And yet it itself is nothing—less than nothing—when its littleness is brought into contrast with the vast bulk of the millions of suns that swim those seas of space wherein it paddles lonely and unnoticed, save by its own sun, its own moon. And what is a sun, and what is a moon? I will tell you. That sun is a hundred thousand times the bulk of that World; it is made of white fire, and flames in the far zenith 92,000,000 miles away, and pours its floods of light upon the World all the day; and when the black darkness of the night comes, then comes the moon, drifting through the distant blue, and clothes the World in mellow light. *You* know no night, and you know no day that is like the World's day. You know a light that is lovelier than these—be grateful! You live in an eternal day of soft and pearly light through which trembles and shimmers unceasingly the dainty and delicate fires of the opal—be grateful! it is your possession, and yours alone—no light that shines on any other land is like it; none possesses its charm, its witchery, none is so gentle, so dreamy, so charged with healing for the hurt mind and the broken spirit.

"There that little World—so unimaginably vast, compared with yours!—paddles about in a shoreless solitude of space; and where are those millions of others? Lost!—vanished! invisible, when the great sun rides in the sky; but at night—oh, there they are! colossal black bulks, lumbering by? No!—turned to mere glinting sparks by distance!—a distance not conceivable by such as you! The vault is sown thick with them, the vault is alive with them, trembles with them, quivers with them! And through their midst rises a broad

belt of their like, uncountable for number—rises and flows up into
the sky, from the one horizon, and pours across and goes flooding
down to the other—a stupendous arch, made all of glittering vast
suns diminished to twinkling points by the awful distance—and
where is that colossal planet of mine? It's *in* that Belt—somewhere,
God knows where! It wanders there somewhere in that immeasur-
able ocean of twinkling fires, and takes up no more room and gets
no more notice than would a firefly that was adrift in the deeps of
the opal skies that bend over imperial Henryland!

"Now then, take it or leave it! I've told you the truth, and there's
not a force in this planet that can make me take back a word of
it!"

All aglow with enthusiasm, Louis burst out—

"By God, there stands the palace!—I believed he could build
it!"

"And by God, there stands the supernatural lie!—I *knew* he
could hatch it!"

XIII.

B Y NOW it was two o'clock in the morning, and my little
thought-recorder girl—always punctual to the minute—entered
and broke up the sitting. The boys rose to go, but they said they
didn't want to, and they said it with the most evident sincerity, too.
Louis said it was inspiring and uplifting to listen to such a poem,
and Lem Gulliver said with fervency, he wished he had my talent,
so help him God he would never speak the truth again. I had never
seen them so moved. Louis said my art was perfect, and Lem said
the same. Louis said he was going to practice it himself, and Lem
said he was, too; but both said they could never hope to get up to
my plane. They both said they had had a wonderful evening.
These great praises made me feel so happy that I seemed [to be]
walking on air, and I had no words to thank the boys enough for
them. What a change it was from that long season of aching

depression and disfavor! My atrophied nerves cast off their apathy, and along them raced and rioted fresh new life and pleasure; I was like one risen from the dead.

The boys wanted to rush away to the fossil-mine and tell the whole thing to the nine others—just what I was hoping for! My original scheme would succeed, now—these missionaries would convert the rest of the comradeship, and I should be in full favor again, I felt sure of it. And now they did me a parting honor: by their own invitation we stood up and clinked glasses, shouting—thus:

Louis. "To Old Times Come Again—to stay!"

Lem. "Bumpers! no heel-taps!"

Huck. "And God bless us all!"

Then they sallied out unsteadily, arm-locked, and singing a song I had taught them in those same Old Times—a song disused this many a heavy day—

"Goblskvet liikdwzan hooooclk!" *

In the enthusiasm born of our great fossil-find, we had agreed to dig right along, twenty-four hours in the day, and day after day indefinitely, in order that we might get as far along as possible with the excavating before the news should get abroad and the interruptions begin; but I was deep in a History of the World which I was dictating, to the end that my knowledge in that matter might not fade out and be lost, and I was minded to finish it, now, and make good my share of the flea-mine agreement when it was done. The history of Japan would complete the formidable enterprise; I would put that together at the present sitting, then I should be free and could devote my energies to the fossil flea with a contented spirit and an undivided mind. Meantime the missionarying would be going on, out there at the mine, and might I not venture to hope that by the time I appeared there the conversions would have been accomplished—provided I strung out the story of Japan pretty elaborately? Seemed so to me.

By good luck the thought-recording machine was out of order; it would take a little time to fix it. It would take more if I taught

---

* Trans. "We won't go home till mor-or-ning—
Till daylight doth appear!"

Catherine of Aragon how to do it herself—so I adopted that plan. She was a dear little thing, with a pretty good head, and quite teachable; for whereas she was a "benevolent" microbe—that is to say, a daughter of the people, the masses, the humble hard-workers, the ill-paid, the oppressed, the despised, the unthanked, the meek and docile bulwark of the Throne, without whose support it would tumble to ruin like the card-house it really was—whereas, as I say, she was of this breed and therefore an ass by right of birth, and by old heredity entitled to be profoundly stupid, she was not stupid at all. She wasn't, because, by reason of an ancestral adventure of ancient date, part of a drop of cancer-blood had trickled down to her which should have trickled down to somebody else, and that little stain was worth much to Catherine. It lifted her mentalities away above the average intellectual level of her caste, for the cancers are bright, and have always been so. The other aristocracies breed a bright specimen now and then, but with the cancers, and with the cancers only, brightness is the rule.

Catherine was a neighbor's child, and she and her *Geschwister* were contemporaries and comrades of our earliest Taylor-litter—I mean the one I first knew. Both of these litters had been my teachers in the local tongues, and in return I had conferred English (pretending it was Major Molar) upon hundreds of kids belonging to the two batches—a *sort* of English, at any rate, and not really bad for "benevolents"—but Catherine learned it the quickest of them all, and was a daisy at it. Indeed, she spoke it like a native. I always used the English language when talking with her, in order to keep her in practice and keep myself from forgetting it.

I did not choose that name for her—Catherine of Aragon. I should not have thought of such a thing, for it was quite unsuitable, she was so little. In a World-microscope she would not have showed up at all until she was magnified eighteen hundred diameters. But when she did show up she would command exclamations of delight and admiration, for the Observer would have to grant that she was very very pretty—pretty as a diatom. No, she chose the name herself. She lit upon it one day when we were doing the History of England, and she was quite carried away by it and said it was the sweetest thing out of doors. She had to

have it, she couldn't do without it; so she took it. Her name, before
that, was Kittie Daisybird Timpleton, and quite suited her petite
and dainty figure and exquisite complexion and frivolousness, and
made her look charming. In replacing unpronounceable native
names with easy human ones I always tried to select such as would
not invoke prejudice and uncharitable comment by being in violent
contrast with the style of the persons decorated with them.

But she wanted to be Catherine of Aragon, and was ready to cry
about it, so I had to let her have her way, though,—so applied,—it
had no more fitness nor point than there was in Lem Gulliver's
latest nick-name for me, which was Nancy. Lem Gulliver is vulgar,
and resents refinement, and thinks any person who is refined is
effeminate.

However, she wanted it, so I yielded and let her have it. It was
just an accident that she ever heard of Catherine of Aragon. It
happened one night when I was dictating historical thoughts into
the Recorder. You do not dictate *words,* you understand, but only
thoughts—*impressions*—and they are not articulated; that is to say,
you do not frame the impressions into words, you deliver them in
blocks, a whole chapter in one blast—in a single second, you know
—and the machine seizes them and records them and perpetuates
them for time and eternity in that form; and there they are, and
there they glow and burn forever; and so luminous are they, and so
clear and limpid and superbly radiant in expression that they make
all articulated speech—even the most brilliant and the most perfect
—seem dull and lifeless and confused by comparison. Ah, if a
person wants to know what an intellectual aurora borealis is like,
with the skies all one tumultuous conflagration and downpour of
divine colors and blinding splendors, let him connect-up a Recorder
and turn on one of those grand poems which the inspired Masters
of a million years ago dreamed into these machines!

Yes, you sit silent and dictate to the machine with your soul, not
with your mouth; but sometimes you utter a chance word without
being aware of it, you are so absorbed. And so that was the way Cat
got her new name. I was doing impressions of Henry VIII, and was
so stirred by some of his cruelties toward his first queen that I
unconsciously exclaimed, "Alas, poor Catherine of Aragon!"

That I should break out in *speech* while dictating, was such a surprise to Kittie that it knocked the self-possession out of her and she stopped turning the crank to look at me and wonder. Then the stately flow and music of the name knocked it in again and she exclaimed with emotion—

"Oh, how sweet, oh, how recherché! Oh, I could die for such a name as that! Oh, I think it is *so* chahming!"

Do you notice? Just a dear little bundle of self-complacencies and affectations,—that was what she was. A single speech is enough to expose her. Even the word "die" is an affectation, for she couldn't *think* die; she was a microbe, and could only think "disintegrate." But you would not catch *her* saying she could disintegrate for such a name as that; no, it would not be foreign enough, not affected enough.

Well, that was some time ago, when we were doing "England, From Brutus to Edward VII." Now then, when she came in, that morning, and interrupted that nice time I was having with Lem and Louis, I noticed an astonishing change in her: she was grave, dignified, calm, reposeful—all her notice-begging fussy little airs and graces and simperings and smirkings were gone, her chewing-gum corals were gone, her brass bracelets were gone, her glass aigrette was gone, the manufactured waves were gone from her hair, the spit-curl was gone from her forehead, her gown was dark and plain and neat, simplicities and sincerities sat upon her everywhere, and looked out of her eyes, and found unconscious utterance in her words and her tones when she spoke. I said to myself, "Here is a mystery, a miracle: lo, Kittie Daisybird Templeton is no more, the bogus Catherine of Aragon is no more: this is that bogus Catherine transmuted into the true metal, and worthy to wear the name!"

While she tinkered at the machine, repairing it under my instructions, I inquired into the cause of the transformation, and she explained the matter at once—simply, frankly, unembarrassedly, even with a sort of glad and grateful eagerness, as it seemed to me. She said she had picked up the book called "Science and Wealth, With Key to the Fixtures," with the idea of finding out, for herself, what there was about it to make the new sect, popularly

and ironically called the Giddyites, set so much store by it—with
the unexpected result that within ten minutes a change began to
take place in her—an etherealizing change—a change which was
volatilizing her flesh and turning it to spirit. She read on and on,
the transforming process continued; within the hour it was complete, and she was all spirit, the last vestige of flesh was gone. I
said—

"Catherine, you don't look it; there must be some mistake."

But she was quite sure there was not; and she was so earnest
about it that I could not doubt, and did not doubt, that she believed
what she was saying. To me it was a delusion; an hour or two
earlier I would have *said* so, and risen superior to her, and looked
down upon her compassionately from that high altitude, and would
have advised her to put the foolish and manifest fraud out of her
head and come back to common sense and reasonableness. But not
now. No. An hour or two ago and *now*—those were two quite
different dates. Within that brief space I had suffered a sea-change
myself. I had seen a certainty of mine dubbed a delusion and
laughed at by a couple of able minds—minds trained to searchingly
and exhaustively examine the phenomena of Nature, and segregate
fact from fancy, truth from illusion, and pronounce final judgment
—and these competent minds had puffed my World away without
a moment's hesitancy, and without the shadow of a misgiving.
They thought they knew it was an illusion. I knew it wasn't.

The list of things which we absolutely know, is not a long one,
and we have not the luck to add a fresh one to it often, but I
recognized that I had added one to mine this day. I knew, now, that
it isn't safe to sit in judgment upon another person's illusion when
you are not on the inside. While you are thinking it is a dream, he
may be knowing it is a planet.

I was well satisfied in my mind that Catherine was the prey of an
illusion, but I had no disposition to say so, and so I didn't say it. My
wounds were too sore for that, as yet. But I talked her new
condition over with her, and she made the matter very interesting.
She said there was no such thing as substance—substance was a
fiction of Mortal Mind, an illusion. It was amusing to hear it!

Whose illusion? Why, anybody's that didn't believe as she did. How simple—and how settling! Oh, dear, we are all like that. Each of us knows it all, and *knows* he knows it all—the rest, to a man, are fools and deluded. One man knows there is a hell, the next one knows there isn't; one man knows high tariff is right, the next man knows it isn't; one man knows monarchy is best, the next one knows it isn't; one age knows there are witches, the next one knows there aren't; one sect knows its religion is the only true one, there are sixty-four thousand five hundred million sects that know it isn't so. There is not a mind present among this multitude of verdict-deliverers that is the superior of the minds that persuade and represent the rest of the divisions of the multitude. Yet this sarcastic fact does not humble the arrogance nor diminish the know-it-all bulk of a single verdict-maker of the lot, by so much as a shade. Mind is plainly an ass, but it will be many ages before it finds it out, no doubt. Why do we respect the opinions of any man or any microbe that ever lived? I swear [I] don't know. Why do I respect my own? Well—that is different.

Catherine said there was no such thing as pain, or hunger, or thirst, or care, or suffering of any kind: these were all fictions of the Mortal Mind; without the presence of substance they could not exist, save as illusions, therefore they had no existence in fact, there being no such thing as substance. She called these fictions "claims"; and said that whenever a claim applied, she could drive it away in a moment. If it was a pain, for instance, she had only to repeat the formula of "the Scientific Statement of Being," as set down in the book, then add the words "there is no such thing as pain," and the detected fiction vanished away. She said there was no so-called disease and no so-called pain in all the long roll of microbic ailment-fictions that could not be routed and dismissed by the method above described. Except teeth-claims. They were fictions like the rest, but it was safest to carry them to the dentist. This was not immoral, not irreligious, for it was permitted by the finder of the Giddyite religion, who took her own teeth to the painless-gas establishment, and in that way made the departure from principle holy.

Catherine said cheerfulness was real, and depression of spirits a fiction. She said there was not a care, not a sorrow, not a worry left in her soul. She looked it; I had to confess it!

I asked her to put the principles of her sect into a few clear sentences, so that I could understand them and keep them in my head, and she did it, quite without effort:

"Mortal Mind, being the idea of Supreme Refraction exhibited and sanctified in the Bacterium in correspondence and co-ordination with Immortal Mind in suspension, which is Truth, All-Good follows, of necessity, precipitating and combining with the elements of the Good-Good, the More-Good and the Ultimate or Most-Good, sin being a fiction of Mortal Mind operating upon Absence of Mind, nothing can be otherwise, Law being Law and hence beyond jurisdiction, wherefore the result is paramount—and being paramount, our spirits are thus freed from Substance, which is an Error of Mortal Mind, and whosoever so desires, can. This is Salvation."

She asked me if I believed it, and I said I did. I didn't really believe it, and I don't now, but it pleased her and was a little thing to say, so I said it. It would have been a sin to tell her the truth, and I think it is not right to commit a sin when there is no occasion for it. If we would observe this rule oftener our lives would be purer.

I was greatly pleased with this conversation, because it contained things which seemed to show that the microbe mind and the human mind were substantially alike and possessed reasoning powers which clearly placed them above the other animals. This was very interesting.

I had an opportunity, now, to look into a matter which had been in my mind a long time—the attitude of the microbe toward the lower animals. In my human state I had wanted to believe that our humble comrades and friends would be forgiven and permitted to be with us in the blessed Land of the Hereafter. I had had difficulty in acquiring this belief, because there was so much opposition to it. In fact I never did get it where it would stick. Still, whenever and wherever there was a friendly dog wagging his affectionate tail, and looking up at me with his kind eyes and asking me to swap love for love with him; or a silken cat that climbed into my lap, uninvited, for a nap, thus flattering me with her trust; or a gracious horse that took me for a friend just by the look of me and pushed his nose into my pocket for possible sugar and made me wish he could impart his nature to my race and give it a lift up toward his own—whenever these things happened they always raised that hope in me again and set it struggling toward concrete belief once more.

When I talked with opposers about this, they said—

"If you admit those because they are innocent of wrong by the law of their make, as you say, what are you going to do about the mosquito, the fly, and those others? Where are you going to draw the line? They are all innocent alike; come—where are you going to draw the line?"

It was my custom to say I didn't draw it at all. I didn't want the fly and his friends, but no matter; what a man could stand here he could stand there, and moreover there was a high matter concerned —common justice. By even the elemental moralities, it would be unjust to let in any creature made honor-worthy by deriving its spirit and life from God's hand and shut any other out.

But it never settled it. The opposer was human, and knew he was right; I was human, and knew I was right. There isn't anybody that isn't right, I don't care what the subject is. It comes of our having reasoning powers.

Once I carried the matter to a good and wise man who. . . .

XIV.

I T WAS a clergyman. He said—

"Let us proceed logically; it is the law of my training, and is a good law. Helter-skeltering is bad: it starts in the middle and goes both ways, it jumbles the points instead of ranking them according to seniority or importance, it gets lost in the woods and doesn't arrive. It is best to start at the beginning. You are a Christian?"

"I am."

"What is a creature?"

"That which has been created."

"That is broad; has it a restricted sense?"

"Yes. The dictionary adds, '*especially* a living being.' "

"Is that what we commonly mean when we use the word?"

"Yes."

"Is it also what we *always* mean when we use it without a qualifying adjective?"

"Yes."

"Used without qualification, then, a dog is a creature?"

"Certainly."

"A cat?"

"Yes."

"A horse, a rat, a fly, and all the rest?"

"Of course."

"What verse is it which authorizes the missionary to carry the gospel to the pagans?—to the willing and to the unwilling alike."

" 'Whatsoever ye would that men should do unto you—' "

"*No!* It is infinitely broader: 'Go ye into *all the world* and preach the gospel to *every* CREATURE.' Is that language plain and clear, or is it foggy and doubtful?"

"Plain and clear, I should say. I cannot see anything doubtful about the meaning of it."

"How would you go about doctoring the meaning of it so as to make it apply to man only, and shut out the other creatures? What art would you employ?"

"Well, the arts of shuffling and indirection, adroitly used, could accomplish it, but I like it best as it is. I would not wish to change it."

"You are aware that the plain meaning stood at its full value, unchanged and unchallenged, during fifteen hundred years?"

"I am."

"You are aware that the intelligence of the Fathers of the Church ranks as high to-day as does the intelligence of any theologian that has followed them, and that they found no fault with that language and did not try to improve its meaning?"

"Yes."

"You are aware that the change is a quite modern freshet of intelligence, and that up to so late a time as three centuries ago the Christian clergy were still including the dumb animals in the privileges of that great commandment, and that both Catholic priest and Protestant were still preaching the gospel to them, in honorable obedience to its uncompromising terms?"

"I am aware of it."

"In commanding that the gospel be carried to all the World and preached to every creature, what was the object in view?"

"The salvation of the hearers."

"Is there any question that that was the object?"

"None has been suggested. It has not been disputed."

"Then not two, but only one inference is deducible from the language of that commandment when it is spared jugglery and is conscientiously examined: that *all* of God's creatures are included in His merciful scheme of salvation. Heaven will not look strange to us; the other animals will be there, and it will look like home, and *be* home."

This was a rational view, at last, a just view, a fair and righteous view, a generous view, and one in accord with the merciful character of the Creator. It removed all my doubts, all my perplexities, it brought conviction to me, and planted my feet upon solid ground. The clergyman was right, I felt it to my marrow, and in the best words I could command I tried to make him understand how grateful I was to him. My feelings were revealed in my words, and *they* at least were eloquent I knew, whether the words were or not, for he was much moved. I wished he would say that pleasant sentence over again, and over again, and still again, it had been so contenting to my spirit; and really, he seemed to divine that thought of mine, for without my saying anything he uttered it at once, and with emphasis—

"Yes, *all* the creatures! Be at rest as to that—they will be there; no creature designed, created, and appointed to a duty in the earth will be barred out of that happy home; they have done the duty they were commissioned to do, they have earned their reward, they will all be there, even to the littlest and the humblest."

"The *littlest.*" The words sent a subtle chill down my hot veins.

Something rose in me: was it a shadowy doubt? I looked up vacantly, muttering absently—

"The disease-germs? the microbes?"

He hesitated—some little time; then changed the subject.

Well, as I have said before, the matter of whether our humble friends go with us to our happy future home or not had never lost its interest with me, and so I thought I would introduce it, now, and talk it over with Catherine. I asked her if she thought the dogs and the horses and so on would go with us microbes and still be our pets and comrades. It raised her interest at once. She said I knew she had formerly belonged to the most widely spread of all the many religions of the planet—the Established Church of Henry-land—and didn't I know that that question was always being privately discussed and fussed over by the membership whenever the authorities were not around? didn't I know that?

Yes, oh, yes, I said, certainly I knew it, but it had escaped my mind. It would have hurt her if I had told her I hadn't even heard of it before, but I think it is not right to hurt a person who is not doing any harm. Lem Gulliver would have told her, for he has no moral sense; it is nothing to him whether he does right or doesn't. It is the way he is made, and so it may be that he is not responsible for it. But I do not do right because I am responsible, and I do not do right because it is right to do right, I think it is a low motive; I do it because—because—well I have a lot of reasons, I do not recollect which ones are the main ones now, but it is of no consequence, anyway. She said she felt a strong interest in the subject, and had very decided notions about it—that is, she *had* had—and would gladly state them for me—that is, her present ones. But not in her own language, for that was not allowed; members of her sect must not exhibit religious matters in their own words, because they would be incompetently put together and would convey error. Then she began, and went along so trippingly that I saw she had her Book by heart:

"As concerns this question, our inspired Founder instructs us that the fealty due from the Ultimate in connection with and subjection to the intermediate and the inferential, these being of necessity subordinate to the Auto-Isothermal, and limited subliminally by this contact, which is in all cases sporadic and incandescent, those that ascend to the Abode of the Blest are assimilated in thought and action by the objective influence of the truth which sets us free, otherwise they could not."

There she stopped. Apparently I had wandered, and missed a cog somewhere, so I apologised and got her to say it again. She said it the same way. It certainly sounded straightforward and simple, yet I couldn't seem to get it, quite. I said—

"Do you understand it, Catherine?"

She said she did.

"Well, I *seem* to, but I can't make sure. Which ones do *you* think it is that ascend to the Abode of the Blest?"

"We are not allowed to explain the text, it would confuse its meaning."

"Well, then, don't do it. I do not pretend to revere it, still I would not like that to happen to it. But you can tell me this much, anyway, without doing any harm. (You needn't speak, you know, just nod your head; I'll understand.) Which ones is it that could not?—could not *otherwise*, I mean? It seems to be the sporadics, but it looks as if it might be the incandescents. *Is* it the sporadics? Don't speak, just nod. Nod, or shake, according to the facts."

But she refrained. She said it would amount to explaining, and was not allowable.

"Well, are they *animals?* Surely you can tell me that, Catherine?"

But she couldn't. She was willing to say the formula over again, and as many times as I pleased, but the rules were strict, and would not allow her to add to the formula, or take from it, or change the place of a word, the whole being divinely conceived and divinely framed, and therefore sacred.

It seemed to me that it would have been a good idea to apply this sensible rule to the other Scriptures and paralyse the tinkers with it: the ones that squeezed the animals out of that good and merciful text.

"Well," I said, "say it again, and say it slow. I'll tally-off as you unwind; that is, when I think you've let out as much of an instalment as I can handle without help, I'll give notice and you'll shut down till I take up the slack and stow it, then you'll let out another one—and so on, and so on, till I've got it all. The instalment plan is the best, with this line of goods. Remember—don't rush—slow and careful is the thing. Now then—ready? Play ball!"

"Which?"

"Oh, that's a technicality. If means, Begin. Once more—ready? Unwind!"

She understood, this time, and performed perfectly. Pretty metalically, as to sound, pretty dead-level and expressionless, like a phonograph saying its prayers, but sharp and definite, and quite satisfactory:

"As concerns—this question—our inspired Founder—instructs us that—the fealty due from—the Ultimate in connection with—and subjection to the—intermediate and the inferential, these—being of necessity sub—"

"Halt! I do believe you've dealt me a sequence. Let me look at my hand."

But it was a disappointment. Good cards, but no two of the same suit. Still, it was a hand that might be patched, perhaps. "Interme-diate—Inferential"—that really looked like a pair. I felt encouraged, and said:

"Go on, Catherine, I'll draw to fill. Give me three."

But she is not educated, and she did not understand. But I did not explain; I said the laws of the cult didn't allow it. This was a sarcasm, but it didn't penetrate. I often fired little things like that at her, but only because she was sarcasm-proof, and they wouldn't hurt. I have a good deal of natural wit, and when a person is that way, he enjoys to listen to himself do it. If such a person gets the right encouragement, there is no limit to how high up he can develop. I think it was owing almost entirely to Uncle Assfalt that I got mine developed so high. He loved to hear me, and that made me keep working at it. The time that I said that about the cow that —that—well, the rest of it has gone out of my memory, now, I can't recollect what it was she did, but it was that funny it seemed like Uncle Assfalt was never going to get done laughing over it. He fairly rolled on the floor in agonies. I said—

"Never mind the three, Catty, it's another technicality. This instalment is a failure; let us try another. Go ahead."

But it was another failure. It was just a snow-flurry on a warm day: every flake was distinct and perfect, but they melted before you could grab enough to make a ball out of them. So I said—

"We will try another way. Sometimes, you know, if you dart a swift glance over a tough foreign sentence you capture the general meaning of it, whereas if you stop to meddle with details you're gone. We'll try that method. Now then—no commas, no dashes, no pauses of any sort: start at the beginning and buzz the whole incantation through just in one solid whiz—swift, you know— Empire Express—no stop this side of Albany. One—two—three— let her *go!*"

My, it was a grand effect! Away off you could hear it coming— next it was in sight and raging down the line like a demon chasing a Christian—next second, *by* she plunges, roaring and thundering, and vomiting black smoke—next, round the corner and out of sight! Apparent dividend: scurrying leaves, whirling dust, a shower of cinders. Even these settle and quiet down, after a little, and then there isn't anything left at all.

When the furniture stopped whirling around and there was only one Catherine instead of a ring of Catherines, I said I was willing to surrender if I could march out with my side-arms. Then, being defeated, I felt malicious, and was going to say I believed the Founder had a "claim," and that it was a mental one, but I didn't say it. It would only hurt Catherine, and she couldn't defend herself, because she wasn't built like some, and hadn't any wit; and so it would not be generous in me to say it. Put *me* in *her* place, and I would be back before you could wink, with a withering "Perhaps it's *you* that's got the claim!" But not many would think of that. They would think of it next day, but that is the difference between talent and the imitation of it. Talent thinks of it at the time.

I could see that Catherine was disappointed about the failure; she had a great affection for her new cult, and it grieved her to see it miss the triumph she had expected it was going to achieve—I thought I could read this in her face, poor thing—so I hadn't the heart to confess I was permanently done trying to strike oil in that formation: I let on that by and by when I got leisure I was going to torpedo that well, and was feeling sure I should turn loose a gusher —a thousand barrels a day, I said; and when I saw how glad it made her, I raised it to four thousand, the expense being the same. I told her to empty the incantation into the recorder—which she did at once—and leave it there. I said I thought that what it needed was, to be *disarticulated,* and resolved into its original elements; that the way it was now, the words broke up the sense—interrupted the flow of meaning, you see—jumbled it all up, you understand, when there was no occasion; the machine would mash the words together into a pulp, and grind the pulp around the way an arastra does with pulverised ores from the mill, and when you come to clean up at the week-end, there you are! there's your virgin gold, caught tight and fast in the amalgam! there's your clean and clear four dollars' worth, a thousand carats fine, *rescued!* Every yellow grain captured, safe and sound, and nothing left behind but eleven tons of slush! It's four dollars, and every dollar worth a hundred cents on the scales; it's not coined, but that's nothing, you've got the full-par *impression,* and when you've got that you've got the whole thing: mint it if you want to, it's your privilege: coin it and stamp Henry's head on it, and it's worth par all over Henryland, but leave it as it is and it's worth par from one end of Blitzowski clean to the other!

Well, it pleased her so, that I wished I had made it nine dollars. For a moment I thought I would do it, but I had scruples about it and refrained. It would be 76 cents a ton, and I knew you couldn't get that out of *that* kind of rock—no, not even with the cyanide. Presently I sighed, and Catherine wanted to know, right away, what was troubling me; she was just that quick in her sympathies, now that her new religion was giving her a chance to stop thinking about her own troubles—in fact she hadn't any, any more, she said. I said—

"I was wishing I had *somebody* that would talk to me about whether the animals are going up there with us or not. You,. see, Catty—"

She made a spring for the window, and cried out—

"Countess! Yonder is Rev. Brother Pjorsky drowsing on the fire-plug. Would you mind asking him to step in here a minute as you pass by him?" Then she returned to her seat, saying, "He'll love to talk with you about it. And he is very nice, too. You remember him, don't you—the time he came here once and took up a collection? No? It was years ago, I thought you would remember it. He is about the same as a priest, but he isn't that—they don't have priests in his sect, but only Brothers, as they call them. He used to be my spiritual father before I was orthodox; or maybe it was before that —or perhaps it was before that again; I remember it was somewhere along there; and so—"

"Why don't you keep a list?"

"List of what?"—proceeding toward the window.

"Salvation-trains. You ought to have a time-table."

"Why?" Oh, that vacant Why! I did hear it *so* often! She could overlook more points than—oh, well she was absolutely immune to wit, it was wasted on her. "There—she's waking him—she's telling him, now. . . . He's nestling, again, but it's all right, he'll come when his nap's out; he won't forget."

"Nap? I thought a microbe never slept. They don't in the Major Molar."

"But he is different. We don't know how to account for it. Nobody knows. It beats the scientists. He is not a native; he comes from the jungles of Mbumbum—emphasis on the antepenultimate —it's a wee little isolated tribe, and almost unknown—its name is Flubbrzwak—"

"Land! what's the matter?" she exclaimed.

I said I was sorry I made her jump; then I explained that I had had a stitch in the side; and it was quite true, too; I did have one once—it was in America, I remember it quite well, though nothing came of it. But that name! It certainly gave me a start, for this is the rare and mysterious microbe that breeds the awful disease called the African Sleeping Sickness—drowses the victim into a dull and heavy lethargy that is steeped with death; he lies there week after week, month after month, his despairing dear ones weeping over him, shaking him, imploring him to wake, beseeching him to open his eyes, if only a moment, and look into theirs once more—just once more—one little look of love and blessing and farewell. But let their hearts break!—it is what the malady was invented for; he will never wake any more.

Isn't it curious and interesting?—the fact that not a microbe in all this microbe-stuffed planet of Blitzowski ever suspects that he is a harmful creature! They would be astonished and cruelly hurt if you should tell them such a thing. The Nobles eat the Ignobles— that is all right, it was intended they should, and so there is no wrong in that, and they would tell you so; in turn, the Ignobles eat *them,* and neither is *that* objectionable; both races feed on Blitzowski's blood and tissue, and that also is proper, foreordained and void of sin; also, they rot him with disease, they poison him, but *that* they do not know, that they do not suspect. *They* don't know he is an animal, they take him for a planet; to them he is rocks and dirt and landscape and one thing and another, they think he has been provided for them, and they honestly admire him, enjoy him, and praise God for him. And why not? they would be ingrates and unworthy of the blessings and the bounties that have been lavished upon them if they did otherwise. Without being a microbe I could not feel this so deeply; before I was a microbe I do not believe I felt it at all. How alike we all are! all we think about is ourselves, we do not care whether others are happy or not. When I was a man, I would have turned a microbe from my door hungry, anytime. Now I see how selfish I was; now I should be ashamed to do such a thing. So would any person that had any religion. The very littleness of a microbe should appeal to a person, let alone his friendlessness. Yet in America you see scientists torturing them, and exposing them naked on microscope slides, before ladies, and culturing them, and harrying them, and hunting up every way they can think of to extirpate them—even doing it on the Sabbath. I have seen it myself. I have seen a doctor do it; and he not cold from church. It was murder. I did not realize it at the time, but that is what it was, it was murder. He conceded it himself, in light words, little dreaming how mighty they were: he called himself a germicide. Some day he will know to his sorrow that there is no moral difference between a germicide and a homicide. He will find that not even a germ falls to the ground unnoticed. There is a Record. It does not draw the line at feathers.

She said he belonged to the sect of the Magnanimites, and that it was a very good sect, and this Brother as good as the best. She said he and she had always had a fondness for each other when she used to be a Magnanimite, and that that feeling still continued, she was glad to say. She said the countess was orthodox, because she was a kind of a sort of a Noble by marriage, and it would not be good form for her to travel the side-trails to the Abode of the Blest, but she was a good creature and liked the Brother, and he liked her. On she rattled:

"She's a foreigner—the countess. She's a GRQ, and—"

"What's a GRQ?"

"Getrichquick—and she was a lady there; though here, people of her family's condition, being SBE's would have to stick to their proper place, and so—"

"What's an SBE?"

"Soiled-Bread Eater."

"Why *soiled* bread?"

"Because it's earned."

"Because it's *earned?*"

"Yes."

"Does the act of earning it soil it?"

It made her laugh—the idea that I, a grown-up, could be ignorant of an ABC fact like that!—but I detected a sudden happy hunger in her eye which we are all acquainted with, and which I was not sorry to see there: it comes when we think we have discovered that we know something the other person doesn't, and are going to have a chance to unload information into him and surprise him and make him admire us. It wasn't very often that Catherine dropped a *fact* that was new to me, but she often threw an interesting new light upon an old one if I kept shady and allowed her to think the fact itself was a valuable contribution to my treasury. So I generally kept shady. Sometimes I got a profit out of this policy, sometimes I didn't, but on the whole it paid.

My question made her laugh. She repeated it—apparently to taste again the refreshing ignorance of it:

" 'Does the act of earning it soil it?' Why, don't you know—"

She stopped, and looked a little ashamed. I said—

"What's the trouble?"

"You are joking with me."

"Joking? Why should I be joking?"

"Because."

"Because what?"

"Ah, you know very well."

"I don't. I give you my word."

She looked straight in the eye, and said—

"If you are joking, I shall see it. Now I will ask you in earnest, and I think you ought to answer in earnest: Have you ever heard of a nation—a *large* nation—where earning the bread didn't soil it?"

It was my turn to laugh! I started to do it, but—Something moved me to wait a minute; something which suggested that maybe it was not so foolish a question as it seemed. I mused for a while. Great nations began to drift past my mind's eye—habitants of both the planets—and I soon reached a decision, and said—

"I thought it was a foolish question, Catherine, but really it isn't, when a body examines it. I reckon we are pretty full of notions which we got at second hand and haven't examined to see whether they are supported by the statistics or not. I know of a country— through talking with natives of it—where the dignity of labor is a phrase which is in everybody's mouth; where the *reality* of that dignity is never questioned; where everybody says it is an honor to a person that he works for the bread he eats; that earned bread is noble bread, and lifts the earner to the level of the highest in the land; that unearned bread, the bread of idleness, is tainted with discredit; a land where the sayers of these things say them with strong emotion, and think they believe what they say, and are proud of their land because it is the sole land where the bread-earners are the only acknowledged aristocracy. And yet I do see, that when you come to examine into it—"

"I know the land you mean! It's GRQ! Honest—isn't it GRQ?"

"Yes, it is."

"I recognised it in a minute! The countess is always talking about it. She used to love it when she lived there, but she despises it now, and says so, but I reckon she has to talk that way to keep people from doubting that she's been changed and is a real, actual

Henryling, now—and you know, she *is* a real one, realer than the born ones themselves, I know it by the way she talks. Well, she told me about the dignity-of-labor gospeling, and says it's all sham. She says a mechanic is the same there as anywhere. They don't ask him to dinner—plumber, carpenter, blacksmith, cobbler, butler, coachman, sailor, soldier, stevedore, it's all the same all around, they don't ask *any* of them. The professionals and merchants and preachers don't, and the idle rich don't invite *them*—not by a dam sight, she says, and—"

"H'sh! I'm astonished at you!"

"Well, she *said* it, anyway; and she said *they* don't give a dam whether—"

"*Will* you be quiet! You *must* stop this habit of picking up and fetching home every dreadful word you—"

"But she *said* it—I *heard* her say it! The way she said it was this: she fetched her fist down—so!—and said 'By—' "

"Never *mind* how she said it! I don't want to hear it. You are certainly the most innocent animal that ever was. You don't seem to have any discrimination—everything that gets in front of your rake is treasure to you. I think there was never such a random scavenger since language was invented. Now then, let those words alone; just let them alone, and start over again where they side-tracked you."

"Well, I will, and I'm sorry if I've done wrong, I wasn't meaning any harm. The rest that she said was, that if the banker's daughter married the plumber, and if the multimillionaire's daughter married the editor, and if the bishop's daughter married the horse-doctor, and if the governor's daughter married the coachman, there was hell to pay!"

"Now *there* you go, again! I—"

"Why, that's what she said."

"Oh, *I* know it, but—"

"And she said there's families that are so awful high-up and swell, that they won't let their daughters marry any native at all, if they can help it. They save them up till a foreign bacillus with a title comes along; then if they can agree on the price they make the trade. But they don't have auctions, she says. Not public ones. She's as nice as she can be, and it's most interesting to hear her talk.

She's good-hearted and malicious and all that, and is never borous, and makes plenty of friends—and keeps them, too. She's got a heart of gold, and false teeth and a glass eye, and *I* think she's perfect."

"Those are the marks. I should recognize them anywhere."

"It's nice to have you say that. And I thought you would. There's a good deal to her. I think she's awfully interesting. She's morganatic."

"Morganatic?"

"Yes. That's what she is—morganatic."

"How do you make that out?"

"Well, it's what they say. Not she herself, but the others. Neighbors, you know. That's what they say. Morganatic."

"Yes, but *how?*"

"Well, her mother was a vermiform appendix—"

"Oh, good land!"

"It's what they say, anyway. They don't know who her father was. Only just her mother. She was a vermiform appendix. That's what they say. Morganatic."

"How in the nation is *that* morganatic?"

"Irregular, you know. They all say it's irregular for a vermiform appendix to have a family anyway, to *begin* with, for it's never happened before, and doctors didn't believe it *could* happen till it *did* happen; and then to go and have it irregular besides—well, it's morganatic, you see. That's what they all say. Morganatic. Some say it's *more* than morganatic, but I reckon it's not so much as that, do you think?"

"Why, hang it there's nothing morganatic about it—nothing that resembles it. The whole thing is insane—absolutely insane. Now how can these germs be cruel enough to ruin the countess's character in this wanton way?"

"Ruin her character? What makes you think it hurts her character?"

"But doesn't it?"

"Why no. How could it affect her character? *She* wasn't to blame. *She* hadn't anything to do with it. Why, she wasn't any more than just *there*, when it happened. I reckon another minute and she'd have been too late."

"What an idea! Hanged if you can't make the most unexpected turns, and pop out in the most unexpected places that ever I—and there's no such *thing* as understanding these mixed up and helter-skelter and involved statements of yours—why, they fuddle a person all up, they make him dizzy, he can't tell them from sacred passages out of Science and Wealth itself, the style is so astonishingly replicated!"

I was so sorry it escaped me! But for only half a second. Why, she was beaming with gratitude! It wasn't a sarcasm to *her*. It fell short—away short! She took it for a compliment. I hastened to get back on our course and said—

"I am very glad it didn't hurt her character; and very sincerely glad to come across *one* civilization which places shame where it belongs, instead of emptying its brutal scorn upon the innocent product of it. So these good and just people respect the countess, do they?"

"Oh yes, they do, as far as *that* incident is concerned. In fact it is a valuable thing to her, because it gives her distinction."

"How?"

"Why, she's the only appendicitis there is. There's plenty *inside* of people, in the hospitals and around, but she's the only one that's outside; the only one that's been *born,* you know.—Irregular, and pretty morganatic, and all that, but never mind, when all's said and done, she's the *only* one in history, and it's a gigantic distinction. I wish I was it, myself."

"Oh, Great Sc—"

XV.

She clattered right along, paying no attention to my attempt to invoke the Great Scott. Also she followed a slovenly fashion of hers, of throwing a back-handspring clear over thirty yards of general conversation and landing right-side-up in front of an unfinished remark of an hour before—then she would hitch-on to

it, and come lumbering along with it the same as if there hadn't
been anything obstructing the line, and no interruption to its
progress—

"So you see, there *isn't* any big nation, after all, where it doesn't
soil the bread to earn it, notwithstanding you stood out so
stubbornly that it wasn't so." (I hadn't done anything of the kind,
but I knew it would save time and wind to leave it so, and not
argue it.) "The countess says it's all a sham, in GRQ, and of course
if there was a big nation anywhere where it *wasn't* a sham, it would
be there, which is a republic and a democracy, and the greatest one
on the planet, and everybody letting on to be equal and some of
them succeeding, God only knows which ones, *she* says! She says
the sham starts at the top and runs straight to the bottom without a
break, and there isn't a da—" ("Look out!" I said)—"isn't a person
in the land that can see it. That's what *she* says—all blind-fuddled
with bogus sentiment.

"Ranks—grades—castes—there's a million of them! that's what
she says. Mesalliances! why, she says it's just the natural native
home of them, on account of there being so many more ranks and
aristocracies there than anywhere else. She says there's families that
the very President isn't good enough to marry into—at least *until*
he's President. They're nearly always SBE's—tanners, or rail-
splitters, or tailors, or prohibitionists, or some other low trade, and
they've got to climb *away* up above that before they can crowd into
those families—and by that time, you know, it's too late, they're
already coupled. *They* consider it climbing, she says, and everybody does. They admire him—admire him immensely—for what
he is *now*, don't you know—admire him for the respectability he's
climbed up to. They don't say, with swelling pride and noble
emotion, 'Look at him, the splendid SBE—he's a rail-splitter!' No,
they say, with swelling pride and noble emotion, 'Look at him—
away up there!—and just think, he used to wasn't anything but a
rail-splitter!' And she says he's not ashamed of what he was, and no
occasion to, it's a distinction and a grand one, now that he's where
he *is*; and you'd think he would make tailors and tanners and rail-
splitters out of his boys. She says she thinks they do, but she don't
remember any instances.

"So there 'tis, and I reckon you've got to come down."

"Come down?"

"Yes. Come down and acknowledge it."

"Acknowledge what?"

"That *earned* bread is soiled bread—everywhere on the planet of Blitzowski, republics and all. It's the soiled bread that *makes* a nation; makes it great, makes it honored, makes it strong, props up its throne and saves it from the junk-shop, makes its waving flag a beautiful thing to see, and bring the proud tears to your eyes to look at it, keeps its da—keeps its Grand Dukes out of the hog-wallow, the jail and the alms-house—if you sh'd sweep the SBE's and their dirty bread away there wouldn't be a solitary valuable thing left in the land! and yet, by God—"

"Oh, for goodness sake!—"

"Well, that's what *she* said. She said, 'By—' "

"*Will* you hush! I tell you—"

"But she *said* it—the countess did. She put up her hand—away up so, with her fist clinched and her eyes snapping, and rips out the doggondest, consoundedest, allfiredest, thunderblast of—"

Thank heaven there was a knock on the door! It was the good Brother, the impressive Sleeping-Sickness germ.

He had a gentle way with him, and a kind and winning face, for he was a Malignant; that is to say, a Noble of the loftiest rank and the deadliest, and the gentle bearing and the kind face are theirs by nature and old heredity. *He* was not aware that he was deadly; he was not aware that *any* Noble was deadly; he was far from suspecting the shocking truth that *all* Nobles are deadly. I was the only person in all Blitzowski that knew these terrible facts, and I knew it only because I had learned it in another World.

He and Catherine gave each other a pleased and affectionate greeting, she going on her knees to him, as etiquette required, she being an SBE and he of dizzily lofty blood, and he patting her bowed head lovingly, and telling her she might rise. Which she did, and waited so, until he told her she could sit. He and I exchanged stately bows, each repeatedly waving a reverent hand toward a chair and accompanying each wave with a courtly "After you, m'lord."

We got it settled presently, by the two of us chairing ourselves with carefully exact simultaneousness. He had a slender long box with him, which Catherine relieved him of—curtsying profoundly.

Ah, he knew things, the wise old gentleman! He knew that when you are in doubt it is safest to lead trumps. He could see that I was of a great blood; I *might* be a Noble, so he treated me as one, without asking any awkward questions. I followed his lead: I made him a Duke, without asking him anything about it.

He was munching an SBE which he had captured as he came along—eating it alive, which is our way—and its cries and struggles made my mouth water, for it was an infant of four weeks and quite fat and tender and juicy, and I hadn't tasted a bite since the boys left at 2 A.M. There was enough of it for a family, therefore no occasion for etiquetical declining and polite lying when he offered me a leg; I took it, and it seemed to me that I had never tasted anything better. It was a *pectin*—a spring pectin—and I think them quite choice when they are well nourished.

I knew Catherine was hungry, but this kind of game was not for her: SBE's eat Nobles when they get a chance—war-prisoners or battle-slain—but SBE's don't eat each other, and she was an SBE. It was a good meal, and we threw the remnants to the mother, who was crying outside. She was very grateful, poor thing, though it was but a trifling kindness, and we claimed no merit for it.

When the Brother learned that I longed to have our humble friends and helpers, the lower animals, accompany us to the Happy Land and partake of its joys with us, it went to his heart. He was deeply moved, and said it was a most noble and compassionate feeling, and that he shared it with me to the uttermost. That was good and strong and cheering language; and when he added that he not only longed for the translation of the animals but believed it would happen and had no shadow of a doubt that it *would* happen, my cup of happiness was full! I had never lacked anything but a support like this to clinch my own belief and make it solid and perfect, and now it *was* solid and perfect. I think there was not a happier microbe than I, at that moment, from Henryland to GRQ, and from the Major Molar to the Great Lone Sea. There was but one question left to ask, and I asked it without fear or misgiving—

"Does your Grace include *all* the creatures, even the meanest and the smallest—mosquito, rat, fly, *all and every?"*

"Yes, *all and every!*—even the invisible and deadly microbe that feeds upon our bodies and rots them with disease!"

x x x x The stars represent the time it took me to get my breath back. Yes, yes, yes, how strangely we are made! I had always *wanted* somebody to say that, and round-out and perfect the scheme of justice, making all innocent and duty-doing life partakers of it, and I had long ago (unsuccessfully) offered an upright and kind-hearted clergyman an opportunity to do it, yet now that somebody *had* said it [at] last, it nearly paralysed me!

The Duke saw it. I couldn't help it—he saw it. I was ashamed, but there it was; so I didn't make any excuses, or venture any lies, I just stood pat. It's the best way, when you know you are caught and there isn't anything you can do. But the Duke was handsomely magnanimous about it; he dealt in no upbraidings, no sarcasms, he did a better thing—he dealt in reasonings: reasonings supported by facts. He said—

"You make a limit, you draw a line; do not let that trouble you, there was a time when I did it too. It was when I lacked knowledge —that is, full knowledge; it was incomplete—like yours. Yours is about to be amended, now—and completed—by me. Then you will see the right, I know you need have no doubts as to that. I will show you the facts. Arguments carry far, but nothing but facts carry home. There are plenty of evidences on view in this room that you are a student of science, m'lord, but you have revealed the fact—unintentionally—that there is one great field of science— bacteriology—which you have neglected—which, at any rate, you have not made yourself altogether familiar with. Is it so?"

Well, what was I to say? As to *World*-bacteriology, I was the expert of experts—I was a past master—I knew more about it in a week than Pasteur ever knew about it in a year. I couldn't tell the Duke that—he wouldn't know what I was talking about. As to bacteriology here in this planet—the infinitely microscopic microbes that infest *microbes*—land, I knew nothing about it! I had sometimes lazily wondered if they were minute duplicates of the World-microbes, and had the same habits and devoted themselves to the same duties, but I had never felt interest enough in the matter to think examining into it worth the trouble. On the whole I thought I would tell the Duke I didn't know anything about germs and such things, and that is what I did.

It didn't surprise him any—I could see that—and it hurt my pride a little, but I stood it and made no moan. He got up and arranged one of my microscopes—remarking casually that he was a bacteriologist of some reputation—by which he meant that he was *the* bacteriologist of the planet—oh, I know *that* tune!—and I know how to dance to it to the singer's satisfaction, too—which I did, in the old shop-worn way: I said I should consider myself the most ignorant of scientists if I was not aware of *that* pretty well-known fact. Then he got a glass slide out of his grooved box— which I had recognized, early, as a slide-box—and put it under the microscope. He worked the screws and made the proper adjustment, then told me to take a look.

Oh, well, there's no use—I *was* astonished! It was one of those old familiar rascals which I had had under the microscope a thousand times in America, and here was his unspeakably littler twin exactly reproduced, to the last detail. He was a pectin—a spring pectin—a baby one, and most ridiculously like the mammoth one (by comparison) which we had just eaten! It was so funny that I wanted to make a joke about him; I wanted to say, let's get that little speck out on a needle-point and make a gnat eat him, then give his remnants to his mother! But I didn't say it. It might be that the Duke was not witty: well, you don't charm *that* kind by reminding them of their defect and making them ashamed and envious. So I held in, but it strained me some.

XVI.

H E MADE a sketchy little introductory layout in the professorial style, in which he generalized, as in an impressionist picture, the great lesson which he was going to particularize for my instruction; then he got down to his work. At this point he discarded the local vernacular, and thenceforth employed the highest and purest dialect of the black plague, which he spoke with a French accent— I mean, it sounded like it. It had long been the court language, all over Blitzowski, and was now becoming the language of science, because of its peculiar richness in several high qualities; among them, precision and flexibility. I will remark, in passing, that in this tongue, the scientific family-name for *all* germ-forms is *swink*. Every microbe is a swink, every bacterium is a swink, and so on; just as in the World every German, Indian, Irishman, and so on, is a *man*.

"Let us begin at the beginning," he said. "This mighty planet which we inhabit, and in which we have set up our democracies, our republics, kingdoms, hierarchies, oligarchies, autocracies and other vanities, was created for a great and wise purpose. It was not chance-work, it proceeded, stage by stage, in accordance with an ordered and systematised plan.

"It was created for a purpose. What was that purpose? That We might have a home. That is the proper expression—a home, not a mere abiding place, stingy of comforts. No, the design was, a home rich in comforts, and in intelligent and hard-working subordinates to provide them for us. No microbe fails to realize this, no microbe forgets to be grateful for it. If the microbe is also a little vain of his high position, a little vain of his august supremacy, it must be allowed that it is pardonable. If the microbe has by his own unanimous consent gilded himself with the large title of Lord of Creation, it must be allowed that that also was pardonable, seeing that it was safer to *take* the title than go before the country with the matter and possibly fail to get elected.

"Very well. The planet was to be created—for a purpose. Was it created—and then the microbe put into possession of it at once? No, he would have starved. It had to be prepared for him. What was the process? Let us *make* a little planet—in fancy—and see.

"Thus. We make some soil, and spread it out. It is going to be a garden, presently. We make air, and put into it moisture; the air and the moisture contain life-nurturing foods in the form of gases —foods for the plants which we are going to raise. We put into the soil some other plant-foods—potassium, phosphorous, nitrates, and such.

"There is plenty of food; the plant eats, is energised, and springs from the soil and flourishes. Presently the garden is wealthy in grains, berries, melons, table-vegetables, and all manner of luscious fruits.

"There being food now for the Lord of Creation and for the horse, the cow and their kind, and for the locust, the weevil, and the countless other destructive insects, we create *them* and set them to the table. Also the tiger, the lion, the snake, the wolf, the cat, the dog, the buzzard, the vulture and their sort?

"Yes, we create them, but it is not a fortunate time for them, because they cannot live on garden-stuff. They have to sacrifice themselves in a great cause. They are martyrs. Though not by request. Being without food, they die.

"At this point we create the *swinks,* and they appear on the scene —with a stupendous mission. They come in countless multitudes, for much is required of them. What would happen if they did not come?

"Why, the catastrophe of catastrophes! The garden would use up and exhaust the supply of essential foods concealed in the soil—the nitrates and the rest of that nutritive menu; then it would have nothing left to live on but the slim menu furnished by the air— carbon dioxide and such—and so it would get hungrier and hungrier, and weaker and weaker, then it would gasp out its remnant of life and die. With it all the animals would perish, the Lord of Creation along with them, and the planet would be a desolate wilderness, without song of bird, or cry of predatory creature, or whir of wing, or any sign of life. The forests would wither and pass away, nothing would be left of all the fair creation but limitless expanses of rocks and sand.

"Is the humble swink important in the scheme, then? Ah, yes—beyond question! What shall we call him? What shall be his title, since he is unmicrobically modest, and has not selected one himself? Let us name him in accordance with the plain facts. He is the Lord Protector of the Lord of Creation, and ex-officio Redeemer of his Planet. Let us now examine his procedure and his methods.

"He arrives on the scene in his due order and at the proper and appointed time. The microbe is well, and well fed; the same is the case with the cow, the horse and the other creatures that can live on vegetable products, but there is a wilderness of tigers, dogs, cats, lions, and other meat-eaters dying, because there isn't meat enough to go around. The swink attacks the carcases and their previous excretions, feeds upon them, decomposes them, and sets free a lot [of] oxygen, nitrogen and other things necessary to the plant-table; the plant-leaves seize upon these foods—with the exception of the nitrogen, which it must get later through the labors of other breeds of swinks.

"Very well, the country is saved. The plants get their foods back again, and thrive. They digest them, building them into albumins, starch, fats and so on; these go back to the animals, who feed upon them and thrive; in digesting them *they* build them into various food-forms; some of these pass to the air in their breath and are re-captured by the plant-leaves and devoured; some of them go from them in their excretions and are recovered by the swink and returned to the plants; when the animals die the swink rots him and sets free the rest of the plant-foods and *they* go back to the garden.

"So, the eternal round goes on: the foods fat-up the plants; they go from the plants to the animals and fat *them* up; the swink recovers them and sends them back to the plants' larder; the plants eat them again, and again forward them to the animals. Nothing is lost, nothing wasted; there's never a new dish, and never *has* been one; it's the same old sumptuous but unchanging bill of fare, and not only the same bill, but the very same old *food* which was set upon the table at creation's first meal, and has been warmed over and chewed and re-chewed, and chewed and chewed and chewed and chewed and chewed again and again and still again and yet again at every single meal that life in any form, in land and water and air has ever sat down to, from that original first day to this.

"It is a marvelous machinery, an amazing machinery; the precision of it, the perfection of it, the wonder of it—put it into your own words, I have none that are sublime enough!

"Remove the swink from the scheme, and what have you? Rocks and sand! Rocks and sand, stripped bare; the forests gone and the flowers, the seas without a fish, the air without a wing, the temples without a worshiper, the thrones empty, the cities crumbled to dust and blown away. And the armies, and the banners, and the shouting—where are they? Do you hear a sound? It is only the wandering wind, the lamenting wind; and do you hear that other sound?—

> " 'The old, old Sea, as one in tears,
> Comes murmuring with foamy lips,
> And knocking at the vacant piers,
> Calls for his long-lost multitude of ships!'

"x x x x We will look at this swink, this giant. Catherine, bring a tin cup. A pint tin cup. Now fill it with wheat—level full. There—it represents a pound, avoirdupois by immemorial tradition. There are 7,000 grains. Take 15 of them, crush them in the mortar. Now wet the pulp, and make a pill of it. It is a small pill, isn't it? You could swallow it without difficulty? Let us suppose it hollow—with a hole in it, pierced by the most delicate needle-point. Let us imagine it the house of the swink, and summon him and his to come forth. Go on with the fancy: behold, he comes—the procession moves! Can you see so minute a creature? No—you must imagine him. Count!

"One—two—three—Three *what?* Individuals? No! It would take a year. You must count him—how? By armies—only by armies—each a million strong. Count!"

"One—two—three." I was counting. I went on counting—counting—counting—monotonously. I got to the forties.

"Go on!"

I got to the seventies.

"Go on!"

I got to the nineties.

"Go on!"

I reached a hundred.

"Stop! There he stands, a hundred million strong—his mass, the mass of a calomel pill! Take off your hat—make reverence: you stand in the presence of his sublime Majesty the Swink, Lord Protector of the Lord of Creation, Redeemer of his Planet, Preserver of all Life!

"Will he be forgiven, and changed to a spirit, and allowed to ascend with us to the Land of Rest—to fold his tired hands and labor no more, his duty done, his mission finished? What do *you* think?"

XVII.

AT LAST my spirit had found perfect repose, perfect peace, perfect contentment—never again to be disturbed, never again to be tossed upon waves of doubt, I hoped and believed. The Lower Animals, big and little, would be *spirits* in the Blessed Land, as intangible as thought; airy, floating forms, wandering hither and thither, leagues apart, in the stupendous solitudes of space, seldom glimpsed, unremarked, inoffensive, intruding upon none—ah, why had not some one thought of this simple and rational solution before? In the human World even the most fastidious churchman would hail with joy and thankfulness the translation of my poor old tramp to the Blessed Land from a repentant deathbed, quite undisturbed by the certainty of having to associate with him there throughout eternity. In what condition? frowsy, drunk, driveling, malodorous?—proper comrade for a disease-germ? No: as a *spirit*— an airy, flitting form, as intangible as thought; in no one's way, offending none. Yet the same charitable churchman who could forecast the tramp as a spirit and purified of offensiveness, could never in all his days happen to hit upon the logical idea of also forecasting the *rest* of the ruck of life as spirits. Plainly a thing not difficult to do after practising on Blitzowski and getting reconciled to the process.

Something roused me out of this reverie, and I found that the Duke was talking. Something like this:

"We have seen that the swink—and the swink alone—saved our planet from denudation and irremediable sterility in the beginning; saved Us and all subordinate life from extinction; is still standing between Us and extinction to-day; and that if ever he deserts Us, that day is Our Doomsday, that day marks the passing of Our Great Race and of Our Noble Planet to the grave of the Things That Were.

"Is that humble mite important, then? Let us confess it: he is in truth the *only* very important personage that exists. What is the suit of clothes which we call Henry the Great, and bow before, reverent and trembling? What are the tribe of kings, and their grandeurs? What are their armies and their navies? What are the multitudinous nations and their pride? Shadows—all shadows—nothing is real but the swink. And their showy might? It is a dream —there is no might but the might of the swink. And their glories? The swink gave them, the swink can take them away. And their riches, their prosperities—

"Let us look at that. There are some strange resemblances between Our Grand Race and those wee creatures. For instance, We have upper classes—so have they. That is a parallel, as far as it goes, but it is not a perfect one, for the reason that Our aristocracy is useful and not often harmful, whereas their aristocracy are disease-germs, and propagate deadly maladies in Our bodies.*

"But the next parallel has no defect. I refer to their lower classes —their laboring poor. They are harmless. They work, they work intelligently, they work unceasingly. We have seen that they save

---

* Listen to that, now! He was a disease-germ himself, and didn't suspect it. The girly innocence of these poisonous Toughs is almost unthinkable.

Us and Our planet; very well, they also create Our wealth for Us, they prepare it for Our hand, We take it and use it.

"For instance. No method of separating the linen fibres in the flax from the wood fibres has yet been devised which dispenses with the aid of the swink. He holds the patent upon that essential. He has always been boss of the whole rich linen industry of this planet; he is still boss of it; he keeps the mills going; he pays the wages, he attends to the dividends. He bosses the sacking industry, too; helps to get the jute ready. The same with other fibre-products of several kinds.

"Swinks of various breeds help in a multitude of Our commercial industries. The yeast-swink helps in every kitchen and every bakery on the planet. You get no good bread without him. He conducts Our wine-business, strong-liquor business, beer-business, vinegar-business, and so on, for Us, and does it on a mighty scale. It is by his grace that those generous floods are poured down the throats of the nations, and the dividends handed over by the train-load to the capitalist.

"He sees to it that your butter is good; and your cream, your cheese, and all sorts of boarding-house essentials.

"When the tobacco leaf sprouts, the swink is there—on duty, and faithful to his trust. He will never leave that leaf until he has helped it with his best strength and judgment through every one of its curing-processes; and when it reaches your mouth the flavor and the aroma that make it delicious to your taste and smell, and fill your spirit with contentment and thanks, are *his* work. He oversees, and superintends, and makes profitable beyond the dreams of the statistician the entire tobacco-industry of this great planet, and every day the smoke of the burnt offerings that go up in praise and worship of this unknown god, this god whose labors are not suspected and whose name is never uttered by these ignorant devotees, transcends in volume all the other altar-smokes that have gone skyward during the preceding thirty years. Pray correct me if I seem to fall into error at any time, for we are all prone to do this when stirred by feeling.

"These are great services which we have been tallying off to the credit of Our benefactor, the humble swink, the puissant swink, the all-providing swink, the all-protecting swink. Is the tale finished? Is there yet another service? Yes—and a greater still. This:

"In their time, the trees and the plants fall, and lie. The swink takes hold. He decomposes them, turns them to dust, mingles them with the soil. Suppose he didn't do this work? The fallen vegetation would not rot, it would lie, and pile up, and up, and up, and by and by the soil would be buried fathoms deep; no food could be grown, all life would perish, the planet would be a lifeless desert. There is but one instrument that can keep this vast planet's soil free and usable—the swink."

"Oh, dear me," I muttered to myself, "the idea of ruling God's most valuable creatures out of heaven, and admitting the Blitzowskis!"

"There. Let us finish. We complain of his aristocracy—his disease-germs. All We can think about, when the swink is mentioned, is his aristocracy's evil doings. When do We ever speak of the laboring swink, Our benefactor, Our prosperity-maker? In effect, never. Our race does not even know that he *is* Our benefactor, none knows it but here and there a student, a scholar, a scientist. The public—why, the public thinks *all* swinks are disease-breeders, and so it has a horror of all the race of swinks. It is a pity, too, for the facts and the figures would modify its hostilities if it had them and would examine them.

"When the plague-swink starts upon a raid, the best he can do, while it lasts, is to kill 2½ per cent of the community attacked—not the nation, merely the few communities visited. Nowadays, I mean. He did a larger trade in bygone ages, before science took hold of his case. He kills 2½ per cent; then he has to lie still for years. The cholera-swink does even a slenderer business; then he also must postpone his next raid for years. Both of these are harshly talked about and dreaded. Why? I don't know. None but mere outlying corners of the planet ever see either of them during entire life-times. Meantime the laborer-swink is supporting all the nations, prospering all the nations—and getting neither thanks nor mention."

He dropped into the vernacular:

"Take all the other disease-germs in a mass, and what do they accomplish? They are responsible for ten graves out of a hundred, that is all. It takes them half a lifetime to bring down the average sooflasky try as hard as they may; and all that time his brother swink the laborer has been feeding him, protecting him, enriching him—and getting neither thanks nor notice for it. To use a figure, the swink gives the public a thousand barrels of apples; the public says nothing—not a word; then it finds a rotten apple in the cargo, and—what does it do *then*, Catherine?"

"Raises—"

"Shut up!" I shouted, just in time.

"It's what the countess says, I heard her say it myself. She said—"

"Never *mind* what she said; we don't want to hear it!"

XVIII.

I WAS CHARMED with the Duke's lecture. Its wonders were new to me, and astonishing. At the same time, they were old to me, and not astonishing. In the World, when I was studying micrology under Prof. H. W. Conn, we knew all these facts, because they were all true of the microbes that infest the human being; but it was new to me to find them exactly duplicated in the life of the microbes that infest the human *being's* microbes. We knew that the human race was saved from destruction in the beginning by the microbe; that the microbe had been saving it from destruction ever since; that the microbe was the protector and preserver and ablest propagator of many of the mightiest industries in the Earth; that he was the personage most heavily interested in the corporations which exploited them, and that his expert service was the most valuable asset such corporations possessed; we knew that he kept the Earth's soil from being covered up and buried out of sight and made unusable; in a word, we knew that the most valuable citizen of the Earth was the microbe, and that the human race could no more do without him than it could do without the sun and the air.

We also knew that the human race took no notice of these benefactions, and only remembered the disease-germ's ten per cent contribution to the death-rate; and didn't even stop with that unfairness, but charged *all* microbes with being disease-germs, and violently abused the entire stock, benefactors and all!

Yes, that was all old to me, but to find that our little old familiar microbes were *themselves* loaded up with microbes that fed *them,* enriched them, and persistently and faithfully preserved them and their poor old tramp-planet from destruction—oh, that was new, and too delicious!

I wanted to see them! I was in a fever to see them! I had lenses of two-million power, but of course the field was no bigger than a person's finger-nail, and so it wasn't possible to do a considerable spectacle or a landscape with them; whereas what I had been craving was a thirty-foot field, which would represent a spread of several miles of country and show up things in a way to make them worth looking at. The boys and I had often tried to contrive this improvement, but had failed.

I mentioned the matter to the Duke, and it made him smile. He said it was a quite simple thing—he had it at home. I was eager to bargain for the secret, but he said it was a trifle and not worth bargaining for. He said—

"Hasn't it occurred to you that all you have to do is to bend an X-ray to an angle-value of 8.4, and refract it with a parabolism, and there you are?"

Upon my word, I had never thought of that simple thing! You could have knocked me down with a feather.

We rigged a microscope for an exhibition at once, and put a drop of my blood under it, which got mashed flat when the lense got shut down upon it. The result was beyond my dreams. The field stretched miles away, green and undulating, threaded with streams and roads, and bordered all down the mellowing distances with picturesque hills. And there was a great white city of tents; and everywhere were parks of artillery, and divisions of cavalry and infantry—waiting. We had hit a lucky moment; evidently there was going to be a march-past, or something like that. At the front where the chief banner flew, there was a large and showy tent, with showy guards on duty, and about it were some other tents of a swell kind.

The warriors—particularly the officers—were lovely to look at, they were so trim-built and so graceful and so handsomely uniformed. They were quite distinct, vividly distinct, for it was a fine day, and they were so immensely magnified that they looked to be fully finger-nail high.*

Everywhere you could see officers moving smartly about, and they looked gay, but the common soldiers looked sad. Many wife-swinks and daughter-swinks and sweetheart-swinks were about—crying, mainly. It seemed to indicate that this was a case of war, not a summer-camp for exercise, and that the poor labor-swinks were being torn from their planet-saving industries to go and distribute civilization and other forms of suffering among the feeble be-nighted, somewhere; else why should the swinkesses cry?

The cavalry was very fine; shiny black horses, shapely and spirited; and presently when a flash of light struck a lifted bugle (delivering a command which we couldn't hear) and a division came tearing down on a gallop it was a stirring and gallant sight, until the dust rose an inch—the Duke thought more—and swallowed it up in a rolling and tumbling long gray cloud, with bright weapons glinting and sparking in it.

Before long the real business of the occasion began. A battalion of priests arrived, carrying sacred pictures. That settled it: this was war; these far-stretching masses of troops were bound for the front. Their little monarch came out now, the sweetest little thing that ever travestied the human shape, I think; and he lifted up his hands and blessed the passing armies, and they looked as grateful as

---

* My own expression, and a quite happy one. I said to the Duke—

"Your grace, they're just about finger-nailers!"

"How do you mean, m'lord?"

"This. You notice the stately General standing there with his hand resting upon the muzzle of a cannon? Well, if you could stick your little finger down against the ground alongside of him, his plumes would just reach up to where your nail joins the flesh."

The Duke said "finger-nailers was good"—good and exact; and he afterward used it several times himself. In about a minute a mounted General rode up alongside of the other one and saluted, and the Duke said—

"There, now—with the horse to help, this one's nearly a nail and a third high."

they could, and made signs of humble and real reverence as they drifted by the holy pictures.

It was beautiful—the whole thing; and wonderful, too, when those serried masses swung into line and went marching down the valley under the long array of fluttering flags.

Evidently they were going somewhere to fight for their country, which was the little manny that blessed them; and to preserve him and his brethren that occupied the other swell tents; and to civilize and grab a valuable little unwatched country for them somewhere. But the little fellow and his brethren didn't fall in—that was a noticeable particular. But the Duke said it was without doubt a case of Henry and Family on a minute scale—*they* didn't fight; they stayed at home, where it was safe, and waited for the swag.

Very well, then—what ought *we* to do? Had we no moral duty to perform? Ought we to allow this war to begin? Was it not our duty to stop it, in the name of right and righteousness? Was it not our duty to administer a rebuke to this selfish and heartless Family?

The Duke was struck by that, and greatly moved. He felt as I did about it, and was ready to do whatever was right, and thought we ought to pour boiling water on the Family and extinguish it, which we did.

It extinguished the armies, too, which was not intended. We both regretted this, but the Duke said that these people were nothing to us, and deserved extinction anyway for being so poorspirited as to serve such a Family. He was loyally doing the like himself, and so was I, but I don't think we thought of that. And it wasn't just the same, anyway, because we were sooflaskies, and they were only swinks.

XIX.

THE DUKE presently went away, and left my latest thought simmering in my mind—simmering along in the form of reverie: "it wasn't just the same, anyway, because we were sooflaskies, and they were only swinks." There it is: it doesn't make any difference who we are or what we are, there's always *somebody* to look down on! somebody to hold in light esteem or no esteem, somebody to be indifferent about. When I was a human being, and recognized with complacency that I was of the Set-Aparts, the Chosen, a Grand Razzledazzle, The Whole Thing, the Deity's Delight, I looked down upon the microbe; he wasn't of any consequence, he wasn't worth a passing thought; his life was nothing, I took it if I wanted to, it ranked with a mark on a slate—rub it out, if you like. Now that I was a microbe myself I looked back upon that insolence, that pert human indifference, with indignation—and imitated it to the letter, dull-witted unconsciousness and all. I was once more looking down; I was once more finding a life that wasn't of any importance, and sponging it out when I was done with it. Once more I was of the Set-Aparts, the Chosen, a Grand Razzledazzle, and all that, and had something to look down upon, be indifferent about. I was a sooflasky; oh, yes, I was The Whole Thing, and away down below me was the insignificant swink—extinguishable at my pleasure— why not? what of it? who's to find fault?

Then the inexorable logic of the situation arrived, and announced itself. The inexorable logic of the situation was this: there being a Man, with a Microbe to infest him, and for him to be indifferent about; and there being a Sooflasky, with a Swink to infest him and for the said Sooflasky to be indifferent about: then it follows, for a certainty, that the Swink is similarly infested, too, and has something to look down upon and be indifferent to and sponge out upon occasion; and it also follows, of a certainty, that below that infester there is yet another infester that infests *him*— and so on down and down and down till you strike the bottomest bottom of created life—if there is one, which is extremely doubtful.

However, I had reached down to comfort, at any rate, and an easy conscience. We had boiled the swinks, poor things, but never mind, it's all right, let them pass it along; let them take it out of *their* infesters—and those out of *theirs*—and those again out of *theirs*—and so on down and down till there has been an indemnifying boiling all the way down to the bottomest bottom, and everybody satisfied; and glad it happened, on the whole.

Well, it's a picture of life. Life everywhere; life under any and all conditions: the king looks down upon the noble, the noble looks down upon the commoner, the commoner at the top looks down upon the next commoner below, and he upon the next, and that one upon the next one; and so on down the fifty castes that constitute the commonalty—the fifty aristocracies that constitute it, to state it with precision, for each commonalty-caste is a little aristocracy by itself, and each has a caste to look down upon, plum all the way down to the bottom, where you find the burglar looking down upon the house-renting landlord, and the landlord looking down upon his oily brown-wigged pal the real estate agent—which is the bottom, so far as ascertained.

XX.

I GLANCED over my paper on the currency, and found it lucid, interesting, and accurate. It had been written long before. In those early days in Blitzowski I made it a point to put upon paper the new things I learned, lay the thing away, then take it out from time to time in after years and examine it. There was generally something to correct—always, I may say; but in the course of time I got all errors weeded out. This paper on the currency had been through that mill. I found it satisfactory, and gave it to Catherine to put away again.

That was 3,000 years ago. Ah, Catherine, poor child, where art thou now? Where art thou, thou pretty creature, thou quaint sprite! Where is thy young bloom, thy tumultuous good heart, thy capricious ways, thine unexpectednesses, oh thou uncatchable globule of frisky quicksilver, thou summer-flurry of shower and sun-shine! You were an allegory! you were Life! just joyous, careless, sparkling, gracious, winning, worshipful Life! and now— thou art dust and ashes these thirty centuries!

This faded old paper brings her back. Her hand was the last that rested upon it. She was a dear child; and just a child—it is what she was; if I knew the place her fingers touched, I would kiss it.

There was a time when a pair of young adventurers, exploring a solitude, found a spot which pleased them, and there they began a village, and it was Rome. The village grew, and was the capital of kings for some centuries; and made a stir in the world, and came to be known far and wide; and became a republic, and produced illustrious men; and produced emperors, next, some of them tolerably tough; and when Rome was seven or eight hundred years old, Jesus was born in one of her   provinces; by and by came the Age of Faith, and the Dark Ages, and the Middle Ages, extending through a procession of centuries, Rome looking on and superintending; and when she was eighteen hundred years old, William the Conqueror visited the British isles on business; and by and by came the Crusades, and lasted two centuries, and filled the world with a splendid noise, then the romantic show faded out and disappeared, with its banners and its noise, and it was as if the whole thing had been a dream; by and by came Dante and Boccacio and Petrarch; and after another by and by came the Hundred Years' War; and after a while Joan of Arc; and soon the Printing Press, that prodigious event; and after another while the Wars of the Roses, with forty years of blood and tears; and straight after it Columbus and a New World; and in the same year Rome decreed the extirpation of the witches, for she was more than twenty-two hundred years old, now, and tired of witches this good while; after that, during two centuries not a lantern was sold in Europe and the art of making them was lost, the tourist traveling at night by the light of roasting old mothers and grandmothers tied to stakes 32 yards apart all over the Christian world, which was gradually getting itself purified and would eventually have accomplished it if some one had not chanced to find out that there wasn't any such thing as a witch, and gone and told; two centuries have dragged by since; Rome, that was once a fresh little village in a solitude, is more than twenty-six hundred years old, now, and is named the Eternal City, and what were her palaces in Christ's time are mouldering humps of weed-grown bricks and masonry in ours, and even Columbus's lonesome continent has put on some age, and acquired some population, and would be a surprise to him if he could come back and see the cities and the railroads and the multitudes.

Musing over these things made it seem a long, long time since the two adventurers had started that village and called it Rome; and yet, I said to myself, "it isn't as long a stretch of centuries as has passed over my head since that girl took this old manuscript from me and put it away; I wish I knew the place her fingers touched."

It is a good chapter, and I will insert it here. Its facts about the money of that day will be valuable in this book.

THE CURRENCY.

In one matter of high importance civilization in Blitzowski can claim a distinct superiority over the civilizations of the World. Blitzowski has, by ancient *Bund*, a *uniform* currency. You don't have to buy a supply of foreign pocket-change when you are preparing for a voyage, nor get your letter of credit made out in currencies you are not familiar with. The money of all the countries goes at par in all the other countries.

When the idea was first suggested it was received with great doubt, for it proposed the simplifying and sanitation of a most crazy and intricate puzzle. Every nation had its own currency, and so had every little tuppenny principality, and the same deplorable condition of things prevailed which must necessarily prevail wherever that kind of a chaos exists. It is illustrated by the experiences of a great-great-grandfather of mine who found himself traveling in Germany, one time.

There were 364 sovereign princes doing business in that State in those days—one per farm. Each had a mint of his own; each coined five or six hundred dollars' worth of money every year and stamped his picture on it; there were 3,230 different breeds of coin in circulation; each had a home-value of its own, each had a name of its own. No man in the country could name all the names, nor spell the half of them; every coin began to lose value when it crossed its own frontier, and the further it went the faster it melted.

My ancestor was an Assfalt, and he was a General, because he had been on the governor's staff when he was young, to fill a vacancy that had three weeks to run. He was in Germany for his health, and by the doctor's orders he had to walk five miles and back every day. Upon inquiry, he found that the cheapest course was nothe-east-and by-nothe, nothe-east-half-east, because it took him across only five frontiers; whereas if he got careless and fell off a point to starboard it took him across seven, and a point to port was worse still, because it took him across nine. These latter were much the best roads, but he was not able to afford them, and had to stick to the muddy one, although it was bad for his health, which he had been sent there on purpose to improve. Any other person would have perceived that the cheap road was really bad economy, but you couldn't ever beat a simple proposition like that into an Assfalt.

He was summering in the capital village of the Grand Duchy of Donnerklapperfeld at the time, and he used to load up with twenty dollars' worth of the local coin every morning, and start, right after breakfast—every alternate day, with a new suit of clothes on, costing about twenty dollars and worth eight and a half. It was an outrage, that price, but he had to buy of the Duke, who was able to have everything his own way, and didn't allow any other tailor to keep shop there.

At the local frontier, 300 yards from the inn, the General had to pay export duty on his clothes, 5 per cent ad valorem. Then they let him through the gate and a uniformed foreigner on the other side of it halted him and collected 5 per cent import duty on the same, and charged him an exchange-discount on his foreign money—another 5 per cent.

The game went right along, like that. He paid export and import duty at every gate, and one discount for exchange-tax each time: two dollars per gate, 5 times repeated. The same, coming back; twenty dollars for the trip. Not a copper left; and yet he hadn't bought a thing on the road. Except just privileges and protection. He could have gotten along without the privileges, and he didn't really get any protection—not from the government, anyway.

Every day ten dollars went for exchange, you see. The General was reconciled to that, but he considered that the daily ten that went for duties was a pure extravagance, a sheer waste; because it ate up the clothes every two days and he had to buy another suit.

Assfalt was there 90 days. Forty-five suits of clothes. But I am a protectionist—which he wasn't—and I think that that was all right; but when you start out with a fat and honest dollar and have it melt entirely away to the last grease-spot just in shaves on exchange, I think it's time to call a halt and establish an international currency, with dollars worth a hundred cents apiece from the North Pole to the South, and from Greenwich straight around, both ways, to 180. Such is Blitzowski style, and nobody can better it, I reckon.

The coin unit of the planet is the *bash,* and is worth one-tenth of a cent, American.

There are six other coins. I will name them, and add their (closely approximate) American values:

Basher—10 *bash.* Value, 1 cent.

Gash—50 *bash.* Value, our nickel.

Gasher—100 *bash.* Value, our dime.

Mash—250 *bash.* Value, our quarter.

Masher—500 *bash.* Value, our half dollar.

Hash—1,000 *bash.* Value, our dollar.

Then comes the paper. It begins with the dollar bill, and runs along up: 1 hash, 2 hash, 5 hash, 10 hash, 20 hash, 50 hash.

Then the name changes, and we have the

Clasher—100,000 *hash.* Value, 100 dollars.

Flasher—1,000,000 *hash.* Value, 1,000 dollars.

Slasher—100,000,000 *hash.* Value, 100,000 dollars.

The purchasing power of a *bash,* in Henryland, equals the purchasing power of a dollar in America.

In the beginning there was a good deal of trouble over selecting the names for the money. It was the poets that made the difficulty. None but business men had been put upon the commission appointed to suggest the names. They put a great deal of time and labor upon the matter, and when they published their proposed list everybody was pleased with it except the poets. They fell foul of it in a solid body, and made remorseless fun of it. They said it would forever mash all sentiment, all pathos, all poetic feeling out of finance, because there wasn't a name in the lot that any language, living or dead, could find a rhyme for. And they proved it. They flooded the land with impassioned couplets whose first lines ended with those coin-names, and went all right and rich and mellow all down the second till they struck the home-stretch, then they pulled a blank, every time, and nobody won out.

The commission was convinced. They decided to sublet the contract to the poets, and that was wisdom; the poets selected the names *bash, mash,* and so on, after a good deal of wrangling among themselves. The names were accepted by the commission and ratified by a referendum, and there they stand, to this day, and will abide. They are excellent for poesy, the best in existence, I think. Compare them with other financial nomenclature, and see:

sovereign,	piastre,	florin,
gulden,	nickel,	groschen,
centime,	obolus,	ruble,
eagle,	shekel,	shinplaster,
doubloon,	bob,	pfennig,

and so on. On a financial epic for a chromo—impromptu, mile heat, single dash—a single sooflaski poet could take the field all by himself against the combined talent of Christendom, and walk over the course in an awful solitude, warbling his gashes and mashes and hashes and ashes just as easy!—and annex that chromo—and where would the others be, I ask you? Still back in the first quarter somewhere, trying to blast rhymes out of that obstinate list, and not the least chance in the living world!

At this point Catherine reminded me that my Advanced Class in Theological Arithmetic would be arriving right after breakfast, and that breakfast was already on the fire. There was no time to spare; so she set herself to the crank and I ground the History of Japan Down to Date into the recorder, and was not sorry to see my gigantic History of the World complete at last. It began with an impressionist cloud which I could make nothing of when I reversed the machine to see how Japan had panned out. The rest was clear, but that was a fog. Then Catherine took the receiver, and recognized that it was that passage from Science and Wealth—boned. Boned of its words and compressed into unarticulated thought. It was a good kind of a nut, in its way, and I left it there for the future history-student to whet his teeth on.

I was impatient to get out to the fossil-field, now, and see what sort of luck my "poem" was having with the boys in full congress assembled; so I thought I would turn my class in Theological Arithmetic over to my assistant and start for the field at once. I had to stay, however; the assistant disappointed me. He was out at the field himself, as it turned out; he was out there listening to the wonderful tale and getting quite carried away by it. He had the soul of a poet, he was born for enthusiasms, and he had an imagination like that microscope I have just been talking about. He was good and true and fine, and by nature all his leanings were toward lofty ideals. It will be perceived by this that he was no twin of his brother, Lem Gulliver. The name I had given him was a pretty large compliment, but it was the right one—Sir Galahad. He didn't know what it stood for, any more than Lem knew what *his* name stood for, but I knew, and was satisfied with my work as a god-father.

Sir Galahad had been my favorite pupil from the beginning, and my brightest. He had risen by his own merit to his high place as my right hand in my little college—if I may call my modest school by so large a name. He was as fond of morals as I was, and as fond of teaching them. I found it safest to be present when he was leading certain of the classes—not because I doubted his honesty, for I didn't, but because it was necessary to put a shrinker upon his imagination from time to time. He never said anything he did not believe to be true, but he could imagine *any* extravagant thing to be true that came into his head; then he immediately believed it was true, and straightway he would come out flat-footed and *say* it was true. But for this infirmity he would have been great—absolutely great—in his class-expositions of certain of our high specialties. It was a charm and a wonder to hear him discourse upon Applied Theology, Theological Arithmetic, Metaphysical Dilutions, and kindred vastnesses, but I could listen with all the more comfort if I had my hand on the air-brake.

When at last I got out to the fossil-mine that afternoon I found the work at a stand-still. All interest was centred in the romance which Louis and Lem had brought from me: the lie, as Lem called it, the poem, as Louis called it. It had made a rousing stir. For hours, now, the boys had been discussing it, some taking Lem's view, some taking Louis', but nobody taking mine. But everybody wanted to hear me tell the rest, and so I was pretty well satisfied with the situation. I began by explaining that in the World, Man was the Great Inhabitant, enjoying there the same supremacy enjoyed in the planet Blitzowski by the Sooflasky. I added—

"The individuals are called Human Beings, the aggregate is called the Human Race. It is a mighty aggregate; it numbers fifteen hundred millions of souls."

"Do you mean that that is all there *are*—in the entire planet?"

The question burst in about that form from the whole clan in one sarcastic voice. I was expecting it, and was not disturbed by it.

"Yes," I said, "it's all there are—fifteen hundred millions."

There was [a] general explosion of laughter, of course, and Lem Gulliver said—

"Why, my land, it doesn't even amount to a family—I've got more blood-kin than that, myself! Fetch the jug, his factory's running dry!"

Louis was troubled—disappointed—my poem wasn't keeping up to standard, in the matter of grandeur; I could see it in his face. I was sorry for him, but I wasn't worrying. Louis said, reluctantly—

"Think, Huck. There's a discrepancy. It is careless art, and no occasion for it. You see, yourself, that so trifling a group is quite out of proportion to the vastness of its habitat; here it would be swallowed up and lost in our meanest village."

"I guess not, Louis. I'm not careless—it's you. You are premature with your conclusion. The returns are not all in yet—there's a detail lacking."

"What detail?"

"The size of those Men."

"Ah—their size. Aren't they like us?"

"Why, yes, they *look* like us, but only as to shape and countenance, but when it comes to bulk—well, that is a different matter. You wouldn't be able to hide that Human Race in our village."

"No? How much of it, then?"

"Well, to be exact, not any of it."

"Now *that's* something like! You are working up to standard, Huck. But don't go too far the other way, now. I—"

"Let him alone, Louis!" said Lem; "he's got his old works going again, don't discourage him, give him full swing. Go it, Huck, pull her wide open! Your reputation's a suffering: you might as well die for a sheep as a lamb—tell us we couldn't even hide *one* of those bullies in our village!"

"Sho," I said, "you make me smile! his mere umbrella would spread from your North Pole far and away below your Equator, and hide two-thirds of your wee Planet entirely from sight!"

There was an immense excitement.

"Shirts! shirts!" the gang shouted, springing to their feet, and the shirts began to sail about me and fall upon me like a snow-flurry.

Louis was beside himself with joy and admiration, and flung his arms about me, murmuring, half-choked with emotion—

"Oh, it's a triumph, a triumph, the poem is redeemed, it is superb, it is unapproachable, its sublime head strikes the very zenith—I *knew* it was in you!"

The others carried on like mad for a while screaming with care-free fun and delight, electing me by acclamation Imperial Hereditary High Chief Liar of Henryland, With Remainder to Heirs Male in Perpetuity, then they began to shout—

"Dimensions! dimensions! hooray for His Nibs, give us his particulars!"

"All right," I said, "any you want. To start with,—supposing this planet of yours wore clothes, I give you my word I've seen more than one Man who couldn't crowd into them without bursting them—yes, sirs, a man who could lie down on Blitzowski and spread over both sides and stick over at both ends."

They were perfectly charmed, and said that *this* kind of lying was something *like,* and they could listen to it by the week; and said there wasn't a liar in all history that could come up to my knee;

and why did I go and hide this splendid talent, this gorgeous talent all this time? and now "go ahead—tell some more!"

I was nothing loath. I entertained them an hour or two with details of the Monster and of his World, naming nations and countries, systems of government, chief religions, and so on— watching Lurbrulgrud out of the corner of my eye all the time, and expecting to hear from him by and by. He was one of your natural doubters, you know. We all knew he was taking notes privately—it was his way. He was always trying to ambush somebody and catch him in contradictions and inveracities. I could see that the boys didn't like it this time. They were plainly annoyed. You see, they thought it very handsome of me to make up all those variegated and intricate lies for their amusement, and it wasn't fair to expect me to remember them, and get called to book for them. By and by, sure enough, Grud fetched out his notes, set his eye upon them, and opened his mouth to begin. But at a sign from the others, Davy Copperfield covered it with his hand and said—

"Never you mind; you hold your yawp. Huck doesn't have to make good. He has given us a wonderful exhibition of what imagination can do when there is genius behind it, and he did it to let us have a good time, and we've had it—is that the straight word, boys?"

"It is *that*—every time!"

"Very well then—hold your yawp, I say it again—you can't spring any traps here, you can't fetch him to book."

"And that's the word with the bark on it!" said the boys. "Take a walk, Grud!"

But I interposed, and said—

"No, let him ask his questions—I don't mind. I'm ready to answer."

They were quite willing, in that case. They wanted to see how I would come out.

"Hold on!" said Lem Gulliver. "There's going to be some bets on this game. Ask your first question, Grud, then stop."

Grud said—

"Huck, along in the beginning you threw out a good deal of brag about the Cuban War, as you called it. You furnished some amusing statistics of that skirmish; will you be kind enough to repeat them?"

"Stop," said Lem. "Two to one on each separate statistic; two bash to one he fails on each. Come—who puts up?"

The boys looked unhappy and didn't say anything. Of course Lem jeered; that was the way he was made. It angered Louis, and he sung out—

"I take you!"

"Hanged if I don't, too!" piped up Sir Galahad.

"Good! Any more?" No answer. Lem rubbed his hands together in malicious glee, and said, "Here—the same odds that he doesn't answer *any* question right, in the entire list! Come—what do I hear?"

I waited a moment, then said—

"I take you."

The boys broke out in a rousing shout and kept it up till Lem's temper was pretty thoroughly tried, but he knew better than to let it slip—oh, no, that would have been nuts for the boys—*any* boys. He allowed the noise to quiet down, then he said—

"*You* take it! *You* do! I like your discretion. Go ahead with your answer."

The boys bunched their heads together over Grud's notes, and waited eagerly. I said—

"We sent 70,000 men to Cuba—"

"Score one!—for Huck!"

That was from the boys.

"We lost of them, killed and wounded together, 268."

"Score two—for Huck!"

"We lost 11 by disease—"

"Score three—for Huck!"

"—and 3,849 by the doctors."

"Score four—for Huck!"

"We mustered-in 130,000 men besides the 70,000 we sent to Cuba—kept them in camp in Florida."

"Score five—for Huck!"

"We added the entire 200,000 to the pension roll."

"Score six—for Huck!"

"We made a major general out of a doctor for gallantry at the great battle of San Juan—"

"Score seven—for Huck!"

"—in sending his pills to the rear and saving life with the bullet."

"Score eight—for Huck!"

"Huck, you furnished some medical statistics of what you called the Jap-Russian War—whatever that may be. Please repeat them."

"Of 9,781 sick Jap soldiers brought from the front in one batch to Japan for military hospital treatment, only 34 died."

"Score nine—for Huck!"

"Of a single batch of 1106 wounded Jap soldiers brought to Japan for military hospital treatment because their wounds were too serious for treatment in the field hospitals, none died. All got well, and the majority of them were able to return to the front and did so. Of the 1106, three had been shot through the abdomen, three through the head, and six through the chest."

"Score ten for Huck! And ten thousand for the Japanese military medical service!"

"Huck, in speaking of the American Medical Service—"

"Wait—I did not speak of it. We haven't any. We have never had any, at any time. What I said was, that the *people* call it the Medical Service sometimes, sometimes they call it The Angels of Death, but they are not in earnest when they use either of the terms. We have a Surgical Service, and there is none better; but the other industry is in two divisions, and has no general name covering both. Each is independent, performs a special service, and has a name of its own—an official name, furnished by the War Department. The War Department calls one of them the Typhoid Service, the other the Dysentery Service. The one provides typhoid for the Reserves-Camps, the other provides dysentery for the armies in the field. At another place in my informations I also told you that the lessons of the Cuban War were not lost upon the Government. Immediately after that conflict it reorganized its military system and greatly improved it. It discarded soldiers, and enlisted doctors only. These it sends against the enemy, unencumbered by muskets and artillery, and carrying 30 days' ammunition in their saddlebags. No other impedimenta. The saving in expense is quite extraordinary. Where whole armies were required before, a single regiment is sufficient now. In the Cuban War it took 142,000 Spanish soldiers five months to kill 268 of our defenders, whereas in the same five months our 141 doctors killed 3,849 of our said defenders, and could have killed the rest but they ran out of ammunition. Under our new system we replace 70,000 soldiers with 69 doctors. As a result we have the smallest army on our planet, and quite the most effective. I wanted to lay these particulars before you because, while they are not required by your list of questions, they throw a valuable general light upon the whole body of interrogatories. Pardon me for interrupting the game with this excursion. Now go on with your questions."

But by this time a decided change had come over the boys, and they burst into an excited chorus of—

"Wait! wait, we're coming in!"

And very eager they were, too, and began to get out their money and push it under Lem's nose, boldly offering to take the whole of the 182 remaining questions on Lem's original proposition. But he declined. He had already lost 20 bash to Louis and 20 to Galahad, and matters were getting pretty serious for him. Yes, he declined. He said—without any considerable sugar in it—

"You had your chance, you didn't take it, you're out, and you'll *stay* out."

Then they got yet more excited, and offered *him* two to one. No —he wouldn't. They raised it. Raised it to 3 to 1; 4 to 1; 5 to 1; 6—7—8 to one! He refused. They gave it up, and quieted down. Then I said—

"I'll give you 50 to 1, Lem."

By George, *that* raised a shout! Lem hesitated. He was tempted. The boys held their breath. He studied as much as a minute. Then he said—

"No-o. I decline."

It fetched another shout. I said—

"Lem, I'll do this: two to one I miss on no detail of the 182. Come—if I miss on a single detail, you take the whole pot; isn't that a fat enough thing for you?—a seasoned old sport like you? Come!"

The taunt fetched him! I was sure it would. He took me up. Then he set his teeth, and held his grip, till I had scored 33 without a miss—the boys breathing hard, and occasionally breaking out into a hasty burst of applause—then he let fly in a rage and swore there was chicane here, and frothed at the mouth, and shook his fist in my face and shouted—

"This whole thing's a swindle—a put-up swindle! I'll pay the others, but not you. You got those lies by heart and laid for me, and I was too dull to see it. You knew I'd offer bets, and you laid for me. But you'll get nothing by it, I can tell you that. Betting on a sure thing *cancels the bet,* in *this* country!"

It was a handsome triumph for me, and I was exceedingly comfortable over it. The boys cried—

"Shame, shame, you shirk!" and were going to force him to hand over my winnings, but I saw my chance to do some good by setting a moral example. To do it might be worth more to me, in the way of trade, if it got talked about among families interested in morals, than the money; so I made the boys let him alone, and said—

"I can't take the money, boys, I can't indeed. My position does not permit me to gamble; indeed it requires me to set my face against gambling. Particularly in public, and I regard this occasion as in a sense public. No, I cannot accept the pot; to me, situated as I am, it would be tainted money. I could not conscientiously use it, except in the missionary cause. And not even in that cause, except under certain restrictions. In my discourse upon the World I spoke of the long and bitter war of words which was waged in America over tainted money and the uses which it might be legitimately put to. In the end it was decided that no restriction at all could properly be put upon its use. For that reason I left the country, and came here. I said these parting words; said them in public: 'I go,' I said— 'to return no more; I renounce my country; I will go where it is clean, I cannot live in a tainted atmosphere.' I departed—I came hither. My first breath of the atmosphere of Blitzowski convinced me that I had made a signal change, my friends and dear comrades!"

The boys took it for a compliment—I had judged they would—and they gave me three times three with enthusiasm, and followed it with a rousing *chckk* (tiger). Then I proceeded.

"Where I disagreed with that verdict of my then-countrymen was upon a detail which persons less inflexibly, less inveterately moral than myself might regard as a quibble. I took the stand that all tainted money lost its taint when it left the hand that tainted it, except when employed abroad to damage a civilization superior to our own. I said, do not send it to China, send it to the other missionary fields, then it will go clean and stay so. I mentioned to you the country called China this afternoon, you may remember.

"No, I cannot take these tainted stakes, because now I am out of reach of China. I never intended to take then anyway; I was only betting for amusement—yours and mine. And I did not win them; I knew, all the time, I wasn't winning them, and wouldn't be entitled to them."

"Hel-lo! how do you make that out?" the boys exclaimed.

"Because it's as Lem said—I *was* betting on a sure thing. Those were merely *facts,* not creations of fancy—merely common historical facts, known to me this long time; I couldn't make a mistake in them, if I tried."

That was a sly and well-considered attempt to undermine and weaken the boys' obstinate conviction that my World and all my details were smart inventions—lies. I glanced at their faces—hopefully; then my spirits went down—I hadn't scored; I could see it. Lem was feeling happier and more respectable than had been his case a little while before, but it was observable that he had his doubts as to my having come into our contest with honest cards unstacked. He said—

"Huck, honor bright. Didn't you cram? Didn't you get that raft of details by heart for this occasion?"

"Honor bright, I didn't, Lem."

"All right, I believe you. Moreover I admire you; and that is honest. It shows that you have a splendid memory and—what is just as valuable—a recollection that answers up promptly when required to produce a thing,—a recollecting-faculty which always instantly knows just which pigeon-hole to find it in. In many a case the professional liar lacks the latter gift, and it beats him in the end, to a certainty; his reputation begins to dwindle, it fades gradually out, and you cease to hear of him."

He stopped there, and began to put on his shirt. I waited for his head to come through, supposing he would finish then. But apparently he had already finished, for he did not say anything more. It took me several seconds to realize that there was a connection between his random remarks about professional liars and me. Yes, there was a connection, I could perceive it now. And he had been paying me a compliment. At least that was his idea of it. I turned to the boys, intending to let them help me enjoy the joke, but—ah, well, they hadn't seen any. They were admiring, too—on the same basis. It was certainly a discouraging lot! The laugh I was arranging turned into a sigh.

Presently Sir Galahad took me aside, and said—trying to suppress his excitement—

"Tell me confidentially, master, I will keep it honorably to myself: *was* it lies, or was it really facts—those wonders, those marvels?"

I replied sadly—

"Why tell you, my poor boy? you would not believe me; none believes me."

"But I *will!* Whatever you tell me, I will believe. It is a promise —and sacred!"

I hugged him to my breast, and wept upon him, saying—

"No language can tell how grateful I am for this! for I have been so depressed, so discouraged, and I was hoping for so different a result. I swear to you, my Galahad, I have not made one statement that was not true!"

"Enough!" he said, with fervor, "it is enough; I believe it, every word. And I long to hear more. I long to hear all about that stupendous World and the Humming Race, those sky-scraping monsters that can step from one end of this planet to the other in two strides. They have a history—I know it, I feel it—an old and great and stirring history—would Grak * I knew it, master!"

"You shall, my precious boy—and at once. Go to Catherine of Aragon, tell her to reverse the recorder, and turn the crank. The entire history of the World is in it. Go—and Grak bless you!"

Straightway he was gone. It was his way, when he was excited.

When I got back to the boys, Lem Gulliver was already busy with a scheme. I sat down and listened. His idea was to get up a company and put my Lie on the market. He called it that. He said there wasn't anything on the planet that could compete with it for a moment. It could absorb all the little concerns in the business, on its own terms, and take the entire trade. It would be a giant monopoly, and you wouldn't have any trouble about the stock, indeed you wouldn't. No trouble about it, and no uncertainties; just get up a little inexpensive syndicate among ourselves, and water the stock, and—

"Water your granny!" said Grud, "it's all water, *now*; you can't find a solid place in a million tons of it. How—"

"Never you mind," said Lem, "you wait—you'll see. All we want is to start right, and she'll go like a hurricane. First, we want a name for her—a grand name; an impressive name—come, make a suggestion, somebody."

"Standard Oil."

I offered that.

"What's Standard Oil?"

"The most colossal corporation in the World, and the richest."

"Good—that's settled. Standard Oil she is! Now then—"

"Huck," said Grud, "you can't market a lie like that, all in one hunk. There isn't any nation that can swallow it whole."

"Who said they could? They don't have to. They'll take it on the instalment plan—there don't any of them have to take any more of it than they can believe at a time. Between rests."

"Well, I reckon that'll do—it looks all right, anyway. Who'll work the flotation?"

---

* One of the principal deities.

"Butters."

"What—that bucket-shop dysentery-germ?"

"Plenty good enough, all the same. He knows the game."

"So he does," said Davy Copperfield; "but would you let him keep our capital in his safe?"

"No. Keep it in the stove, and have two firemen, in two watches, four hours off and four on."

"Well, I reckon that'll answer. But wouldn't Butters feel humiliated?"

"The Butterses ain't that kind."

Hang them, they were actually getting ready to chip in! I never saw such a volatile lot; you could persuade them to anything in five minutes. Their scheme would absolutely destroy me! Parents would not send their young sons to my Institute to be taught morals by an incorporated liar.* If the Standard Oil should fail of success, my ease and comfort would be gone, there would be nothing left but the organ, the monkey, and bitter hard toil with little rest.

I was in a sort of panic, and well I might be. I must stop this disastrous scheme at once.

How? by persuasion? Not on your life! Golden dreams are not blown out of frenzied heads by *that* process. No—there is a way— one way, and only one, not two: you must see that golden dream and raise it—raise it to the limit!

My mind was working with a rush, by now—working full head

---

*About the middle of the second decade I began to teach morals. The additional money thus earned furnished me some lacking little comforts which were very welcome. I painted my sign myself, on a square of tin, and at first I displayed it on my back when I was around with my organ, but for some reason it did not draw; so then I nailed it on the house door:

INSTRUCTION GIVEN IN
Political Morals
Commercial Morals
Ecclesiastical Morals
and
Morals

Pupils applied at once, and I soon had my classes going. Many of the people said my morals were better than my music, if anything. It sounds like flattery but they were in earnest, I think. I generally found the people to be straight-speakers.

—you could hear it rumble. Swiftly I turned over this, that and the other project—no good! . . . Time was flying! But at last, just in the nick of time I struck it, and knew I was saved! My anxiety, my worry, my terror, vanished; and I was calm.

"Boys," I said,

XXI.

THEN I stopped.

That is the way to get the attention of a fussy and excited young crowd. Start to say something; then pause; they notice *that,* though they hadn't noticed your words—nor cared for them, either. Their clack ceases; they set their eyes upon you, intently, expectantly. You let them do that for about eight seconds, or maybe nine, you meantime putting on the expression of a person whose mind has wandered off and gotten lost in a reverie. You wake up, now, give a little start,—that whets them up! you can see their mouths water. Then you say, quite indifferently, "Well, shall we be starting along?—what time is it?" and the game is in your hands.

It's a disappointment. They are sure you came within an ace of saying something important, and are trying to keep it back, now— out of prudence, maybe. Naturally, then, they are eager to know what it was. You say, oh, it wasn't anything. Of course, then, they are just bound to find out; so they insist and insist, and say they won't stir a step until you've told them what it was. Everything is safe, now. You've got their whole attention; also their curiosity; also their sympathy; they've got an appetite. You can begin. Which I did. I said—

"It's really of no consequence, but if you want to hear it, you shall; but don't blame me if it isn't interesting; I've already indicated that it isn't. That is, *now.*"

"What do you mean by *now?*" said Davy Copperfield.

"Well, I mean it *would* have been interesting if—well, it was a scheme I happened on when I was on my way out here this afternoon, and I was rather full of it for a while, for I thought maybe we could scrape together a little capital among us, and—and —I confess it looked pretty promising, but—well, it isn't any matter *now*, and there's no hurry, there isn't a person that knows how to find it but me—I'd give him ten years and he couldn't find it!—so it's perfectly safe; it'll keep, and in a year or two or three when we've got the Standard Oil on its legs and going, we—gee, but that's a good name! It'll make it go—you'll see. If we hadn't anything but just that name it would be enough. I feel just as certain that three years from now—or maybe four,—the Standard Oil—"

"*Hang* the Standard Oil—stick to the scheme!" cried Lem Gulliver, with peppery impatience; "what *is* the scheme?"

"That's it!" they all chimed in together, "fetch it out, Huck, *tell us!*"

"Oh, I've no objection to telling you, for it'll keep, years and years; nobody knows where it is but me, and as for *keeping*, the best thing about gold is—"

"*Gold!*"

It took their breath, it made them gasp.

"Gold!" they shouted, hot-eyed, dry-throated, "Where is it? tell us where! stop fooling around and get to the point!"

"Boys, be calm, do not get excited, I beg of you. We must be prudent; one thing at a time is best. This will keep, I assure you it will. Let it wait—that is wisest; then, in six or seven years, just as soon as the Standard Oil—"

"Thunder and blazes, let the Standard *Oil* do the waiting!" they cried. "Out with it, Huck. Where is it?"

"Ah, well," I said, "of course if it is your unanimous desire and decision to postpone the Standard Oil utterly until after we—"

"It is! it is!—utterly, entirely, never to be touched until we've made that scoop, and you give the word. Go ahead now and tell us —tell us everything!"

I recognized that the Institute of Applied Morals was saved.

"Very well, then, I will place the thing before you, and I think you will like it."

I bound them to secrecy, with proper solemnities, then I told them a tale that crisped their hair, it was of such a heating nature. The interest was intense. Sometimes they breathed, but generally they forgot to. I said the Major Molar was a section of a curving range of stupendous brown cliffs which stretched away, no one knew how far—thousands of miles. The rock was a conglomerate of granite, sandstone, feldspar, pitchblend, lapis lazuli, 'dobies, verde antique, freestone, soapstone, grindstone, basalt, rock salt, epsom salts, and every other ore that contains gold, either free or in a matrix. The country was exceedingly rough and forbidding and desolate, and it had taken me several months to explore a hundred miles of it, but what I had seen of it had satisfied me. I had marked one place, in particular, where I would sink a shaft some day if I lived and ever got hold of capital enough for the job. And now, in my belief, that happy day was come. Were the boys content with the scheme?

Were they! Oh, well!

So *that* was settled. The enthusiasm was away up—away high up—up to the topmost top. Standard Oil was flat. We went home gay.

The truth was, I couldn't really tell whether the scheme was worth anything or not. Still, I had pretty fair hopes. I got them from putting this and that together and drawing an inference. Blitzowski had almost certainly seen better days, at some time or other, for he had the dentist-habit. Among the poor and defeated, none but people who have been well off, and well up, have that expensive habit.

I was satisfied with the way I had played that game. People who are on fire with a splendid new scheme are cynical and chilly toward a new one if you spring it on them suddenly and beseech them to look at it. It is best to be indifferent, and disinclined, then they get an appetite, and do the begging themselves.

XXII.

CATHERINE SAID she had turned the crank a while for Sir Galahad and he went wild with delight and astonishment over my History of the World, then he rushed away with the Recorder and said he was going to shut himself up with it at home and master its entire contents before ever he rested.

I had saved my College of Morals, by interposing a gold mine between it and the dangerous Standard Oil; it was only an emergency-gold mine, I only invented it to stop that gap; but now that it was invented, and the boys joyfully insane about it, I must stand by it or invent something still richer and better, to take its place. I thought over a lot of substitutes, such as emerald mines and opal mines, and diamond mines, but I had to give them up, Blitzowski would turn out to be quite barren of those things, for sure. I fell back on the gold. I got to working up a hope. The more I worked at it, and coaxed it, and reasoned with it, the less and less chimerical it seemed. It is the right way to do with a hope; it is like any other agriculture: if you hoe it and harrow it and water it enough, you can make three blades of it grow where none grew before. If you've got nothing to plant, the process is slow and difficult, but if you've got a seed of some kind or other—any kind will answer—you get along a good deal faster. I had one. It was a dream. I planted the dream. It turned up in my memory just at the right time. I believe something in dreams. Sometimes. I had not believed in this one when it happened, but that was because I hadn't any use for it then. It was different, now. A dream that comes only once is oftenest only an idle accident, and hasn't any message, but the recurrent dream is quite another matter—oftener than not it has come on business. This one was that kind. I wondered, now, that I hadn't had this thought at the time. It was a good dream, and well put together.

First I dreamed that I was patiently chewing my way through a

very long and delicate nerve in one of Blitzowski's back teeth—
lower jaw—and feeling him rock and sway mountainously in
response to the pain; this went on for some weeks, and at last I
fetched out into a vast cavity, a cavity of imposing grandeur, with
walls that stretched up and up and up through an ever-dimming
twilight until lost in the ultimate thick darkness, for his mouth was
shut at the time.

By and by the dream came again. But this time I found the
stupendous Cave filled; Blitzowski had been to the dream-dentist.

After an interval it came a third time. In my dream the plug was
transparent. It was disposed in three vast strata, each about a third
of a mile thick, (microbe measure). The top one was dove-colored,
the next one had the tint of oxydized silver, the bottom one was
yellow.

I called up those dreams, now, and studied them; a little
doubtfully at first, but under painstaking and intelligent cultivation
they improved. In the end, the crop arrived at puberty, and was
satisfactory. I was in a condition of mind bordering on enthusiasm.
The mine was there, sure—pretty dreamy, yes, pretty dreamy, but
there, anyway; I could *see* it! just as if it were before my eyes: top
stratum, a third of a mile deep—cement; next stratum, amalgam;
bottom stratum, gold! good, straight, honest dentist's gold, 23
carats fine!

And as for the quantity. I fell to measuring it—for fun. Very
soon the towering figures began to take hold of my imagination!
How natural that was! It is the way we are made. I began in fun; in
fifteen minutes I was sobering down to earnest. And how natural
that was, too! In the alembic of my fancy—without my noticing it,
so absorbed was I in my ciphering—my dream-gold was turning
into the real metal, and my dream was turning into a fact. At least
into a persuasion. Very well, it didn't take the persuasion long to
harden into a conviction. So there is where I had presently arrived:
I was convinced that the dream was a straight and honorable and
perfectly trustworthy photograph of an existent actuality. Which is
to say, all doubts and questionings had sifted out of my mind, by
now, and disappeared, and I was believing, up to the hilt, that that

mighty treasure was really yonder and waiting for us in the sub-cellar of Blitzowski's tooth. Between believing a thing and thinking you *know* it is only a small step and quickly taken. I soon took it, and was prepared to say to all comers, "It isn't a mere probability, I *know* the gold is there." It's the way we are made. We could be better made, but we wouldn't be interesting, then.

By my stingiest and most conservative and exacting measurement, I was obliged to admit that that wad of gold was not a shade less than half the bigness of a human buckshot! It was titanic—colossal—unthinkable—it was absolutely breath-taking! Yet there it was—there were the figures—there was no getting around them.

What might I compare this astonishing deposit with? Klondike? It made me smile. Klondike was but a peanut-pedlar's till, alongside of it. The Big Bonanza, then? Let us consider. The Big Bonanza was discovered in Nevada seven years before I was born—a stupendous body of rich silver ore, the like of which had never been heard of in the world before. Two day-laborers discovered it, and took into partnership in the secret a saloon keeper and a broker; they bought the ground for a song, and in two weeks they were hundred-millionaires. But the Big Bonanza was nothing—you might say, less than nothing—compared with the measureless mass of wealth packed away in the deeps of Blitzowski's tush. A speck of gold worth 2,000 *slasher* would not be detectible under a human microscope until magnified seventeen hundred and fifty-six diameters. Let some one else go on now, and cipher out the whole value of that tooth, if desired, it makes me tired.

The spectacle of this incredible wealth dazed me, I was like one drunk—drunk with delight, with exultation! I had never had any money before, to speak of, and I didn't know what to do with it, it was a positive embarrassment—for some minutes. I had never cared for money before, but now I cared for it. So suddenly as this I was changed like that! We *are* strangely made!

What would the boys say when I told them! How would they feel, what would they say, when they pulled their stampeded wits together and realized how limitlessly rich they were! Oh, how *would* they feel when they realized that they couldn't possibly spend their yearly income, even though they should hire the imperial Henryland Family to help!

I was impatient to summon them and tell them the great news. I reached out my hand to touch the bell—

Wait! Something in me seemed to say, don't be precipitate—reflect!

I obeyed the mysterious impulse, and reflected.

x   x   x   x

I reflected hard, for an hour. Then I sighed, and said to myself "It is only fair; it is I that discovered the mine; if it had not been for me it would never have been discovered at all; it would not be just for them to have a twelfth apiece, and I no more."

I reflected further, and decided to keep half, and let them have the other half among them. It seemed to me that that was right and fair, and I felt quite satisfied.

I was going to ring, now—

That warning stopped me again.

x   x   x   x

I reflected another hour. Then I saw that they could never use so much money—it would be impossible. A third of the property would be quite sufficient for them, modest as were their needs, unfamiliar as they were with m—

I reached for the bell.

x   x   x   x

After a season of deep reflection I recognized that they would never be able to spend judiciously any more than a fourth of that mass of riches—

x   x   x   perhaps not even a tenth. Indeed, with so much as a tenth, would not the poisonous spirit of speculation enter insidiously into them? would it not undermine their morals? had I a *right* to place such a temptation before such young and inex—

x x x ah, no, no, I must not betray them, I must do my duty by them, I should never be able to sleep again if I should be the instrument of their moral ruin. Oh, the bare thought of it is more than I—

x x x Yes, it would be best for them that I keep the gold. No harm would come to them then, and the reflection that I had saved them pure would always be my sufficient reward—I could ask no other, no sweeter, no nobler.

x x x But I would not allow them to go wholly shareless in this good fortune that was come to me; no, they should have part of the amalgam mine. They should do the work on both mines, and have part of the amalgam for their labor. I would determine what part, upon further reflection. And they could have all the cement.

I then went to bed.

(1905)

The Refuge of the Derelicts

Chapter 1

"TELL HIM to go to hell!"

"So *that* was the message the footman brought you from the Admiral!" said Shipman, keeping as straight a face as he could, for he saw that his friend the young poet-artist was deeply wounded, therefore this was not a proper time for levity. He loved the poet-artist better than he loved any other creature; loved him as a mother loves her child; loved to touch him, pat him, look into his eyes, loved to listen to his voice, knew his footstep from any other, and thrilled to it. And so, for him, this was not a time to laugh, this was not a time to add a pang to that smarting wound. He made him sit down on the sofa by him, laid a caressing hand upon his knee, and said, "You have been so excited, George, that you haven't been altogether clear in your narrative. You called at the Admiral's house—that much is clear—you sent in your request for a ten-minute interview—that is clear, too—the footman came back with an invitation—"

"Yes"—bitterly—"invitation to go to hell!"

"Clear again. But the rest of it is confused. You *think* you have explained to me how you came to go there without an introduction, and you also think you have made me understand what your project was, but it's a mistake; I didn't get it. You are calmer, now, George; tell me the whole thing; maybe I can help you."

"No," said George, "You are mistaken as to the project, I only said I had a project, I didn't tell you what it was. I was coming to that. It is great and fine and will be costly; it may be a dream, but it is a noble dream—that I know." The thought of it lit the poet's deep eyes as with a sunbeam. "I went there to ask him to subscribe to it."

"What is the project?"

"A monument."

"A monument?"

"Yes."

"To whom?"

"Adam."

Shipman was caught unprepared, and he burst out with—

"Gr-reat Scott!"

He was almost startled from his base, but he immediately followed his give-away exclamation with a remark intended to express pure admiration, and "save his face," which it did. The poet was visibly pleased, and said—

"I'm so glad you like the idea, David."

"Why, I couldn't help but like it, George. I think it's one of the greatest and most unusual ideas I have ever heard of. I wonder it has never been thought of before."

"So do I. But I am glad it wasn't."

"You may well be. It is an august idea, there's nothing to compare with it, nothing that approaches it. None but a poet's mind could ever have conceived it!" and he seized the dreamer's hand and crushed into it the rest of the enthusiasm he was persuading himself to feel.

"It *is* wonderful, isn't it, David?" said George, flushing with pleasure.

"Boy, it's *great!* And you will succeed, too."

"Do you really think so, David?"

"Think it? I *know* it! Another couldn't, but you will. Because your heart is in it; and when your heart is in a thing, George, you've got the words to match, words that persuade, words that convince. Is that a list of people you hope to round-up? Give it to me."

He ran his eye down it.

"Do you know any of these, George?"

"Well, no—I don't."

"It's no matter, I know them, and I'll steer you. It's a large thing, and will take us both. I'll furnish the bait, and you'll land the fish. Tell me—what was your plan? As regards the Admiral, for instance."

"Plan, David? Why—I hadn't any."

"Hadn't any *plan!* How did you mean to go at him?"

"I was only going to tell him the idea, and ask him to subscribe. That was all."

"And you a perfect stranger! Why, George, *that* was no way to do. How could you be so innocent? Don't you know that in all cases where you are interested and the other person isn't, there are four thousand wrong ways to go at him, and only one right one?"

"Why, no, I didn't know it. It wouldn't ever have occurred to me, David. Do you mean that the one right way to go at one person is the *same* way to go at all the others?"

"Broadly speaking, yes. You must apply the same persuader in all the cases."

"David, you surely can't mean *all?*"

"Yes, all. The whole human race."

"David, if you are not joking, what is the one right way?"

"*Purchase.* Bribery. Bribery and corruption."

The poet was dumb for a minute—paralysed. Then he said, gravely—

"I was in earnest, David. It isn't kind to treat it like this."

Shipman laid an affectionate hand upon his shoulder, and said—

"Forgive me, lad, I meant no harm, I wouldn't hurt you for the world—you know that. I was too abrupt, that was all. It misled you. I was not joking, I meant what I said, and what I said is true—I give you my word it is. Now, as soon as I come to expl—"

"But David! Look at that list. Think what you are saying. The purest people, the noblest people, the—some of them not rich, but there isn't gold enough in Klondike to—"

"*Money?* Dear me, I didn't say anything about money—I wasn't thinking of it. I—"

"Why, David, you *said*—"

"*Buy? Bribe?* So I did, but I didn't say buy with money."

"Oh, well, goodness knows *I* don't know what you are driving at. If you think you know, yourself, I do wish you—"

"I do know, George, I do indeed. What I was meaning was, that every human being has his price, every human being can be bought—"

"Now you are saying it again! yet you said, only a minute ago—"

"Hush! Let me talk. You interrupt me so, I can't arrive anywhere. Now then, the thing is perfectly simple. Listen. Every human being has a weak place in him, a soft spot. In one it is avarice—you buy him with money; in another it is vanity—you beguile him through that; in another it is a compassionate heart—you work him to your will through that; in another—a mother, for instance—it is adoration of a child, perhaps a crippled one, an idiot—she sells a politician her husband's vote for a judas-kiss bestowed upon her bratling; she doesn't know she is being bribed, but she is; the others don't suspect that they are selling themselves, but they are. It is as I tell you: every person has his price, every person can be bought, if you know where his weak spot is. Do you get the idea now?"

There was no answer; the poet was lost in thought. The burden of his thought was: "How true it is, no doubt . . . . poor human nature! . . . . what children we are—and don't know it, don't suspect it . . . . the proudest of us, the biggest of us, purchasable! . . . . purchasable with a toy! . . . . Even the old Admiral, too?—bronzed by the storms of all the seas, old, white-headed, beloved of his friends as Arthur was by his knights, brave as Launcelot, pure as Galahad . . . . what might *his* price be!"

Meantime Shipman had retired to his den with the list, and was making skeleton notes. He finished them, then sat musing a moment. His thoughts ran something like this:

"God knows it's the insanest idea that ever . . . . but it's colossal, there's no denying that . . . . and new—oh, yes indeed, there's nothing stale about it! . . . . How *can* he be so serious over it? But he is. He sees only the dignity of it, the grandeur of it; to him it has no frivolous side, to him there is no glimmer of the humorous about it. My, but he is innocent!—poet to the marrow, dreamer, enthusiast . . . . conceive of his selecting *these* people to place such a project before, and strike them for contributions! No matter, they are bribable—for this queer project or any other, if he follows my instructions—borrowed from Lord Bacon—and concentrates his forces upon their weak spots."

A minute or two later he was saying to his pupil:

"Now then, here we have the campaign planned out. Take these notes, and think them over at your leisure—they point out the weak spots of each person in your list—come whenever you like, and we will elaborate the matter with talk. To each in turn I will certify you before your visit—then you will be expected, and your road will be smooth."

"Oh, it's ever so lovable in you, David!"

"I know it. First,—and right away—you will assault the Admiral again. I will telephone him. As you didn't give your name before, he won't know it was you he sent that invitation to." The poet colored, and shifted his body nervously, but said nothing. "Now I will post you about the Admiral. He is a fine and bluff old sailor, honest, unworldly, simple, innocent as a child—but doesn't know it, of course—knows not a thing outside of his profession, but *thinks* he knows a lot—you must humor that superstition of course—and he *does* know his Bible, (just well enough to misquote it with confidence,) and frankly thinks he can beat the band at explaining it, whereas his explanations simply make the listener dizzy, they are so astronomically wide of the mark; he is profoundly religious, sincerely religious, but swears a good deal, and competently—you mustn't notice that; drinks like a fish, but is a fervent and honest advocate and supporter of the temperance cause, and does what he can to reclaim the fallen by taking the pledge every now and then as an example, with the idea that it is a great encouragement to them; he can't sing, but he doesn't know it—you must ask him to sing; is a composer—good land!—and believes he is a musician; he thinks he is deep, and worldly-wise, and sharp, and sly, and cunning, and underhanded, and furtive, and not to be seen through by any art, whereas he is just glass, for transparency—and lovable? he is the most lovable old thing in the universe."

"My word, what a person! David, is he insane?"

"He? If he is, he has never suspected it. And the man that suggests it to him will do well to take a basket along to carry what's left of him home in. Do you want a basket? There's one in the other room."

"No. I am not going to need it. David, he seems to have quite a lot of vulnerable points—bribable points—"

"No he hasn't. He has only one. I haven't spoken of it yet. These others are to show you what to talk about, when you get started, and *how* to talk—they are aids, helpers, and very useful—but the one I haven't mentioned is the one that opens the door to his heart and puts him up for sale. That one, properly handled, will thaw him out and start his talking-mill—then you've got him!"

"I see! It's his magnificent achievements, his illustrious record, his great deeds in the war, his—"

"No, it isn't; it's his cat."

The poet was paralysed again, for a moment; then he regained his voice—

"His *cat?*"

"That's it. You get at him through his cat. He is bribable through his cat, but in no other way. In all other ways, his probity is adamant, he is as chaste as the driven snow, he is unpurchasable. But don't forget the cat. Work the cat; work him for all he is worth. Go along, now; I will telephone the Admiral you are on the way."

Chapter 2

The Admiral

He was eighty years old. Tall; large; all brawn, muscle and health; powerful bass voice, deep and resonant. He was born at sea, in the family's home, which was a Fairhaven whaleship, owned and commanded by his father. He was never at school; such education as he had, he had picked up by odds and ends, and it was rather a junk-shop than a treasury; though that was not his idea of it. He had very decided opinions upon most matters, and he had architected them himself. Sometimes they were not sound, but what they lacked in soundness they generally made up in originality.

He spent seventy years at sea, and then retired. He had now been retired ten years. He had never served in a warship, and did not get his title from the government; it was a token of love and homage, and was conferred upon him by the captains of the whaling fleet.

He was sitting in an arm-chair when George entered, and close at hand were various objects which were necessary to his comfort: grog, a

Bible, a Dibdin, a compass, a barometer, a chronometer, pipes, tobacco, matches, and so on. His ancient face was mottled with pinks, reds, purples and intermediate tints, and wrinkled on the plan of a railroad map; his head was wonderfully bald and slick and shiny and dome-like, and stood up out of a fence of silky white hair in a way to remind one of a watermelon in a bucket. Friends who liked to pester him said —not in his hearing, but to get it reported to him—that the flies used to slip, on his baldness, and fall and cripple themselves, and that in his native good-heartedness he rigged shrouds, made of thread, so that they could go aloft and return without risk.

He motioned George to a chair, then snuggled back into his own, with a contented grunt, and began to examine his guest with a calm and unblinking and prejudiced eye. This silent inquest was a little em-barrassing for the guest; an effect which was distinctly enhanced when the Admiral presently began to reinforce it with audible comments— under the impression that he was thinking to himself:

"Pale . . . . slim . . . . anemic . . . . half-fed . . . . timid. Lawyer? . . . . doctor? . . . . school-teacher? No. Not those. Hard to make him out. . . . . Good enough face, all but the eye. Has a malignant eye. What's his game, should you say? Has a game, of course; they all have. . . . . . Wants my influence, I reckon—most of them do. Wants to get a billet in the navy. They all think I've been in the navy. . . . . . Job where he'll have a salary and nothing to do . . . . it's the usual thing. Well, to come down to business, what does this one want, do you reckon? Paymaster? no. Captain's secretary? no. Those require work. Not in this one's line. . . . . Ah, ten to one he wants to be chaplain. Yes, that's it. Well, I'll beat his game." Without taking his eye from the uncomfortable poet the Admiral reached for a pipe, lit it, and resumed. "That chair makes him squirm. They all squirm when they sit in that chair. They think I put them in it by accident. . . . . Chaplain—*him!* Probably couldn't expound a miracle to save his life. But that's nothing, I've never seen one that could. No—and when I show them the trick they are jealous, and resent it; and they feel their ambition stirring in them, and they pipe to quarters and clear for action, and start in all cocky and conceited and do their idiotic damdest to put me in the wrong; and when I break in and tell them to go to—

I say!—" (this in a trumpet-blast that made the poet jump), "can you expound the miracles?"

"Can I, sir?"

"Yes, you. Can you do it?"

"Really, I am afraid not, sir."

The Admiral stared at him with astonishment, the sternness in his face perceptibly relaxing a little, and muttered to himself—audibly —"a *modest* one, at last!—I never expected to see it." Then to the poet, with the eager light of controversy rising in his eyes—

"Try it, young man, try it! Let's see what you can do; take any in the lot—pick your own miracle, and make sail. Try an easy one, first-off."

George found himself feeling relieved and measurably comfortable all at once. The Admiral's soliloquy and David's instructions had furnished him a safe cue, and he knew how to proceed. He said, with judicious humility—

"Anywhere but here, Admiral Stormfield. But here, if you will excuse me—"

"And why not here?"

"Because David Shipman warned me. He said 'Keep out of that subject if you don't want to come to grief, you would only expose yourself; Admiral Stormfield could give any man of your calibre ninety in the game and win out with one hand tied behind him.'"

"Did he say that? Did he?" The old gentleman was profoundly pleased.

"Yes, that is what he said. And he—"

The cat came loafing in—just at the right time, the fortunate time. George forgot all about the Admiral, and cut his sentence off in the middle; for by birth and heredity he was a worshiper of cats, and when a fine animal of that species strays into the cat-lover's field of vision it is the one and only object the cat-lover is conscious of for one while; he can't take his eyes off it, nor his mind. The Admiral noted the admiration and the welcome in George's face, and was a proud man; his own face relaxed, softened, sweetened, and became as the face of a mother whose child is being praised. George made a swift step, gathered the cat up in his arms, gave him a hug or two, then sat down and spread him out across his lap, and began to caress his silken body with lingering long strokes, murmuring, "Beautiful creature . . . . wonderful creature!" and such things as that, the Admiral watching him with grateful eyes and a conquered heart. Watching him, and talking to himself—aloud:

"Good face—full of intelligence . . . . good eye, too—honest, kind, couldn't be a better one . . . . a rare person, and superior—superior all around—very different from the run of lubbers that come here legging for influence—tadpoles that think they are goldfish—"

And so on and so on. What was become of the poet's "malignant eye" all of a sudden? If the question entered the Admiral's head at all, it created no disturbance there, aroused no concern; the Admiral's latest view of a thing was the only one he cared for; he had never been a slave to consistency.

The caressing of the purring cat went on, its flexile body hanging over at both ends, its amber eyes blinking slowly and contentedly, its strong claws working in and out of the gloved paws in unutterable satisfaction, the pearl-lined ears taking in the murmured ecstasies of the stranger and understanding them perfectly, and deeply approving them, the Admiral looking on enchanted, moist-eyed, soaked to the bone with happiness.

By and by he sprang up abruptly and shook himself together with the air and look of one who is pulling himself out of a dream, and began to move briskly about, muttering, "Manners? What the hell have I been thinking about?—and him a guest?"

He got a feather-duster and zealously dusted off a leathern armchair that had no dust on it, handling the duster not like a housemaid who is purifying furniture but like a chief of police who is dispersing a mob with a club; then he polished the leather with his silk handkerchief until it was as shiny as his own head; finally he stood aside and said, with a wave of his hand—

"Do me the honor. I'm ashamed. I don't know how I came to give you that chair, it's not fitting for the likes of you."

George began a polite protest, and got as far as that he was "quite comfortably seated, and—" The Admiral interrupted, with a burst as of thunder—

"Do as I *tell* you!" and the poet had accomplished the change before the curtains had stopped quaking.

The Admiral was pacified, and muttered to himself, "he don't mean any harm, all he wants is discipline—has been brought up loose and harum-scarum, the way they do on land." Meantime he was busy stuffing a pipe. He handed it to George, lifted a leg, gave a strenuous forward-rake upon its under-half with a match—successfully; in fact that kind of a rake would have lit a nail. He held the match to the pipe, while he worded another apology—

"You mustn't mind—I never meant any unpoliteness, but just as I was going to reach for a pipe for you, Bags came a-loafing in, and when a cat comes my way I forget myself for a minute."

"So do I!" responded the poet, eagerly. "Why, I shouldn't ever be able to keep my head, with a cat like *this* one anywhere between me and the horizon."

The emphasis on that word fell with a most pleasant thrill upon the Admiral's ear, and he said, with affectionate pride in his tone—

"Now he *is* a daisy, ain't he?"

The response to this was up to standard. The Admiral, chatting comfortably about his cat, and weaving into the meshes of his theme another apology as he went along, got a little table and placed it between his chair and George's, set bottle and glasses on it, seated himself, brewed a couple of punches, remarked, "now we'll take a bit of comfort," then got some photographs of the cat out of his pocket and spread them out on the table for inspection. The cat was interested at once. He leaped upon the table, sniffed at the bottle and at each punch in turn, then arched his neck, curved a paw, and flirted the photographs off the table one at a time, the Admiral observing the performance admiringly, and remarking, "graceful? it ain't any *name* for it!" The cat bent down over the edge, inspecting the fallen cards longingly and turning his lively head this way and that, then he cast an eloquent glance at the Admiral, who said, "he's asking me to get them for him, you see?" and proceeded to pick them up and replace them, saying "notice that thankfulness in his eye and the way he acts? *talk* ain't any plainer;" the cat eagerly flirted them off as fast as they were restored, the Admiral remarking "notice that? You'll see he'll keep it up as long as it int'rests him—always does." The patient picking-up and the cheerful flirting-off continued for a minute or two, then the cat sat up and began to lick his paws and use them to rake forward

his ears and scrub his cheeks, paying no further attention to the replacing of the cards. "You notice?" said the Admiral, with a successful
prophet's satisfaction, "didn't I tell you he would? oh, I know *him*,
I reckon! now I'll show you the pictures."

But he was disappointed. The cat lay down and stretched himself
out lengthwise of the table, which was only about two and a half feet
long—stretched himself to his utmost length, with each end of him
projecting a trifle beyond the edge. His body covered the cards and
left but scant room for the bottle and glasses. The Admiral sighed, and
said—

"Well, I wanted to show them to you, but it ain't any matter; there's
plenty of time, and maybe he'll think of something else he wants to do,
pretty soon. Often he does. Every night when we play cards on this
little table—me and my grand-niece or her Aunt Martha—he comes
and spreads out all over it the way he's doing now, and is most uncom-
monly in the way; you have to play *on* him, you know, because there
isn't any other place, he flats out so; and if he gets a chance he flirts
off the tricks with his paw; and if he lays down on a trick, the game's
up; you can't get at it, because he don't like to be disturbed. . . . Well,
we can talk, anyway, whilst he's thinking up something fresh to do—
say! now the light's coming just right—look at him! *ain't* he the very
blackest object that ever cast a gloom in the daytime? Do you know,
he's just solid midnight-black all over, from cutwater to tip-end of
spanker-boom. Except that he's got a faint and delicate little fringe of
white hairs on his breast, which you can't find at all except when the
light strikes them just right and you know where to look. Black? why,
you know, Satan looks faded alongside of Bags."

"Is that his n—"

"Look at him *now!* Velvet—satin—sealskin; can't you pick them out
on him? Notice that brilliant sheen all down his forrard starboard paw,
and a flash of it in the hollow of his side, and another one on his flank:
is it satin, or *ain't* it?—just you answer me that!"

"It *is* satin, it's exactly the name for it!"

"Right you are. Now then, look at that port shoulder, where the
light don't strike direct—sort of twilight as you may say: does it just
pre-cisely counterfeit imperial Lyons velvet, forty dollars a yard, or
don't it: come!"

"It does, I take my oath!"

"Right, again. The thickest fur and the softest you ever s— there! catch it in the shadow! in the deep shadow, under his chin—ain't it sealskin, *ain't* it? ain't it the very richest sealskin you—*say!* look at him now. He's just perfect now; wait till he gets through with that comfortable long summer-Sunday-afternoon stretch and curls his paw around his nose, then you'll see something. You'll *never* know how black he is, nor how big and splendid and trim-built he is till he puts on his *accent*. . . . . Th—there it is—just the wee tip of his pink tongue showing between his lips—now he's *all* there!—sheen and gloom and twilight—satin, sealskin, velvet—and the tip of his tongue like a fire-coal to accent him, *just* the blackest black outlay this side of the sub-cellars of perdition,—now I ask you honest, *ain't* he?"

The poet granted it, and poured out praise upon praise, rapture upon rapture, from his sincere soul, closing with—

"He *is* the last possibility of the beautiful! But oh, Admiral! how did you ever come to name him—"

"Bags? Sho, *that's* not his name, it's only his nom de plume. His name's Bagheera."

"Bagheera! Admiral, I could hug you for that! And he's worthy of it, too. If anybody can add anything to that praise, all right, let him try."

"You forgive me, don't you?" said the Admiral, oozing gratification from every pore; "I reckon I knew what I was about when I promoted him to that." He rose and moved toward his book-shelves. He took out a volume and patted its brown back. "Here she is," he said. "Kipling. Volume VII, Collected Works. Jungle Book. Immortal?"

"It's the right word, Admiral, in my opinion."

"You bet you! It'll outlast the rocks. Now I'm going to read to you out of this book. You look at the cat, and listen: 'A black shadow dropped down into the circle. It was Bagheera the Black Panther, inky black all over,'—*now notice, keep your eye on the cat*—'inky black all over, but with the panther markings showing up in certain lights like the pattern of watered silk.' There—don't he fill the bill? ain't he watered silk? look at his high-lights—look at his twilights—look at his deep glooms! Now you listen again: 'He had a voice as soft as wild honey dripping from a tree, and a skin softer than down.' *Bags!*"

The cat raised a sleepy head, and delivered an inquiring look from a blinking eye.

"Speak!"

The cat uttered a quivery-silvery mew.

"You hear that? is it soft as wild honey dripping from a tree? fills the bill don't it? Times, it is that rich and soft and pathetic and musical you wouldn't think it was a cat at all, but a spirit—spirit of a cat that's gone before, as the saying is. You ought to hear him when he's lonesome and goes mourning around empty rooms hunting for us; why, it just breaks your heart. And he's full of talent; full of tricks and oddities that don't belong in a cat's line, which he invented out of his own head."

"Could I see him do some of them?"

"—*sh!*" said the Admiral, putting his finger to his lips. "Change the subject. He *seems* to be asleep, this last half-a-minute, but that ain't any proof; it's just as likely he's awake, and listening. In that case you couldn't get him to do a thing. He's just like a child about that; the more you want him to show off, the more he won't do it to save your life."

"Admiral, is he so bright that he—"

"Understands? Every word!"

"I think, myself," George began, doubtfully, "that some animals understand a good deal of what we say—"

The Admiral stepped over and whispered at the poet's ear—

"*Every word!* Wasn't *that* what I said?"

"Yes, but—"

"I *said* it, didn't I? Well, it means par. He understands every word. Now I'll prove it"—still whispering. "It's a fad of his, to play with fire, and—"

"What, a cat play with fire?"

"Not so loud! Yes; it's because he found out that other cats don't. That's the way he's made—originality's his long suit; he don't give a damn for routine; you show him a thing that's old and settled and orthodox, and you can't get him to take any int'rest in it, but he'll trade his liver for anything that's fresh and showy. Now I'll light a little alcohol lamp and set it over yonder on the floor, and if he hasn't overheard us he'll put it out with his paw when he gets up; but if he is shamming and listening, now, he'll put up a disappointment on us, sure: he'll go over and give it an indifferent look and pass by on the other side, like the Good Samaritan."

The little lamp was duly lighted and placed, and the experimenters waited, in a solemn silence, for the result. Pretty soon—

"Watch him!" said the Admiral. "He's turning on his back to— look at that! when he gets that stretch completed and everything taut, he'll be twice as long as you think he is. There—how is that? as long and stiff as a deer-carcass that's frozen for transportation, ain't it? Notice the flash of that sheen on his garboard strake, port side of his keelson, just forrard of the mizzen channels—ain't that a gloss for you! Now then—stand by for a surge, he's going to gape. When he gets his mouth full-spread, look in, and see how pink he is inside, and what a contrast it is to his thunder-black head. There you are! ain't it pretty? ain't it like a slice out of a watermelon? . . . . Now—stand by again— he's going to break out his spinnaker."

The cat rose, added some fancy touches to his luxurious stretch, then he skipped to the floor and started across the room, making long final stretch-strides which extended first one hind leg and then the other far to the rear—then he discovered the lamp, and made straight for it with strong interest. The Admiral whispered, in high gratification—

"I bet you he didn't hear a word we said! Come, this is luck!"

The cat approached to within a foot of the lamp, then began to circle warily around it and sniff at it.

"It's the way he always does," whispered the Admiral, "he'll attack it in a minute."

The cat presently stopped, stood high, raised a paw—

"You see that? ain't it a pretty curve? he'll hold that paw that way as much as a half-a-minute, measuring his distance—sometimes he'll hold it out as straight as a stunsl-boom and—there, see him strike? Didn't fetch it this time, but you'll see he'll never let up till he does."

"Admiral, he burnt his fur; I smell it."

"That's nothing, he always does; he don't care. Another whack! ain't it graceful? ain't it resolute, ain't it determined? He's going to try with the other paw, now. He was left-handed when he was born, but

I learnt him ambidexterousness when he was little. . . . . There!—that was a good spat, you could hear it! That's four—about next time he'll fetch it. . . . . There! what'd I tell you?—he's done it."

The cat gave his paws a lick or two, then loafed off to a corner and stretched himself out on the floor. George said he could not have believed in this extraordinary performance if he hadn't seen it; that he had never heard of a cat before that would attack fire. He wanted to know who taught him.

"Nobody. It was his own idea. Took it up when he was a kitten. But never mind that—that ain't the thing that's before the house." The Admiral gave his head a prideful toss, and added, "the thing that is before the house is, did I *prove* it? That's the thing for you to answer: did I, or didn't I?"

"Prove what?"

The Admiral was a little nettled.

"Come! what did I start *out* to prove?"

"Well, I don't qui—I—"

"You've *forgot,* by gracious!—that's it—forgot it a'ready! Didn't I say he understood every word? Didn't I say I would prove it? Well, then—have I, or *haven't* I?"

George began to stammer and hesitate, showing that the proof had missed him; that he didn't know what it consisted in, and was fighting for time and revelation. The Admiral was surprised at his stupidity, and said with severity—

"Didn't I *tell* you, that if he was actually awake and overhearing us he would understand every word and wouldn't do a thing? Well, didn't he put out the lamp? Now then, what does it prove? It proves that he *didn't* overhear us, don't it? And *that* proves that he understands every word when he *does* overhear, don't it? I knew perfectly well I could prove it, I told you so before."

The Admiral had him under his severe and unrelenting eye, and so he was obliged to confess the "proof," for diplomacy's sake, though deep down in his heart he couldn't seem to see any convincing connection between the evidence and the alleged fact. However, he had wit enough to throw out a nicely buttered remark which beguiled the Admiral away from the danger-line and saved the situation: he said it was perfectly wonderful the way the Admiral could "argue." The old gentleman melted to that rather gross contribution; he was pleased to the midriff, and said complacently—

"Well, they all say the old man can do a tidy thing in that line now and then, but I don't know—I don't know."

The poet followed up his advantage with more butter, and still more butter, until all possible peril was overpassed, and quite new and safe ground reached. To-wit, music. The poet was fond of it, the Admiral was fond of it—here was a new tie; the two men were already friends, through the ministrations of the cat, their mutual passion for music added several degrees of Fahrenheit to the friendship; by this time the Admiral had dropped all formalities and was calling the poet by his first name. Also, he was requiring George to come often—"the oftener the better." George was more delighted than he could tell in words. It seemed a good time to bring forward his great project, and he did it. His delivery accomplished, he watched the Admiral's face with anxious solicitude. That patch-quilt remained calm. No lights, no shadows, no changes of any kind moved across its surface. The Admiral was thinking. Thought he was thinking. He was often calm and expressionless, like that, when he thought he was thinking. After a silence so extended that the poet was beginning to lose heart and wish he had not ventured so soon, the Admiral lifted his glass and said gravely—

"I have examined it, I have looked it all over in my mind, carefully. I see the grandeur of it. Drink!—then we will talk."

The poet was profoundly relieved; his spirits revived, and he cried—

"Thank you, thank you, Admiral, for being willing to discuss it!"

"Willing, yes, and glad to. Discussion throws light. I always want to discuss a thing, no matter how well I am disposed to it; it's best to feel your way on a strange coast, so I always take soundings."

"It's the wise course—I know it. I wish I did it more myself."

"You'll come to it—you're young, yet, and we don't learn such things early." He disposed himself comfortably, and took a pipe, and passed one to George; then he resumed. "A monument to Adam, says you. Very well, let's look at the case. Now then, I'm going to admit, to start with, that of all the minor sacred characters, I think the most of Adam. Except Satan."

"Satan?"

"Yes. Jimmy differs. That's all right, it's her privilege."

"Her?"

"Yes—*her*. What of it? She's an orphaness. Also, Aunt Martha differs. That's all right, too, it's her privilege—although she's only a second cousin, and not an aunt at all. It's what we call her—aunt. Yet she's no more an aunt than you be, although she's a Prisbyterian. It's only a formality—her being an aunt is. It's only her being it through being a second cousin to some of our ancestors, I don't know which ones. But she's gold!—and don't you forget it. She's been with me twenty years; ten at sea, and ten here on land. She has mothered Jimmy ever since she was a baby."

"Ever since—since—*she* was a baby?"

"Certainly. Didn't I just say it?"

"I know; but I mean, *which* she?"

"*Which* she? What are you talking about with your *which* she?"

"I—well, I don't quite know. I mean the one that was a baby. Was *she* the one?"

The Admiral nearly choked with vexation; his face turned storm-blue, its railroad-lines turned fire-red and quivered over it like lightnings; then he did the thundering himself:

"By God, if you say it again I'll scalp you! you've got me so tangled up that I—*say!* can you understand *this?* Aunt Martha—SHE—understand?—mothered Jimmy ever since she was a baby—ever since SHE was a baby! SHE—get it?"

The poet—still uncertain—gave up, and falsely indicated comprehension with a strenuous nod, to pacify the Admiral and avert war. Things quieted down, then, and the Admiral growled his satisfaction:

"I'm glad. Glad I've succeeded. It's been admitted before this, that I can state a thing pretty limpid when I try. . . . . Very well, then. As I was saying, she did the thing I said. And nobody could have done it better—I'll say that, too. Jimmy's twenty-one, now. Baby on shore, first; then all of a sudden an orphaness, and so remains to this day, although at sea ten years, as I told you before. Aboard my ship. Along with Aunt Martha, who fetched her. I've been her father, Martha's been her mother; mother, old maid, and a Prisbyterian, all at the same time, a combination to beat the band. Heart of gold, too, as I told you before. Sixty years old, and sound as a nut. As for the name, I thought of it myself. I gave it to her."

"Martha is a good name," suggested the poet, in order to say something, it being his turn.

"Martha? Who said anything about Martha? Can't you keep the run of the ordinariest conversation?—say, can't you?"

"Oh, I—you see—well I understood you to say that she—"

"Hang it, what you understand a person to say hasn't got anything to do with what the person says, don't you know that? I was talking about Jimmy—my grand-niece."

"Oh, I see, now. I quite misunderstood, before, for I thought you said she was only twenty-one, and—"

"I *did* say it! George, take something; damned if you don't need it; your mind is failing. Now then, listen, and I'll try to put it so that even you can understand it. Aunt Martha is sixty—second cousin out of sources of antiquity—old maid, Prisbyterian from cat-heads to counter —get it? Very well. Jimmy is twenty-one—grand-niece—ex-fathered by me, ex-mothered by Martha—orphaness to this day—orphaness to this *day*—get it? Very well. Now we come to the place where you stuck: it was *her* I named, not Martha—get it? Named her James Fletcher Stormfield; named her for her little brother that had gone before, as the saying is. It broke my heart when he went—the dearest little fellow! but I saved the name, and there's comfort in that, I can tell you. As long as I've got Jimmy and the name, the world ain't going to get blacker than I can stand, although she's nothing but an orphaness when all's said and done, poor little thing. *But*—gold, all gold, like our Aunt Martha out of the geological period. Got it *all*, now, haven't you George?"

"All, and a thousand thanks, Admiral—you're ever so good."

He stopped with that, and thought he would economise words whenever he could, now, so as to keep out of trouble, and also trick the Admiral into sticking to his subject. The Admiral resumed:

"Now that we've got that settled, we'll return back to Adam and see if we can pull *him* off. I wish Aunt Martha was on deck, but it's her watch below. You see, she— *Bags!*" In the midst of the black velvet mask two disks of fire appeared—gleamed intensely for a moment, then the mask closed upon them and blotted them out. "He heard me, you see. Bags! turn out and tell your Aunt Martha to report in the chart room." The Admiral waited a moment, the fires did not reappear; then he explained, regretfully: "That's the way with a cat, you know—any cat; they don't give a damn for discipline. And they can't help it, they're made so. But it ain't really insubordination, when you come to look at it right and fair—it's a word that don't apply to a cat. A cat ain't ever anybody's slave or serf or servant, and *can't* be—it ain't *in* him to be. And so, he don't have to obey anybody. He is the only creature in heaven or earth or anywhere that don't have to obey *somebody* or other, including the angels. It sets him above the whole ruck, it puts him in a class by himself. He is independent. You understand the size of it? He is the only independent person there is. In heaven or any-where else. There's always somebody a king has to obey—a trollop, or a priest, or a ring, or a nation, or a deity or what not—but it ain't so with a cat. A cat ain't servant nor slave to anybody at all. He's got all the independence there is, in heaven or anywhere else, there ain't any left over for anybody else. He's your friend, if you like, but that's the limit—equal terms, too, be you king or be you cobbler; you can't play any I'm-better-than-you on a cat—*no*, sir! Yes, he's your friend, if you like, but you've got to treat him like a gentleman, there ain't any other terms. The minute you don't, he pulls his freight. And he—*say!* you get that new tint?—on the curve of his counter—see it? delicate coppery mist, faint as dream-stuff—just like you catch it for a second in a mesh of the purple-black hair of a girl when the slant of the sun is right, ain't it so? Gone, now. Aunt Martha says—George, you'll like Aunt Martha."

"I'll be glad to, Admiral, and I'm sure I shall."

"Oh, yes, you will, there's no doubt about it." After a moment, he added, casually, "she has a ferocious temper."

"Is that so?"

"The worst there is. I wouldn't blame her, for she didn't make her temper, it was born in her; I wouldn't blame her if she didn't *hide* it; but I have to blame her for that, because it's deception."

George tried to say the kindly and modifying thing—

"Maybe she is only trying to keep it *down*, Admiral, instead of con-cealing it—and there should be merit in that."

"No, I know her—she just hides it, lets on it ain't there; she don't let a sign of it slip. She's deep, Martha is; you could be with her years and years and never find out she had it if I hadn't told you." A silence ensued; George could not think of any appropriate thing to say. The Admiral added, "she swears a good deal." George started, but ventured nothing. "You can't break her now," continued the Admiral, "it's too late; she's sixty, you see, and she's been at it twenty years. Picked it up from the sailors."

George thought of saying, "and from you, perhaps?" but concluded to stay on safe ground, now that he was doing well. He had been wanting to know Aunt Martha, on account of her heart of gold, but he hoped for better luck, now. He was afraid of her. The Admiral drifted tranquilly along with his treasonable revelations.

"Well, she's been through a lot, poor thing, and it's only right to make allowances. You see, she got a blight."

Pause.

"A blight?"

"That's it." (Pause.) "Got a blight."

This conversation was difficult.

"Got—er—got a—"

"That's it. Blight." (Pause.) "Early."

"How—er—how sor—unfortunate."

"Right again. She wasn't quite seventeen, he was just the same age."

"Oh—I see: unhappy love-passage."

"Yes, that was the trouble. Reefing a gasket in a gale, and fell off the foretogallantstunslboom. No-o—come to think, that was another one —the first one. This one's boat was smashed by a bull whale after he was struck, and a wave washed him down his throat—unhurt. He was never seen again."

"How dreadful!"

"Yes. You don't want to speak of it to her, she can't bear it."

"I can easily believe it, poor lady."

"No, she can't. It blighted her. Blighted yet. They were to 've been married as soon as he got to be mate, and he was already boat-steerer. It's the uncertainty that makes her life so mournful."

"Un— What uncertainty?"

"About his fate, you know."

"Why—I thought he went down the whale's throat?"

"Yes, that's it; that's what happened to him, poor boy."

"Yes, I understand that, but what I meant was, what was the uncertainty?"

"Why—well, as to what went with him after that, you know."

"Why, Admiral, there *couldn't* be any uncertainty as to that, could there?"

"I don't rightly know. At bottom, as between you and me, *I* don't think him likely to turn up again, but I don't *say* it, of course, and—"

"Does *anybody* think it likely that he—"

"*She* does; yes, she can't give up the hope that he'll fetch around yet, poor thing. She's to be pitied, I think."

"Indeed with all my heart I pity her. It is one of the saddest things I have ever heard of. But surely, after all these many many unrevealing years she—"

"No, nothing can convince her. You see, she's a Prisbyterian, and it makes her feel near to Job in the whale's belly—nearer than you and me can ever feel, not being situated like her—and she can't help feeling that what's happened once can happen again."

"True—but in that other case it was only three days, whereas in this one it is a whole generation and more. The cases are very different."

"I know it, but she holds to it that Job was old, and maybe, being superannuated, that way, he would have struck the limit before this, but her Eddy being young and hardy it could be different with him. But I know you wouldn't ever find any way to comfort her anyhow, because he was the only one the whale got. The others escaped, you see, and got drowned."

George struggled with this proposition, but could not work his way through the fog of it. He finally said—

"I don't quite see how his being the only one the whale got affected his unhappy case either one way or the other."

"That's what I think; but she keeps brooding over his being in there so long without any company. So lonesome, you see."

"I—yes—yes, I seem to see it, but I should not have thought of that," said George, bewildered.

"Well, it troubles her, every time she thinks of it. So dark in there, you see, and nothing doing. Night all the time, you know, and such a sameness and so dull. She longs to be with him."

George was not able to drum up a comment.

"Yes, it's a hard life for her, George; hard for her, hard for him, if he's there yet, which is far from likely, in my opinion, and I've thought it over a good deal. She always sees him the same way."

"How do you mean, Admiral?"

"Young, you know—not seventeen. Sees him the same way: young, fresh, rosy, brim full of life and the joy of it; always sees him the way he was when she saw him last, swinging down the road after his kiss, with his white ducks, and his tarpaulin with a dangling ribbon, and his blue neck-scarf, and his blue-bordered broad collar spreading upon his shoulders; sees him like that, with the sunset painting him all red and gold and glorious—the last sight of him she was ever going to see, George."

"How pitiful, how pathetic!"

"Yes, that is what I say. Sees him always just so—blooming, boyish, beautiful. Always the same—never adds a day; stands still in his youth, and she gets old and older, and gray and grayer, and—"

"*That's* pitiful, too!"

"It's the right name for it, George. Well, for ten years it was sweetheart and sweetheart; then she reconnized that she was outgrowing him—twenty-seven too old for seventeen—so she had to make a change; so she gradually got to regarding him as her son."

"How curious!"

"Yes. Well, that was all right and satisfactory till she drifted away from him wider and wider till last year she reconnized that the whole gap between them was forty-two years; then she shifted him to grandson. And there he is now. If she lives, he's good for a twenty-year rest. Then she'll promote him again. George, she's had a bitter hard time, and I want you to try to overlook her defect and feel the best and charitablest you can towards her, considering everything."

"O, God knows I would not add a pain to her sorrows for anything this world has to give!"

"I'm glad to hear you say that, George, it shows you've got a good heart. Jimmy's always kind and gentle to her. She's got the devil's own temper, too, but never shows it. I want you to know Jimmy."

"I shall be g—glad to, I'm sure."

It didn't sound quite like it.

"She'll play the penola for you. She's musical, like the rest of the breed. When she's a little further along I'm going to learn her to work the squawkestrelle. *Say!* look at him! look at his eyes!—locomotive head-lights, ain't it? Look at his attitude: whole body advanced and rigid; one front paw lifted and curved and motionless—looks so, but it ain't; he's putting it down, but you can't detect any motion to it; he's letting on that I'm a bird and he's creeping up on me and I don't know it; see him whimper and whicker with his lips and not make anything but just barely a little flicker of sound—a cat never does that but when it's slipping up on a bird and lusting after it; starboard paw's down at last—lifting the port one, now, but you can't perceive it; see him glare at me—never budges his eyes from me nor winks; six feet to come, and it'll take him five minutes; see him droop his belly, now, most to the floor, and whimper with his mouth and quiver his tail; I'll turn my face away, now and let on I don't know there's any danger around—it's part of the game—he expects it."

By and by the cat completed his imperceptible journey; then squatted close to the floor, worked his haunches and twitched his lithe tail a moment, then launched himself like a missile from a catapult and landed with a smashing impact upon the Admiral's shoulder. Before he could be seized he was away again. The Admiral was as vain of the performance as if it was the world's last wonder and he the proprietor of the sole miracle-monger that could achieve it.

"Does it every day!" said he. "Often he—*come in!*"

It was Aunt Martha. Seeing the stranger, she was going to retreat, but the Admiral gripped her by the hand and led her in, saying cordially—

"Don't you mind, it's nobody but George. Here she is, her own self, George—Martha Fletcher, heart of gold, chief mate, brains of the house—there! ain't she a daisy?" He swept her figure with an admiring look, gave a wave of his hand as if to say, "what did I tell you?—up to sample, ain't she?" then he bustled her into a chair and finished the introduction.

The poet had been expecting to be afraid of her if chance should some day bring him face to face with her, but he was pleasantly disappointed. There was nothing formidable about her, nothing to frighten any one; on the contrary, she was charming. Her hair was white and wavy and silky, she had a soft voice, her face was beautiful with the beauty of kindliness, human sympathy and the grace of peace, and upon her sat a gentle dignity which any could see belonged to her by right of birth. The Admiral beamed affection and admiration upon her, and the poet could not help doing the same—tempered, in some degree, by the remembrance of what he had heard about her profanities and her temper. His interest in her grew by swift stages, and in no long time he found himself condoning those defects, and even trying to believe they were not really defects at all, but only eccentricities, and not important. By and by she arrived at the errand she had come about: she wanted to advertise for a lodger. George pricked up his ears.

The Admiral said there was no occasion—there was money enough, and to spare. Aunt Martha said, no matter, the empty rooms were a reproach—some one ought to be enjoying them; even a charity-lodger who paid nothing would answer; she was not particular, as to that, but it was on her conscience that those good rooms were going to waste— and so she gently stuck to her point. The Admiral wavered, then surrendered, saying—

"All right, Aunt Martha, you would have it your own way sooner or later, anyhow, you are so obstinate when you are set. Go ahead and advertise."

She thanked him sweetly, and rose to go. George thought that now was his chance or never; so he made bold to say—

"If the Admiral would be willing, Miss Fletcher, do you think you could try *me* for a month and see if I would do? I am leaving my lodgings to-day." Which was not true.

"The very thing!" This from the Admiral. "Get your kit aboard and begin right away. I'll not let her overcharge you."

"Abner, I was not going to do it,—you know that," said the aunt in gentle reproach.

"Yes, you had it in your mind, I saw it. Go and fetch your things, George, you can look to me for protection. Another plate for supper, Martha—you hear?"

George brought his belongings and delivered them to the old sailor who did duty as the Admiral's butler, bos'n, second mate and one thing or another, then he called on his friend David and reported his great luck in securing lodgings in the Admiral's house. David asked why he had needed to do that, and George explained:

"It took me two hours to get him down *to* Adam and the monument, and that is as far as I've got, he scatters so. I hope to land him, but it will take time. He's worth it, though; he's worth no end of effort, I think. So I call it good luck that I got the lodgings. And there's another reason: I was lonesome where I was."

"Well, *that's* at an end, now, sure!" said David. "Sure—whether you like each other or not."

"I'll tell you our talk, David, then you can judge which it is."

When he had finished, David conceded that the new relationship did not seem to have anything cold about it. Then he added:

"You have done well, George, you have indeed. Well and judiciously. You've gone far with the Admiral. It is good diplomacy and a creditable performance. I hope you will land him, and I also believe you will."

"I am glad to hear you say it, David. It will take time, as I've said, but that's nothing; it's not going to be dull."

"Oh, on the contrary. Inasmuch as you want society, you are in even better luck than you think for, George."

"How is that? Are you thinking of Aunt Martha?"

"No—outsiders. Protégés of the Admiral."

"Protégés?"

"Yes. Life's failures. Shipwrecks. Derelicts, old and battered and broken, that wander the ocean of life lonely and forlorn. They all drift to him; and are made welcome."

"David, it is beautiful! He didn't mention this."

"He? No, he wouldn't be likely."

"Then it's all the more beautiful!"

"So it is. They drop in on him, whenever they please, and he comforts them. A poor old pathetic lot."

"I want to see them, David; I'd like to know them."

"Well, you will, if the Admiral sees that sort of spirit in you. Otherwise not. It is thought that he helps them with his purse as well as with his sympathies; in fact, between you and me, I know he does, but you will keep this knowledge to yourself. He's a man, George—he's a whole man. There's delicacies in him that you wouldn't suspect, he seems so rough."

"*I* suspected them, the minute the cat came in, David!" said George, proud of his penetration. "Delicacies are of the heart; and the minute the cat came in, his heart was exposed. He was not much better than a pirate when he was talking to himself before that; but afterwards it was very different. And a good deal of a relief to me, too. Once he started to reveal to me how Bags stands in the matter of morals, but changed the subject when Bags let an eye fall open, showing that he wasn't asleep. I recognized, then, that what he had been going to let out was something shady, or partially so, and he didn't want to hurt Bags's feelings."

"It was like the Admiral. Privately his friends have a name or two for his house,—half a dozen, in fact—founded on his special compassion for life's failures—ironical names, but there's no sting in them: 'Haven of the Derelict,' 'Refuge of the Broken Reed'—that's a couple of them."

"Why, they're lovely, David! It's the lead of irony transmuted into the gold of homage. Do you—"

"Wait—I want to give you a point, while I think of it. Talk temperance—*general* temperance—with the Admiral, if you want to—he likes the subject—but don't go into the history of it; at least don't go away back; don't go back as far as Father Matthew. Because mention of that name is a thing he can't stand. It has been tried. By an ignorant person. Ignorant and innocent. He was fooled into doing it by a friend of the Admiral's who knew a secret and tender spot in the old mariner's history and wanted to get some effects out of it without taking the risk of putting his own finger on it. They say that the eruption of profanity that ensued lasted several hours and has not been equaled since Vesuvius buried Herculaneum. Do as I tell you: leave Father Matthew alone—let the Admiral's volcano sleep."

"All right, I will, but tell me about it. Why should the name rouse him so?"

"Because it reminds him of an incident of his early life which he hates the memory of. It was like this. Away back, fifty or sixty years ago, when the Admiral was about twenty-five, he came back from a three-year voyage to find a melancholy change at home in New Bedford and Fairhaven: Father Matthew, the great apostle of temperance, had been sweeping New England like a prairie-fire, and everybody had joined the Father Matthew Societies and stopped drinking. When Stormfield realized the situation, his heart almost broke. Not a comrade would drink with him, he had to drink all alone, and you know what that means to a sociable soul. He wandered the streets disconsolate, bereft, forsaken; nobody wanted his company, the girls cut him, he was not asked to the parties and the dances.

"And he had come home so triumphant, so joyful! For he had been promoted from mate to captain, and was full of the glory of it, and now there was nobody interested in his honors, no one cared to hear about them. He endured his sufferings as long as he could, then he broke his jug and surrendered, and sent in his name to be balloted for at the Father Matthew Society's next meeting. That same night his crew arrived—Portuguese and Kanakas from the Azores—and at daybreak in the morning he sailed.

"He was gone three years. He was firm; he drank not a drop the whole time, but it was a bitter hard battle, from the first day to the last—with the grog circulating among those brown men every few hours, and his mouth watering for it unspeakably! For he had begun to repent of what he had done before he was out of sight of land; he repented every day and all the days, for three years—and most deeply of all on the last one, which was fearfully cold, with a driving storm of wind and snow, and he had to plow the fleecy deck and face the gale, *dry*—oh, so dry! and those brown people comforting themselves with hot grog every little while and he getting the whiff of it; and so, the minute he made port he bought a jug and rushed to the Society and hit the secretary's desk with his fist and shouted—

" 'Take my name off your cussed books, I'm dying of a three-years' thirst!'

"The secretary said, tranquilly—

" 'Hasn't ever been on—*you were black-balled.*'

"Those are the facts, George." That far in his talk David was serious; possibly he was serious in the rest of it; most people would have doubted it; George might have doubted it himself if he had been differently made. "You would think, George, that after the incident had had a year's wear, the soreness would have passed out of it and left nothing behind but a text for the Admiral to joke about; it is what would have happened if anybody else had been in the Admiral's place, but in his case it did not happen. With him it has remained a serious matter, and when you consider the make of him you can understand why. To him the thing stands for one thing only: bitter *loss*, irreparable loss. Suppose a happy bridegroom should lie in a trance three years: would not he recognize that he could never catch up, in this life? Well, that is the way the Admiral feels."

There was a sigh, and George said—

"I am glad you have shown me this aspect of it, David. At first I saw only one side, and so it seemed funny, but I see now that it is not. It would pain me to laugh at it now; I think it would pain any one who has any heart."

"Yes, I am sure it would. George, he has borne this sorrow for fifty years, without outward complaint; borne it with dignity, borne it with a certain composure. One cannot reflect upon this and not revere him."

"You could not say a truer thing than that, David. I feel just as you do about it."

"In a large sense it is a blighted life. Yet it has been blest to him, and richly blest to others, for it has borne precious fruit. It has made him the friend and brother of all upon whom disaster and blight have fallen; out of it has grown the 'Haven of the Derelict,' the 'Refuge of the Broken Reed.' "

"David," said George, deeply touched, and awed, "that incident of the long ago was not an accident, it was *meant*, and it had a purpose. The hand of Providence was in it—I know it, I see it. It was no earthly hand that black-balled him."

"I have never doubted it," said David, impressively; "there are no accidents, all things have a deep and calculated purpose; sometimes the methods employed by Providence seem strange and incongruous, but we have only to be patient and wait for the result: then we recognize that no others would have answered the purpose, and we are rebuked and humbled."

Chapter 3

From George's Diary

I WAS in time for supper. The Admiral sat at the head of the table,
Aunt Martha at the foot; I and the cat (the latter on a high baby-
chair) sat on one side, and Jimmy and a middle-aged lady in rather
loud and aggressive young-girl dress on the other. The Admiral made
the introductions. He called the elderly girl the Mar*cheez*a di Bianca
—"otherwise White," he added, "Eyetalian for White." The marchesa
corrected his pronunciation—

"Mar*kay*za," she said, unpleasantly.

The Admiral was not troubled. He nodded at me and said, tranquilly—

"In a way, she's right; they say it that way over there, they being
backward in their spelling, but over here it's not right, because the
Constitution don't allow it. The Constitution says we've got to pronounce words the way they are spelt." Jimmy and the aunt glanced up
at him doubtfully, (or maybe it was reproachfully,) and the marchesa
opened her mouth—"Close it!" said the Admiral fiercely, and was
obeyed. "It's spelt the same as cheese, and when I heave it out, cheese
it *is*." He glared around, from face to face. "Any objections?"

None were offered. The ancient sailor-butler was serving. He was
tall, grave, grizzled, muscular, he wore sailor-clothes, was stiff-legged
on the near side, and had the gait of a carpenter's compass when it is
semi-circling its course across a ground-plan; for one of his legs was
made of wood, or iron, or some other rigid material. The Admiral and
his family called him Bos'n, and he always answered "aye-aye, s'r," re-
gardless of sex. George noticed that he skipped the cat. The Admiral
noticed that George noticed. He explained:

"Bags don't eat with the rest of the family, he waits, and eats by himself. It's his own idea. But he most always comes and looks on, because
he likes company, and wants to hear the talk. Often he takes a hand in
it himself."

Jimmy and the aunt cast that mystic glance at him again. It seemed to me that it might mean "Remember, there is a stranger present; he is not used to you, and will misunderstand." If that was the look's message, there was nothing to show that it reached port; the Admiral went on talking about the cat's interest in dinner-conversations and participation in them, and pretty soon he was enlarging. It did not take him long to enlarge to where he was giving samples of what the cat had actually *said* on one or another occasion. Then the ladies seemed to give it up. They looked resigned; and I did not see them employ that glance any more. I felt sorry for them, but there was nothing I could do; at least nothing but try to relieve the situation by changing the subject. I did that a couple of times, but it did no good, the Admiral changed it back as soon as it suited him. He got to reporting political and theological views—of the cat's—which were manifestly beyond and above a cat's reach, and although I could easily see that this distressed his ladies and made them bend their heads and look at their plates, he did not seem to be aware of it himself. He quoted remarks—of the cat's —which were often discreditable and sometimes profane, and then made the matter worse by approving and defending them. It was a sufficiently embarrassing situation. Now and then he would throw out a remark of the cat's that was really and extravagantly outrageous; then he would look aggressively around upon the company, as if he were expecting a revolt, and wishing for it. But it never happened, and he had to put up with his disappointment the best he could. He realized that there was doubt in the air, and it annoyed him, and made him want to remove it. Instead of reasoning the matter with *us*, he sought refuge in a transparent absurdity; he asked the *cat* if he had quoted him correctly. The cat always said something back; then the Admiral would cast a lurid look of triumph upon the company and say, "I reckon that settles it!" whereas it settled nothing, for we could not understand the cat. But we had to leave it his way, there was no other course. By help of our silence, which he translated into assent, he was able to establish all his points. This pleased him, and made him periodically happy, and saved us from getting flung out of the window.

When the dinner was ended, with its procession of alternating storms and calms, fearful perils and blessed rescues, I realized that I had had an interesting time, and said so. The Admiral was perceptibly flattered and gratified, and confessed, on his part, that he had seldom participated in a more informing and satisfying "discussion." That was his word. If he had searched the dictionary through, he could not have found a more fiendishly inappropriate one. It was the kind of discussion a saw has with a saw-log. My indignation rose, for a moment, for it was very trying to have him empty that offensive word upon me in that bland way, but I held my peace and put my feelings away, and it was better so. To have challenged the word would merely have brought on another discussion—of his kind—with no profit to any one.

He was feeling good and sociable, now, and we all went to his parlor in a promisingly comfortable condition of mind. Under the pleasant influences of punch and pipe the Admiral presently broke ground on the monument scheme of his own volition, and explained it to the ladies. It produced effects—one could see it in their faces. The Admiral then proceeded, without waiting for comments:

"When you come to consider the minor sacred characters, it seems to me that Satan and Adam—"

"Abner!" This from Aunt Martha, with gentle surprise.

"Now then, what's the matter with *you?*"

"Abner, Satan is not one of the sacred characters."

"The h—alifax he ain't!"

"Why, no, he isn't. But don't lose your temper, dear heart."

The mild admonition and the affectionate epithet modified the Admiral, and he dropped into what I suspected was his favorite argumentative plan of hunting an objection down:

"Martha, ain't he in the Book?"

"Yes."

"Martha, is it a holy Book?"

"Yes."

"*All* holy?"

"Yes, it is all holy."

"Is there another word for it?"

Aunt Martha hesitated; as one might who is becoming uncertain of his ground. The Admiral took notice, gave a complacent nod, and furnished the word himself:

"*Sacred* Scriptures, ain't it?"

"Ye-s."

"*The*, ain't it?"

"I—I know; yes."

"What does *the* stand for? The *only* one that's sacred, ain't it?"

Aunt Martha's gun was silent.

"Well, then!" and he began to tally-off the conceded points on his fingers, point by point: "One, it's in the Book—you give in to that. Two, the Book's *holy*. Three, it's *all* holy, says you. Four, it's the *sacred* Scriptures. Five, it's *the* sacred Scriptures. Grand total: holy, all holy, sacred, *the* sacred. Very well, then; when a thing is so utterly and altogether and absolutely and uncompromisingly and all-solitary-and-alone sacred, without any competition in the business, how are you going to make out that there's anything in it that *ain't* sacred? You just answer me that, if you think you can!"

This burst of remorseless logic seemed to wither Martha. One might imagine her a rumpled and collapsed flag that has been hauled down; whereas the Admiral looked as pleased as a mine might that has done its job well and blown up an assaulting party. Smiling benignantly upon the wreckage, he was about to start his talk again, when the marchesa sniffed and dropped a comment:

"Putting buttons in the contribution-plate don't make them holy."

Martha and Jimmy glanced at her. As to what the glances meant I could not be sure, but to me they seemed to mean, "*Don't* do that!" Then, before the Admiral could open up on the marchesa—which he was evidently going to do—Jimmy said, persuasively—

"Please begin over again, Uncle Abner, I want to hear all I can about the monument before bedtime, and no one can make it so interesting as you."

The storm-cloud flitted out of his face and he went at his work at once, quite evidently gratified by that just remark.

"As concerns Satan and Adam, I was going to say I rank them about on a par among the minor prophets, and—"

"Prophets!" scoffed the marchesa, and was going to enlarge, when the Admiral turned a warning eye upon her and put the ends of his thumbs and of his middle fingers together in the form of an open mouth—for a moment, then impressively brought the parts together, thus closing that mouth. The marchesa closed hers. The Admiral resumed:

"I rank them about on a par, as regards intelligence. And yet Satan was one of the oldest of the sacred characters, and therefore—"

He stopped and glanced around, apparently to see if that word was going to be attacked again. It didn't happen.

"The idea that he ain't a sacred character! Suppose you handle him in a humorous lightsome way just once,—only just once—in a magazine, if you want to know! You'll have all the pulpits and deacons and congregations on your back in a minute, in the correspondence-columns, for trifling in that unsolemn way about a person that's in the Bible. Haven't you seen it? Don't you know it's so?"

Nobody ventured dissent.

"You know mighty well it is. That's the reason you don't try to call the hand. Very well then. As I was saying, Satan was very old and experienced, yet he didn't outrank Adam in intelligence, which was only a child, as you may say, though grown up. How do I make it out? I will tell you. Satan offered all the kingdoms to our Savior if he would fall down and worship him. Did he own them? No. Could he give title? No. Could he deliver the goods? No. Now I'll ask you a question. If a slave was to go to a king and offer to trade him his own kingdom for a dollar and a half, how would we rank him for intelligence? Way, way, *way* down! ain't it so?"

He polled the company; there was not an opposition vote.

"Carried. Now then, I'll ask you another question. Can you find anything anywhere in Satan's history that's above that mark, for intelligence? No. In the Middle Ages he was always building bridges for monks in a single night, on a contract—and getting left. Ain't it so? And always finishing cathedrals for bishops in a single night, on a contract—and getting left. Ain't it so? And always buying Christian souls, on contracts signed with red Christian blood—and getting left. Every time. Can you find a case where they didn't *do* him, as the saying is? There isn't one. Did he ever learn anything? No. Experience was wasted on him. Look at his trades; he was as inadequate in the last one as he was when he first started. Finally—I'll ask your attention to this: didn't he start in to convert this whole world to sin and pull in everybody and range them under his banner? Certainly. Hasn't he been hard at it for centuries and centuries? Certainly. Well, how does the thing stand now—is it his world? No, sir! if he has converted nine-tenths of it it's the most you can say. *There!* Now then, you answer me this: is he one of life's failures?" He paused, took a drink, wiped his lips thoughtfully, and added: "*One* of them? why, he's *It!*"

Then the idea of Satan's being a life's failure seemed to touch him, and he said with a little quiver in his voice:

"Well, he's out of luck—like so many—like so many—and a body has to pity him, you can't help it."

I was not expecting to be moved by any gentle word said about Satan, but the Admiral surprised me into it. It was ridiculous, but at the moment it seemed a natural thing and a matter-of-course. Well, I suppose that it isn't so much *what* a man says that affects us as the *way* he says it. I will make a note of it.

The Admiral began—

"We will now examine Adam. As far as—"

The soft rich note of a Japanese temple-bell interrupted: "plung-plung—plung-plung—plung-plung—plung-plung!" Then the bos'n's deep voice pealed through the house—

"E-i-g-h-t bells—starboard watch turn out!"

"Divine service," said the Admiral, and rose and took his place behind a stand that had some religious books on it. The young girl Jimmy seated herself at the piano, which was equipped with a pianola attachment. Footsteps were heard approaching, and a rustling of gowns, and several servants entered softly and stood against the wall. The Admiral read a prayer from the Episcopal prayer-book, and did it nobly. To me it seemed a marvelous performance. Where did he get that great art, that rare art? David says there are only a hundred and thirteen people in the world who know how to read. When he hears the Admiral he will add one to his list.

Then the Admiral read a familiar hymn. This was the first time that the deeps and graces and sublimities of that hymn were ever revealed to me. The congregation—save the Admiral—sang the piece, Jimmy playing it with the pianola-thing which the renowned musical professionals puff so much. Then the Admiral prayed a prayer of his own make. With a word or two it invoked a blessing upon the national government. Next, it implored salvation for the "anchor watch"—

apparently a brevity-title for his college of derelicts; then he implored salvation for his mother and father, dead a generation ago; then for the household, servants and all; then for me. He paused, now, and there was silence for some seconds. Then he bowed his head, and added in a low voice—

"And humbly I beseech, O Lord, salvation for one other . . . . not named."

It startled me. Who was the unnamed one? Ah—Satan? No. I put that out of my mind. The sentiment for Satan had of course been an accidental thing born of his discourse about him, and not permanent. Then—why, it must have been himself! I was sorry. It suggested theatrical humility—show-off humility, for people to admire—and he so finely and faultlessly genuine, so worshipfully genuine, up to that moment! It was as if the robes of an image of gold had blown aside and exposed legs of clay. I was sorrier than I can tell. I went to bed depressed.

Chapter 4

From George's Diary, a Week Later

Tʜɪs is not a dull house. The human interest is pervasive here, pervasive and constant. I did not know, before, how interesting our race can be; I only knew how uninteresting it can be. I see, now, that it was uninteresting merely because I had no close contact with it, and not because the people of my acquaintanceship were commonplace. In a single week I have come to doubt if there *are* any uninteresting people. Certainly most people are commonplace,—a word which, taken apart and examined, merely means that their tastes, ideals, sympathies and mental capacities are below your standard—a word which contains and conveys the fact that those people are dull to you—but when you get *on the inside of them*—well, I begin to think that that is quite another country. If to be interesting is to be uncommonplace, it is becoming a question, with me, if there *are* any commonplace people.

Broadly speaking, my previous contacts have been with persons whose ways and standards did not tally with mine, and I thought that that was the reason their company was a weariness to me. But I see that that could have been a mistake. If I had happened to get at their insides I think I should have found interesting things hidden there. Books? Yes, books. So the bos'n says. He says a man's experiences of life are a book, and there was never yet an uninteresting life. Such a thing is an impossibility. Inside of the dullest exterior there is a drama, a comedy, and a tragedy. The bos'n says there is no exception to the rule. But how difficult it is to get at those poems!

My life was dull before luck got me into this house; I had only outsides to contemplate, but here it is the other way. Here I have opportunity to penetrate beyond the skin. The contacts with the household are frequent, and the same is the case with the derelicts and their intimates. As a rule I have not had friends before, but only acquaintances; they talked the news and gossip of the day—which was natural—and hid their hurts and their intimate joys—which was also natural—and so I took them for light-weights and commonplace, and was not glad of their society. Lord, they all had their tragedies!—every one of them, but how could I suspect it?

Formerly if a person had said to me, "Would you like to know Smith the letter-carrier?" it would not have occurred to me to say yes. But I should say it now, believing as I now do that a man's occupation is not a mirror of his inside; and so I should want to know Smith and try to get at his interior, expecting it to be well charged with interest for me.

The fact is, I do know Smith the (ex-)letter-carrier, though it is only by accident that I have used him as an illustration. He is a derelict. I asked him to sit, and am painting his portrait. He is from a distant State and city. His young wife is there. He is silent and abstracted, and usually sits apart, with his head bent, and thinks his thoughts, and does not smile. When he supposed I was meaning to charge him for the portrait he looked up, pulled his wandering mind home with an effort, and said no, he had no money; I explained that it was not a matter of money, I only wanted to paint it for practice and he could have it when it was done. The idea did not seem to take hold.

I could see that he was vaguely wondering what use it could be to him; he looked up vacantly—the problem had baffled him; I said "for your wife"—then his eyes filled.

The first sitting thawed him a little; before the second one was ended he was telling me how he was occupying himself and how the Admiral came to run across him and add him to his accumulation of human wreckage; in the third sitting the thawing reached still further into his mass and he talked about his boyhood and his parents, his playmates and his brothers and sisters; in the fourth the melting was nearly complete and he talked freely and trustingly of some of the things hidden away in the deeps of his heart—such as the happinesses of his married life, and how Mary looked, and how she talked, and what her opinions were, on this and that and the other matter of moment, and how sterling she was, and how sane, and how good-hearted, and all that; and in the fifth—in the fifth the last ice-shield broke away and out came the tragedy! There is always one, if you can get at it. Often it looks trivial on paper, but never is trivial when it trickles out before you tinged with heart's blood.

This tragedy will look trivial to an outsider. It cannot be put in words that could save it from that. The conventions are in the way; they blur our vision, and keep us from perceiving that the sole tragic thing about a hurt is the hurt itself and its effect upon the sufferer, not the noble or ignoble factors and conditions involved in the infliction of it. The present tragedy is a brief story. This is what happened.

Smith was nineteen years old, and was already a journeyman machinist, with a year's savings laid up. He had a good reputation as a workman, a good wage, a permanent job, and a sweetheart to his taste. He had reached the very top of his ambition, his dearest dream was realized; he was grateful, proud, satisfied, happy, to a degree beyond any words of his to express. His family were proud of him, his friends were proud of him; this was the best and the most that a duke or a king could have, and so he believed he felt just as kings feel. What could he want more? Nothing.

He lived, moved, and had his being in this delicious incense, the approval, amounting to deference, of his family and friends. He and they were all of humble estate—mechanics and laborers. His father was a day laborer and unschooled; his mother took in washing; his

Mary's people were conditioned in like way; her father was a pavior, her mother a washerwoman, Mary was a helper. The two families lived high up in mean tenement houses.

Young Smith had given himself a pretty fair education, by sitting up nights, and was fond of study. He and Mary spent their evenings in study together. They married—he nineteen and she a year younger. They went on with their studies, and were perfectly happy. For a year. Smith repeated that. "For a year."

I noted it; it foretold disaster. There was a competitive examination, for the office of letter-carrier. Smith entered the competition—"just to see what he could do," he said; he did not need the place, and did not want it. To his and Mary's astonishment—and joy—he came out on top and got it! With something near to a moan he added, "that was where our ruin began—lord, if I had only lost it!"

The pride and exultation of the two families and the friends exceeded all bounds. Smith's and Mary's happiness soared to the limit of human endurance; they thought they felt as kings feel when accident promotes them to emperorship. When Smith appeared for the first time in his uniform the families and the friends did not stop with admiration, they were *awed*; so awed that they acted more like strangers than friends; they were constrained, their tongues were crippled, they talked disjointedly, they were embarrassed, and they embarrassed him. He was an officer of the government of the United States, and they were —what they were; they could not bridge the chasm. It took the old-time easy familiarity all out of them.

That was the beginning of the tragedy. Next, the uniform introduced certain compulsions. Among other things, it—I can't recal his precise words, I wish I could, for they were beyond all art for innocent quaintness; but the sense of them was this: it raised them to a higher and more exacting social plane than they had been occupying before and they had to live up to the change, which was costly. I risked a delicate question and asked him who these exclusives might be— though of course I did not use that word. The inquiry did not disturb him; he was quite simple and frank about it, and said—

"Shop-clerks, sales-ladies, and such. And there was a steamboat mate and a type-writer."

Mary had to get some suitable clothes. Smith had to take to cigarettes—he had not smoked at all, before. Also, he had to rise above five-cent drinks, which made treating a noticeable burden. He paused, at this point, reflected, then recalled another detail—collars; he had to wear white ones.

The next step was inevitable: they had to move into better quarters, they must live up to the uniform, and to the new social altitude. Slight as the added rent was, it was a burden. They visited their new associates, and were visited by them. This had a foreseeable result: it presently broke off intercourse with the old friends, for between these and the new people were several inharmonies—discords in the matter of clothes and manners, furniture, upholstery, ideals, interests, and so on. When the two classes met at Smith's there were embarrassments and a frost. Intercourse between the Smiths and their ancient and cordial friends ceased, by and by, and the couple were left to the new people and a frivolous and empty and cheerless life.

Next stage. The added expenses were infinitely trifling,—would have seemed so to the reader's ear, at any rate—but no matter, they strained Smith's purse beyond its strength. He could not bear to reveal this to Mary, and he didn't. When he was depressed and sore and she put her arms about his neck and begged him to tell her what was the matter, he said it was headache and made him feel a little down. Then, with a loving desire to cheer him up, she would take the worst way she could have found: she would invite their fashionables to cake and tea, and make another expense. When at last he was at his wits' end—

"What do you reckon I did?" he asked, looking at me out of what one might have mistaken for the face of a dead man, so wan and white it was. "Lord God forgive me, I began to rob the letters!"

Mary did not know, nor suspect—until the black day when the officers came, and tore him from her clinging arms and his heart almost broke under the misery of hearing her despairing shrieks and moans and sobs.

He was in prison two years. When he got out, not even his light fashionables would associate with him, and they had cut Mary long before. The brand was upon him, the machinists' union rejected him, he could get no work. For three years he "has been in hell." The words are his. He has drifted hither and thither, and earned bread when he could. But for the Admiral, who happened upon him when he was at his lowest, death by starvation would have been his fate, he thinks. It is seven months since he last saw Mary; and then she did not know him. A fall on the ice injured her spine, and she is a helpless invalid. Her mind has failed. She is in the tenement again, with her old father and mother.

Chapter 5

From George's Diary—the Same Day

AT THIS point I shifted the subject, for it was bearing too hard upon the young fellow's spirits—and upon mine too. I tried a reference to the monument, hoping that the change would change his mood. It did. At the mere mention of Adam's name his temper rose with a flash, and it was wonderful to see what a customarily reserved man can do with his tongue when an inspiring theme comes its way. It was like Vesuvius in eruption. Lava, flame, earthquake, sulphurous smoke, volleying explosions—it was all there, and all vindictive and unappeasable hostility and aversion. I sat enchanted, dumb, astonished, glad to be there, sorry when the show was over.

One would have supposed Smith was talking about an intimate enemy—an enemy of last week, of yesterday, of to-day, not of a man whom he had never seen, and who had been dust and ashes for thousands of years. The reason for all this bitter feeling? It was very simple.

"*He brought life into the world*," said Smith. "But for him I should not have been born—nor Mary. Life is a swindle. I hate him."

After a panting moment or two he brought forth another surprise for me. To-wit, he was unreservedly and enthusiastically in favor of the monument! In a moment he was in eruption again. This time it was praises of Adam, gratitude to Adam, exaltation of his name. The reason of *this* attitude? Smith explained it without difficulty:

"*He brought death into the world*. I love him for it." After a little he muttered, like one in a reverie, "death the compassionate . . . . the

healer of hurts . . . . man's only friend . . . ." He was interrupted, there
—the bos'n came in for a sitting.

The bos'n didn't think much of me the first day or two, because
there was an impression around (emanating from David,) that I
was a poet; but when he found that my trade was artist in paints the
atmosphere changed at once and he apologised quite handsomely. He
had a great opinion of artists, and said the Admiral was one. I said I was
glad, and would like to see his pictures, and the bos'n said—introducing
a caution—

"That's all right, but don't let on. When you want anything that's
private out of the Admiral, don't let on. He might be in the mood,
and he mightn't. As soon as the mood takes him he'll open up on it
himself—you'll see—but not any sooner. There ain't anybody that
can unlock him on a private lay till he's ready. Not even Miss Jimmy,
not even Aunt Martha."

I said I should remember, and be careful. I repeated that I was glad
the Admiral was an artist. The bos'n responded, with feeling and
emphasis.

"An artist he *is*—I can tell you that. Born to it, *I* think. And he ain't
only *just* an artist, he's a hell of an artist!"

The form of a compliment has nothing to do with its value—it is the
spirit that is in it that makes it gold or dross. This one was gold. This
one was out of the heart, and I have found that an ignorant hot one
out of the heart tastes just as good as does a calm, judicial, reasoned
one out of an educated head. I hope to be a hell of an artist myself
some day, and hear the bos'n concede it.

As I was saying, the bos'n arrived. The ex-postman went away. I
settled myself for a stage-wait. The bos'n was just from the looking-
glass, but no matter, he would prink again; his first sitting had taught
me this. But it was no matter, he couldn't well be uninteresting, no
matter what he might be doing, for he was good to look at; besides, he
was generally talking, and his talk was not borous. He was past sixty,
but looked considerably younger, and had a fine and tall figure and an
athletic body—a most shapely man when standing before the glass,
with his artificial leg quiet. He had a handsome face and an iron jaw,
and that tranquil and business-like eye which men and tigers have so

much respect for. He is very likeable. We chatted while he prinked. Mainly about Smith. Presently I said I was sorry to see that Smith was a pessimist.

"A whichimist?" inquired the bos'n, turning a glance of interest at me over his shoulder, while rearranging for the fourth time the sailor-knot in his flowing neckerchief.

"Pessimist."

"Good word. As good as they make. What's a pessimist?"

"The opposite of an optimist."

"Another one. What are they both?"

"An optimist is cheery and hopeful—looks on the bright side of things. A pessimist is just the other way. Smith has no business to be a pessimist, he is too young."

"Is—is he? What's your age, Mr. Sterling?"

"Twenty-six."

"What's his?"

"About the same."

He came and took his seat and arranged his pose.

"He oughtn't to be a pes—pes—"

"Pessimist. No, he oughtn't. He has had trouble, he is in trouble, but at his age he oughtn't to give himself up body and soul to his sorrows. He ought to be more of a man. Shutting himself up to selfishly brood over his troubles and pet them and magnify them is a poor business, and foolish. He ought to look on the bright side of life."

"Now then," said the bos'n, "I'll set you right. Aunt Martha set me right when I was thinking the same as you, and I'll pass it along—then you'll see the rights of it, too. Smith's made on another pattern from you. Well, he can't help that. He didn't make his pattern, it was born to him, the same as yours was born to you. Smith *don't* brood mainly over his troubles; he's built so's 't he's got to suffer and sweat over everybody else's. You read the papers, don't you?"

"Yes."

"So does Smith. Do you read the telegraph news—all of it?"

"Yes, all of it."

"This morning, as usual?"

"Yes."

"How did you feel, after it—cheerful?"

"Yes. Why?"

"Comfortable?"

"I—well, I don't remember that I didn't."

"All right. It's the difference between you and Smith. *He* can't read the paper and not break his heart. Other people's troubles near kill him. It's because he was born tender, you see—not indifferent." I winced a little. He took up the paper and began a search, turning it this way and that, and still talking along. "You see, if a person shuts himself up inside of himself and don't worry about anybody's troubles but his own, he . . . . I can't seem to find the telegraphs . . . . he can get to be considerable of an octopus—"

"Optimist."

—"optimist, by and by, you know; and manly, and all that . . . . oh, now I'm striking the telegraphs . . . . and can look on the bright side of life and . . . . here they are! . . . . admire himself."

He uttered that vicious sarcasm so absently and so colorlessly that for a quarter of a second I hardly felt its teeth go in; then the bite took hold. I tried to look unaware, but I probably merely looked ashamed, and sorry I had exposed my self-complacency so brashly. He began to read the head-lines; not with energy and emphasis, but with a studied seeming of indifference and lack of interest which I took for a hint that perhaps that was my way of reading and feeling such things:

"Child crushed by mobile before its mother's eyes."

"Factory burned, 14 young work-girls roasted alive; thousands looking on, powerless to help."

"Little Mary Walker not found yet; search relaxing; no hope left; father prostrate, mother demented."

"Aged couple turned out in the snow with their small effects by landlord for lack of rent-money; found at midnight by police, unconscious; rent-money due, $1.75."

I recognized all these items; I had already read them, but only with my eyes, my feelings had not been interested, the sufferers being strangers; but the effect was different, now. The words were the same, but each of them left a blister where it struck. I was ashamed, and begged the bos'n to stop, and said I was a dog, and willing and even anxious to confess it. And so he softened, and put away the paper and said—

"Oh, I beg pardon; but as you said you'd already read them, I thought it wouldn't be any harm to—to—why, Smith was up at daylight reading them. And b'god he was near to *crying* over them!"

"Hang it, so am I, *now*, but—but—well, I never took the thing *in*, before."

"Oh, *that's* all right," said the bos'n, soothingly, "you ain't to blame, you can't help the way you're made. And Smith, he can't help the way *he's* made. Land, he takes the whole suffering world into his heart, and it gives him hell's-bells, *I* can tell you! Why, Mr. Sterling, that man takes into his inside enough of the human race's miseries in a day to last a real manly man thirty years!"

"Oh, rub it in, I'm down, rub it in!"

"No,"—appealingly—"*don't* talk like that, Mr. Sterling, *I'm* not saying anything, I'm only trying to *show* you that a person ain't to blame that's made—made—well, that's made the way you be. So's 't you'll feel good."

"Oh, thanks, it's ever so kind of you! I haven't felt so good in a year."

"Now I'm right down glad of that. Say—Mr. Sterling, Smith ain't twenty-six, he's sixty."

"Lord, I understand, I understand!"

"Yes, that breed—people that's made that way—people that have to bear the world's miseries on top of their own—why, it makes them old long before their time; *they* can't find any bright side of life. Lord, yes, it makes them old, long, *long* before their time. But it's different with your make, you know; *you* might live a thou—"

"Oh, let up, and change the subject! Haven't I *said* I'm a dog? Well, then, have some pity!"

Chapter 6

George's Diary—Continued

THE PAST few days have been like all the days I have spent in this house—full of satisfactions for me. Every day the feeling of the day before is renewed to me—the feeling of having been in a half-trance all

my life before—numb, sluggish-blooded, sluggish-minded—a feeling
which is followed at once by a brisk sense of being out of that syncope
and awake! awake and alive; alive to my finger-ends. I realize that I am
a veteran trader in shadows who has struck the substance. I have found
the human race. It was all around me before, but vague and spectral; I
have found it now, with the blood in it, and the bones; and am getting
acquainted with it. That is, with the facts of it; I had the theories before. It is pleasant, charming, engrossing. Incidentally, I am also getting acquainted with myself. But it is no matter, it could not well be
helped, the bos'n is around so much. I do not really care.

I have not lost my interest in the monument—that will stay alive,
there is no fear as to that—but the human race has pushed it to second
place.

The Admiral, of his own motion, is allowing me to use what he calls
the ward-room as a studio. It is spacious and airy, and has plenty of
light. The derelicts and the friends of the derelicts have the freedom of
it, night and day. They come when they please, they sit around and
chat, they smoke and read, and the Admiral "pays the freight," as the
slang phrase goes. And they sit to me. They take an interest in each
other's portraits, and are candid with criticisms. They talk to me about
themselves, and about each other. Thus I get the entire man—four-
fifths of him from himself and the other fifth from the others. I find
that no man discloses the completing fifth himself. Sometimes that
fifth is to his credit, sometimes it isn't; but let it be whichever it may,
you will never get it out of the man himself. It is the make of the man
that determines it. The bos'n says there are no exceptions to this law.
He says every man is a moon and has a side which he turns toward nobody: you have to slip around behind if you want to see it.

I began on the Admiral's portrait this morning. Every derelict that
happened in was at once interested. They sat around and kept one eye
on the brush, the other on the sitter, and talked. It was very pleasant.
"Uncle 'Rastus" was one of the group—'Rastus Timson. He is a colored man; 70 years old; large, compact, all big bone and muscle, *very*
broad-shouldered, prodigiously strong—can take up a barrel of beer
and drink from the bung; shrewd, good-natured, has a sense of humor;
gets up his opinions for himself, and is courageous enough to change

them when he thinks he has found something better; is plain, sincere, and honest; is ready and willing to debate deep questions, and gets along pretty well at it; has a pronounced Atlas-stoop, from carrying mighty burdens upon his shoulders; wears what is left of a once hat—a soft ruin which slumps to a shapeless rumple like a collapsed toy balloon when he drops it on the floor; the remains of his once clothes hang in fringed rags and rotting shreds from his booms and yard-arms, and give him the sorrowfully picturesque look of a ship that has been through a Cape Horn hurricane—not recently, but in Columbus's time. He lives by such now-and-then whitewashing jobs as he can pick up; was a Maryland slave before the War. In those distant times he was a Dunker Baptist; later, a modified Methodist; later still, a Unitarian, with reservations; he is a freethinker now, and unattached—"goes in a procession by himself, like Jackson's hog," as the bos'n phrases it. A good man and a cheerful spirit; the other derelicts like him; his is a welcome face here.

He lives at "Aunty Phyllis's" humble boarding house, where the derelicts Jacobs and Cully put up—"the Twins," as the bos'n calls them. Aunty Phyllis was born and brought up in Maryland—Eastern Shore. She was a slave, before the War. She is toward seventy, stands six feet one in her stockings, is as straight as a grenadier, and has the grit and the stride and the warlike bearing of one. But, being black, she is good-natured, to the bone. It is the born privilege and prerogative of her adorable race. She is cheerful, indestructibly cheerful and lively; and what a refreshment she is! Her laugh—her breezy laugh, her inspiring and uplifting laugh—is always ready, always on tap, and comes pealing out, peal upon peal, right from her heart, let the occasion for it be big or little; and it is so cordial and so catching that derelict after derelict has to forget his troubles and join in—even the ex-postman.

She is a Methodist, and as profoundly and strenuously religious as Uncle 'Rastus isn't. The pair are close friends in other things, but in the greater matter of religion—well, they debate that. Pretty much all the time; at least Aunty Phyllis debates it and 'Rastus listens; he does not get much chance to air his side. There is apparently but one text: are there such things as special providences, or aren't there? Aunty Phyllis "knows" there are, 'Rastus denies it. It is going to take time to settle this. Both belligerents were on hand to-day, and of course there was a debate; but when I began on the Admiral's portrait the new interest suspended it.

After some general chat the Admiral drifted into the matter of the monument, and I was glad of that, for his views regarding Adam had only been hinted, as yet, not developed.

"As concerns Adam in general," said the Admiral, "I have been thinking him over, several days, and I have to stand where I stood before; I have to rank him with the minor sacred characters, like Satan. But I want to be fair to Adam, and I make allowances; he hadn't had Satan's experiences, he hadn't Satan's age; if he *had* have had, I don't say but what it might have been different. But we have to judge by the facts we have, we can't go behind the record; we have to look at what he did, not at his might-have-dones. Adam was only a child, when you do him square justice, and so I don't hold him down to the mark the way I do Satan—I make allowances. Now then, you want to put Adam out of your minds, and take *another* child—it's the only way to get a right focus on the situation and understand it, because you've always been bred up to the fact that Adam was a full grown *man*, and so you forget to remember that he could be a man and a child both at the same time, and *was*. Well, put another child in his place. You say to that child, 'let this orange alone.' The child understands that—ain't it so? Ain't it so, Aunty Phyllis?"

"Yes, marse Stormfield, de child un'stan'."

"Next, you say to the child, 'if you disobey, arrested development and ultimate extinction shall be your portion.' What does that mean, Aunty Phyllis?"

"Umhh! Bless yo' soul, honey, if I was to die for it I couldn't tell you!"

Of course those long words compelled her wonder and admiration and brought out of her a powerful laugh—it was her way of expressing applause.

"What does it mean, 'Rastus?"

"Deed'n'deed, *I* don't know, marse Stormfield."

"*Why* don't you know?"

"Becaze I hain't ever struck dem words befo'."

"Very well, that was the case with Adam. How was he going to know what 'surely die' meant? *Die!* He hadn't ever struck that word before; he hadn't ever seen a dead creature, there hadn't ever been a dead creature for him to see; there hadn't ever been any talk about dead things, because there hadn't ever *been* any dead things to talk about."

He paused, and waited for the new idea to take hold. Presently Aunty Phyllis said—

"Well, dat do beat me! But it's *so*—I never see it befo'. It's so, sure as you bawn. Po' thing, it didn't mean nothin' to him, no mo'n de 'rested distinction mean to me when I hain't ever hearn 'bout it befo'."

The other derelicts granted that this was a new view, and sound. Sound and surprising. The Admiral was charmed. He resumed.

"Now then, Adam didn't understand. Why didn't he come out and *say* so? Why didn't he ask what 'surely die' meant? Wouldn't he, if he had felt scared? If he had understood those awful words he would have been scared deaf and dumb and paralysed, wouldn't he? Aunty Phyllis, if they had been said to you, you would have left the apple alone, wouldn't you?"

"Yes, marse Stormfield, I mos' sholy would."

"I wouldn't tetched it if it was de las' act," said Uncle 'Rastus, fervently.

"Very well, it shows that he didn't suppose it was anything serious. The same with Eve. Just two heedless children, you see. They supposed it was some little ordinary punishment—they hadn't ever had any other kind; they didn't know there was any other kind. And so it was easy for Satan to get around them and persuade them to disobey."

The mother-heart of Aunt Phyllis was touched, and she said—

"Po' little Adam—po' little Eve! It was de same like my little Henry: if I say, 'dah you is, a-snoopin' 'roun' dat sugar agin; you dast to tetch it once, I lay I'll skin you!' 'Cose de minute my back's turned he's got de sugar; 'caze *he* don't k'yer nothin' for de skinnin', de way *I* skun him. Yes-suh, I kin see it all, now—*dey* didn't k'yer nothin' for de skinnin', de way de good Lord allays skun 'em befo'."

Uncle 'Rastus highly admired this speech, and admitted it, which greatly pleased Aunt Phyllis. 'Rastus added—

"It's plain to me, dey warn't fa'rly treated. If de' *was* a Adam—which people says nowadays de' wasn't. But dat ain't nothin', justice is justice, en I want him to have de monument."

"Me too!" from Aunt Phyllis.

Two new converts. I was prospering. The Admiral proceeded with his examination of Adam.

"As far as I can see, he showed up best in naming animals. Considering that he hadn't ever seen any animals before, I am of the opinion that he did it very well indeed, as far as he got. He had a sure touch, on the common ones—named them with insight and judacity, and the names stick, to this day, after all the wear and tear they've been through; it was when he struck the big ones and the long ones that he couldn't cash-in. Take the ornithorhyncus, for instance."

The music of it and the majestic outlandishness of it broke Aunty Phyllis up again, and it took her a while to laugh out her admiring astonishment.

"Ornithorhyncus." The Admiral paid out the great word lingeringly; it tasted good to him. "As we know, he skipped the ornithorhyncus. Left him out of the invoice. Why?"

He looked blandly around for answers. The others showed diffidence about entering the field, but Aunty Phyllis ventured—

" 'Fraid of him, *I* bet you! I wouldn't gone anear him, not for pie!"

'Rastus turned upon her and said argumentatively—

"You old fool, what does *you* know about him?"

"You mine yo' manners, 'Rastus Timson, er I lay I'll take 'n wipe de flo' wid you! What does *I* know 'bout him! I reckon I knows dis much: dey never gin him no name like dat less'n he *deserve* it. So dah, now!"

'Rastus—with the grateful air of one who has received new light—

"Well, it—yas, it sutt'nly do look reasonable. When a body git a name like dat, a body deserve it." (Thoughtful pause.) "Same like *Phyllis*."

The Admiral lifted his hand, and Phyllis quenched the battle-light in her eye, and reserved her retort. The dipsomaniac Strother, a dreamy and melancholy wreck, muttered absently, with a sigh—

"Ornitho ... tho ... rhyncus. Sounds like ... like ... well, I know I've *had* it."

The Admiral resumed—

"In my judgment the alphabet was just beginning to accumulate, in that early day, and there wasn't much of it yet, and so it seems reasonable that he had to skip it because he couldn't spell it." The company did not need to speak out their praise of this striking and happy solution, their faces did the office of their tongues, and did it with an eloquence beyond the arts of speech. After a little, Jimson Flinders—young colored gentleman—stenographer, sub-editor of his race's paper—visitor—dressy—thinker, in a way—somewhat educated —said, with honest admiration—

"Why, it's so simple and plain and dead-sure, that what makes me wonder, is, that there didn't somebody hit on it long and long ago."

This brought emphatic nods of agreement and approval, and the Admiral could not entirely conceal his pleasure. He took up his theme again.

"Adam skipped a lot of the creatures. This has been the astonishment of the world for—well, from away back. Ages, as you may say. But you can see, now, how it was. He didn't want to skip, he wanted to do his honest duty, but there he *was*—he hadn't the ammunition. He was equipped for short names, but not the others. If a bear came along —all right, he was loaded for bear. There was no embarrassment. The same if a cow came along; or a cat, or a horse, or a lion, or a tiger, or a hog, or a frog, or a worm, or a bat, or a snipe, or an ant, or a bee, or a trout, or a shark, or a whale, or a tadpole—anything that didn't strain his alphabet, you know: they would find him on post and tranquil; he would register them and they would pass on, discussing their names, most of them pleased—such as leopards and scarlet tanagers and such, some of them pained—such as buzzards, and alligators, and so on, the others ashamed—such as squids, and polecats, and that kind; but all resigned, in a way, and reconciled, reconnizing that he was new to the business and doing the best he could. Plain sailing, and satisfactory, you see. But in the course of trade, along comes the pterodactyl—"

There was a general gasp.

"Could he spell that? *No*, sir. Solomon couldn't. Nor no other early Christian—not in *that* early time. It was very different from now, in those days. Anybody can spell pterodactyl *now*, but—"

The eager and the ignorant interrupted the Admiral and asked him
to instruct them in that formidable orthography, but he shivered
slightly and hastened on, without seeming to hear—

—"but in those old early geological times the alphabet hadn't even
got up to the Old Red Sandstone period yet, and it was worse in Adam's
time, of course; so, as he didn't want to let on that he couldn't spell it,
he just said, 'Call again, office hours over for to-day,' and pulled down
the shades and locked up and went home, the same as if nothing had
happened.

"It was natural, I think, and right enough, too. I would have done it;
most people would. Well, he had a difficult time, limited the way he
was, and it is only fair for us to take that into account. Every few days
along would come an animal as big as a house—grazing along, eating
elephants and pulling down the synagogues and things: 'Dinosaurium-
iguanodon,' says Adam; 'tell him to come Sunday;' and would close up
and take a walk. And the very next day, like enough, along comes a creation a mile long, chewing rocks and scraping the hills away with its
tail, and lightening and thundering with its eyes and its lungs, and Eve
scoops up her hair over her arm and takes to the woods, and Adam says
'Megatheriomylodonticoplesiosauriasticum—give him his first syllable
and get him to take the rest on the instalment plan,' which it seems to
me was one of the best ideas Adam ever had, and in every way creditable to him. He had to save *some* of the alphabet, he couldn't let one
animal have it all, it would not have been fair, anyway.

"I will say it again, I think Adam was at his level best when he was
naming the creatures, and most to be praised. If you look up your
fossiliferous paleontology, I acknowledge you will have to admit that
where he registered one creature he skipped three hundred and fifty,
but that is not his fault, it was the fault of his alphabet-plant. You
can't build a battleship out of a scrap-heap. Necessarily he couldn't
take the whole of one of those thirteen-syllabers and pay spot cash; the
most he could do was to put up a margin. Well, you know what happens to that kind of financing."

Chapter 7

George's Diary—Continued

At this point the marchesa came tripping girlishly forward from the other end of the ward-room, the bos'n half-spiraling along after her, pivoting on his game leg—with a corky squeak—and fetching a curve with his good one, in accordance with the requirements of his loco-motion-plant. The poor old girl was girlishly indignant about some-thing—one could see it in her eyes and in her manner. She came straight to the Admiral and broke into his discourse with a complaint against the bos'n. Another man would have been annoyed; the Admiral was not. He is frequently a little sharp with the marchesa, but as a rule he soon softens and looks remorseful and begins to betray his discomfort and repentance in ways which beg forgiveness without humbling him to the spoken prayer. It is a mystery; I don't understand it. She is fretful, offensive, ungracious, disagreeable, ungrateful, impossible to please, and I can't see why these people don't fly out at her every day and give her what she deserves. But they don't. They put up with it, they are mistakenly gentle with her, and of course she goes right on. Every time I think the bos'n is going to let her have it, he most strangely doesn't. He says irritating things to her whenever he can think of any to say, but there is no viciousness in them, no temper; often they are merely idiotic, yet *he* is not idiotic. He doesn't seem to know they are idiotic; they seem to drop out of him without inten-tion and without consciousness. But they irritate the marchesa, and then he doesn't seem to understand why they should. If he would give her a dressing-down once, it would do her good. And he is quite competent. But no, she can't seem to exasperate him into a harshness. The same with Jimmy and Aunt Martha: they are persistently and devilishly kind to her, in spite of all she can do. They even strain the human possibilities to be benevolent to her: for they go with her daily on her long and objectless tramps about the streets, and she in that outrage that she wears—tricked out in a gay and girly costume which is all of twenty years too young for her; and stared at, and she and her escort laughed at, by everybody that comes along, of course. What can the mystery be? Every time I think the bos'n is going to explain it, he doesn't. The same with Jimmy and Aunt Martha. And they are all like what the bos'n said about the Admiral: if you want to get at his privacies, wait till it suits him to start the subject himself—you will get nothing by trying to start it. Every night the Admiral prays for the salvation of that unnamed person again, and I would like to know if it is himself, but I suppose I must wait until some member of the family starts the subject. This only keeps my curiosity fretting, and does no good. I have to assume that it is the Admiral, and it is not pleasant—a bluff and open self-appreciation is more in his line.

The marchesa's temper was pretty well up; she was flushed, and her lips quivered nervously. The Admiral listened patiently to her charges; respectfully, too, though there was nothing in them. It turned out that she and the bos'n had been having a scrap over the Rev. Caleb Parsons—again. This was a visitor—not a derelict. He is what we call a "regular," as distinguished from casual visitors to the Anchor Watch. He is disliked. That is enough for the marchesa: she always manages to like—or think she likes—whoever or whatever is disliked by the rest of us. So she is championing Mr. Parsons in these days—just as she had championed Satan until the Admiral took him under his wing that night, then she turned against him, horns, hoofs and all, and was so bitter that she said she wouldn't lend him a shovel of coal if he was freezing to death. That is what the bos'n said she said, but she denied it and was in a great fury about it, and said she never said coal at all, she said brimstone. As if that made any great difference! And she complained to the Admiral and said the bos'n was always distorting her words and making them seem worse than they were, and she wanted him punished; whereas the bos'n complained that she was always distorting *his* words. And he was right. So was she. Both of them were persistently guilty of that same offence.

As I have said, the Watch did not like Rev. Mr. Parsons; it was not because he wasn't a good enough man, and well-meaning, but because he hadn't any talent and was over-sentimental. He was always getting thunderstruck over the commonest every-day things the Creator did, and saying "Lo, what God hath wrought!" The bos'n called him Lo, for short, the Anchor Watch adopted it, and this aggravated the marchesa, and she added it to her list of grudges against the bos'n, and between them they made it do good service in their debates. It was upon trifles like this that the marchesa lived and throve.

As usual, the present charges were of no consequence, and not worth coming to the Admiral about, but he listened, good man, without fret. She wanted the bos'n put in irons—a thing she was always longing to accomplish, but she never could. She had two or three of these little charges this time. To begin with, she said she was remarking upon Mr. Parsons's early history and how good he was, and at last had his reward and heard God call him to His ministry; and she said the bos'n interrupted her and said it was probably an *echo*, the call was from the other direction—

And she was going on to give the bos'n down the banks, when the Admiral put up his hand for silence. Then he sat there and thought it out. Thought it out, and gave his verdict. To this effect: that the *sky* can't produce an echo, for the sky is made of air and emptiness; a call coming from below would have to have something hard and solid to hit against and rebound from, otherwise it would keep on going and never be heard of again: so, as this call *was* heard, it is proof that it did not come from below; not coming from below, it could not be an echo, and wasn't; not being an echo, it *had* to come down from above, and did; therefore, the bos'n was "in the wrong, and is decided against. But there is no punishment, no harm being intended. We will pass to the next charge if you please, madam."

The marchesa blazed out and denounced the verdict as being "rotten with nepotism;" and on top of that she shook her little nubbin of a fist in the Admiral's face and called him plainly and squarely a "hardened and shameless old nepot."

The Admiral winced, but made no retort. Everybody was shocked and offended, and Aunty Phyllis spoke out without reserve and said it warn't to nobody's credit to live on the Admiral's goodness and hostility and then call him a teapot. The marchesa would have resented this, and Aunty Phyllis cleared for action and invited her to come on, but the Admiral interfered. Then once more he asked for the next charge, and the marchesa furnished it:

"He said I was so deaf I couldn't read fine print."

The Admiral's face clouded up and he gave the bos'n a severe look and said—

"Tom Larkin, what do you say to this charge?"

The bos'n answered, without bitterness, but in a wounded tone—

"I give you the honest truth, sir, I never said it. She is always distorting my words. All I said was, that she was so near-sighted she couldn't hear it thunder."

The Admiral went away down down into this difficult thing with a patience and a judicial calm that were beyond belief. He reasoned it out, detail by detail, and decided that both parties were in the wrong—because:

"Deafness has nothing to do with reading fine print—it is a matter of vision, not auricularity. Therefore the charge has no legal standing, no basis; it falls to the ground of its own weight. The defendant was in the wrong to make it, it not being true; but the plaintiff cannot claim that it is a slander, because, true or untrue, it is merely an infirmity, and innocent of criminality, all infirmities being visitations of God and visitations of God being not actionable, by reason of lack of jurisdiction. The other charge is of the same nature, substantially. Whether true or false, the act of not being able to hear it thunder on the part of a near-sighted person is not reprehensible, because not intentional, not dependent the one upon the other, and both coming under the head of infirmities—hence properly recognizable as visitations of God and not actionable, therefore not slanderous, by reason of lack of jurisdiction. And so it is manifest that both parties to these charges are guilty: the defendant for making them with probable intent to slander, and the plaintiff for claiming them as slanders when they are not slanders because based upon infirmities and not avoidable. And both parties are innocent, of a necessity, considering the circumstances; the defendant being innocent of accomplishing his probable design, and the plaintiff through not being able to convict him of it, although such was her intention. The cases are dismissed."

Sometimes he makes my head ache, it is so difficult to understand him. And I can't see how he understands himself, when he strips and goes floundering out into these tumbling seas of complexities, but he probably does; thinks he does, I know; and certainly he always gets through, and wades ashore looking refreshed and all right.

Chapter 8

George's Diary—Continued

I HAD the hope that we were going to get back to Adam, now, but it failed. The marchesa was not in any degree satisfied with the way things had gone with her, and she could not reconcile herself to the idea of leaving them so; and so she begged for one more chance. The Admiral sighed, and told her to go ahead; go ahead, and try to let this be the last, for the present. Whereupon she accused the bos'n to this effect:

"He said I said the lack of money is the root of all evil. I never said it. I was quoting, and said the *love* of money is the root of all evil."

The Admiral's eyes flashed angrily and he burst out with—

"*Another* of your damned trivialities! Now look here, marcheesa—"

He stopped there. His lips remained parted, the fire in his eyes sank down to a smoulder. He sat like that—thinking—and he had that faraway look which comes upon him when something has hit his thought a blow and stunned it, or sent it wandering in other fields. In the stillness he loomed there on his raised platform like that, looking like a bronze image, he was so motionless. We sat looking at him, and waiting. You could hear the faint wailing of the winds outside, rising and falling, rising and falling, you could catch the rumble and murmur of the distant traffic. Presently he muttered, as to himself—

"The lack of money .... the *lack* .... is the root of all evil. The ...."

He fell silent again. There was no passion in his face, now; the harshness had passed out of it and left only gentleness. As one in a reverie, his eyes began to drift to this figure and that and the other, and dwell a little space upon each—dreamily, and no words uttered. Naturally my gaze journeyed with his.

Lord, those pathetic figures! Here, and there and yonder they hung

limp upon their chairs, lost to the present, busy with the past, the un-
returning past—there, brooding, they hung, the defeated, the derelicts!
They all had a droop; each a droop of his own, and each telling its
own story, without need of speech. How eloquent is an attitude—how
much it can say! When a silence falls, we who are alive start out of
our thoughts and look about us, but it descends upon these dead-in-
hope like the benediction of night, and conveys them gently out of this
workaday world and the consciousness of it.

There sat Strother the dipsomaniac, his graying head drooped, gazing at the floor—and not seeing it. He was awake only a moment ago,
he is dreaming now, already. A flabby ruin, his flesh colorless and puffy
with drink, his nerves lax, his hands uncertain and quivery. You would
not think it, but he was a man, once; and held up his head with the
best; and had money to waste—and wasted it; and had a wife who lived
in the light of his eyes; and four children who loved him with a love
that made him proud, and paid him a homage that made him humble,
so innocent and honest and exaggerated it was. Well, his money is
gone, the respect of men is gone, his self-respect is gone, his life is
bankrupt; of all his possessions nothing is left but five accusing graves,
and memories that tear his heart!

Near by, droop "the Twins." They are always together. In a bygone
time Jacobs was rich, and his money made him happy—happier than
anything else could have made him. Cully was his coachman. Speculation impoverished Jacobs; sudden and great wealth came to Cully
from a departed Australian uncle, and Jacobs became Cully's coachman. By and by, speculation made a pauper of Cully. Now in their
gray age they are derelicts. The Admiral finds odd jobs for them when
he can, their brother derelicts helping in this when opportunity offers.
They board cheaply with Aunty Phyllis's humble colored waifs and
hand-to-mouths, and come here to dream their great days over again,
and count up the money they used to have, and mourn over this and
that and the other disastrous investment, and reason out, for the thousandth time, just how each mistake came to be made, and how each
and all of them could have been so easily avoided if they had *only* done
so and so. Then they sigh and sorrow over those dreary "onlies" . . . .
and take up the tale again, and go wearying over it, and over it, and

over it, in the same old weather-worn and goalless track, poor old fellows!

Other derelicts sit drooping, here and there—the forgotten ex-Senator, once so illustrious and so powerful; the ragged General, once so great, once so honored—long ago; the Poet, once so popular and so prosperous, until he took a stand for straight talk and principle, and lost his place on the magazine and never could get another start. And so on and so on, derelict after derelict—a melancholy landscape to cast your eye over. And beyond them, walking wearily to and fro, to and fro, to and fro, like a tired animal in a cage, is Peters the inventor. He is always doing that. I wonder when he rests? If you speak to him he gives you a dazed look and a wan smile, and takes up his dreary tramp again. He scraped and scraped, spent and spent, and was always going to get his great invention launched—next month—the month after, sure—*then*, oh, then the roses would come back to his young wife's cheeks, and she would have silks to her back, only just wait a little while! And he saw her youth pass, and age come, and the patient face fade toward the inevitable—and *that* came, and left him forlorn, to fight his fight alone. Always the vision was rising before him of a capitalist—a capitalist who would give his great invention to the world and add another splendid factor to its advancing civilization and its fabulous forces. There was nothing needed but that capitalist—who never came. In his desperation, Peters committed a forgery, and sat in a prison five years, eating his heart out. Now he walks the floor, and dreams of what might have been—what might have been—what might have been! if only the capitalist had come!

The ex-postman haunts his neighborhood—out of a natural fellow-feeling for him, perhaps; and droops his head and dreams of his ruined life, and of how it came about.

The Admiral was still gazing, lost in thought. He came to himself, now, and said, very quietly—

"The lack of . . . . *both* are true! The case is dismissed."

I thought it a good verdict, but the marchesa was of another opinion —mainly because she was disappointed again, most likely—and she began to rail against it fiercely. Nobody interrupted her, and she kept it up until she ran out of vitriol. But it did good service. Its electricity cleared the air; drove away the gloom, and let in some cheerfulness. We all felt better, the Admiral chirked up and was himself again. I think he was grateful to the marchesa; he looked so, and he said to her, in almost a petting way, as it seemed to me—

"Let it go, marcheesa, put it behind you and let's go about and try a slant up to wind'ard, so to speak, and forget about it—change the subject, you understand, if we can find one. It's wholesome—a change is —if a person hits it right."

Two or three suggested a return to Adam, and wanted to hear the rest about him, in case there was anything lacking to make his rehabilitation complete. It flattered the Admiral, and he looked nearly as gratified as he was.

"Well," he said, reflectively, "let me see. Since you want it, I think there's a word more that I would like to say. Only just a word, in palliation of his simpleness and unworldliness, as you may say. Eve's, too. I think it was beautiful, the amount they didn't know about common ordinary things. Take the matter of clothes, for instance. It is perfectly astonishing, the way they would go about like—like that. And perfectly unconcerned, too. But I am not reproaching them for it—no, just the contrary. They are to be praised. They had the right kind of modesty, to my mind—the kind that ain't aware of itself. I think it's a much better sort than these statutes that stand around in parks with a fig-leaf on to set a good example. I believe it's a mistake. Who ever follows it? Nobody. Adam and Eve didn't think about their modesty, didn't fuss about it, didn't even know they had it; and so it was sound modesty, real modesty; whereas some people would have gone blustering around. The more I think of those beautiful lives of theirs, the more I lean to the idea of the monument.

"And there's other reasons. Adam is fading out. It is on account of Darwin and that crowd. I can see that he is not going to last much longer. There's a plenty of signs. He is getting belittled to a germ— a little bit of a speck that you can't see without a microscope powerful enough to raise a gnat to the size of a church. They take that speck and breed from it: first a flea, then a fly, then a bug, then cross these and get a fish, then a raft of fishes, all kinds, then cross the whole lot and get a reptile, then work up the reptiles till you've got a supply of lizards and spiders and toads and alligators and Congressmen and so on, then cross the entire lot again and get a plant of amphibiums, which are half-breeds and do business both wet and dry, such as turtles and frogs and ornithorhyncuses and so on, and cross-up again and get a mongrel bird, sired by a snake and dam'd by a bat, resulting in a ptero-dactyl, then they develop *him*, and water his stock till they've got the air filled with a million things that wear feathers, then they cross-up all the accumulated animal life to date and fetch out a mammal, and start-in diluting again till there's cows and tigers and rats and elephants and monkeys and everything you want down to the Missing Link, and out of him and a mermaid they propagate Man, and there you are! Everything ship-shape and finished-up, and nothing to do but lay low and wait and see if it was worth the time and expense.

"Well, then, was it? To my mind, it don't stand to reason. They say it took a hundred million years. Suppose you ordered a Man at the start, and had a chance to look over the plans and specifications—which would you take, Adam or the germ? Naturally you would say Adam is business, the germ ain't; one is immediate and sure, the other is speculative and uncertain. Well, I have thought these things all over, and my sympathies are with Adam. Adam was like *us*, and so he seems near to us, and dear. He is kin, blood kin, and my heart goes out to him in affection. But I don't feel that way about that germ. The germ is too far away—and not only that, but such a wilderness of reptiles between. You can't skip the reptiles and set your love on the germ; no, if they are ancestors, it is your duty to include them and love them. Well, you can't do that. You would come up against the dino-saur and your affections would cool off. You couldn't love a dinosaur the way you would another relative. There would always be a gap. Nothing could ever bridge it. Why, it gives a person the dry gripes just to look at him!

"Very well, then, where do we arrive? Where do we arrive with our respect, our homage, our filial affection? At Adam! At Adam, every time. We can't build a monument to a germ, but we can build one to Adam, who is in the way to turn myth in fifty years and be entirely forgotten in two hundred. We can build a monument and save his name to the world forever, and we'll do it! What do you say?"

It was carried, with a fine enthusiasm; and it was beautiful to see the pleasure beam out all over the Admiral when that tribute burst forth. My own pleasure was no less than his; for with his favor enlisted in my enterprise, it was recognizable that a great step had been made toward the accomplishment of the grandest dream of my life.

Chapter 9

The Diary Continued

TEN DAYS LATER. The derelicts get a certain easment by talking to me about their sorrows. I can see it. I thought it was because my sympathy was honest and prompt. That is true, it is a part of it, the bos'n says, but not all of it. The rest of it, he says, is, that I am new. They have told their stories to each other many times, for grief is repetitious; and this kind of wear eventually blunts a listener's interest and discourages the teller, then both parties retire within their shells and feed upon that slow-starving diet, Introspection. But a new ear, an untired ear, a fresh and willing and sympathetic ear—they like that!

About a week ago the bos'n said another thing:

"They've all one burden to their song, haven't they?"

"Yes. Sorrow."

"Right enough, but there's more than one kind of sorrow. There's the kind that you haven't helped to bring about—family bereavements, and such; and then there's the kind that comes of things you did, your own self, and would do so different if it was to do over again."

"Yes, I get the idea. That kind is repentance. It's when you have done a wrong thing."

"You've got the name right—repentance. But you don't cover enough ground with it. Repentance ain't confined to doing wrong, sometimes you catch it just as sharp for doing right."

I doubted that, and said it was against experience.

"No—against teaching," the bos'n retorted. "You get taught, right along up, that if you always do the rightest you can, your conscience will pat you on the back and be satisfied; but experience learns a person that there's exceptions to the rule. We've got both kinds here."

We couldn't argue it any further, because there was an interruption. Aunt Martha of the welcome face and the lovely spirit shone in upon us like another sunbeam, for a moment, to say the Admiral wanted the large Atlas and couldn't find it, and did the bos'n know where it was? Yes, and said he would go and send for it right away, adding, "it got left behind at Hell's Delight when we broke camp there—I forgot it."

That was a private summer resort, instituted by the Admiral for the derelicts. Hell's Delight was not its official name; in fact it never had one. In the beginning the Rev. Lo-what-God-hath-Wrought had called it "The Isles of the Blest," and every one liked it, but when the bos'n got to referring to it by that other name it was soon adopted because it was short and unpretentious, and the pretty one fell into disuse and was forgotten.

I began to take note, and presently found that the bos'n was right about the conflicting sources of repentance. The revealments of my sitters showed that several of them were penitents of the class that regret and grieve over righteous things done. It cost me a pang to have to register these exceptions to the fairer and pleasanter law of my teaching and training, but it had to be done, the hard facts of experience put in their claim and stood by it and made it good.

For instance, there was the case of Henry Clarkson, Poet: the derelict with the deep eyes, the melancholy eyes, the haunting eyes, the hollow face, the thin hands, the frail figure—draped in that kind of clothes that hang, droop, shift about the person in unstable folds and wrinkles with every movement, take a grip nowhere, and seem to have nothing in them. He is old, yet is not gray, and that unpleasant incongruity makes him seem older than he really is; his hair is long and black, and hangs lank and straight down beside his face and reminds one of Louis Stevenson.

The first stage of his life went well enough. He struggled up, poor and unaware of it, his heart full of the joy of life and the dance-music of hope, his head full of dreams. He climbed and climbed, diligently, laboriously, up through mean employments, toward a high and distant goal, and there was pleasure in it. He kept his eye fixed steadily on that goal, expecting to make it, determined to make it, and he did make it; and stood on that high place exultant, and looked out over the world he had conquered with his two hands. Far down on the earth stood the memory of him, the vision of him—shop-boy, errand-boy, anything you please; and here he stood, now, on this dizzy alp, at twenty-eight, his utmost ambition attained: literary person, rising poet, first assistant editor of a magazine!

It was a wonderful thing to see, how the old dead fires flamed up in his eyes when he got to that proud climax and stood again in fancy upon that great summit and surveyed his vanquished world! And he lingered there lovingly, and told me all about the sublimities of the position, and the honors and attentions it brought him; told me how the greatest in the region round about fellowed him with themselves, and familiarly chatted and laughed with him, and consulted him on large affairs; and how there was a seat for him at the dais-table of every banquet, and his name on the program for a stirring poem; and how satisfied with him the aging editor-in-chief was, and how it was well understood and accepted that he was to be that great functionary's successor, all in good time . . . .

He was so eager, so earnest, so inspired, so happy, so proud, in the pouring forth of these moving memories, that he made me lose myself! I was no longer I, he was no longer the mouldering derelict: he lived his sumptuous and coruscating romance over again under my eyes, and it was all as if I was in it and living it with him! How real it was!

Then all of a sudden we crumbled to ashes, as it were! For his tale turned down-hill on the sunset side; his voice and his face lost their animation; the pet of fortune, the courted of men, was gone, the faded derelict was back again—all in a moment. It seemed to make a chill in the air.

He told me how his ruin came about, and how little he was expecting it, how poorly prepared for it. Everything was going well with him. He had recently seen one of his grandest dreams come to fruit: he had issued his poems in a volume; a fine large step for a person who had been of the ephemerals before; he felt that permanent fame, real fame, even national fame, was close ahead of him, now. The poems wouldn't bring money, but that was nothing, poems are not written for that. And he had made still another large step—his idol had appointed the wedding day. The pair had been waiting until the editorial salary should reach a figure that would support two in a fairly adequate way. It had reached it, now, and would by and by double with the impending chief-editorship. Well, it was at this time of all times, when the poet's sun was blazing at high noon, that the disaster fell.

He made a discovery one morning, while reading proof. It was an article in praise of an enterprise which some unusually good people were getting up for the profit of the working girl, the mechanic, the day laborer, the widow, the orphan—for all, indeed, who might have poor little hoards earning mere pennies in savings banks. These could get into the enterprise on the instalment plan, and on terms so easy that the poorest could not feel the burden. For the first year the dividend would be ten per cent—not a mere possible or probable ten per cent, but "guaranteed." In the second year this would certainly be increased by fifty per cent, and in all probability doubled. Parties proposing to subscribe for the stock must lose no time. It could be had at par during thirty days; after that, for thirty days, the price would be 1.25; after which the price would be augmented by another 25.

The discoverer was as happy as Columbus. He had saved the magazine! But for the accident that he had happened to be reading proof that morning, to relieve the proof-reader of a part of his burden and hasten the "make-up," this vile masked advertisement would almost certainly have gone into the forms, escaping detection until too late. He carried the poisonous thing to the sanctum, and laid it before the chief editor. Without a word; for he did not want to betray his joy and pride in his lucky achievement. The chief ran his eye over the opening paragraph, then looked blandly up and said—

"Well?"

That was all. No astonishment, no outraged feelings, no—well, no nothing. Just tranquillity. Not even a compliment to the discoverer. Young Clarkson was very much surprised—not to say stunned. It took him a little while to find some words to say. Then, said he—

"Please read a little more of it, and you will see that it is really a masked advertisement—smuggled past the staff by the advertising agent, without doubt."

"Umm. You think so, do you?"

"I feel sure of it, sir. It came near getting into the forms; I stopped it just in time."

"You did, did you?"

"Yes, sir."

The chief's manner was very calm, very placid, almost uncomfortably so.

"Mr. Clarkson, have you been officially authorized to stop articles?" A faint red tinge appeared in the chief's cheek and a just perceptible glimmer as of summer lightnings in his eye when he said this.

"Oh, no, sir, certainly not! I only thought—"

"Then will you be kind enough to tell me why you took it upon yourself to stop this one?"

"I—I—why, I hardly know what to say, I am so—so unpre—I thought I was doing the magazine a great service to stop it—and time was precious."

"Umm. What was your objection to the article?"

"If you would only read it, Mr. Haskell! then you would see what it is, and you would approve what I did. I meant no harm, I was only— If you will read it, you will see that it is just the old wrecked "Prize-Guess" swindle hidden under a new name. It robbed hundreds of thousands of poor people of their savings before, and is starting out now to do the like again. The magazine's moral character and reputation are without spot, and this article could heavily damage these great assets; and so I at once—"

"Yes, you did. . . . . Well, well, let it go, I think you meant well. Sit down; I will throw some light."

Henry took a seat, wondering what kind of light he was going to get. The chief said—

"I do not wish to mince matters, and I will be perfectly frank. This is a great and prosperous periodical; to continue so, it must sail with the times. The times are changing—we must change with them, or drop behind in the race. Very well, this *is* immoral advertising and iniquitous, but the others are engaging in it, and we've got to fall into line. Our board of directors have so decided. It pays quintuple rates, you see; that hits them where they live. It is odious, it is infamous, it kept me awake several nights, thinking of the shame of it—that this should come upon my gray head after an honorable life! . . . . But it is bread and butter; I have a family; I am old, I could not get another place at my time of life if I should lose this one; I must stick to it while my strength lasts. I have had principles, and have never dishonored them— you will grant me that?"

"Indeed I do—oh, out of my heart!"

"Well, they are gone, I have turned them out of doors—I could not afford them. Ah, you *stung* me so, when you brought this accusing thing here! I was getting wonted to my chains, my slavery, by keeping them out of sight. I wanted to strike you for reminding me."

"Forgive me! I did not know what I was doing."

"Oh, it wasn't you—it was myself, slapping my own face over your shoulder, so to speak. I have succumbed, Benson has succumbed. He wrote that article—by command of the directors. Henry, you have a good place here. In time you will step into my shoes, Benson into yours. I will not advise you—that is, urge you—I cannot venture such a re-sponsibility as that—but if you are willing to stay with us under the new conditions, I shall be glad—more glad than I can say. Will you stay?"

"It is hard to part with you, sir, for you have been a good friend to me, but I feel I must not stay. Indeed I could not. I could not bear it."

"How right you are, my boy, how absolutely right! I am grown so uncertain of my species of late that I was afraid—half afraid, at any rate—that you would stay. You are young, you can get another place— this world is for the young, they are its kings."

Henry went to the counting-room, got his money, left his resigna-tion, and went forth into the world a clean man and free.

Then, proud and light of step, he went to his bride-elect, and told her his news. . . .

Those dots are to indicate that a blank in Henry's tale occurred at that point.

I felt that blank. The derelicts are always leaving such. They skip a great episode—maybe the greatest in their lives—and pass, without dropping so much as a crumb of that feast, to their next stage. You get not a trace of that episode except what your imagination can furnish you.

Henry supposed he could get a new berth right away. He was mistaken; it did not happen. He went seeking, from town to town. For a while he was merely surprised at his non-success; but by and by he was dismayed. Terror succeeded dismay. They turned him out of his last boarding house; his money was all gone. He wandered everywhither—further and still further away, subsisting as he could, doing what he could find to do, in whatever corner of the earth he chanced to be—shoveling sand, scouring pavements, sawing wood, selling papers, finally doing clog dances and general utility in a "nigger" show.

After three years of this, he surrendered; from Australia he wrote Mr. Haskell and begged for his place again, saying he was done with virtue and its rewards, and wanted to eat dirt the rest of his days.

After a month or two the answer came—from Benson: Haskell was dead, Benson was chief, now, and sorry there was no vacancy on the staff.

It is thirty-three years since Henry resigned, on that proud day, that unforgettable day; he has never had another literary situation since. He has wandered and wandered, regretting, lamenting, and at last he is here, member of the Anchor Watch, a forlorn and cheerless derelict—with all hope of better things gone out of him long ago.

So ends his tale. Now then, he is one of those people the bos'n classified to me: people who do a thing they know to be clearly right, absolutely right and clean and honorable, and later come to grieve over it and repent it. Henry has been miserably grieving over that good and righteous act of his for thirty years. Benson is well off, influential, important, honored, stands high in his guild from one ocean to the other, is a deacon or a church committee or something, and has children and a grandchild. It makes me wretched to see this poor derelict clasp his head with his hands and impotently cry out in his anguish—

"Oh, to think *I* could be in his place, if only I had not been such a fool—oh, *such* a fool, such a vain, stupid, conceited fool! Oh, why did I ever do that insane thing!"

It seems a tragic tale to me. I think it *is* tragic. When he finished it my mind ran back over it and again I saw him make his eager climb, a hopeful and happy boy; and I climbed with him, and felt for him, hoped for him; when he stood on his great summit a victor, I was there, and seemed to be in the sky, we were so far aloft and the spread of plain and mountain stretched so wide and dwindled to such dreams in the fading distances; and I turned with him when his trouble came; I was with him when he reached the abyss, his life ruined, his hopes all dead —and behind us that stately summit still glittering in the blue!

How could it affect me like that? how could it seem a tragedy to me? Because it contained a disappointed life, and the woe of a human heart—that was all. Apparently that is all that is necessary to make tragedy; apparently conditions and altitudes have nothing to do with the size and the reality of the disaster—they are conventions, their measurements are without a determining standard.

If I had gone into particulars about that "summit," the conventions would have belittled the tragedy and made it seem to you inconsequential. But I will furnish the particulars now. The summit was a summit to the boy who made the fight for it, and to the man who conquered it and lost it; but it would not have been a summit to you who are reading this. The magazine was a religious periodical in an interior city; as important as any other religious magazine, but a place on its staff or at the staff's head would not have been considered a Matterhorn by the average budding hero.

Yet—toward it this poor defeated poet has looked for thirty years, and seen it coldly glinting in the sky, and wished he had thrown away his fatal honor and stayed there—there where would be with him now, in his loveless age, those children and that grandchild, destined for him, lost to him by his own act, whose faces he has never seen and will never see. To him this is tragedy.

Chapter 10

Diary—Continued

THERE IS a new face or two every day—gone the next, perhaps. When they are derelicts, they are usually members of the Watch who have been off wandering in the world for refreshment. Some are gone a week, or a month or two, some are gone half a year. Then they come back eager to see the old stay-at-homes and tell their adventures; they bring fresh new blood, you see, and are very welcome. There are perhaps thirty stay-at-homes. These lodge not far away, and they drift to the house at one time or another every day and every night when the weather will let them. Their desultory occupations are not much of a hindrance. They use the ward-room as a club; they loaf in and out at their pleasure; from breakfast till midnight some of them are always on hand, weather or no weather; on pleasant nights, and at the Admiral's two Sunday services, they gather in force. Members only, and the household, are allowed at those services. A good while ago chance visitors used to come, some out of general curiosity, some to stare at the derelicts, some to hear the Admiral read, and get the thrill of his organ-voice and his expression. He would not have that; so no visitors get in, now, not even the "regulars," with the exception of Lo and two or three other clergymen. Some of the aged derelicts who had a religion once, haven't any now, but they all come. It is their tribute of reverence to the Admiral, and does them credit. Once, in the days when outsiders were admitted, one of the strangers smiled superciliously when the Admiral mispronounced a word; Bates, the infidel, who sat near, leaned over and whispered to him, "Straighten your face—if you want any of it left when you leave this place!" He was obeyed; he was a man-o'-warsman before his derelict days, and can still furnish to an offender the kind of look that carries persuasion with it. The bos'n says all the derelicts are loyal to the Admiral.

The flitters—Members that come and go—are very numerous. They bring tales and tidings from all over the continent and from all about the globe. It is astonishing, the miles they cover, and the things they see and hear and experience. My days here seem rather a brisk dream than a flesh-and-blood reality. I believe I have not had a dull day yet, nor one that hadn't part of a romance in it somewhere.

The bos'n claims that there isn't an entirely bad person in the whole Membership, flitters and all. He says there is a good spot in each one; that in a lot of cases many people can't find it and don't, but that the Admiral can and does—every time; and Martha too. He says it isn't smartness, it's instinct, sympathy, fellow-feeling—which is to say, it is a gift, and has to be born in a person, can't be manufactured. He says it can be trained, and developed, away up—but you have to have the gift to start with, there's no other terms.

I said it would probably puzzle a person to find the good spot in the marchesa.

"No," he said, "she's got it. She loves children; she'll do anything for a child—anybody's."

"Give it candy, perhaps. Is that it?"

"More than that—go through fire for it."

"Bos'n, aren't you romancing, now?"

"No—there's those that saw her do it. It was a tenement house. She went in and helped, just like a fireman—she did indeed. A woman with a child in her arms slumped down on a hall floor, smothered by the smoke. A fireman saved her, but the marcheesa saved the child. She gathered it up and fetched it down three iron fire-escape ladders, through black smoke that hid her half the time, the crowd cheering; and that mother was laying for her at the bottom and nearly hugged the life out of her when she got down, being one of those Irish mothers with a heart in her the size of a watermelon, and the crowd cheered her over and over again, and the firemen said she was a brick; and she's honorary member of No. 29 ever since, and can wear the badge and go in the procession and ride the engine if she wants to—yes, sir, and welcome."

"My word!"

"Good spot, ain't it?"

"I should say so! Who could ever have believed it?"

"Well, she's so full of ginger and general hellishness a person naturally wouldn't—but there 't is, you see. You can't ever tell what's in a person till you find out. Look at Satan, for instance."

"Satan?"

"Oh, helm-a-lee—hard-a-port! Of course I don't mean the sacred one, I mean the derelict that *thinks* he's it. Now to look at his wild eye and hear him talk, you'd think there's nothing in him but everlasting schemes for hogging money—hogging it by the cart load, the ship load, the train load, though dern seldom it is he sees a cent that's his own—yet he's got his good spot, Martha will tell you so. Why, the very reason he's so unfamiliar with a cent is that the minute he's got it he gives it away to any poor devil that comes along. It's the way he's made, you see; it's his good spot; they've all got it. Including you."

"Thanks, awfully! What is my good spot?"

"Damned if *I* know. But you've got it—everybody has. You know a cat's passion is fish. Particularly somebody else's fish. There's an awful lot to a cat—anybody knows that. Now then, you can train a cat up, in an ecclesiastical way, till it is that sunk in righteousness you couldn't any more get him to break the Sabbath than you could get a cowboy to keep it; but all the same, you lay a fish down and turn your back and there ain't real religion enough in that whole ornithological species to save that cat from falling. Especially a tomcat. For they're the limit, you know. Look at Bags. He don't miss the services, does he? No; you couldn't get him to. And as for self-sacrifice, why, in the coldest weather he'll quit a warming-pan to sleep on a sermon. It shows you how earnest he is; it shows you how anxious he is to do just right. But all the same, although he *looks* purified, he ain't transmuted all through, and when the time of stress comes you'll find there's hunks of unconverted cat in him yet. Now you lay out a fish handy, and you'll see. He would hog that fish if it was his last act. Well, what fish is to a cat, cigars are to Satan—just a wild unmeasurable passion. So you know by that, that for him to give away his last cigar is to give away his blood —ain't it so? Well, I've seen him *do* it! It's just as I told you—there's a good spot tucked away somewhere in everybody. You'll be a long time finding it, sometimes, if you ain't born to it, like the Admiral and Martha, but I haven't spent twenty years with that pair, and ten of it here and in Hell's Delight, not to get convinced it's so."

I said I felt bound to believe him, "but who is this Satan—and where is he?"

"Oh, there's no telling. He's a flitter. But he'll turn up; he's never gone for very long. I was thinking he was here when you came, but I remember, now, he was just gone. He's a busy cuss—as busy as the other one."

"Why do they call him by that name?"

"They? Because it's what he calls himself. He thinks he *is* Satan."

"Oh—I understand it, now."

"Understand what?"

"Why, the reason of it. He's crazy."

The bos'n gave me a solemnly inquisitive look, and then translated the look into words:

"Well . . . . are you acquainted with anybody that ain't?"

"That ain't? What do you mean?"

"Oh, when you come down to it fine, there's some that ain't as crazy as others, but as far as I've come along the road I haven't run across any yet that was perfectly straight in their minds. You see, everybody is a *little* crazy—some about one fool thing, some about another, and nearly all of them harmless—but as for a person that ain't any way crazy *at all*, damn'd if there's any such!"

"Oh, come!"

"Well, now, honor bright, do you know anybody that's right down sane—to the bottom?"

"Very well, then, honor bright, I am quite sure *I* am, myself."

"Oh, you—with your Adam monument!"

I thought that this was carrying jesting a little too far; so I made a stiff bow whose meaning could not be easily misunderstood, and strode away pretty haughtily.

Chapter 11

Diary Continued

Perhaps it was natural enough and human enough for the Poet to feed daily for thirty years upon the memory of a disaster which wrecked his life, and for the General, the ex-Senator, the inventor and others of our derelicts to do the same. But is it natural and human for a couple of persons to keep up a mere dispute that long?—a dispute that can never be settled?—a dispute about a matter of not the least consequence?

Well, natural or unnatural, we have a case of it here. Thirty years ago Uncle 'Rastus hired himself out to work on a farm on top of a high hill in a New England State, and there he found Aunt Phyllis, who was the farmer's cook. They at once began to dispute about the question of special providences, and from that day to this they have continued the debate whenever there was opportunity.

Two years later, luck added another matter to argue about. They discussed it a few weeks; dropped it, took it up again a year later; and again after two or three years; once more after a longer interval; then gave it a rest—apparently for good and all. But not so. After a quiescent interval of as much as half a decade, they got out that hoary mossback once more, to-day, and gave it a final overhauling. This aged contention had its origin in a heroic act performed by 'Rastus twenty-eight years ago. These are the details.

One summer afternoon a pair of visitors drove up from the town down below in the valley—the charming and beautiful young wife of a wealthy citizen, and her child, aged two years. Toward sunset the lady started homeward. The horse was young and nervous, and unacquainted with hill-work. The farmer and his family stood on the porch and watched the start with some uneasiness. There was a straight stretch of slanting road for a third of a mile, downward from the house, and the first half of it was visible from the porch, but at that point a curtain of trees intervened and hid the rest.

The buggy made the first two or three hundred yards at a safe gait, then it began to move faster—faster—still faster; soon it began to fly; then the dust rose up in a cloud and hid it, just as it was reaching those intervening trees. It was a narrow road; at the end of the straight slant there was a very sharp turn and an unfenced precipice.

The farmer said, "Oh, my God, there is no hope for them—no power on earth can save their lives!" and he and his family sprang from the porch and went racing down the hill through the dust-cloud—not to help, but to mourn; not to save, but to seek the dead and do such reverent service as they might. When they reached that sharp elbow, —right there, right at that deadly spot—they saw, dim and spectral in the settling dust, the horse standing at ease, with 'Rastus at its head, and nobody hurt!

It was unbelievable—clearly unbelievable—yet it was so. 'Rastus had been coming up from town with his farm-team, and had halted at the turn to rest. He heard a noise, and looked up the road and saw the dust-cloud sweeping down upon him. When the interval between him and it had diminished to fifty steps, he got a vague glimpse of the horse's head, and understood. With an undisturbed head, and all his wits about him, he stepped to the right spot and braced himself; and the next second he grabbed the flying horse and stood him up on his hind legs!

The news sped to the town, but was not believed. Every one said the feat was impossible; that it was beyond the strength of the strongest man on the continent. But no matter, it had actually been performed, the proofs of it were unassailable, and had to be accepted. The newspapers applauded it; for several days people climbed up from the town to look at the spot, and wonder how the incredible thing was done; 'Rastus was a hero; there was not a white man nor a white woman in the region round about who was ashamed to shake hands with him; wherever he appeared the people took him by his horny black hand and gave it a good grip, and many said, "I'm proud to do it!" Last happiness of all, the rich man handed 'Rastus his check for a thousand dollars—the first time in his life that 'Rastus had ever owned above thirty dollars at one time.

Then that dispute began. Aunt Phyllis charged 'Rastus with cheating. He was indignant, and said—

"It's a lie. Who has I cheated?"

"Dat gen'lman. De idea o' you takin' a thousan' dollars! De hoss en harness en buggy warn't wuth it, en you knows it mighty well."

"Woman, what's de matter wid yo' brains? What is you talkin' 'bout?"

"Nemmine 'bout my brains, you stick to de pint, dat's all. You ain't gwyneter dodge it whah I is. You cheated, en I ain't gwyneter let you fo'git it, mind *I* tell you!"

"I didn't!"

"You did!"

"I didn't!"

"You did! Dey warn't wuth mo'n eight hund'd dollars—anybody'll tell you so. Now look at dat. You save' eight hund'd dollars for de gen'lman, en take a thousan'. It's cheatin', dat's what it is. No Christian wouldn't 'a' done it, nobody but a low-down inf'del would. S'pose you was to die—right now? Dat's it—s'pose you was to die?"

"Well, s'pose I *was* to? *Den* what?"

"Ain't you got no shame, 'Rastus? How'd you like to 'pear up dah, wid dem two hund'd dollars stickin' to yo' han's?"

"I'd hole my head up, dat's what I'd do. Hain't you got no sense, can't you git nothin' thoo yo' head? You's got de whole thing hindside fust—can't you see dat?"

"Who? me? How has I got it hindside fust?"

"Becaze you keep arguin' dat de gen'lman gimme de thousan' dollars for savin' de hoss en de buggy, but if you had any sense you'd know he didn't gimme it for *dat*, at all."

"De nation he didn't!"

"No, he didn't."

"Well den, you 'splain to me what he did give it to you for, if you think you kin."

"Why, for savin' his *fambly*."

"For savin' his *fambly*, you puddn'head!"

"Yes, for savin' his fambly. Anybody'll tell you so."

"In my bawn days I never see sich a numskull. 'Rastus, don't you know it don't stan' to reason? Now you pay 'tention—I's gwyneter show you. It's a new hoss en a good one, ain't it?"

"Yas."

"Cost five hund'd en fifty dollars, didn't it?"

"Yas."

"New buggy, ain't it?"

"Yas."

"Cost two hund'd en fifty, didn't it?"

"Yas."

"Dat make eight hund'd widout de harness, don't it?"

"Yas."

"You save' de whole outfit, didn't you?"

"Yas."

"Dat's eight hund'd dollars wuth ain't it?"

"Yas."

"Now den, we's got down to de fambly. How much is de lady's clo'es wuth?"

"How's I gwyneter know?"

"Well, I knows. Dey's spang-bang new, en dey cost a hund'd en sebenty-fo' dollars. How much is de chile's clo'es wuth?"

"I don't know nothin' 'bout de chile's clo'es."

"Well, I does. Dey cost twenty-five dollars. So, den, all de clo'es cost a hund'd en ninety-nine, ain't it?"

"Oh, yas, yas, yas, I reckin so. Git done wid de business!"

"Now den, what's de *lady* wuth?"

"Lan', you make me tired wid dis foolishness! How's I gwyneter know what she's wuth?"

"What's de *chile* wuth?"

"I don't k'yer nothin' 'bout it, en I ain't gwyneter *say* nothin' 'bout it."

"Now den, I's gwyneter come back to de harness. I knows what de harness cost, and so does you, en I's gwyneter c'rect you if you tries to fo'git en make a mistake 'bout it. What did de harness cost, 'Rastus?"

"It cost—cost—"

"I has my eye on you, 'Rastus."

"Cost fifteen dollars. . . . *Damn* de harness!"

"Now den, 'Rastus, de fac's is all in. All de thousan' dollars is 'counted for. You been 'cusin' me o' gittin' de matter hindside fust, en it hurt me to hear you say dat, 'caze it make it seem like I ain't got good sense; but 'Rastus, de figgers *shows* you was in de wrong en I was in de right. Dey shows you he didn't give you de thousan' dollars for savin' de fambly, he give it to you for savin' de *truck*. En he didn't pay full up, nuther, 'caze *he owes you fo'teen dollars on de harness!*"

. . . . It all happened twenty-eight years ago, when these dear old things were young—only forty. 'Rastus bought a farm for sixteen hundred dollars, paid a thousand down and borrowed the six hundred on mortgage. During eighteen years, by working sixteen hours a day and watching the pennies and economising on clothes and tobacco, he made enough to pay the interest each year and reduce the mortgage-debt ten dollars per annum; then the rheumatism claimed him for her own and he gave the property to a nephew and wandered out into the world. He turned up here, in the course of time, and has been free of the ward-room ever since, and has had the Anchor Watch's privileges here and in Hell's Delight—as good a man and as contented a soul as I know. The nephew still runs the farm, pays the interest, and in ten years has reduced the mortgage by thirty dollars. The child that survived the runaway through 'Rastus's once famous miracle has a prosperous huband and a family, is beautiful in character and in person, is happy, and to this day does not know that any one ever saved her life.

As I have said, that long-neglected dispute was resurrected to-day. At the close of it Aunty Phyllis had a happy idea, and fetched it out with glee, and confidence, and vast expectations. But 'Rastus was loaded, *that* time! Phyllis said—

"You is de man dat's allays sayin' de' ain't no sich thing as special providence. If 'twarn't for special providence, what would 'a' went wid dat buggy en harness? Who put you in dat road, right exackly in de right spot, right exackly at de right half-a-second?—you answer me dat, if you kin!"

"Who de nation sent de *hoss* down dah in sich a blame' fool fashion?"

Chapter 12

From Intermittent Diary

I HAVE skipped a week. Trifles of interest got in the way, and it was easier to skip than to write. One of the trifles was a "regular"—Stanchfield Garvey, called "Governor." The title dates from away back, years and years ago. He served four years as Secretary of a territory, and meantime as Acting Governor twice or thrice, during brief absences of the actual Governor. Once "Governor" Garvey, always Governor Garvey; once General on a Governor's staff, always General; once justice of the peace for a year, always "Judge" thenceforth to the grave—such is our American system. We have a thoroughly human passion for titles; turning us into democrats doesn't dislodge that passion, nor even modify it. A title is a title, and we value it; if it chance to be pinchbeck, no matter, we are glad to have it anyway, and proud to wear it, and hear people utter it. It is music to us.

Governor Garvey is eighty years old, but does not look nearly so old. He is a good six feet high, and very slender; he has the bearing of a gentleman; his hair is short and thick, and is silver-white; his face is Emersonian, and he has intellect, but as it is of an ill-ordered and capricious and unstable sort, his face mis-states and over-states its character and bulk. However, his eyes correct these errors. They are kind and beautiful and unsteady, and they tell you he is weak and a visionary. He is not a derelict, but that is because the Admiral saved him from it several years ago by getting him a job as rough-proof reader on an evening paper—an easy berth which pays him ten dollars a week and supports him. He has a bed and an oil stove in a small room in a tenement house, and is his own chambermaid and cook.

He be gan life as a printer's apprentice in a western city. He was sixteen or seventeen, then, and had a common-school education of a meagre sort, which he tried to enlarge by studying, nights. Without serious success; for he was shavings, not anthracite. That is to say, that whatsoever thing he undertook, he went at it in a blaze of eagerness and enthusiasm and burnt the interest all out of it in forty-eight hours, then dropped it and went at something else in another consuming blaze. During the four years of his apprenticeship he carried his conflagrations into the first chapter of every useful book in the Mechanic's Library, but never any further than that in any instance. And so, whereas he picked up a slight smattering of many breeds of knowledge, his accumulation was valueless and unusable, it was a mere helter-skelter scrap-heap.

For a week or two, in the beginning, he had a burning ambition to be a Franklin; so he lived strictly on bread and water, studied by the firelight instead of using candles, and practised swimming on the floor. Then he discarded Franklin, and imitated somebody else a while. This time an orator; and went around orating to his furniture with pebbles in his mouth. Next, he proposed to be a great lawyer, and with this idea he read Blackstone a couple of weeks. Next, with an earnest desire to make men better and save them from the pains of that fierce hell which all believed in in those days, he studied for the ministry for a while. But his path was beset with difficulties. Not his path, his wash; for he washed from one religion to another faster than he could keep count, and never landed on the shore of any one of them long enough to dry his feet. He has kept up these excursions all his life. He has sampled all the religions, he has been an infidel, he is a Christian Scientist, now. I mean, this week.

Nobody could ever tell what he would do next. His friends and family expected much of him, for he was bright above the average, but he disappointed every hope of theirs as fast as it was born. He was always dreaming—of doing good to his fellow-man, as he supposed—whereas at bottom his longing was for distinction, though he didn't suspect it. When he was studying to be a Franklin, he copied Franklin's brief and pregnant rules of conduct and stuck them in the frame of his mirror. He lived by them until he recovered from the Franklin disease, then he lived by the next model's rules, and the next and the next. When a model hadn't a set of rules, he supplied him with one. In his time he has lived by more different kinds of rules than has any other experimenter in right and rigid conduct. He has a set now, drawn from "Science and Health," and thinks he understands what they mean.

When he was twenty years old, he resolved upon a visit to his people. They lived in a village a hundred miles away. It was in the winter time. He gave no notice that he was coming. He thought it would be romantic to arrive at midnight, and surprise them in the morning. This was not well conceived, for the family had moved to another house, and the one which they had been occupying was now occupied by an old doctor who hadn't any romance in him, and by his two maiden sisters who had long ago outlived their romantic days. Stanchfield slipped into the house the back way, and up stairs with his boots in his hands. He undressed in the dark in his room, and got into bed with the old maids, whom he supposed were his brothers. Presently one of them said, drowsily—

"Mary, don't crowd so!"

Stanchfield began to scramble out, and he was feeling very sick and scared, and much ashamed. He had been nurturing a beard, and one result of this was that the other maid cried out "There's a man in the bed!" and both maids began to scream. Stanchfield fled, just as he was, and met the doctor on the stairs, with a candle in one hand and a butcher knife in the other. An explanation followed, and the doctor brought the clothes.

Two or three nights afterward, Stanchfield sat in his room at home, reading, also dreaming. At four in the morning he started out to call on a young lady—without looking at the clock. He hammered on her door a good while, then her father appeared, shivering in his dressing-gown, learned his business, admitted him to a freezing parlor, and sat there silent and lowering for an hour—waiting for an opportunity to say something cruel. At last Stanchfield timidly asked when Miss Louise would be down.

"As soon as she's done dressing for breakfast! Won't you wait?— oh, do!"

Stanchfield was in the town a fortnight. In that time he joined the Sons of Temperance, agreed to make a speech at a temperance mass meeting, and meantime he furnished the mottoes for the torchlight procession; but when the time came he was on the other side and made an impassioned plea for unlimited whisky.

When he was twenty-three and had been a journeyman printer a year, he returned to his village home, bought the weekly paper for five

hundred dollars, borrowing the money at ten per cent, and at once reduced the subscription price one half. He made a clean paper, and
worked hard; but he got but a meagre subsistence out of it for his
widowed mother and her young family. He paid his interest every year,
but was never able to pay any of the principal. At the end of six years
he gave the paper to his creditor and moved to another town. There he
bought a part of a paper on credit, and fell in love with a girl in a neighboring town and engaged himself to her. A few weeks afterward he engaged himself to a girl in his new home-town. He found himself in a
difficulty, now, and did not quite know how to get out of it. It seemed
to him that the right way, the honorable way, would be for him to go
and explain to girl No. 1 and abide by her decision as to what he should
do. He told his project to girl No. 2, who remarked that he would
marry *her*—and now—and he could afterward go and explain to No. 1
at his leisure, if he wanted to.

So said, so done. No. 2 was a good and patient and valuable wife to
him—as far as any wife could be valuable to such a weather-vane. After
three years he gave his share of the paper to his creditor and moved to
another town, where he bought a wee little business, on credit, and at
once cut prices till there was no profit in it. He scrambled along for
four years, meantime making and losing friends continually by changing his religion and his politics every three months; then he chanced
upon a new opening. In his apprenticeship-days, eighteen years before,
a great lawyer had taken an interest in him, and this acquaintanceship
came good, now. The lawyer got him appointed Secretary of one of the
new territories.

He made a good Secretary, for he performed his duties well and
faithfully, and was a strictly honest man where honest men were scarce.
He was very popular, he had the confidence and the friendship of the
whole territory, and for four years he and his wife knew to the full what
comfort and happiness were. Then the territory was elevated to State-
hood. There was much fussing at slates for other State officers in his
party, but none about the Secretaryship: no one thought of giving that
post to anybody but him.

But he had to have a freak on nomination-night—he wouldn't have
been himself if he had failed of that. He would not go to the conven-

tion. For two reasons: he thought candidates ought to keep away from conventions—they ought to leave the delegates unembarrassed to choose the candidates. Also, the convention was to meet in a liquor saloon, and he could not conscientiously enter there, for his turn to be a prohibitionist had come around again, lately. His friends could not persuade him, his wife could not persuade him. Very well, the thing happened which all expected except himself: he was left off the ticket.

A few months later the State assumed command, the territory went out of business, and he with it. There was nothing for him to do; he could find no employment. By and by he and his wife gave up and went home—expensively; so recklessly expensively that they spent all their savings on the road. Poor creatures, they had never had a real holiday in their lives, before, and knew they might never have another one. It turned their heads and abolished their prudence. For thirty years Garvey's friends stood by him, for he was good at heart, and without stain, and well beloved. During all that time they found place after place for him, but he lost them all. Lost them by throwing them away to hunt for something better. He always gave satisfaction to others, but could never be satisfied himself.

Eight years ago his wife died. After that, he had nothing to care for, nothing to live for, and he went wandering. Her devotion had been his stay and support; such courage as ever he had had she gave him; after each of his thousand failures she lifted him out of his abysses of despondency and found for him a new hope. For three years he drifted in a starless gloom, rudderless; then the Admiral found that proof-reading job for him, and he holds it yet; his old hankering to throw away good things to hunt for better ones is dead in him. He spends all his evening with the Anchor Watch, and has, for company and sympathisers, the General, the ex-Senator, the Poet, and one or two other derelicts who look back upon a special disaster which ruined their lives, and which they only live to regret and repent and mourn over. From the day that the Governor stood stanchly by his principles and lost the Secretaryship he has lamented that righteous act, and cursed it and bitterly grieved over it. It has wrung his heart for forty years. If he could only get back there and have that chance again! That is the dirge he sings. That, and how much of sorrow and privation and humiliation he could have saved his patient and faithful wife if he had not been such a fool, "oh, *such* a fool!" And who knows? she might be with him now and blessing him! Ah, yes; and what would he not give to see that dear face once more! And so he murmurs along, and it is pitiful to hear.

Chapter 13

Intermittent Diary—Continued

INTERRUPTING myself to gossip about the Governor has made a blank where the Plum Duff occurred. By help of Jimson Flinders the colored stenographer and sub-editor, I can fill it now. The bos'n says plum duff is the sailor's luxury-dish in whaleships, and is a dough pudding with raisins in it, as distinguished from dough pudding plain. It is served once a week—usually on Sundays. Duff is probably the fo'-castle way of pronouncing *dough*; and a good enough way, too, if it be righteous to pronounce tough *tuff*. Plum Duff, here in the Haven of the Derelicts, is the Anchor Watch's name for Entertainment-Night. And well named, too. It is the night that has the intellectual raisins in it, and is as welcome here as is plum duff at sea.

The weather was bad, but no matter, we had a full house. All the derelicts were present, all the "regulars," and all the "casuals"—in fact, everybody possessing the high privilege of assisting at Plum Duffs. We had as many as fifty people on hand. This time the feature of the evening was to be a lecture, in the form of a story, illustrated by "living pictures" thrown upon a screen. Subject, "The Benevolence of Nature." Lecturer, Rev. Lo-what-God-hath-Wrought. Edgar Billings, amateur naturalist, was to manage the picture-machinery. He stood at one end of the great room with his apparatus, and the lecturer stood by the vast white screen at the other.

The idea of illustrating the story was a late thought; so late that there was no time for lecturer and illustrator to go over the ground in detail together, but apparently this kind of particularity was not going to be needed. Lo gave Billings a synopsis of the story, and Billings said it was a plenty; said he had just the pictures for it, and could flash the right one onto the canvas every time, sure, and fit every incident of the tale to a dot as it went along. Billings is an earnest and sincere and good-hearted creature, but hasn't much judgment.

First we had some music, as usual, Jimmy doing the pianola-business and the Admiral the orchestrelle, then the lecturer began. He said it was most wonderful, most touching and beautiful, our dear old Mother Nature's love for her creatures—for *all* of them, from the highest all the way down the long procession of humbler animated nature to the very worms and insects. He dwelt at some length upon her unfailing goodness to her wards, and said he wished especially to note one feature of it, her intricate and marvelous system of providing food for the animal world; her selection of just the right and best food for each creature, and placing each creature where its particular kind of food could never fail it. Her tender protection, he said, was over all—the humble spider, the wasp, the worm, all the myriads of tiny and helpless life, were under her watchful eye, and partakers of her loving care. By Mr. Billings's help he would exhibit this love as exercised toward two or three of the lowliest of these creatures, and would ask the house to remember that the same love and the same protection were exercised in the same way toward the unspecified myriads and millions that creep and fly about the earth. Should these little creatures be grateful? Yes. If we understood their language we should hear them express that gratitude, should we not? Without a doubt, yes, without a doubt. Might he try to put himself in their place and speak for them? He would make the effort, putting it in the form of a little story.

The room was then darkened; an intensely bright great circle appeared upon the white screen; the lecturer began to read:

THE STORY

Once there was a dear little spider, who lived in a web pleasantly situated, and was expecting a family; and she was very happy—happy, and tenderly grateful to the dear Mother Nature that gave her so lovely a world to live in, and surrounded her with so many comforts, and made her little life so sweet and beautiful—

Instantly a wide-spreading web appeared upon the screen, and in the middle of it a hairy fat spider as big as a watermelon, with bunches of crumpled legs which seemed to be all elbows. It made the audience start, it was so alive, and sharp-eyed and real. The lecturer glanced at it, looked uncomfortable, and moved a little away. After a pause to recover his serenity, he resumed his reading.

She was lonely, and sweetly sad, for her dearest, her heart's own, her young husband, was absent, and she was fondly dreaming of him and longing for his return—

A smaller devil of the spider species—evidently the husband—appeared on the frontier of the web, took a hesitating step or two toward his wife, then changed his mind and began to crawl slowly and almost imperceptibly backward toward foreign parts.

She was very hungry, for she had been without food for a whole day; but did she lose faith? did she complain, as we too often do? No; dropping her eyes meekly, she murmured, "Our dear Mother Nature will provide—"

A sudden commotion on the screen attracted all eyes. With a rush which broke the smooth web into waves the big wife swept down upon the poor cowering little husband, and as she sunk her fangs into him and began to suck he struggled and squirmed in so pitiful a way that many of the audience turned away their eyes, not being able to bear the sight of it. There were some subdued and scarcely audible chucklings here and there, but they lasted only a moment. The lecturer took one glance, and looked embarrassed—as one could see, for his face came within the circle of light—also he looked as if he was not comfortable in his stomach. Soon he went on with his reading. He had to stick to his text; he was not a person who could change it to meet an emergency.

Now came an event which filled her mother-heart with joy—the birth of the expected family. Out from the silken bag attached to her body poured a flood of little darlings, dainty little spiderlings, hundreds and hundreds of them, and she gathered them to her maternal breast in a rapture of gratitude and joy—

And in an instant there it was, on the screen!—a mighty swarm of frisky little spiders the size of horseflies—just a tumultuous confusion of ten thousand legs all squirming at once. They attacked their mother.

She tried to get away, but they overflowed her, overwhelmed her, and began to chew her legs and her body—a horrible sight! The lecturer did not take a look this time. No, he made a half-motion to do it, but changed his mind and went on reading.

Her first thought, poor little mother, was, how should she find food for her nine hundred little darlings; but her second was, "Nature will provide." What a lesson for us it is! Ah, my friends, when the larder is empty and in our despair we know not where to turn, let us remember the faith of this humble insect and imitate it and be strengthened by it; let us be brave, and believe, with her, that nourishment will be provided for our little ones.

At this moment, dear friends, arrived a wasp. In a sunny meadow she had digged a hole and prepared a cosy home for the dear offspring she was expecting. Now she was abroad to secure food for that offspring. Her happy heart was singing, and the burden of that grateful song was, "Nature will provide." She hovered over our mother-spider, then descended upon her—

Instantly it was on the screen! A wasp the size of a calf swooped down upon wide-spreading wings, gripped the struggling mother-spider, and slowly drove a sting as long as a sword, deep into her body. The audience gasped with horror to see that hideous weapon sink in like that and the spider strain and quiver and rumple its legs in its agony, but the lecturer ventured no look; he went right on with his reading.

The spider was not killed, my friends, it was only rendered helpless. That was the intention. It was to serve as food for the wasp's child, and would live a week or two—until half eaten up, in fact. She deposited an egg on the spider's body, carried her prey to her dark home in the ground, crammed the prisoner in there and went for more, radiant with that spiritual joy which is the reward of duty done. In two days the wasp's child was born, and was hungry; and there at hand was its food, the melancholy spider, faintly struggling and weary. With a deep hymn of gratitude to kind and ever-watchful Nature, who allows none of her children to suffer, the larva gnawed a hole in the spider's abdomen, and began to suck her juices while she moaned and wept—

Straightway the revolting banquet was pictured upon the screen, the larva munching its way, most comfortable and content, into the spider's vitals, and the helpless spider feebly working its legs and probably trying to think of a grateful sentiment to utter that would not sound too grossly insincere.

Has the spider been forgotten? is the spider forsaken in its time of sorrow and distress? Ah, no, my friends, neither she nor any other creature is ever forgotten or ever forsaken. Soon the spider will have the reward of its patience, its faith, its loving trust. In six days the half of it will have been eaten up, then it will die, and pass forever to that sweet peace, that painless repose which is provided for all, howsoever humble and undeserving, who keep a contented spirit and cheerfully do the duties allotted to them in their sphere. I will now show you, with Mr. Billings's help, how wonderfully we have been provided with yellow fever and malaria by the ministrations of a humble little mosquito which—

And so on, and so on. It would take me too long to write down the rest of it, but it was very interesting. Everybody was pleased, and many said they shouldn't want to eat anything for a week. It seemed to me that it was a most charming and elevating entertainment, and others thought the same, and said it was ennobling. They said they never should have thought of such ways to feed animals, and regarded it as most intelligent and grand. I think the Rev. Mr. Lo will stand on a higher plane with us hereafter than he did before. Many shook hands with him and congratulated him, and he was greatly pleased and thankful. Bates the unbeliever conceded that the lecture had given him a new view of the benevolence of Nature.

(1905 and 1906)

The Fable of the Yellow Terror

A LONG, long time ago the Butterflies held a vast territory which was flowery and fragrant and beautiful. The Butterflies were of many kinds, but all the kinds were richly clothed and all had a fine and cultivated taste in colors and were highly trained in etiquette, and deportment and in the other graces and accomplishments which make the charm of life in an advanced and elegant civilization. There was not another civilization among the animals that approached that of the Butterflies. They were very proud of it, insufferably proud of it, and always anxious to spread it around the planet and cram it down other people's throats and improve them.

They had an idea that they were the only people that knew the true way to be happy and how to lam happiness into other people and make them good. So they sent missionaries to all the pagan insects to teach them how to be tranquil and unafraid on a deathbed, and then sent trader-bugs to make them long for the deathbed, and then followed up the trader-bugs with diplomat-bugs and undertaker-bugs to perfect the blessings of the conferred civilization and furnish the deathbed, and charge for the funeral. There was hardly a single Butterfly of all the millions that did not boast of this civilization with his mouth, and laugh at it in private. For truly it was a whitewashed humbug, and few there were that prayed for it. Except with the mouth.

369

The Butterflies had what is called a cinch on a great and profitable art. This was the art of making honey. Also a cinch on another great and profitable art. This was the art of killing. For in those days the Butterfly had a sting. He not only had a sting but he was the only bird in the world that had studied out how to use it scientifically and devastatingly. It made him Boss. There was not a weak and ignorant nation that could stand against him. Multitudes were nothing to him —nothing at all. If they had a property he wanted, he went there and took it, and gave them his civilization in the place of it, and was pleased with himself, and praised his Maker for being always on his side, which was quite true, and for giving him such a chance to be noble and do good.

His whole time was taken up in shoving his civilization and his honey. His whole ambition was to widen and ever widen the market for his honey, and get richer and richer and richer and holier and holier and holier all the time.

At last he had covered all the ground but one. That was the vast empire of the Bees. He tried to get in there, but was warned away. He kept trying, but the Bees kept discouraging him. Courteously, but firmly. The Bees were a simple and peaceable folk, poor and hard-working and honest, and they did not want any civilization. They begged to be let alone; they held out against all persuasions. They wanted no honey, and said so. They did not know how to make it themselves, and did not wish to learn. They still held out. Courteously and kindly, but firmly.

At last the Butterflies were tired of this. They said that a nation that had a chance to get civilization and buy honey and didn't take it was a block in the way of progress and enlightenment and the yearning desires of God, and must be *made* to accept the boon and bless the booner; so they set about working up a moral-plated pretext, and soon they found a good one, and advertised it. They said that those fat and diligent and contented Bees, munching grass and cabbage, ignorant of honey, ignorant of civilization and rapacity and treachery and robbery and murder and prayer and one thing and another, and joying in their eventless life and in the sumptuous beauty of their golden jackets, were a Yellow Peril.

It took. It went like wildfire. It was a splendid phrase. It didn't seem to have any meaning, as applied to a far-away and unoffending mighty multitude that hadn't a desire in the world but to stay by themselves and be let alone, but that did not signify: a Yellow Peril is a Yellow Peril, and a shuddery and awful thing to think of, and has to be crushed, mashed, obliterated, whether there is any such thing or not.

So each of the different tribes of Butterflies sent in a two-hundred-dollar missionary with the private purpose of getting him massacred and collecting a million dollars cash damages on him, along with a couple of provinces and such other things as might be lying around; and when the Bees resisted, civilization had its chance! When it got through, there wasn't a Bee that wasn't bruised and battered and sore, and most humble and apologetic and submissive.

The enlightened world of Butterflydom rejoiced and gave thanks. And properly; for wasn't the Yellow Peril over and done with, for good and all?

It looked so. Then there was a great peace, and a holy tranquillity, and the Finger of God was visible in it all, as usual. When a paying job is finished and rounded up, he is a cross-eyed short-sighted person indeed who can't find the Finger of God in it.

Things went on handsomely. And handsomer and handsomer all the time. The Bees began to like honey and buy it. And they liked it better and better, and bought more and more of it, and civilization was happy to the marrow. One clever tribe of Bees even began to learn how to make honey itself—which made civilization proud, and it said "They are rising out of their darkness—we have lifted them up—how noble we are, and how good." Next that tribe wanted to learn the other great art, the sacred monopoly of the loftiest of civilizations—the art of how to kill and cripple and mutilate, scientifically. And they did learn it, and with astonishing quickness and brilliancy. Whereupon civilization rejoiced yet more, and was prouder of its nobleness and beneficence than ever.

For a time. Then there was an episode. This progressive tribe of Bees had picked up another specialty of all high civilizations, ancient and modern—land-grabbing; and presently, while working this specialty it came into collision with a vast tribe of Butterflies who were likewise out grabbing territory, and a fight resulted. The Bees showed that they had learned to be remarkably prompt and handy with their stings, those little weapons which had been so harmless until education taught them what God had intended the weapons for.

There was a market for wise observations, now, and a grave gray Grasshopper supplied it. He said to a prominent Butterfly—

"You have taught one tribe of Bees how to use its sting, it will teach its brother-tribe. The two together will be able to banish all the Butterflies some day, and keep them out; for they are uncountable in numbers and will be unconquerable when educated. Also, you have given the Bees the honey-appetite—forced it upon them—and now the frenzy of it will never leave them. Also, you have taught the brilliant tribe how to make it, and you will see results. They will make as prime an article of honey as any Butterfly can turn out; they will make it cheaper than any Butterfly can make it; they are here on the spot, you are the other side of the world, transportation will cost them nothing—you can't compete. They will get this vast market, and starve you out, and make you stay at home, where they used to beg you to stay, and you wouldn't listen. That will happen, no matter how this present scuffle may turn out. Whether Bee or Butterfly win, it is all the same, the Butterfly will have lost the market. There are five hundred million Bees; it is not likely that you can whip them without combining, and there is nothing in your history to indicate that your tribes can combine, even when conferring enlightenment and annexing swag are the prize. Yet if you do not subdue them now, before they get well trained and civilized, they may break over the frontiers some day and go land-grabbing in Europe, to do honor to your teaching. It may be that you will lose your stings and your honey-art by and by, from lack of practice, and be and remain merely elegant and ornamental. Maybe you ought to have let the Yellow Peril alone, as long as there wasn't any. Yet you ought to be proud, for in creating a something out of a nothing, you have done what was never done before, save by the Creator of all things."

The Butterfly gave thanks, coldly, and the Grasshopper asked for his passports.

(1904–1905)

Passage from "Glances at History" (suppressed.)

Date, 9th century

X X X IN A SPEECH which he made more than 500 years ago, and which has come down to us intact, he said:

We, free citizens of the Great Republic, feel an honest pride in her greatness, her strength, her just and gentle government, her wide liberties, her honored name, her stainless history, her unsmirched flag, her hands clean from oppression of the weak and from malicious conquest, her hospitable door that stands open to the hunted and the persecuted of all nations; we are proud of the judicious respect in which she is held by the monarchies which hem her in on every side, and proudest of all of that lofty patriotism which we inherited from our fathers, which we have kept pure, and which won our liberties in the beginning and has preserved them unto this day. While that patriotism endures the Republic is safe, her greatness is secure, and against them the powers of the earth cannot prevail.

I pray you to pause and consider. Against our traditions we are now entering upon an unjust and trivial war, a war against a helpless people, and for a base object—robbery. At first our citizens spoke out against this thing, by an impulse natural to their training. To-day they have turned, and their voice is the other way. What caused the change? Merely a politician's trick—a high-sounding phrase, a blood-stirring

373

phrase which turned their uncritical heads: *Our Country, right or wrong!* An empty phrase, a silly phrase. It was shouted by every newspaper, it was thundered from the pulpit, the Superintendent of Public Instruction placarded it in every school-house in the land, the War Department inscribed it upon the flag. And every man who failed to shout it or who was silent, was proclaimed a traitor—none but those others were patriots. To be a patriot, one had to say, and keep on saying, "Our Country, right or wrong," and urge on the little war. Have you not perceived that that phrase is an insult to the nation?

For in a republic, who *is* "the country?" Is it the Government which is for the moment in the saddle? Why, the Government is merely a *servant*—merely a temporary servant; it cannot be its prerogative to determine what is right and what is wrong, and decide who is a patriot and who isn't. Its function is to obey orders, not originate them. Who, then, is "the country?" Is it the newspaper? is it the pulpit? is it the school-superintendent? Why, these are mere parts of the country, not the whole of it; they have not command, they have only their little share in the command. They are but one in the thousand; it is in the thousand that command is lodged; *they* must determine what is right and what is wrong; they must decide who is a patriot and who isn't.

Who are the thousand—that is to say, who are "the country?" In a monarchy, the king and his family are the country; in a republic it is the common voice of the people. Each of you, for himself, by himself and on his own responsibility, must speak. And it is a solemn and weighty responsibility, and not lightly to be flung aside at the bullying of pulpit, press, government, or the empty catch-phrases of politicians. Each must for himself alone decide what is right and what is wrong, and which course is patriotic and which isn't. You cannot shirk this and be a man. To decide it against your convictions is to be an unqualified and inexcusable traitor, both to yourself and to your country, let men label you as they may. If you alone of all the nation shall decide one way, and that way be the right way according to your convictions of the right, you have done your duty by yourself and by your country—hold up your head! you have nothing to be ashamed of.

Only when a republic's *life* is in danger should a man uphold his government when it is in the wrong. There is no other time.

This republic's life is not in peril. The nation has sold its honor for a phrase. It has swung itself loose from its safe anchorage and is drifting, its helm is in pirate hands. The stupid phrase needed help, and it got another one: "Even if the war be wrong we are in it and must fight it out: *we cannot retire from it without dishonor.*" Why, not even a burglar could have said it better. We cannot withdraw from this sordid raid because to grant peace to those little people upon their terms—independence—would dishonor us. You have flung away Adam's phrase—you should take it up and examine it again. He said, "*An inglorious peace is better than a dishonorable war.*"

You have planted a seed, and it will grow.

(early 1900s)

Passage from "Outlines of History" (suppressed.)

Date, 9th century

X X X Bᴜᴛ ɪᴛ ᴡᴀꜱ impossible to save the Great Republic. She was rotten to the heart. Lust of conquest had long ago done its work; trampling upon the helpless abroad had taught her, by a natural process, to endure with apathy the like at home; multitudes who had applauded the crushing of other people's liberties, lived to suffer for their mistake in their own persons. The government was irrevocably in the hands of the prodigiously rich and their hangers-on, the suffrage was become a mere machine, which they used as they chose. There was no principle but commercialism, no patriotism but of the pocket. From showily and sumptuously entertaining neighboring titled aristocracies, and from trading their daughters to them, the plutocrats came in the course of time to hunger for titles and heredities themselves. The drift toward monarchy, in some form or other, began; it was spoken of in whispers at first, later in a bolder voice.

It was now that that portent called "The Prodigy" rose in the far South. Army after army, sovereignty after sovereignty went down under the mighty tread of the shoemaker, and still he held his conquering way—North, always North. The sleeping republic awoke at last, but too late. It drove the money-changers from the temple, and put the government into clean hands—but all to no purpose. To keep the power in their own hands, the money-changers had long before bought up half the country with soldier-pensions and turned a measure which had originally been a righteous one into a machine for the manufacture of bond-slaves—a machine which was at the same time an irremovable instrument of tyranny—for every pensioner had a vote, and every man and woman who had ever been acquainted with a soldier was a pensioner; pensions were dated back to the Fall, and hordes of men who had never handled a weapon in their lives came forward and drew three hundred years' back-pay. The country's conquests, so far from being profitable to the Treasury, had been an intolerable burden from the beginning. The pensions, the conquests, and corruption together, had brought bankruptcy in spite of the maddest taxation, the government's credit was gone, the arsenals were empty, the country unprepared for war. The military and naval schools, and all commissioned offices in the army and navy, were the preserve of the money-changers; and the standing army—the creation of the conquest-days—was their property.

The army and navy refused to serve the new Congress and the new Administration, and said ironically, "What are you going to do about it?" A difficult question to answer. Landsmen manned such ships as were not abroad watching the conquests—and sunk them all, in honest attempts to do their duty. A civilian army, officered by civilians, rose brimming with the patriotism of an old forgotten day and rushed multitudinously to the front, armed with sporting-guns and pitchforks—and the standing army swept it into space. For the money-changers had privately sold out to the shoemaker. He conferred titles of nobility upon the money-changers, and mounted the republic's throne without firing a shot.

It was thus that Popoatahualpacatapetl became our master; whose mastership descended in a little while to the Second of that name, who still holds it by his Viceroy this day.

(early 1900s)

Passage from a Lecture

THE MONTHLY meeting of the Imperial Institute took place on the 18th. With but two exceptions the seats of the Forty Immortals were occupied. The lecturer of the evening was the distinguished Professor of the Science of Historical Forecast. A part of his subject concerned two of the Laws of Angina Pectoris, commonly called the Mad Philosopher; namely, the "Law of Intellectual Averages" and the "Law of Periodical Repetition." After a consideration, at some length, of cognate matters, he said:

I regard these Laws as established. By the terms of the Law of Periodical Repetition nothing whatever can happen a single time only; everything happens again, and yet again, and still again—monotonously. Nature has no originality—I mean, no large ability in the matter of inventing new things, new ideas, new stage-effects. She has a superb and amazing and infinitely varied equipment of old ones, but she never adds to them. She repeats—repeats—repeats—repeats. Examine your memory and your experience, you will find it is true. When she puts together a man, and is satisfied with him, she is loyal to him, she stands by him through thick and thin forevermore, she repeats him by billions and billions of examples; and physically and mentally the *average* remains exactly the same, it doesn't vary a hair between the first batch, the middle batch and the last batch. If you ask—

"But really—do you think all men are alike?" I reply—

"I said the *average* does not vary."

"But you will have to admit that some individuals do far overtop the average—intellectually, at least."

Yes, I answer, and Nature repeats *those*. There is nothing that she doesn't repeat. If I may use a figure, she has established the general intellectual level of the race at say, six feet. Take any billion men and stand them in a mass, and their head-tops will make a floor—a floor as level as a table. That floor represents the intellectual altitude of the masses—and it never changes. Here and there, miles apart, a head will project above it a matter of one intellectual inch, so to speak—men of mark in science, law, war, commerce, etc.; in a spread of five thousand miles you will find three heads that project still an inch higher,—men of national fame—and *one* that is higher than *those* by two inches, maybe three—a man of (temporarily) world-wide renown; and finally, somewhere around the circumference of the globe, you will find, once in five centuries of waiting, one majestic head which overtops the highest of all the others—an author, a teacher, an artist, a martyr, a conqueror, whose fame towers to the stars, and whose name will never perish, never fade, while time shall last; some colossus supreme above all the human herd, some unmated and unmateable prodigy like him who, by magic of the forces born in him, turned his shoe-hammer into the sceptre of universal dominion. Now in that view you have the ordinary man of all nations; you have the here-and-there man that is larger-brained and becomes distinguished; you have the still rarer man of still wider and more lasting distinction; and in that final head rising solitary out of the stretch of the ages, you have the limit of Nature's output.

Will she change this program? Not while time lasts. Will she repeat it forever? Yes. Forever and ever she will do those grades over and over again, always in the same proportions, and always with the regularity of a machine. In each million of people, just so many inch-superiorities; in each billion, just so many 2 inch superiorities—and so on; and always that recurrent solitary star once in an age, never oftener, never two of them at a time.

Nature, when pleased with an idea, never tires of applying it. She

makes plains; she makes hills; she makes mountains; raises a conspicuous peak at wide intervals; then loftier and rarer ones, continents
apart; and finally a supreme one six miles high. She uses this grading
process in horses: she turns out myriads of them that are all of one
common dull gait; with here and there a faster one; at enormous intervals a conspicuously faster one; and once in a half century a celebrity
that does a mile in two minutes. She will repeat that horse every fifty
years to the end of time.

By the Law of Periodical Repetition, everything which has happened
once must happen again and again and again—and not capriciously,
but at regular periods, and each thing in its own period, not another's,
and each obeying its own law. The eclipse of the sun, the occultation of
Venus, the arrival and departure of the comets, the annual shower of
stars—all these things hint to us that the same Nature which delights
in periodical repetition in the skies is the Nature which orders the affairs of the earth. Let us not underrate the value of that hint.

Are there any ingenuities whereby you can discredit the law of suicide? No. It is established. If there was such and such a number in
such and such a town last year, that number, substantially, will be repeated this year. That number will keep step, arbitrarily, with the increase of population, year after year. Given the population a century
hence, you can determine the crop of suicides that will be harvested in
that distant year.

Will this wonderful civilization of to-day perish? Yes, everything
perishes. Will it rise and exist again? It will—for nothing can happen
that will not happen again. And again, and still again, forever. It took
more than eight centuries to prepare this civilization—then it suddenly
began to grow, and in less than a century it is become a bewildering
marvel. In time, it will pass away and be forgotten. Ages will elapse,
then it will come again; and not incomplete, but complete; not an invention nor discovery nor any smallest detail of it missing. Again it will
pass away, and after ages will rise and dazzle the world again as it
dazzles it now—perfect in all its parts once more. It is the Law of
Periodical Repetition.

It is even possible that the mere *names* of things will be reproduced.
Did not the Science of Health rise, in the old time, and did it not pass

into oblivion, and has it not latterly come again and brought with it its forgotten name? Will it perish once more? Many times, I think, as the ages drift on; and still come again and again. And the forgotten book, Science and Health, With Key to the Scriptures—is it not with us once more, revised, corrected, and its orgies of style and construction tamed by an educated disciple? Will it not yet die, once, twice, a dozen times, and still at vast intervals rise again and successfully challenge the mind of man to understand it? We may not doubt it. By the Law of Periodical Repetition it must happen.

(early 1900s)

History 1,000 Years from Now

A translation

THE COMPLETION of the twenty-ninth century has had at least
one effect which was no doubt common to the completion of all the
centuries which have preceded it: it has suddenly concentrated the
thoughts of the whole thinking and dreaming world upon the past.
To-day no subject but the one—the past—can get much attention.
We began, a couple of years ago, with a quarrel as to whether the
dying century closed with the 31st of December 2899, or whether it
would close with the last day of last year, and it took the entire world
the best part of a year to settle it; then the past was taken hold of with
interest, and that interest has increased in strength and in fascination
ever since. To-day men are reading histories who never cared for them
before, and men are writing them who had found no call to work such
veins previously. Every day brings forth a new history—or shall we
say a dozen new ones? Indeed we are floundering in a flood of history.

It will be difficult to condense these narratives into a sketch, but
the effort is worthwhile; at least it seems so to the present writer. This
sketch must be drawn, fact by fact, trifle by trifle, from the great general mass, therefore it will not be possible to quote the authorities,
the number of names and books would be too great for that. And we
must make a bare sketch answer, we cannot expand much; we must
content ourselves with a mere synopsis.

It is now a thousand years since the happy accident—or series of accidents—occurred which after many years rescued our nation from democracy and gave it the blessed refuge and shelter of a crown. We say a thousand years, and it was in effect that, though the histories are not agreed as to the dates. Some of them place the initial events at nine centuries ago, some at ten, others at eleven. As to the events themselves, however, there is less disagreement.

It is conceded that the first of these incidents was the seizure, by the government in power at the time, of the group of islands now called the Vashington Archipelago. Vashington—some say George, some say Archibald—was the reigning President, hence the name. What the group was called before is not now known with certainty, but there is a tradition that our vast Empire was not always called Filipino, and there are those who believe that this was once the name of that archipelago, and that our forefathers adopted it in celebration of the conquest, and out of pride in it. The universal destruction of historical records which occurred during the long and bloody struggle which released us from the cruel grip of democracy makes our history guess-work mainly—alas that it should be so!—still, enough of apparently trustworthy information has survived to enable us to properly estimate the grandeur of that conquest and to sketch the principal details of it with a close approach to exactness.

It appears, then, that somewhere about a thousand years ago the Filipino group—if we may use the legendary name—had a population of 260,000,000—Hawkshaw places it at more than this, as does also Dawes—a population higher in civilization and in the arts of war and manufacture than any other in existence.

(January 1901)

Old Age

I THINK it likely that people who have not been here will be interested to know what it is like. I arrived on the thirtieth of November, fresh from care-free and frivolous 69, and was disappointed.

There is nothing novel about it, nothing striking, nothing to thrill you and make your eye glitter and your tongue cry out, "Oh, but it *is* wonderful, perfectly wonderful!" Yes, it is disappointing. You say, "Is *this* it?—*this*? after all this talk and fuss of a thousand generations of travelers who have crossed this frontier and looked about them and told what they saw and felt? why, it looks just like 69."

And that is true. Also it is natural; for you have not come by the fast express, you have been lagging and dragging across the world's continents behind oxen; when that is your pace one country melts into the next one so gradually that you are not able to notice the change: 70 looks like 69; 69 looked like 68; 68 looked like 67—and so on, back, and back, to the beginning. If you climb to a summit and look back—ah, then you see!

Down that far-reaching perspective you can make out each country and climate that you crossed, all the way up from the hot equator to the ice-summit where you are perched. You can make out where Infancy merged into Boyhood; Boyhood into down-lipped Youth; Youth into indefinite Young-Manhood; indefinite Young-Manhood into

384

definite Manhood; definite Manhood with aggressive ambitions into sobered and heedful Husbandhood and Fatherhood; these into troubled and foreboding Age, with graying hair; this into Old Age, whiteheaded, the temple empty, the idols broken, the worshippers in their graves, nothing left but You, a remnant, a tradition, belated fag-end of a foolish dream, a dream that was so ingeniously dreamed that it seemed real all the time; nothing left but You, centre of a snowy desolation, perched on the ice-summit, gazing out over the stages of that long *trek* and asking Yourself "would you do it again if you had the chance?"

(December 1905)